Human Spoken Interaction as a Complex Adaptive System

Studies in Social Interaction
Series Editors: Steve Walsh, Paul Seedhouse and Christopher Jenks

Presenting data from a range of social contexts including education, the media, the workplace, and professional development, the *Studies in Social Interaction* series uncovers, among other things, the ways in which tasks are accomplished, identities formed and communities established. Each volume in the series places social interaction at the centre of discussion and presents a clear overview of the work which has been done in a particular context. Books in the series provide examples of how data can be approached and used to uncover social-interaction themes and issues, and explore how research in social interaction can feed into a better understanding of professional practices and develop new research agendas. Through stimulating tasks and accompanying commentaries, readers are engaged and challenged to reflect on particular themes and relate the discussion to their own context.

Series Editors
Steve Walsh is Professor of Applied Linguistics at Newcastle University

Paul Seedhouse is Professor of Educational and Applied Linguistics at Newcastle University

Christopher Jenks is Professor of Intercultural Communication at the Utrecht University

Titles available in the series:

Social Interaction in Second Language Chat Rooms	Christopher Jenks
Social Interaction and L2 Classroom Discourse	Olcay Sert
Social Interaction and Teacher Cognition	Li Li
Social Interaction and English Language Teacher Identity	John Gray and Tom Morton
Social Interaction in Language Teacher Education	Fiona Farr, Angela Farrell and Elaine Riordan
Intercultural Transitions in Higher Education	Alina Schartner and Tony Johnstone Young
Multimodal Participation and Engagement	Christine M. Jacknick
Human Spoken Interaction as a Complex Adaptive System	Aki Siegel and Paul Seedhouse

Visit the Studies in Social Interaction website at
www.edinburghuniversitypress.com/series/SSINT

Human Spoken Interaction as a Complex Adaptive System
A Longitudinal Study of L2 Interaction

Aki Siegel and Paul Seedhouse

Edinburgh University Press is one of the leading university presses in the UK. We publish academic books and journals in our selected subject areas across the humanities and social sciences, combining cutting-edge scholarship with high editorial and production values to produce academic works of lasting importance. For more information visit our website: edinburghuniversitypress.com

© Aki Siegel and Paul Seedhouse, 2024, 2025

Edinburgh University Press Ltd
13 Infirmary Street
Edinburgh EH1 1LT

First published in hardback by Edinburgh University Press 2024

Typeset in Minion Pro by
Cheshire Typesetting Ltd, Cuddington, Cheshire

A CIP record for this book is available from the British Library

ISBN 978 1 3995 2268 7 (hardback)
ISBN 978 1 3995 2269 4 (paperback)
ISBN 978 1 3995 2270 0 (webready PDF)
ISBN 978 1 3995 2271 7 (epub)

The right of Aki Siegel and Paul Seedhouse to be identified as the authors of this work has been asserted in accordance with the Copyright, Designs and Patents Act 1988, and the Copyright and Related Rights Regulations 2003 (SI No. 2498).

CONTENTS

Dedications	vii
List of Figures and Tables	viii
Acknowledgements	xi
Overview	xii

1 Introduction to Human Spoken Interaction as a Complex Adaptive System   1
    1.1 Introduction   1
    1.2 Human Spoken Interaction in a Superdiverse World   3
    1.3 Complex Dynamic Systems Theory   4
    1.4 The Study Context   6
    1.5 The Participants and Corpus   7
    1.6 Rationale for the Corpus   9
    1.7 Purpose and Overview of the Book   11

2 L2 Interaction: Word Searches, Development and CDST   14
    2.1 Word Search Sequences   14
    2.2 Patterns of Word Search Sequences   19
    2.3 Developmental Studies on Interactional Competence   28
    2.4 Complex Dynamic Systems Theory and L2 Interaction   36
    2.5 Summary and Research Gap   47

3 Mirroring Methodology   49
    3.1 Introduction   49
    3.2 Basic Principles and Procedures of Conversation Analysis   49
    3.3 Basic Interactional Mechanisms   53
    3.4 Socially Distributed Cognition, Information Exchange and Topic Development   59
    3.5 Adapting CA Methodology to Social and Institutional Goals   64
    3.6 The Relationship between CA and CDST   70

4 Patterns of Word Search Sequences at the Group Level   79
    4.1 Introduction   79
    4.2 Word Search Initiations   80
    4.3 Candidate Solution of Word Searches   90

4.4 Responses to Candidate Solutions	116
4.5 Summary and Discussion	124

5 Longitudinal Changes in Word Search Sequences — 126
   5.1 Introduction — 126
   5.2 Quantified Changes in the Participants over Time — 127
   5.3 Ami's Case — 132
   5.4 Maya's Case — 140
   5.5 Yoko's Case — 155
   5.6 Tomoko's Case — 164
   5.7 Discussion: Variation and Patterns of Change — 174

6 Seeing Human Spoken Interaction as a Complex Adaptive System — 176
   6.1 Introduction — 176
   6.2 Matching the Ten CDST Principles to Findings from the Data Analyses — 177
   6.3 How Do All the Components Combine in Spoken Interaction? — 185
   6.4 Chapter Summary and Conclusions — 193

7 Conclusions and Implications — 196
   7.1 Introduction — 196
   7.2 Summary of Findings — 196
   7.3 Methodological Issues — 198
   7.4 Implications — 201
   7.5 Limitations and Directions for Future Research — 204

Appendix 1: Recordings of Participants — 208
Appendix 2: Transcription Conventions — 211
References — 212
Index — 227

DEDICATIONS

Aki Siegel: I dedicate this book to Joe, Ken and Hal for their love and patience throughout the years of conducting this project. I am also indebted to my parents who supported me during the writing process. I want to express my sincere thanks to Professor Paul Seedhouse for understanding my vision and perspective on the world, and for supporting me throughout this project. Last but not least, I am grateful to the participants of the project for their time and allowing me to have a glimpse of their community.

Paul Seedhouse: This book is about the universality of the human experience, as embodied in the universal interaction engine. I dedicate this book to all of my extended family, to all of my ancestors and to all of my future descendants!

FIGURES AND TABLES

FIGURES

3.1	Fractal shape form of a Romanesco broccoli (Source: Reproduced from http://commons.wikimedia.org/wiki/File:Fractal_Broccoli.jpg)	71
4.1	Line 5 'how do you say that'	82
4.2	Line 3 'how do you say'	83
4.3	Line 3 'ah::'	83
4.4	Line 5 'sappa?'	83
4.5	Line 2 'and (1.0)'	86
4.6	Line 4 '*nandakke*'	86
4.7	Line 8 'not teach but'	86
4.8	Line 9 'like teacher assistant'	86
4.9	Lines 9–10 'what (0.5)'	88
4.10	Line 3 Ami claps	92
4.11	Line 4 Ami tilts head	92
4.12	Line 7 'how do you say'	95
4.13	Line 7 'ah:::'	95
4.14	Line 9 'sappa?'	95
4.15	Line 14 'supper?'	95
4.16	Line 15 Ami holds mouth	96
4.17	Line 6 Typing	98
4.18	Line 7 (2.0)	100
4.19	Line 8 'ahula'	100
4.20	Line 10 '*kira kira kira*'	100
4.21	Frequency of code-switching use in resolving a word search by Japanese participants	103
4.22	Line 1 'steak'	107
4.23	Line 2 'very sick'	107
4.24	Lines 5–9 'thick'	107
4.25	Line 11 hamburger	107
4.26	Example of electronic dictionary use	109
4.27	Line 5 '*nani* ah *nandakke*'	110
4.28	Line 3 'fish'	114
4.29	Line 38 'please my dictionary'	114

4.30	Line 46 Showing dictionary	114
4.31	Line 51 Kei looks at dictionary. Maya fish gesture	114
5.1	Average of TOEFL ITP scores	128
5.2	Individual TOEFL scores	128
5.3	Frequency of word search sequences and candidate solutions	129
5.4	Frequency of strategies used as candidate solutions	130
5.5	Individual frequency of word searches and prosody-marked candidate solutions	131
5.6	Individual frequency of strategies used as candidate solutions	132
5.7	Ami's word searches with Hang	133
5.8	Line 4 (0.6)	134
5.9	Line 2 (1.0) gap gesture	136
5.10	Line 8 'mmm'	136
5.11	Line 12 (1.0) gap gesture	137
5.12	Line 13 'gap?'	137
5.13	Line 5 Roof	139
5.14	Line 5 Walls	139
5.15	Maya word search sequences with Kei and Yanti	141
5.16	Line 14 Launching of fireworks	143
5.17	Line 7 Picks up dictionary	146
5.18	Line 7 Puts dictionary down	146
5.19	Line 3 (1.2)	149
5.20	Line 5 'long sentence'	149
5.21	Line 7 'paragraph'	149
5.22	Line 9 'paragraph'	149
5.23	Line 6 (0.6)	152
5.24	Yoko's word search sequences with Shitora	156
5.25	Candidate solutions with Shitora	156
5.26	Line 10 (3.7)	159
5.27	Line 11 'can'	159
5.28	Line 15 'is about'	159
5.29	Line 16 (3.0)	159
5.30	Tomoko's frequency of word search sequences	164
5.31	Line 7 Swom	167
5.32	Line 8 (1.4)	167
5.33	Line 9 Swum	168
5.34	Line 11 (1.7)	168
5.35	Line 20 Looks away	170
5.36	Line 22 Looks at nails	170
5.37	Line 1 'ku-'	172
5.38	Line 1 '-ri'	172
5.39	Line 4 'ma-'	172
5.40	Line 4 '-ron'	172
6.1	Line 3 'hmm'. An embodied display of 'thinking'	186

TABLES

1	Ami's recordings	208
2	Yoko's recordings	209
3	Maya's recordings	209
4	Tomoko's recordings	210

ACKNOWLEDGEMENTS

This project was supported by JSPS Grant-in-Aid for Scientific Research (Kaken), Young Scientists (B), 2011–2012, Grant number 23720303, Aki Siegel.

The authors would like to thank:

Keith Richards for his expert feedback, ideas and editing. Indeed, Paul would like to thank Keith for 36 years of expert feedback and guidance!;

Helmut Czekay for his expert editing work;

Gabi Kasper for first suggesting that the authors should work together in this area;

Adam Brandt, who was second supervisor for Aki Siegel's dissertation;

Salla Kurhila for examining Aki Siegel's dissertation;

Alison Whelan for indexing the text;

anonymous reviewers for their suggestions and expert reviews of drafts;

Steve Walsh and Chris Jenks as Series Editors;

Helena Heald, Sam Johnson, Laura Quinn and Joannah Duncan at Edinburgh University Press and Cheshire Typesetting Ltd for their excellent work in taking the manuscript through many stages to publication.

OVERVIEW

Most people believe they think and speak **in** a particular language and that our world is divided by the 7,000 languages spoken in different countries. However, in this book we show that language is only one of the two complex adaptive systems (of equal importance) which we all use in combination during human spoken interaction. Moreover, the other system –which Levinson (2006) calls the 'interaction engine' – is the universal, foundational system which we all learn as infants as a prerequisite before we learn languages. The interaction engine evolved before language and forms the 'natural ecological niche for language' (Schegloff 2006: 70). Language is a separate complex adaptive system described elsewhere (e.g., N.C. Ellis and Larsen-Freeman 2009b). The interaction engine provides the infrastructure for speakers to mirror their communicative intentions to each other multimodally in talk and to resolve problems.

We explain how the interaction engine uses the same basic procedures as other life-related complex systems in the world; these are described in the substantial literature on Complex Dynamic Systems Theory (CDST). Human beings are complex adaptive systems, so it is important for us to understand how such systems work. We specify how exactly the interaction engine functions and how its component mechanisms combine and adapt to enable speakers to perform their social actions and to understand each other. For this, we use the substantial literature on Conversation Analysis (CA) and present a combined 'CA-CDST' approach to spoken interaction, providing examples of how to analyse spoken interaction on both the micro and macro levels simultaneously.

Focusing on L2 users of English engaged in interaction in a 'superdiverse' context, we zoom in on how the speakers utilise and adapt word search sequences over time in the informal English as a lingua franca (ELF) setting of an international dormitory. We analyse the patterns and changes of the users as individuals and as a cohort in terms of their use of word search sequences as a system. We find that L2 speakers adapt their language use and epistemic stance both moment to moment and across a longer time span based on feedback. We also demonstrate the dual nature of word search sequences as speakers seamlessly and mutually move in and out of learning and socialising.

Our data reveal a discrepancy: the speakers make expert, inventive use of the universal interaction engine to convey sophisticated levels of meaning, even though they are not expert level speakers of the L2 and do not share the same linguistic or cultural background. We argue that this is because they are employing two separate complex adaptive systems: the interaction engine and language.

We also introduce the practices of treating research methodologies themselves as complex adaptive systems and of using self-similarity as a methodological principle. These practices reveal how CA methodology adapts itself to mirror the adaptations of the complex system of human spoken interaction, as well as explaining the nature of the relationship between CA and CDST.

In contrast to the diverse languages which have tended to separate us as a human race, the interaction engine is what brings us all together in a communal human experience and is what enables us to communicate with others whenever language is a problem. We explain why the interaction engine is the most revealing of all life-related complex systems on planet Earth.

1
INTRODUCTION TO HUMAN SPOKEN INTERACTION AS A COMPLEX ADAPTIVE SYSTEM

1.1 INTRODUCTION

Human spoken interaction is a phenomenon with which we are all too familiar from our everyday experience; we take it for granted as we are immersed in it. In this book we view human spoken interaction afresh as both an object of research and as a remarkable phenomenon worthy of wonder. We show how it functions as a complex adaptive system in similar ways to other life-related systems, how it enables us to communicate with each other and perform a vast range of intricate social actions. We are **not** looking at how **language** functions as a complex adaptive system, which has been the focus of other studies (e.g., N.C. Ellis and Larsen-Freeman 2009b). Rather, we align with Levinson's (2006, 2023) conception of the 'interaction engine' as the more fundamental, more primal system which evolved before language and languages and which is acquired by infants before language(s).

Levinson (2022) writes that 'it is not language that has made human social interaction possible, it is rather our interactional abilities that have enabled language' (3). The interaction engine is the structure of everyday human spoken interaction and is the underlying resource we all use to conduct our spoken business with each other, together with overlaid language(s). The functioning of the interaction engine has already been described in detail in the vast literature on Conversation Analysis (CA) (e.g., Sidnell and Stivers 2013). We describe in detail how the interaction engine works in Chapter 3, and how it is founded on the inter-related mechanisms of turn-taking, sequence and repair, among others. The interaction engine is 'nearly uniform across the species' (Levinson 2022: 1) with some cultural variation, as shown in Dingemanse et al. (2015), Kendrick et al. (2020) and Stivers et al. (2009). This homogeneous universal foundation for human communication enables everyone to orientate themselves when interacting with people of different cultures, languages and traditions. We argue that the interaction engine is the foundational complex system as far as human spoken communication is concerned; specific languages are overlaid onto the same interaction engine. Languages are portable in spoken interaction; as long as all participants use the universal bedrock of the interaction engine, they can switch in and out of any language or lect that they like, mixing them at will. Schegloff (2006) refers to interaction as the 'natural ecological niche for language' (70). We may think we are conversing **in** a language. However, we are actually designing our turns using two separate systems, namely the interaction engine and language. The interaction engine is universal but languages are variable. We can switch languages in mid-turn and still make sense because we are working with both a universal and a variable system, the combination of which gives our talk enormous generative potential. Further evidence of the importance of the interaction engine is as follows: when people do not share any language, successful transactions can still be managed by replacing language with multimodal resources like mime and gesture. Indeed, travellers have managed this for many millennia. When language is lost in adults (e.g., aphasia), interaction can still continue; C. Goodwin (1995) shows how someone with a vocabulary of only three words can still interact successfully by using the resources of the interaction engine. Infants communicate verbally, non-verbally and multimodally before they learn to use language. In the pre-linguistic stage (Bruner 1974), they learn how to use the interaction engine through turn-taking and sequence games such as 'peekaboo'.

In this study, we describe the complex adaptive system for spoken interaction which all humans use, whichever language they speak, and exemplify how this is adapted over time by a specific cohort of users for their own purposes. We analyse pairs of speakers with different L1s in a 'superdiverse' (Vertovec 2007) setting, each of whom is speaking English as a lingua franca (ELF). We examine data in which one might expect significant cross-linguistic and cross-cultural trouble to occur in interaction. We show that, in spite of this, they are able to perform their social actions, develop topics, exchange meanings and understand each other. They do so in sophisticated and sometimes inventive ways. Most importantly, we show how speakers adapt to the interaction and their interlocutor over time in order to maintain intersubjectivity and to progress the interaction. We argue that this is possible because they are employing the same universal interaction engine to orientate themselves; the system is infinitely adaptable across languages and cultures. The discrepancy between the speakers' expert knowledge of the universal interaction engine and inexpert knowledge of L2 English reinforces our argument that they are employing two separate (though related) complex adaptive systems.

The methodology we use to analyse our spoken interactional data is Conversation Analysis (CA)[1] (Levinson 1983; Schegloff 2007). We describe how CA works in great detail in Chapter 3. Briefly for now, CA studies the organisation and order of social action in interaction. This organisation and order is one produced by the interactants by means of their talk and is oriented to by them. The analyst's task is to develop an 'emic' or participants' perspective, to uncover and describe this organisation and order; the main interest is in uncovering the underlying 'machinery' (Sacks 1984) which enables interactants to achieve this organisation and order. We describe CA as a 'mirroring methodology' because it aims to describe how the interaction engine functions, employing the same procedures and perspectives as the participants in the interaction. CA analysts aim to provide a 'holistic' portrayal of language use which reveals the reflexive relationships between form, function, sequence and social identity and social/institutional context. That is, the organisation of the talk is seen to relate directly and reflexively to the social goals of the participants, whether

---

[1] In Section 3.6 we explain how we merge CA with CDST to form a combined CA-CDST approach.

institutional or otherwise. CA is now a mature methodology dating from the 1960s which has been used to analyse a huge variety of social actions being performed through spoken interaction in innumerable settings, both institutional and non-institutional. The essential question which we must ask at all stages of CA analysis of data is, 'Why that, in that way, right now?' (Seedhouse 2004: 16). This encapsulates the perspective of interaction as action (why that) which is expressed by means of linguistic forms (in that way) in a developing sequence (right now). Talk is conceived of as social action, which is delivered in particular linguistic formatting, as part of an unfolding sequence.

This is the first book-length study to present how **human spoken interaction** (the interaction engine) functions as a complex adaptive system. What does this mean? Complexity science, or Complex Dynamic Systems Theory (CDST), states that almost all systems which support life are complex adaptive systems (West 2017) and show surprising similarities in the way they function, once scale is taken into account; we introduce CDST in Section 1.3. In this book we compare (1) what is known about the functioning of human spoken interaction from the CA literature with (2) what is known about the functioning of complex adaptive systems from the CDST literature; we argue that they mirror each other. They are both engaged in the same business of showing how systems work, but on vastly different scales and using different terminologies. CA has been focusing narrowly and uniquely on showing how the interaction engine functions as a complex adaptive system (without using such terminology) whilst CDST has been operating on an incomparably broader scale, showing how complex adaptive systems function throughout life on Earth. From Chapter 3 we therefore merge CA and CDST into a single 'CA-CDST' approach which can analyse the system of human spoken interaction on both the micro and macro scales and exemplify its use.

1.2 HUMAN SPOKEN INTERACTION IN A SUPERDIVERSE WORLD

In order to demonstrate how human spoken interaction functions as a complex adaptive system and how to take a CA-CDST approach to data, we focus on the word search sequences used among speakers in the 'superdiverse' setting of an ELF context over time.

ELF is the use of English in a lingua franca language scenario (Mortensen 2013) where English is the language shared by all interactants of the moment and is used in order to communicate (Seidlhofer 2011). In this context, English is used as an initial contact language where speakers come from different linguistic and cultural backgrounds, which includes L1 users of English who are using English in this multilingual multicultural community (Jenkins 2007). We do not see ELF as its own language system nor aim to examine it. Rather, we examine how speakers engage in interaction and co-construct intersubjectivity in ELF contexts and the changes that occur over time. Therefore, we use ELF to refer to the broader context in which the interaction is situated, and refer to the speakers' languages (e.g., L1–L2/L2–L2 interaction) when introducing the literature related to language use.

We also recognise that ELF contexts are 'superdiverse' and that no two contexts are the same. Superdiversity refers to the variability, fluidity and complexity of the people, language and community (Cogo 2012; Vertovec 2007). It reflects the 'multi-dimensional perspective on diversity' (Vertovec 2007: 1026) where a single variable or a category does not capture the dynamicity of the actual population, the language use, nor how the people interact with each other. Individuals bring their rich (socio)linguistic repertoire and diverse experiences to the conversation (Blommaert 2009; Blommaert and Rampton 2011; Cogo 2012). However, often these discussions of 'superdiversity' are limited to the individual level, referring to the multi-layeredness of one's language and culture that cannot be summarised into one category such as 'ethnicity' (Vertovec 2007). In these diverse interactional contexts, where there is no clear single 'standard' language (or culture) shared among the speakers, how do second language (L2) users use English to communicate and reach mutual understandings, and how does their language use evolve over time based on the feedback they receive? As we show in Chapter 2, there is limited literature on this point.

The significance of the superdiverse L2 setting is that it is an ideal test case for the universality of the interaction engine. Can we note a difference between adult speakers' expert use of the universal interaction engine and their inexpert use of L2? Can speakers of different L1s using English as a lingua franca successfully communicate with each other and perform their social actions? If so, how are they employing the mechanisms of interaction? How do speakers construct intersubjectivity, and build a mutual linguistic repertoire that adds to the superdiversity of the individual and the community? How do the interaction engine, the speakers and the conversations co-adapt and co-evolve over time? How can we understand the interaction and its changes from a CDST perspective? These are a few of the questions we aim to tackle through this book.

1.3 COMPLEX DYNAMIC SYSTEMS THEORY

At this point, we provide a basic introduction to Complex Dynamic Systems Theory (CDST) for those not familiar with it, prior to a lengthier discussion in Chapter 2. Below, we list some of the typical characteristics and behaviours of complex adaptive systems.

Living systems (including humans) are complex adaptive systems (West 2017) which must adapt to evolve and survive. Complex systems share some properties because they evolved on Earth from the same source. By contrast, the Newtonian laws of gravitation and motion are **not** complex adaptive systems. They apply equally on planets where there is no life and are linear systems; a change in input is proportional to the change in output. Their behaviour can be calculated and predicted, which is essential to building and flying aeroplanes, for example. Complex adaptive systems are non-linear and therefore less predictable because they must adapt and evolve to changes in their environment or 'deal with life'.

CDST is a science which aims to explain the non-linear interactions of microscopic elements in complex systems (Mainzer 1997) or a science of the global nature of systems (Gleick 1993). CDST is a 'meta-theory' (Larsen-Freeman 2013), which is 'a set of coherent principles of reality (i.e. ontological ideas) and principles of knowing (i.e. epistemological ideas)' (Hiver and Al-Hoorie 2020: 20). It reveals the subtle relationships between simplicity and complexity and between orderliness and randomness (N. Hall 1992: 7). A defining characteristic of a complex system is that its behaviour emerges from the interactions of its components (Larsen-Freeman and Cameron 2008a: 9–10) and so complexity theory always develops a holistic or ecological perspective rather than a reductionist or atomistic one (Gleick 1993: 7).

Within the framework of CDST, the term 'complex adaptive systems' refers to adaptive systems where a system's overall structure is influenced by the context and the independent components within the system, causing changes in the system's rules and behaviour. Complex adaptive systems of many different kinds have been studied so far and include: weather systems; the rise and fall of animal populations; the organisation and functioning of the human brain; language, learning and thinking in humans; the rise and fall of civilisations. Larsen-Freeman and Cameron (2008a) provide a detailed study of the relationship between complexity theory and applied linguistics and discussion of possible applications, as well as the suggestion that spoken interaction is a complex adaptive system. Seedhouse (2010) provides a study of L2 classroom interaction as a complex adaptive system.

Complex adaptive systems share certain crucial properties. They self-organise and involve the adaptation of many interacting agents. Coherent, self-organising clusters at one level combine to form new clusters at a higher level. They are adaptive, in that they do not just passively respond to events. They are non-linear, meaning that small changes in the external environment can produce large changes in the system (Gribbin 2004: 106). Non-linear systems express relationships that are not strictly proportional (Gleick 1993: 23), in which the result is not proportionate to the cause. Moreover, extremely simple systems can generate extremely complex and intricate patterns (Gribbin 2004). Complex adaptive systems show sensitivity to initial conditions where small inputs can lead to dramatically large consequences and very slight differences in initial conditions can produce very different outcomes (Lewin 1993). There are universal properties of non-linear systems: different systems behave in the same ways. Complex adaptive systems arise from the interaction of their parts and function as a whole which is more than the sum of its parts (West 2017: 21). In other words, complex adaptive systems in general cannot be successfully analysed by isolating properties or variables that are studied separately and then combining those partial approaches. Complex adaptive systems simultaneously display both homogeneity and heterogeneity. At the lowest level, no two complex adaptive systems are ever absolutely identical: each starts from slightly different starting conditions and interacts with a slightly different external environment. Yet complex adaptive systems of the same genus display certain similarities. This is because complex adaptive systems display self-similarity on various scales and levels. The patterns or shapes of complex adaptive systems look similar from different scales, perspectives and levels.

CDST has become established as a conceptual framework which is relevant to many areas of applied linguistics as well as to many other academic disciplines. The field of second language acquisition (SLA) also seemed to have reached a tipping point of a new paradigm shift. CDST and its relation to L2 language learning and development has increasingly become a topic of investigation in recent years (e.g., Hiver et al. 2022; Ortega and Han 2017). In the social world, the relationship between cause and effect is complex, since effects or outcomes derive from multiple causes and vary depending on the context. Traditionally, applied linguistic research has oversimplified these aspects of language development, and has conceptualised learning as an individualistic linear-progressive phenomenon. However, accumulating studies have demonstrated how various areas of L2 research can be understood from a CDST perspective and have shown that language development is dynamic and non-linear (e.g., Larsen-Freeman and Cameron 2008a). Scholars have also demonstrated how pre-existing research methods can be applied to data to analyse these dynamic phenomena (e.g., Hiver and Al-Hoorie 2020).

In recent years, research on L2 interaction and development has gained increasing importance and interest, especially in the area of interactional competence. Longitudinal Conversation Analysis for Second Language Acquisition (CA-for-SLA) is now an established area where CA is applied to longitudinal interactional data in seeking change over time (see Chapter 2 for a literature review). However, these studies tend to focus their analysis on the individual and adopt a linear approach towards 'learning' that does not necessarily consider changes in context and/or the interlocutors over time. Attempting to understand longitudinal L2 interaction from a CDST perspective has been overlooked, and there is no established approach yet that has suggested how to conceptualise this. Therefore, through theoretical discussion and empirical data analyses, we suggest and demonstrate a Conversation Analysis – Complex Dynamic Systems Theory (CA-CDST) approach to analysing interaction.

We have provided a brief introduction to CDST here and provide further detail in Chapter 2. In Chapter 3, we present how human spoken interaction (the interaction engine) functions as a complex adaptive system. In Chapter 6, we return to the characteristics of complex adaptive systems described here and verify whether the interaction analysed in Chapters 4 and 5 does indeed display these characteristics. Next, we outline the context of the project and the rationale for the corpus we will be using to demonstrate the CA-CDST approach.

1.4 THE STUDY CONTEXT

Superdiverse contexts are becoming increasingly familiar at workplaces and universities. However, such contexts are still very limited in Japan. Japan continues to be a predominantly monolingual nation where Japanese is used as the common language. Moreover, despite the six years of compulsory English language education, not all Japanese can use English for even the most basic conversational exchanges.

The university where the project takes place is located in Southern Japan, in a relatively rural area. The university is unique in its student demographics, where enrolment is controlled to balance the number of international and domestic (i.e., Japanese) students; thus it professes to be a 'bilingual' environment where English is used as the common language. International students represented over 90 countries at the time of the data collection. Many of the international students are from the

Asia Pacific region, such as Korea, China, India, Indonesia, Mongolia, Thailand and Vietnam, while there are also students from North America, Europe and Africa, giving the campus a multicultural atmosphere.

Entrance examinations are common practice for universities in Japan. When taking the entrance examination of this university, students have the choice of taking the exam in English or in Japanese. Most of the Japanese students take the exam in Japanese, whereas most international students take it in English. For this reason, some international students arrive in Japan with little or no Japanese ability, while all Japanese students have at least six years of formal English instruction prior to enrolment and can use English to some degree. Therefore, according to casual discussions with students and observations, at the beginning of the semester, the common language used on campus and in the dormitory is mainly English. However, as the international students improve their Japanese skills, and the domestic students improve their additional language skills, such as Chinese or Korean, the language choice becomes more fluid and mixed.

The university dormitory where the study took place reflects the student demographic of the university. There are approximately 3,000 residents in this dormitory, approximately half of whom are Japanese, the other half being international students. Almost all the students are first-year students, along with some second- and third-year students who live there as resident assistants (RAs). Most students living in the dormitory live in 'shared rooms', which are rooms where Japanese students are paired up with international students to support each other with campus life and adjustment to the new culture.

1.5 THE PARTICIPANTS AND CORPUS

Four female Japanese first-year students volunteered to join the project as the 'core participants' who would be the main focus of the study. The participants were Ami, Maya, Tomoko and Yoko (all pseudonyms). They saw a flyer passed out during a pre-enrolment session by the researcher to students who arrived on campus prior to the beginning of classes at the middle to end of March 2010. The requirements were that they lived in the university dormitory and were willing to record their conversations with international students. The four students were the only ones who signed up and there was no selection process for the participants.

Data collection took a longitudinal approach for a detailed tracking of the participants. Participants were asked to record themselves talking with an international student in the dormitory approximately for 30 minutes each time, twice a month, over the course of one academic year. Following C.H. Young et al.'s (1991) suggestion of a one-year benchmark for longitudinal studies, and Brouwer and Wagner's (2004) suggestion of conducting recordings with the same interlocutor with frequent intervals, one of the two recordings every month involved the same partner across the whole academic year. The second recording could then be a different partner every month.

The first recording took place in early April 2010, during the first few weeks when the four participants entered the university and moved into the dormitory.

Subsequent recordings were made in the following months up to January 2011. However, since many of the students do not stay on campus during summer and spring holidays, there was a two-month gap during the summer vacation. All core participants conducted 16 recordings for the initial one-year data collection. Three of the four participants (Ami, Maya and Yoko) then joined for a delayed recording with their fixed partner a year after the last recording, in January or February 2012. The core Japanese participants each selected different student partners from their on-campus dormitories as their conversation partners.

The partners of the core participants were 32 different students from 10 countries. The non-Japanese partners represent countries including: Botswana, Canada, China, Korea, Indonesia, Romania, Thailand, United States, Uzbekistan and Vietnam. Some partners had experience living in more than one country for an extended period of time or had parents of different nationalities, and thus represent more than one culture or country. The majority of the recordings were pair conversations, some were in threes, and one recording was done in a group of four. Furthermore, the core participants were responsible for receiving permission from their partner to record their conversation and for explaining that the recording would be used for research purposes. Some participants could not maintain the same intervals between the recordings or keep the same fixed partner throughout the whole project. For instance, in Maya's case, the fixed partner at the beginning could not continue, and she had to change her fixed partner for the second half of the data collection. A few recordings were non-usable and thus not transcribed due to the poor recording condition of the voices, damage to the tape, and non-conversational data (e.g., singing session) (see Appendix 1 for details on partner, date and length of recordings).

Recordings were made by the participants in the dormitory using a video camera. Video cameras are distracting and known to interfere with participants' talk (Landsberger 1958; Richards and Renandya 2002). However, in order to capture any non-verbal communication that was being used during the interaction, which is invaluable in order to understand human interaction, video cameras were used. Participants were asked to place the camera where all of the participants in the conversation could be seen to some degree, but not so close as to distract them during the conversation. Instructions by the researcher were limited to the length of the recording and positioning of the camera. Participants were free to choose conversation topics on their own. The researcher was never present at the recording sessions.

The majority of the recordings were done in the participants' or their partners' rooms. They would often sit on the bed or the floor, and would place the camera on the desk. Occasionally, the recordings were done in the shared kitchen and dining area. The recording sessions were planned by the participants and recorded with consent, thus this knowledge may have influenced what the participants talked about and how. However, at times non-planned students would stop by to talk to the participants or join the ongoing conversation and stay for the rest of the recording. Students who only joined the conversation briefly were not asked their names or backgrounds, and thus are not included as part of the data analysis. The recording lengths varied from 22 minutes to 69 minutes. In total there were approximately 37 hours' worth of usable conversation data collected across 22 months at the longest duration.

In addition to their conversational data, TOEFL ITP scores used for the university English programme were collected from the participants throughout the data collection period. Furthermore, after each recording participants were asked to write a short reflection on their conversation. Finally, simple non-structured interviews were conducted at the beginning and end of the first academic year, and then at the final recording 22 months after the first recording. Interviews were conducted in order to have a better understanding of the participants' living environment, their emotions and their self-perceptions.

The collected recordings were fully transcribed first, then word search sequences were transcribed in detail based on Jefferson's (2004) transcription format and Mondada (2018) and Greer (2019a) for transcribing non-verbal cues (see Appendix 2). In cases where non-English languages were used in a full sentence, a three-line layout was used: the original sentence on the top, followed by a literal word-by-word translation, and last the English translation in bold face letters. If it was a single word or phrase, a two-line layout was used with the direct translation below the word.

Below, we clarify the rationale for this particular data set as suitable for examining the interaction engine underlying human interactions in a superdiverse context.

1.6 RATIONALE FOR THE CORPUS

Our aim in collecting and analysing data was to understand how the interaction engine functions and adapts itself over time. We chose a setting in which the participants are **not** expert L2 users but **are** still expert users of the universal interaction engine. This is intended to determine any possible discrepancies in usage between the complex adaptive systems of language and the interaction engine.

As we show in Chapter 3, the interaction engine consists of many interacting components, so to enable in-depth analysis we have chosen the mechanism of repair,[2] which is one of the fundamental, universal components of the interaction engine. Trouble in the running of a system and how it is repaired are ideal points to examine the overall functioning of that system because they are the points where systems start to feed back on themselves, becoming self-referential and reflexive. Within the repair mechanism we have chosen to focus on word searches in particular as they display a clear embodiment of how socially distributed cognition works as a collaborative, jointly constructed process. Trouble and repair also represent a particular point of stress in L2 talk; if a particular L2 word is not known by a speaker, how can they proceed to convey meaning? As we show in Chapters 4 and 5, the speakers are highly inventive and collaborative in negotiating word search sequences, employing a wide range of resources and strategies. This demonstrates that the mechanism of repair is highly adaptable across languages, cultures and settings; we argue that this is possible because it is part of the bedrock of the universal interaction engine. Essentially our choices of sample, setting and specific focus on word search sequences function as a test case of how exactly the human interaction engine facilitates communication across cultures and languages involving lingua

---

[2] See Chapters 2 and 3 for a detailed discussion.

franca use. This provides a sound basis for understanding the nature of the interaction engine and its workings. In Chapter 3, we provide a more general overview of the engine and its components.

Why are we using a longitudinal perspective on the development of word search sequences over time? We are studying the complex adaptive system of human spoken interaction, and one implication of this is that complex systems evolve and adapt themselves to changes in the environment over time. We therefore hope to uncover systemic evolution in word searches over time in relation to environmental change.

Why is this dataset suitable for our CDST focus? We have pairs of speakers with different L1s, each of whom is speaking English as a lingua franca. We show that in spite of this, they are able to perform their social actions, develop topics and meanings, mutually adapt to the interaction and maintain intersubjectivity. We argue that this is possible because there is a fundamental and universal 'interaction engine' (Levinson 2006) or complex adaptive system governing all human spoken interaction. This functions as a homogeneous foundation for human communication which enables everyone to orientate themselves when interacting with people of different cultures, languages and traditions. The discrepancy between the speakers' expert knowledge of the universal interaction engine and their inexpert knowledge of L2 English reinforces our argument that they are employing two separate (though related) complex adaptive systems.

Why do we use CA? One way in which we can observe people making adaptations to other people and contexts is by examining how they adapt the fundamental CA mechanisms of interaction (turn-taking, sequence and repair). In this study, we examine adaptations of the system of word search, which is part of the mechanism of repair. One clear adaptation of the word search system to this ELF context is in developing a dual nature. Word searches may orient primarily to progressing the topic but may also orient primarily to learning a new L2 word, or do both.

In this study, our priority is to show how human spoken interaction functions as a complex adaptive system. We use a CA-CDST empirical perspective on language development and interactional competence. If and when it is clear that the participants themselves display an orientation to language learning processes in the details of their talk, then and only then is it relevant to discuss language learning and development (see Section 3.5.3). We show in Chapters 4 and 5 how the complex adaptive system of human spoken interaction in this setting evolves over time by using CA with a specific focus on word searches. In this study, however, we are **not** looking primarily at the language or its development, since our focus is tightly on a different complex adaptive system, namely that of human spoken interaction. Nonetheless, there are episodes in which the speakers themselves focus on L2 learning, specifically engaging in word search sequences for L2 words. In these cases, we do bring L2 learning into the discussion since the participants themselves are orienting to this. As our focus is tightly on the interaction engine, we do not draw pedagogical conclusions in this study and leave this for future research.

1.7 PURPOSE AND OVERVIEW OF THE BOOK

This book is **not** about language (which has already been studied as a complex system) or about language learning. Rather, it is about the complex system which underlies and enables language, languages and language learning, namely the universal human interaction engine. We describe how the interaction engine functions as a complex adaptive system and we explain and exemplify how its functioning in talk can be analysed. Because we acquire the interaction engine before language(s), its procedures are so deeply embedded and so implicit that we have difficulty in realising that we are employing them constantly; our aim is to make these procedures and this complex system explicit.

This book aims to:

1. describe how the interaction engine works as a complex adaptive system using complexity science (CDST)
2. demonstrate how we can do microanalysis of talk (using CA) to show how the interaction engine functions
3. explain how it is possible to analyse talk on both the general and particular, the micro and macro levels, using the combination of (1) and (2), namely the CA-CDST approach
4. demonstrate that it is possible to distinguish the impacts of the interaction engine and language in talk, by analysing talk in which users are experts in the interaction engine but non-expert learners of L2
5. explain why it is important to demonstrate that the interaction engine functions in the same basic ways as other life-related systems on Earth.

One of the themes of our study is the importance of scale (West 2017) in understanding how complex adaptive systems work and relate to each other, and our book itself operates on two scales; this reflects the use of both CDST and CA. The book has both large-scale and 'narrow-focus' aims, which are intended to feed each other reflexively. On the large scale, we aim to describe how the interaction engine functions as a complex adaptive system by combining CA findings on the 'machinery' of talk with CDST findings on the functioning of complex systems. We combine these in a CA-CDST approach from Chapter 3 and illustrate its use through analyses of interaction. The narrow-focus aim of the book is to demonstrate how the use and development of word search sequences in informal L2 interaction in this specific ELF setting operates as a complex adaptive system. We do this by investigating both (1) the patterns of L2 interaction of an ELF context as they attempt to reclaim intersubjectivity in situations when the speaker shows trouble locating a lexical item and (2) the changes over time to the patterns of word search sequences used by L2 speakers of English in an ELF context. While using longitudinal CA as the main method of analysis, we employ CDST at various points during the analysis of empirical data in order to help us conceptualise the system as a whole and to consider how it compares with other systems. We refer to CDST at various points in the following chapters when this is able to shed light on the functioning of the interaction engine, identifying the properties and characteristics of complex adaptive systems when these become apparent. Finally, we reconceptualise the relationship between CA and CDST in Chapter 6 and exemplify the CA-CDST approach to data analysis.

On a broader conceptual level, this book tackles a universal problem facing anyone who wants to analyse human spoken interaction: how is it possible to analyse talk on both the micro (particular) scale and the macro (general) scale simultaneously, with the two levels feeding each other reflexively? We do this in five ways: (1) we employ CDST as a meta-theory to conceptualise how the system of human spoken interaction works at a macro or general scale in similar ways to other complex adaptive systems; (2) we employ CA as an empirical methodology to analyse spoken interaction on the micro or particular scale; (3) we use the CDST concept of self-similarity or fractality as a methodological principle to reveal connections between macro and micro scales and to reconceptualise the relationship between CA and CDST as a self-similar one; (4) we demonstrate how the combined CA-CDST approach works on the micro level by analysing an extract of interaction in Section 6.3; (5) we present in Chapter 7 an approach to employing multiple lenses and scales to represent homogeneity and heterogeneity, the macro and micro, the general and particular.

The structure of the book interweaves a CA component with a CDST component. Chapter 1 introduces CDST as meta-theory and CA as empirical methodology. Chapter 2 introduces the underlying theories and the phenomenon of word search sequences and synthesises recent developments in CDST and related literatures. In Chapter 3, we will have a detailed discussion of the CA methodological approach and the relationship between CA and CDST. The chapter thereby explains the basics of how human spoken interaction functions as a complex adaptive system. Chapters 4 and 5 use CA to examine the micro-detail of how word searches are organised by this cohort of learners and how their use changes over time. Chapter 6 then re-examines the findings of Chapters 4 and 5 through a CDST lens and explains how the joint CA-CDST approach works through an example of analysis in Section 6.3. Chapter 7 brings the interwoven strands together, explains how to use multiple lenses and scales, and presents implications.

Our conceptual arguments are as follows. Firstly, it is possible to analyse spoken interaction on both the micro (particular) scale and the macro (general) scale by employing a combined approach of CDST meta-theory and CA microanalysis. However, this approach works better if the CDST concept of self-similarity/fractality is employed as a guiding and connecting principle at all scales and if CDST and CA are **themselves** viewed as complex adaptive systems. From this perspective, CA is a self-similar fractal of CDST and self-similarity illuminates many of CA's principles and procedures. We develop this argument from Chapter 3 onwards. Secondly, there is a universal complex adaptive system (interaction engine) for human spoken interaction, the mechanisms and workings of which we describe in Chapter 3. We examine (in Chapters 4 and 5) data in which one might expect significant cross-linguistic and cross-cultural trouble to occur in interaction. We analyse pairs of speakers with different L1s in a superdiverse setting, each of whom is speaking English as a lingua franca, but none of whom is an expert speaker of English L2. We show that in spite of this, they are able to perform their social actions, develop topics and exchange meanings very effectively and sometimes very inventively. We argue that this is possible because they all have expert knowledge of the universal interaction engine which they are employing to orientate themselves; the system is infinitely adaptable across languages and cultures. Levinson (2023) argues that 'the interaction engine provides a stable cross-cultural base for the use and acquisition of language' (7). We explain in Chapter 3 how exactly the interaction engine is able to adapt itself to superdiverse settings and to enable intersubjectivity, and we trace usage of word search sequences over time in Chapters 4 and 5.

On the narrow scale, the book will illuminate the dynamics of ELF interactions outside institutional language learning settings, and the naturally occurring interactional methods employed by speakers in achieving intersubjectivity. The study also contributes to the field in understanding the longitudinal changes that occur in and through repeated interactions from an early stage of joining an ELF context. On the broad scale, this is the first study to explain in detail how exactly the interaction engine functions as a complex adaptive system, combining CA and CDST in an empirical approach. The methodological innovations we introduce in this study are to employ the CDST concept of self-similarity/fractality as a guiding principle at all scales and to consider both CDST and CA as complex adaptive systems; we explain this in detail in Chapter 3.

2

L2 INTERACTION: WORD SEARCHES, DEVELOPMENT AND CDST

In this chapter we establish what is already known about the phenomena and issues which we will be studying in later chapters; we also identify what is not known, that is, the research gaps. Following on from the brief introductions in Chapter 1, we review the literature on word search sequences as well as on CDST and its principles. We also examine relevant CA and CDST studies on L2 development.

2.1 WORD SEARCH SEQUENCES

We begin by reviewing the literature on word search sequences, as this is the phenomenon we will be studying in Chapters 4 and 5. We begin by introducing the basic definitions of word searches in the CA and applied linguistics literature. We show how word search sequences, especially the interactional methods employed to resolve word searches, can be understood as an interactional competence from the perspective of discursive pragmatics where meaning and actions are co-constructed in the talk-in-interaction. This is followed by an outline of the architecture of word search sequences based on CA studies. Details of the methodology of CA will be introduced in Chapter 3.

Through outlining the common patterns found regarding word search sequences, we discuss our perspective of word searches as an interactional competence and also their dualistic nature in L2/ELF interaction. Word search sequences by L2 speakers share much in common with L1 speakers' word searches. However, in L2/ELF interactions, word searches can serve a dual purpose: they can be used to identify the word to progress the interaction and/or be utilised as an opportunity for learning (Brouwer 2003). Word searches are not necessarily indications of lack of linguistic knowledge, even in L2/ELF interaction (Kurhila 2006). Rather, participants need to mutually orient to the moment as having a learning aim in order for word searches to become a learning opportunity. Word search sequences are therefore of interest as a target research phenomenon because they have the potential to expose the speaker's linguistic capabilities and create learning opportunities, and because word search sequences are moments in interaction when socially shared cognition becomes visible and relevant. What is the word I want to say, what does the hearer know, how can I say it so that the other person understands, what does the speaker want to say and do – these individualised thoughts become visible through the process of speaking, attempting to understand each other and adapt, adjust and work towards reaching a mutual understanding. Word searches display a clear embodiment of how socially distributed cognition works as a collaborative, jointly constructed process. This process of the speakers to mutually agree on the aim of the word search and to co-adapt to the moment in order to complete the word search, we argue, reflects the perspective and processes of CDST.

2.1.1 WORD SEARCHES AS REPAIR

From the Conversation Analysis (CA) approach, word search sequences are referred to as a type of 'repair' sequence. 'Repair' can generally be defined as a modification mechanism of a prior speech production (Schegloff et al. 1977). It is 'the set of practices whereby a co-interactant interrupts the ongoing course of action to attend to possible trouble in speaking, hearing or understanding the talk' (Kitzinger 2013: 229). Repair is thus a mechanism used to restore or achieve mutual understanding among the participants in the interaction, and to return and progress the ongoing talk. This mutual understanding, or 'intersubjectivity' (Garfinkel 1967), refers to the shared perspective of the social world reality by the interlocutors.

Conversation analysts have distinguished between initiation of repair and the actual production of a repair (Schegloff et al. 1977). The initiation of the repair is when one speaker highlights the trouble source in the prior talk and thus stops the flow of the conversation. The speaker can initiate (self-initiated) or the hearer can initiate (other-initiated) a repair. Similarly, the repair work can be completed by the speaker (self-repair) or by the hearer (other-repair). Therefore, generally, repairs can be categorised into these four trajectories:

- self-initiated self-repair
- self-initiated other-repair
- other-initiated self-repair
- other-initiated other-repair.

Word search sequences are a type of self-initiated repair sequence, where the current speaker displays trouble locating a lexical item and moves on to a side sequence (Jefferson 1972) in order to locate the word. The sequence then can be resolved by the current speaker locating the word (self-repair) or the interlocutor providing a candidate solution (other-repair). Word search sequence in this study is used differently from sequences which seek mutual understanding of referentials, such as object, place and people names (e.g., Hayashi 2005; Heritage 2007; Y. Kim 2009). The action of word search, as mentioned previously, can be understood as interactional competence, where interactional work from the speaker and the listener is necessary in order to achieve mutual understanding.

Because the process of word searches is performed publicly, CA analysts understand that they have 'significant interactional consequences' (Hayashi 2003: 114). That is, the participation framework of the conversation shifts to solving the word search. As a result, the conversation is usually interrupted until the word search is completed or the interlocutors reach a mutual understanding. When both parties are satisfied that a common understanding has been reached, or there is no more need to pursue the word, the interlocutors will typically return to the main topic of conversation.

The other-repairs during word searches (i.e., second or third turn) have been distinguished in terms of 'repair' and 'correction' and their significance in language learning (e.g., Hosoda 2006; Seo and Koshik 2010). While 'correction' refers to the replacement of an 'error' or 'mistake' with the correct form (Kurhila 2006; Schegloff et al. 1977), 'repair' encompasses a broader range of strategies used achieve mutual understanding (MacBeth 2004). As such, we use correction in a narrow sense of repair focusing on indications of errors in interaction by a speaker, and speakers orienting to the word search as a language learning sequence. This distinction becomes important as the act of correction exposes the speakers' perspectives with respect to the interaction and each other regarding their language proficiencies. Linguistic corrections are not common in L2 interaction, as they can hinder the flow of conversation (Brouwer et al. 2004; Hauser 2010; Hosoda 2006; Wagner and Gardner 2004) and expose an expert–novice relationship (Siegel 2015). Yet, they do occur more frequently in L2 conversations than in L1 conversations, but when they do occur, they are often embedded rather than exposed (Brouwer et al. 2004; Hauser 2010).

Embedded and exposed other-repairs (corrections) are distinguished based on how the repair is presented. Embedded repairs or corrections are cases where the 'utterances are not occupied by the doing of correcting' (Jefferson 1987: 95) and the conversation progresses while the correction is done in the ongoing course of talk. In contrast, exposed repairs or corrections are when the '"correcting" has become the business' (Jefferson 1987: 97) of the talk and is isolated from the prior topic of interaction. Exposed repairs can be understood by the hearer as disagreements (M.H. Goodwin 1983a) or instruction (MacBeth 2004).

In terms of L2 interaction, embedded repairs can serve a dual purpose for confirming understanding and progressing the conversation while avoiding exposing linguistic differences. Firth (2009) suggests that embedded repair is more frequent in L2 interactions, 'because it does not implicate in any overt way the repairee's language competence; nor does it make the repairer look as though he or she is interactionally taking the proficiency high ground' (147). As such, the repair is designed to be 'under cover' and orients to the preference for self-repair (Brouwer et al. 2004).

From a CDST perspective, word searches are adaptations of the mechanism of repair to the participants' progressing their interaction, performing social actions and (where relevant) learning L2. Word searches can therefore be seen as displaying fractal features in relation to the mechanism of repair. We examine the mechanism of repair in more detail in Section 3.3.3, and the sequential architecture of word searches will be discussed in Section 2.2.

2.1.2 WORD SEARCHES AS DISFLUENCY OR A STRATEGY

Studies have found that L2 word searches are not significantly different from L1 word searches (Gullberg 2011; Kurhila 2006), yet there are also features that are specific to L2 speech, especially how word searches are conceptualised and how word search sequences can create language learning opportunities (Brouwer 2003; Sert and Amri 2021; Svennevig 2018).

The term 'word search' is often conceptualised in the field of applied linguistics as 'disfluency', 'strategic competence' or 'communication strategies'. Often word searches are understood from a language deficiency viewpoint and considered as a sign of 'disfluency', 'trouble' and a 'display of lack of linguistic knowledge' of the L2 learner (e.g., Hilton 2008; Koizumi and In'nami 2013). Oral fluency, which is characterised by a person's perceptions of ease, eloquence and smoothness of speech, has been associated with person's general language proficiency (Housen and Kuiken 2009). Therefore, from this perspective, hesitation markers and pauses in speech, which are components of word search sequences, are typical signs of lower language proficiency. This perspective is reflected in L2 testing where the use of word searches is conceptualised as a lack of fluency (IELTS n.d.).

In contrast, coming from a communicative competence perspective, actions used by L2 learners to deal with referential or lexical identification problems during talk have been labelled as 'strategic competence' (Canale and Swain 1980) or 'communication strategies'(Færch and Kasper 1983; Tarone 1983). These are strategies that speakers use to overcome problems in communicating a message due to a lack in their linguistic system and involve an attempt to solve or avoid the problem. Kasper and Kellerman (1997) observe that word searches occur when 'a speaker wishes to label a concept for which she does not have the lexical resources, or where these resources are available but cannot be recalled, or where available and retrievable resources cannot be used successfully because of contextual constraints' (8). However, these perspectives of word search in L2 interaction view the L2 speaker's activities and attempts to reach mutual understanding with the interlocutor as an individual activity; in other words, little consideration is given to the immediate interactional environment, including the speech of the interlocutor (Tarone 1983).

2.1.3 WORD SEARCH AS INTERACTIONAL COMPETENCE

The use of word search sequences by L2 users can also be conceptualised as a type of 'interactional competence' (e.g., Pekarek Doehler and Berger 2019; Skogmyr Marian and Pekarek Doehler 2022). We briefly explain the background and our stance on interactional competence before describing what has been found regarding word searches from this perspective.

Kramsch (1986) was the first to suggest the term 'interactional competence' and describes it as 'the discourse parameters of language in use' (369). It builds upon the notion of communicative competence (Canale and Swain 1980; Hymes 1972, 1974), which aimed to understand the influence of social dimensions on language and language use. But interactional competence is different from communicative competence in that it focuses on what people actually 'do' in comparison with what people may 'know', such as being able to (1) negotiate intended meanings (for instance, by adapting one's speech to the listener), (2) anticipate the listener's response and possible misunderstandings, (3) clarify one's own and the other's intentions, and (4) achieve mutual understanding among the participants (Kramsch 1986).

He and Young (1998) take a slightly different approach to interactional competence by emphasising the co-construction aspect of interactional competence. They also stress that interactional competence cannot be attributed to an individual and cannot be measured individually out of context. R.F. Young (2008) further describes interactional competence as the 'knowledge of the relation between language forms and the social context in which they are used' (105). He understands that an individual's competence varies according to the interlocutor and the specific interactional practice, and underscores that it is 'not what a person knows, it is what a person does together with *others*' (R.F. Young 2008: 106; emphasis added).

Coming from a CA perspective, Kasper (2006a) and J.K. Hall and Pekarek Doehler (2011) take a discursive pragmatic perspective to interactional competence. A discursive approach is a perspective deriving from discursive sociology (Bilmes 1986) and discursive psychology (Edwards and Potter 1992) that is based on the premise that social and psychological phenomena are constructed through and together in the turn-taking between the interlocutors. Therefore, interactional competence is recognised not only as an individual's linguistic ability in the sequential activity and sociocultural awareness of the interactional environment, but also a co-constructed practice between the interlocutors through the interaction in achieving and maintaining mutual understanding. In other words, interactional competence is the speaker's capacity to construct meaning and action not only constructed *in* but also *through* social interaction.

In this study, we adopt the perspective of interactional competence proposed by R.F. Young (2008), Kasper (2006b), and J.K. Hall and Pekarek Doehler (2011), and will use it to refer to discursive pragmatics, that is, word searches as an interactional practice used *through* interaction in co-constructing meaning and action. Although we will be using the term 'interactional competence' in this book to label the focal phenomena (i.e., word search sequences) and to enable comparison with other similar studies, we also recognise the potential limitations it may create when surveying the literature, and will include studies that use different terminologies to study a similar phenomenon.

From this interactional competence perspective (J.K. Hall and Pekarek Doehler 2011; Kasper 2006b; R.F. Young 2008) on word searches, studies have shown that word searches are not necessarily indications of lack of linguistic knowledge. Rather, they display the cooperative nature of the interaction and ability of the speakers to work collaboratively to reach a mutual understanding (Kurhila 2006). Moreover, word search sequences are moments in talk where the speaker's linguistic preferences and awareness of others' linguistic preferences (Greer 2013b) can be utilised as opportunities for language learning with mutual agreement (e.g., Kurhila 2006; Theodórsdóttir 2018). For example, Brouwer (2004) investigated instances which she calls 'doing pronunciation', where the L2 speaker repairs her pronunciation based on the L1 speaker's correction. Such cases resonate with the disfluency model of word searches. However, she also found that not all pronunciation errors are corrected by the L1 speaker, and L2 speakers will pursue other-correction. Similar findings have been reported where the L2 speaker will pursue other-repair regarding vocabulary and grammar features from the L1 speaker (e.g., Kurhila 2006; Theodórsdóttir 2018).

Brouwer (2004) indicates that it is 'necessary for the interlocutors to agree on the nature of the trouble, and how it may be repaired' (103-4). As will be discussed later in this chapter, this co-adaptive nature of word searches as an interactional competence aligns with the perspective and approach of CA and CDST.

2.2 PATTERNS OF WORD SEARCH SEQUENCES

Now that we have established the conceptualisation of word searches as an interactional competence (rather than as a deficit), in this section we move on to describing the features and patterns of word search sequences identified through CA analyses.

2.2.1 THE OBJECTS OF WORD SEARCH SEQUENCES

A wide range of objects become the target of word searches: lexical items, grammar, pronunciation. Kurhila (2006) indicates that L1 speakers usually search for lexical items while L2 speakers search for lexical and syntactic items. Moreover, data presented in L1 word search suggest that L1 speakers (with no language related issues such as aphasia) often search for referentials rather than general lexical items (M.H. Goodwin 1983a; Schegloff 1984; Schegloff et al. 1977).

L2 speakers also often initiate a search for the appropriate form of the word, thus initiating grammatical searches, even when L1 speakers are not responding to ungrammaticality in their speech (Kurhila 2006). This tendency of L2 speakers to self-repair grammar is also found in L2–L2 speaker interaction (e.g., Kaur 2009), suggesting that L2 speakers consider grammatical accurateness as being important for communication.

Pronunciation of a word also often becomes the object of a word search. In her study of L1–L2 speaker interaction, Brouwer (2004) investigated instances of 'doing pronunciation' where the L2 speaker initiates a search for the 'correct' pronunciation of a word repair. Not all pronunciation errors by the L2 speaker were corrected by the L1 speaker; and the 'corrections' by the L1 speaker were not regarding the L2 speaker's foreign accent. Rather, the corrections focused on phonemes, such as /ryksa;k/ and /rygsæk/, thus 'engaging in learning which sounds of the language are distinctive' (Brouwer 2004: 108).

2.2.2 THE SEQUENTIAL PATTERN OF WORD SEARCH SEQUENCES

In terms of the sequential pattern, Koshik and Seo (2012) identified three types of word search sequence patterns in L2 interaction as shown below:

> Type 1. Self-initiated/self-completed
> A: initiates word search
> A: provides solution
>
> Type 2. Self-initiated/other-completed
> A: initiates word search

> B: provides candidate solution
> A: confirms/disconfirms candidate solution

> Type 3. Self-initiated self-candidate solution/other-completed
> A: initiates word search
> A: provides candidate solution
> B: confirms/corrects candidate solution

The first type is when the current speaker initiates a word search and then finds the word themselves to complete the word search and returns to the main conversation. The second type is when the current speaker initiates the word search and the second speaker provides a candidate solution. Then the first speaker has the option of confirming or disconfirming the candidate word. The third type of word search is when the first speaker initiates a word search and attempts to solve the word search by providing a candidate word, often accompanied with a rising intonation or 'try-marking'. Then the second speaker confirms or disconfirms the candidate word. This third turn in word search sequences (in both Type 2 and Type 3) is critical to complete the word search and for the speakers to return to the main topic of conversation. The returning to the main topic in or after this third turn position (when the candidate solution is confirmed) also signals that the speakers have reached a moment of intersubjectivity in relation to what they are talking about (Kurhila 2006), or at least the speakers have reached a point where they are ready to move on (Siegel 2018).

Below, we go through these sequential turns and outline findings from the literature on how word searches are initiated, candidate solutions are provided, and third turns are conducted.

2.2.3 INITIATING A WORD SEARCH

In L1 speech, as well as L2 speech, the start of a word search sequence is usually initiated through turns-at-talk and embodiment in talk when the speakers display difficulty in finding or producing a relatively lexically or syntactically appropriate word or phrase to complete the turn. The L2 speaker would occasionally stop the turn construction unit in progress or start a side sequence to check the correctness of a lexical item or invite the other speaker to the word in search (Hosoda 2006). Below, we will outline some examples of how this is done.

2.2.3.1 Non-lexical speech perturbations

Word searches are also frequently initiated or marked with the use of non-lexical speech perturbations (Schegloff et al. 1977). These include, for instance, short pauses, elongated vowel sounds, brief hesitation markers that are less noticeable to the hearer or 'uh's and 'uhm's (M.H. Goodwin 1983b; Schegloff et al. 1977; Schegloff 1984). 'Uh's are also commonly found in the position of the object of the search (Schegloff 1979). Brouwer (2004) suggests that speech perturbations such as 'uh' can be considered as 'possible pre-indicators of repair initiation' (95) due to the tendency that repair initiations occur right after them, but not always. These speech perturbations are often followed by wh-questions (e.g., 'what was her name') (M.H. Goodwin 1983b) or 'response cries' such as 'tch' (Goffman 1981b).

Carroll (2005) found Japanese learners of English initiate word searches while attempting to keep their turn by elongating vowel sounds of word endings. Below is an excerpt from Carroll (2005) between Japanese learners of English.

Excerpt 2.1 (Carroll 2005: 210)
```
1    S:    I wen' to::: Bedorow's university?
2          (0.13)
3    K:    ohn yeah good
```

In line 1, S initiates and sustains a word search through an elongated vowel ending. S then presents the solution with a rising intonation. S's use of rising intonation is ambiguous, checking the pronunciation or checking K's knowledge of the school's name. Nevertheless, S is able to keep and complete her turn and to progress the conversation. The candidate solution is then confirmed by K in line 3. Carroll (2005) also highlights that the elongated vowel endings are indicating an ongoing independent word search, and not necessarily inviting an other-completion of a word search.

2.2.3.2 Word search markers

In L1 CA literature, wh-questions are frequently identified in data when the speaker indicates that they are searching for a word (e.g., M.H. Goodwin 1983b; M.H. Goodwin and C. Goodwin 1986). L2 speakers, on the other hand, often are reported to use explicit 'word search markers' (Brouwer 2003) to indicate that the speaker has trouble locating a word. These include multi-word expressions such as 'I don't know what it is in Danish', 'Is it Danish?', 'I don't know how to say it', 'How does one say it?', 'What does one say' (Brouwer 2003: 540) or 'What's it called in Norwegian' (Svennevig 2018). These word search markers can be used to request help from the interlocutor or to indicate an ongoing self-search, depending on the interactional environment and embodiment (Skogmyr Marian and Pekarek Doehler 2022). Moreover, the use of these word search markers can change over time, indicating a move from other-reliance to self-reliance (Pekarek Doehler and Skogmyr Marian 2022). As a variation of the use of the word search marker, Wong (2000b) found L2 speakers (L1 Mandarin) inserting 'yeah' in the slot for a candidate solution; for example, 'how can I say/explain + yeah'. She suggests that this indicates the continuation of the search and failure of finding a candidate solution.

Hayashi (2003) notes that the above mentioned pattern of word search sequences can also be found in L1 Japanese interactions. For instance, he found speakers using 'ano' (uhm) or 'nanka' (like) to indicate a possible trouble or as a delaying device, followed by self-addressed questions such as 'nandakke' (what is it). However, he also found distinct features of Japanese word searches of using of distal pronouns such as 'are' (that one) and 'asoko' (that place) as 'prospective indexicals' (C. Goodwin 1996). This was accompanied by simultaneous iconic gestures to not only initiate a word search, but also to simultaneously (1) indicate the domain of the word, (2) enhance the specifiability of the word at search, and (3) invite co-participation to complete the word search.

2.2.3.3 Multimodality

Embodiment that accompanies word searches has also been found to be a key element. Whilst the speaker is conducting a 'solitary word search' (M.H. Goodwin 1983a), the gaze tends to go elsewhere than the interlocutor's eyes and the speaker displays a 'thinking face' (M.H. Goodwin and C. Goodwin 1986). The speaker often seeks mutual gaze when they invite the interlocutor to join the word search (C. Goodwin 1980; M.H. Goodwin 1983b; M.H. Goodwin and C. Goodwin 1986).

M.H. Goodwin and C. Goodwin (1986) have found that the sequence afterwards may change, depending on this existence of mutual gaze. For instance, if there is mutual gaze and the speaker is ready, and they invite the interlocutor to contribute to the word search, their contributions are acknowledged with tokens such as 'yeah' and 'right'. In contrast, if there is not a mutual gaze and the interlocutor contributes to the word search, there is no acknowledgement.

Both L1 (Bolden 2003; Dressel and Kalkhoff 2019; Dressel 2020) and L2 (Auer and Zima 2021; Hosoda 2000; Rydell 2019; Skogmyr Marian and Pekarek Doehler 2022) studies have confirmed these findings that gaze can be used to regulate the interlocutor's participation in word searches. A detailed study of gaze using an eye-tracker device has also partially supported the findings of the key role of gaze use during word searches. Auer and Zima (2021) confirm that the use of gaze can control the degree of (non-)collaboration of the hearer with the word searches, especially when sitting side-by-side and during co-tellings (i.e., when the hearer knows the topic). However, they also found that in other contexts, this was not always the case, and collaborations in solving the word search can occur despite initially not having mutual gaze (Auer and Zima 2021).

Other embodiment during repair sequences has also been found to be relevant to the interaction, including change in the torso position (Hosoda 2000), self-touching and hand movements (Greer and Nanbu 2022; Skogmyr Marian and Pekarek Doehler 2022), and smiling (Hosoda 2000). Hand gestures during the initiation of the word search can also indicate the word they are searching for through the action of the verb (Kotilainen and Kurhila 2020) or writing the word with the finger (Greer and Nanbu 2022).

2.2.4 COMPLETING A WORD SEARCH AND CANDIDATE SOLUTIONS

The completion of a word search could be done through self-repair, other-repair, or at times no explicit repair but through an indication of understanding from the interlocutor. Other-repair will either be a correction or a display of a candidate solution. However, in terms of preference organisation (Pomerantz 1984), studies have shown that self-correction or self-repair is the preferred action in word search sequences (Schegloff et al. 1977); thus, compared with other-corrections, self-corrections occur earlier in the sequence with little hesitation and fewer turns and, as a result, more frequently. Below, we will summarise what has been reported on how this is done in L2 talk especially in cases when the candidate solution is presented with uncertainty.

2.2.4.1 Try-marking
One of the common ways candidate words are presented is through use of a 'try-marker' (Sacks and Schegloff 1979). Try-marking is done by presenting a candidate understanding with raising of intonation, and occasionally followed by a brief pause. Try-marking is used when 'a speaker anticipates that the recognitional form being used will on this occasion, for this recipient, possibly be inadequate for securing recognition' (Sacks and Schegloff 1979: 18). In other words, a try-marker in L1 speech 'marks' a word when the speaker believes that the particular word choice may not be understood by the hearer.

In L2 interaction, Koshik and Seo (2012) warn that the learner's use of try-marking in a word search is ambiguous and could be used in four different ways. When used at the end of the word search, it could be (1) proffering a candidate solution for confirmation or (2) eliciting a particular term by proffering a more general term or synonym. When used at the end of a possible candidate solution, it can be (3) eliciting confirmation of the content of their talk or (4) eliciting confirmation of understanding. In other words, it could be used to self-repair or initiate other-repair.

2.2.4.2 Code-switching
Code-switching is another feature frequently found in an L2 speaker's word searches, especially when attempting to self-repair (Funayama 2002; Greer 2008, 2013b; Mori and Hasegawa 2009). It involves the use of a different language than the one used in the ongoing conversation to indicate the word they are searching for. The code-switching is usually identified in the position of the sought-for word, and its interpretation is contingent on the interactional context: it can be an initiation of the word search, a display of an ongoing self-search or a candidate solution (i.e., self-repair).

Providing a word in a different language from the ongoing conversation can be seen as a strategy used by speakers to indicate that they are searching for a word in the language that the other speaker prefers (Funayama 2002; Greer 2013b). Greer (2013b) found bilingual interactions where a speaker would switch to another commonly shared language to resolve a word search, reflecting the speaker's own preference of language as well as 'the knowledge of recipients' language preferences' (115). Mondada (2004) states, 'practices of repair initiated within a team and in the language of the team are a recurrent technique to restrict participation to the co-members of that team' (31). Therefore, code-switching is a resource that participants refer to in cross-cultural interactions during word search sequences, and reflects the speaker's (1) own linguistic knowledge and preference and (2) interpretation of the hearer's linguistic knowledge and membership.

2.2.4.3 Semantic contiguity
'Semantic contiguity' is also used by L2 speakers to initiate or resolve the word searches. These are used 'to describe an unknown referent so that the speaker tries to make the referent identifiable through synonymic, metonymic, anatomic or

superordinate relations to other words she knows and remembers' (Kurhila 2006: 117). Semantic contiguity thus can be seen as a circumlocution strategy. However, Kurhila (2006) also notes how speakers use negated semantic contiguity in word searches, for example saying, 'not really trees buts' when searching for the word 'bushes'.

2.2.4.4 Delayed and abandoned other-repair (normalising and let it pass)

Although, in general, the other-repair is done immediately after a trouble source, this can be delayed (Schegloff 2000b; Wong 2000a). For instance, 'let it pass' strategies in ELF interactions are often used where 'the hearer lets the unknown or unclear action, word or utterance "pass" on the (common-sense) assumption that it will either become clear or redundant as talk progresses' (Firth 1996: 243). As a result, the other-repair may be done later in the sequence.

In other cases, other-repair may be abandoned to prioritise progressivity of the talk. This could be done by 'normalising' (Firth 1996) non-conventional words by the hearer starting to use the non-conventional word together in the interaction; however, for critical information, other-repair was conducted immediately. Breiteneder (2005) argues that ELF communication is content-oriented, and 'there is a focus on the content rather than the form of the message' (22–3). Therefore, L2–L2 interactions demonstrate fewer uptakes of 'non-native like' linguistic usage compared with L1–L2 interactions, and have the tendency towards mutual orientation to the content and progressivity of the conversation.

Similar instances were found in conversations between aphasia patients and their families (e.g., C. Goodwin 1995; Oelschlaeger and Damico 2000). Oelschlaeger and Damico (2000) found the wife of an aphasia patient showing 'constructive adaptation' to the husband's aphasia, thus carrying out a 'normalised' conversation. The authors found the wife not repairing immediately after the initiation of a word search, but rather nodding and providing visual feedback to support the speaking effort. As a result, by just reading the transcript, it is difficult to distinguish that one of the speakers is an aphasia patient. Word search sequences in L2 interactions can be similar to aphasia patient interactions in terms of (1) word search initiation behaviours of the speaker, (2) normalisation actions of the hearer, and (3) their membership categories of 'non-native speaker' or 'patient' being ambiguous depending on the cooperation of the interlocutor.

2.2.5 THIRD POSITION IN WORD SEARCH SEQUENCES

We have seen how word searches can be self-initiated and self- or other-repaired. Here, we look at the responses to the other-repair, or the candidate solution in the third position of word search sequences. This is a critical position of the word search sequence where the candidate word provided by the first or second speaker needs to be accepted or rejected. If it is rejected, the speakers will be required to continue with their negotiation, while if it is accepted, the speakers will mutually and publicly display that they have reached an agreement and a shared cognitive state. Then, and only then, can the speakers return to the main topic of conversation.

Several studies have shown that L2 speakers confirm the repair or candidate solution in word search sequences through various means, such as repeating the candidate word (Kristiansen et al. 2017; Svennevig 2018), repeating the gesture (Gullberg 2011), producing acceptance tokens (Hosoda 2000), raising eyebrows (Gudmundsen and Svennevig 2020) or smiling (Gudmundsen and Svennevig 2020). However, different interactional goals may affect the third turn post-other-repair response. Kurhila (2006) found L2 speakers not repeating the other-repair in institutional conversations, while repeating 'corrections' in everyday talk, suggesting there are different interactional goals for different situations. Moreover, lack of comprehension can be a factor that can lead to no uptake of the other-repair by the L2 speaker (Hosoda 2000).

Studies have also noted the asymmetrical dynamics between L1 and L2 speakers during word searches (Funayama 2002; Kurhila 2006). For example, L2 speakers were found accepting candidate solutions from L1 speakers even when they were searching for a different word (Kurhila 2005). Kurhila argues that this behaviour echoes the linguistic authority that the L1 speaker possesses in L1–L2 interactions.

2.2.6 PRE-EMPTIVE REPAIR

Beyond the three types of sequential patterns described above, previous studies have found another distinct type of sequence in ELF data, that is, pre-emptive repairs. Participants in L2 talk are found using 'proactive' (Mauranen 2006) or 'pre-empting' (Kaur 2009) strategies in order to avoid misunderstanding or non-understanding. They are often done by providing a translation in the common language or additional explanation regarding a possible problematic word that is going to be said. Pre-emptive repairs are often done prior to a speaker using a word in an unconventional way (Mauranen 2006), when there is minimal response from the hearer through soft repetitions, backchannelling or silence (Kaur 2009), when new concepts are introduced which could possibly cause non-understanding (Cogo 2010), or when ideas are introduced in a language which other members may not understand (Greer 2008). For example, in Cogo's (2010) multinational interaction data, one of the speakers in the study translates the expression *'fleur bleu'* into English first, then provides the original expression in her L1 French, and finally provides the explanation of the expression. The speaker thus shows high sensitivity and awareness of this expression being culturally sensitive and prompts her to pre-empt, which leads to avoiding any non-understandings. Pre-empting repairs are relevant to word search sequences since they can be used to avoid or minimise moving into a word search side sequence and avoid misunderstandings, thus progressing the conversation.

Moreover, the use of these strategies suggests a high level of language awareness of the participants and a willingness to cooperate and work towards preventing misunderstanding and incomprehension (Mauranen 2006; Murray 2012). At the same time, it highlights the speakers' awareness of the different membership categories of the other speakers based on their language proficiencies in the talk, while working to include the 'othered' member (Greer 2008). These pre-empting strategies 'show how mutual understanding in ELF is not taken for granted, but that speakers engage in a joint effort to monitor understanding at every stage of communication, even before nonunderstanding has taken place' (Jenkins et al. 2011: 294).

2.2.7 SOCIAL EPISTEMICS AND MEMBERSHIP CATEGORISATION: LANGUAGE EXPERTISE

The final but also important feature of L2 word search sequences is related to social epistemics (Heritage 2012a, 2013; Raymond and Heritage 2006) and self- and other-positioning in the interactions in relation to linguistic expertise and goal orientation. As mentioned briefly in the previous sections, during word searches in L2 interactions, the member's identity, especially their so-called 'native speaker' or 'non-native speaker' categories, comes into play. CA studies have demonstrated that L1–L2 speaker categories are closely situated in interaction (Zimmerman 1998) and are negotiated through talk. In particular, during word search sequences, the language becomes the topic of discussion, consequently identities (or membership categories (Sacks 1989)) related to linguistic knowledge or cultural expertise become evident (e.g., Hosoda 2006; Park 2007; Siegel 2015; Taleghani-Nikazm 2014).

Funayama (2002) maintains that in cross-linguistic interactions, 'a word search initiated by a non-native speaker contains, perhaps more clearly, a request–answer dynamic between the less knowledgeable and the more knowledgeable, although this does not eliminate the collaborative, competitive, and negotiable nature of a word-search' (53). In other words, the imbalance of linguistic knowledge is manifested in the initiation of word search sequences. However, there are other scenarios: L2 speakers' word searches could be regarding the content of the talk (i.e., referential) (Y. Kim 2009; Park 2007), and the positioning of the L2 speaker as the less knowledgeable by the L1 speaker could be refuted (Park 2007). These observations are related to the notion of 'epistemics'.

'Epistemics', which refers to the way knowledge is managed in interaction, is demonstrated through the different ways in which commitment is shown towards what one is saying and in which the speaker attitudes towards knowledge are reflected (Kärkkäinen 2003). Epistemics, thus, can be understood as 'identity bound knowledge' (Raymond and Heritage 2006: 678), which was first introduced by Labov and Fanshel (1977) through A-events (A knows but B does not) and B-events (B knows but A does not). Kamio (1994, 1997) expanded on this idea by describing the knowing and unknowing positions being on a continuum, and interactants having domains of information ('territories of information') that are relatively close or distant to them compared with their interlocutor. He further argues that this concept also incorporates the understanding of not only who knows, but also who has the right to know the information and the right to express it (Kamio 1997).

Heritage (2012b) further developed this notion by addressing relative epistemic access on a scale ranging from a more knowledgeable state (K+) to a less knowledgeable one (K-). He refers to this as 'epistemic status' where 'persons recognise one another to be more or less knowledgeable concerning some domain of knowledge as a more or less settled matter of fact' (Heritage 2012b: 32). Heritage further differentiates epistemic status from epistemic stance, and uses epistemic stance in regards to how speakers position themselves or others. An example of this is Heritage's (1984a) finding of 'change of state' displayed by an 'oh' token, where an unknown (K-) recipient of information visibly shifts to a known (K+) position. Heritage (2012b) demonstrates that the K+ and K- positions or categories are displayed through the sequential organisation of talk, and the giving and receiving of information are monitored minutely and publicly. Therefore, analysing assessment sequences and participants' display of K+ and K- positions in conversations have made participants' identities visible. Furthermore, the K+ and K- imbalance between the interlocutors drives the conversation forward (Heritage 2012b).

This notion is exemplified during a conversation between a grandmother and another interlocutor in Raymond and Heritage (2006). The grandmother claims more knowledge of the grandchildren over the interlocutor, thus presenting her ownership of the grandchildren or her identity as their grandmother. As Raymond and Heritage (2006) note:

> By examining how such rights to knowledge and action are shared by speakers, or how they are distributed between them, how they are respected or how they might be violated, and how they are used to establish agreement or how they might be used to foster conflict, we can begin to explicate how identities are produced and reproduced in specific episodes of interaction. In turn, this provides a window into how the complexity of social structure is produced and reproduced through actual conduct. (701)

In other words, knowledge and situated identities are closely connected, and become apparent through the orientation of the participants.

This concept of epistemics is highly relevant for L2 speakers and L2 interaction during word search sequences. Hosoda (2006) analysed word search sequence or repair work related to lexical items between Japanese L2 speakers and L1 Japanese speakers. She found a similar phenomenon where the L2 speakers 'orient to themselves as a "novice"' and their L1 friend 'at that moment, as a language expert' (Hosoda 2006: 33) and these identities were co-constructed. Hosoda (2006) argues that a request for confirmation of a lexical item occurs when a current speaker considers that the information is within the hearer's 'territory' (Kamio 1994, 1997).

Kurhila (2006) found L1 speakers immediately addressing the L2 speaker when looking for a name or a word, whereas L2 speakers initially addressed themselves and then turned to the L1 speaker. She suggests that the L2 speaker, by referring to herself first, can demonstrate that she is potentially able to resolve the problem and display her competence as a responsible interactant. Longitudinal studies have shown this shift from other-reliance to self-reliance indicated through the change in the use of explicit word search markers and gaze work (e.g., Pekarek Doehler and Berger 2019; Siegel 2015; Skogmyr Marian and Pekarek Doehler 2022) as well as the change in recognition by the interlocutor of the speaker's possible ability to self-complete the search (Siegel 2015).

Speaker identities are co-constructed and shift during interaction. For instance, during word search sequences, speakers may undertake expert/L1 speaker and novice/L2 speaker identities, but these expert–novice or L1–L2 speaker roles shift depending on the topic (Park 2007; Siegel 2016) and depending on the interlocutor (Shea 1994), thereby influencing how one speaks. Therefore, analysing the interaction from an emic perspective can highlight self- and other-positioning in terms of social membership and orientation towards 'territory of information' (Kamio 1994). Furthermore, the ways in which epistemic stance in terms of linguistic knowledge may be negotiated and change over time has not been investigated in depth, especially in ELF environments (Pekarek Doehler and Berger 2019; Siegel 2015).

2.2.8 WORD SEARCHES IN ELF CONTEXTS

We have outlined the target linguistic phenomenon of word search sequences, and its features have been identified using CA. The majority of these findings come from research on L1–L1 or L1–L2 interactions. Only a handful of studies have examined word searches in L2–L2 interaction (e.g., Eskildsen 2011; Hellermann 2009a; Kaur 2009) or multilingual interactions (e.g., Greer 2013b). All these studies take place in a language learning context. Other studies have explicitly mentioned that the studies were conducted in an ELF context (e.g., Pietikäinen 2020; Siegel 2015, 2021). For example, in ELF context interactions between speakers with a close relationship, the second speaker does not immediately provide the candidate solution during word searches, and would only provide a corrective repair when explicitly prompted (Pietikäinen 2020; Siegel 2015).

However, there is limited understanding of how word searches are conducted in L2–L2 interactions/ELF contexts, and even less of how word searches change over time, as will be discussed below in the next sections. The current project aims to fill these gaps.

2.3 DEVELOPMENTAL STUDIES ON INTERACTIONAL COMPETENCE

Now that we have conceptualised word search sequences as an interactional competence, we move on to conceptualise 'development' when conducting longitudinal analysis of L2 interaction. In the following sections, we review the developing area of longitudinal Conversation Analysis for Second Language Acquisition (CA-for-SLA) studies, focusing on their approaches to collecting and analysing data. We will review the ways in which developmental theories are used in analysing development of L2 interactional competence and synthesise how development is described through empirical data in longitudinal CA studies. We then provide the definitions of 'development' and 'learning' used in this study and introduce the framework of CDST used for the analysis.

2.3.1 LONGITUDINAL CA FOR SLA STUDIES

CA was not originally intended to be used for tracking language development, and CA's classical assumption is the speakers' skills remain the same and thus analysts can examine the organisation of interaction (Brouwer 2004). According to He (2004), 'CA is not concerned with the cognitive processes that enable the learner to absorb the interactional data internally; nor does CA address the process of learning over an extended period of time' (578). Nevertheless, researchers have demonstrated ways in which language developmental research might be approached using CA.

Wootton (1997) was one of the first to conduct a longitudinal study of development of interactional competence using CA. He conducted a detailed analysis of his child's L1 speech and interaction across 12 months. By taking this approach, he was able to unfold the process of the child's development of the use of requests as part of the development of interactional and social cognitive competencies (Wootton 1997). Since this study, increasing numbers of longitudinal studies of L2 development adopting a CA analytical approach have been conducted, and have repeatedly demonstrated that CA can be applied to interactions taking place across time to analyse changes in language use and participation practices.

Longitudinal CA or 'macro-longitudinal CA' (Markee 2010) has been applied not only to analyse L2 development, but also to L1 speakers who are: new to a certain context (e.g., Nguyen 2008, 2011), aphasia patients (e.g., Wilkinson et al. 2007) or children (e.g., Carlin and Kim 2021; Kılıç and Balaman 2023). However, the majority of longitudinal CA (or CA-inspired) studies are conducted on L1–L2 or L2–L2 interaction with the aim of identifying change over time.

At the time this book was written, 55 studies were identified that used longitudinal CA to analyse L2 interactional competence. The duration of data collection ranges from 1 week to 3.5 years, with an average length of approximately 38 weeks, a little over 9 months. Intervals of data collection vary greatly, with some studies only collecting data at two time points, while others use shorter and more frequent intervals. The status of interactional partners differed also, with some studies having fixed interlocutors and others having alternating interlocutors. Research contexts frequently take place in the classroom (Hellermann and Cole 2008; Hellermann 2008, 2009a, 2009b) or a language learning related context including tutoring sessions, study groups or out of class tasks, online study platforms, language exchanges and office hours. An increasing number of studies, however, have started to investigate language development in non-institutional settings of everyday life, that is, 'in the wild'. These contexts include the home or homestays (Greer 2019a; Pekarek Doehler and Skogmyr Marian 2022), hair salons (Greer 2013a), dormitories (Siegel 2015), stores (S. Kim 2019) and hotels (Nguyen 2019).

Longitudinal CA-for-SLA studies focus on various aspects of interactional competence including: the use of multimodality such as gaze and body use (e.g., Skogmyr Marian and Pekarek Doehler 2022); participation methods to social activities, for example how to engage in an office hour talk or classroom discussion (e.g., Nguyen 2012; Watanabe 2017); and language use, such as the use of lexical items (e.g., Eskildsen 2009; Hauser 2017; Theodórsdóttir and Eskildsen 2022), repair (e.g., Pekarek Doehler and Berger 2018, 2019) and turn design (e.g., Greer 2019a; Taguchi 2014) to demonstrate an increase in effectiveness in communication in the L2. These longitudinal studies have shown how speakers adjust their language over time to increase the effectiveness of their communication skills (i.e., interactional competence). These studies have noted improvements in conversational smoothness, reduced reliance on the interlocutor, and increased participation and turn-taking abilities. These changes in the use of linguistic items and approaches to participation have been described as 'development'. Below, we explain these theories and approach, then we reconceptualise the notion of 'development' in relation to the empirical data of the studies.

2.3.2 DEVELOPMENTAL THEORIES AND APPROACHES

2.3.2.1 Sociocultural theory

One of the fundamental conceptualisations of language development is rooted in Vygotsky's (1978) sociocultural theory. Vygotsky takes the perspective that development is observable and the learning process is necessary for the developmental process to occur. However, learning and development are not coincidental; the developmental process lags behind the learning process. Furthermore, he suggests that development is never ending, that is, an initial mastery of a certain skill or knowledge 'provides the basis for the subsequent development of a variety of highly complex internal processes' (Vygotsky 1978: 90). Ishida (2011) and Ohta (2001) in their study of L2 interactional competence align their view to Vygotsky (1978), and differentiate learning from development. Ohta (2001), based on the interviews with the participants, argues that the learners are doing 'learning' that cannot be seen only from the recordings and they are 'developing' from cumulative efforts and challenges.

2.3.2.2 Situated learning theory

In contrast, in situated learning theory, 'learning' is viewed as the activities that the learners do to 'participate in the communities of practitioners and that the mastery of knowledge and skills requires newcomers to move towards full participation in the sociocultural practices of a community' (Lave and Wenger 1991: 29) with the guidance of a member of the community. In other words, language learning is seen as participation (Sfard 1998) and a mutual engagement in a joint enterprise in achieving a shared repertoire (Wenger 1998) for a certain community. Thus, 'development' entails becoming a fuller participant in the social practices of a community.

These studies using the situated learning theory have shown CA's capacity in locating change and development over time in talk-in-interaction in terms of participation of learners and sequential word usage including turn-taking patterns in relation to the interlocutor. Furthermore, the studies have shown that learning and participation are closely connected. For instance, with an adult Vietnamese learner of English during writing workshops, Young and Miller (2004) found an increase in turn-taking skills and sequential organisation (e.g., transition between topics). Similarly, Cekaite (2007) found child L2 learners moving towards fuller participation through turn-taking behaviour. More specifically, she found the learner being silent in class at first, then using inappropriate turn-takings, and at the end of three semesters the learner was using appropriate turn-takings. Hellermann (2008) in his study of ESL classroom dyadic tasks found a newcomer to the USA 'adjusting practices for participation in subsequent engagements in the particular action based on what was required and provided by the local context for the engagement' (154), and developing new task-openings and closings in their interactions.

Nevertheless, concerns have been raised regarding the applicability of this theory when analysing development using CA. For instance, Appel (2010) argues that participation and learning are not synonymous and that participation can actually constrain learning in some cases, especially in classroom settings, where members can be denied access to learning opportunities or have difficulty accomplishing tasks due to the different participation styles they are used to from previous classroom experiences. Moreover, concerns have been raised that CA studies are data-driven in nature, and by using exogenous theories such as the situated learning theory, analyses could become theory 'driven' rather than theory 'informed' (Hauser 2011). In other words, the study may not always be based on conversational achievements but uses the theory to claim that the identified language use phenomenon is a developmental feature.

Finally, in the ELF context, such as the current study, an additional aspect needs to be taken into account. The situated learning theory assumes the presence of a pre-existing community and a mentor or expert. However, in situations where the community and its members are not predetermined or are more fluid and dynamic, it becomes challenging to establish a clear benchmark for determining 'development'.

2.3.2.3 Usage-based theory

Longitudinal CA studies, more recently, seem to be divided into two strands in terms of how they theorise 'development', one of which is the 'usage-based theory' (Tomasello 2000, 2009), and the other is the data-driven approach (Markee 2008). The usage-based perspective views language as a collection of semiotic resources that are acquired through language use (Eskildsen 2012; Eskildsen and Cadierno 2015; Tomasello 2000), thus seeing language development as non-linear and grounded in language use (e.g., Roehr-Brackin 2014; Tomasello 2009; Verspoor et al. 2012). Tomasello (2000) lays out the perspective of usage-based models and describes:

1. the units of language with which people operate are not presupposed or prejudged
2. there is an explicit concern with processes of communication in usage events
3. the primary research questions are how human linguistic competence has evolved historically and how today it develops ontogenetically. (78)

In essence, usage-based models understand that language emerges from communication and communicative needs, and traditional language acquisition distinctions of competence and performance are transcended.

Studies that adopt the usage-based approach to longitudinal CA have demonstrated the gradual expansion of the use of a certain word or a phrase (e.g., 'how do you say', 'what do you say') from a specific use to a wider range of contexts and functions (e.g., Eskildsen 2009, 2011, 2018; Pekarek Doehler 2018; Pekarek Doehler and Skogmyr Marian 2022), and adapting news ways of conducting similar actions, such as story-openings (Pekarek Doehler and Berger 2018). These studies have indicated a certain trajectory of development: from a limited range of literal use of a certain grammatical or phrasal construction towards a diversified range of uses (Pekarek Doehler 2018; Pekarek Doehler and Berger 2018). At the same time, they have demonstrated individual differences and non-standard language use emerging and stabilising as a repertoire through multiple interactions across time, demonstrating non-linear development (Eskildsen 2012).

As will be shown below, the concerns and perspectives towards language and language development of the usage-based approach are not significantly different from data-driven longitudinal CA studies. One thing that does differentiate the approaches, however, is that the usage-based approach focuses on the individual speaker's change, while the interlocutor's language use or changes are not incorporated into the analysis.

2.3.2.4 Data-driven or learning behaviour tracking

Other longitudinal CA studies that do not claim to use any explicit developmental theory assert that CA is sufficient to document the change and (social) cognition of the participants. The authors often use the terms 'data-driven' (e.g., Hauser 2011; Jenks 2010) or 'learning behaviour tracking' (Markee 2008) to explain their approach to emphasise that the researchers do not hold preconceptualised learning theories about the data or the participants.

CA was not originally developed with an intent to document change of language use over time (Brouwer and Wagner 2004), nor is it associated with any theories of development or learning (He 2004). However, CA is not 'strictly anti-cognitive' (Kasper 1997: 310) either. CA understands cognition as socially shared, that is:

> participants in interaction constantly analyse each other's conduct for its locally emerging meanings, monitor their own, and display their understandings to each other through the details of their talk. In this way, cognition goes public as participants' joint enterprise and becomes available to researchers for analysis. (Kasper 2009: 12)

For instance in Markee's (2008) study, the word 'prerequisite' is introduced in an orientation session through a PowerPoint presentation and lecture. Two days later, the student shows her attempt in using and understanding of usage of the new word, and it becomes an object of a repair sequence between student and teacher. Although Markee does not have recorded data, it was then later reported by the teacher that the student was found autonomously using the word 'prerequisite'.

2.3.3 ACTUAL PORTRAYAL OF DEVELOPMENT OF L2 INTERACTIONAL COMPETENCE IN LONGITUDINAL CA-FOR-SLA STUDIES

Studies that employ sociocultural theory, situated learning theory and usage-based understanding of L2 development describe the ways in which L2 speakers change within their immediate interactional environment to improve mutual understanding and the progressivity of the conversation. These studies are all empirically based and provide insights into 'development' of L2 interactional competence. When focusing on the empirical data that is displayed in these studies, regardless of the learning theories employed (or not) when synthesising the analyses of longitudinal CA-for-SLA studies, the ways in which 'development' is conceptualised in the studies can be synthesised into one of the following categories. That is, L2 development is:

1. the diversification of lexical or syntactic formulations to convey a concept or functional meaning
2. the increase in contexts in which the same or similar lexical items are employed
3. the expansion of linguistic or behavioural versatility that enables increased participation in communicative events
4. co-adaptation between the speakers.

The first category includes studies where 'development' is identified when the learner shows increase in the variety of expressions to convey a similar concept (Balaman 2018; Eskildsen 2012; Hauser 2013b, 2013c; König 2013). For example, Hauser documented an L2 learner of English shifting their use of negation from 'no understand' to 'don't understand' (Hauser 2013c) and expanding his variation of doing direct reported speech (Hauser 2013b) over multiple encounters.

The second category pertains to studies that demonstrate the expansion of the use of a specific lexical item across different contexts and is regarded as a process of linguistic 'development' (e.g., Hauser 2017; Ishida 2009; Pekarek Doehler and Berger 2018, 2019; Pekarek Doehler and Skogmyr Marian 2022; Theodórsdóttir and Eskildsen 2022). For instance, in Ishida's (2009) investigation, a student during a study abroad was observed using the Japanese discourse marker '*ne*' first in a limited context, but then in various interactional settings and for different communicative purposes. Similarly, Theodórsdóttir and Eskildsen's (2022) study documents an L2 learner of Icelandic who, after being taught the expression '*ég ætla*' in the context of making requests in service encounters, eventually masters it, but then later on re-learns it to use it in a different context of peer conversations and for a different function of making an account.

The third category presents L2 development of L2 speakers shifting their participatory actions for a similar task over time, such as task openings, so as to make the activity more efficient or 'appropriate' for the context (Greer 2016, 2019a; Hellermann and Cole 2008; Nguyen 2012; Watanabe 2017). For example, Watanabe (2017) documented how a child in an EFL classroom changed when and how to respond to the teacher's prompts over time and increased the uptake of his contributions by the teacher. Similarly, Nguyen (2012) presents a case where an L2 learner engages in an office hour for their first time having a slower reaction to the cues of shifting from doing updates to talking about the writing. Later in the semester, the student shows increased sensitivity to the verbal and non-verbal cues of the teacher and shows smoother transition between the two tasks. Therefore, these studies demonstrate the changes not only in students' speaking ability, but also in their listening ability and context awareness. Moreover, many of these studies adopt situated learning theory to make connections between the different data points and to bring a developmental perspective to it.

The developmental features described in the above three categories are all indeed changes in interactional competence from the perspective of discursive practice. The studies show the linear and also the non-linear process development where language use may stabilise in a non-standard-like manner. Nevertheless, the studies outlined above rarely consider the changes that may be occurring to the interlocutor and how that may be affecting the focal speaker. Furthermore, longitudinal CA-for-SLA studies have frequently failed to track the same participant group over time for accurate comparison to be possible (Brouwer and Wagner 2004). This issue persists despite learning theories (e.g., Lave and Wenger 1991; Vygotsky 1978) and empirical findings from CA research demonstrating that the surrounding interactional environment, especially the interlocutor, affects how people converse.

The final category, however, includes studies incorporating the core aspects of CDST and interactional competence (R.F. Young 2019), but it is rarely discussed as 'development'. This is the aspect of *mutual* adaptation and incorporating the analysis and changes of the interlocutor into the analysis of 'change'. Greer (2013a) observes how a hairdresser and a customer over multiple encounters mutually shift their language use to match the other speaker's preference or proficiency. The Japanese L1 speaking hairdresser starts to use English in repetition turns for confirmation, which is the customer's preferred language. The customer, in contrast, attempts to use Japanese at the beginning, but then starts to use more English after noticing the high English comprehension ability of the hairdresser. As a result, the two speakers display mutual accommodation through multilingual use and code-mixing. Similarly in an ELF context, Siegel (2021) tracks a gradual increase in utilisation of a shared L2, Japanese, as a means of communication between a Japanese and Thai speaker. This phenomenon occurs as the Japanese speaker recognises the Thai speaker's growing proficiency in Japanese over time. Additionally, as the Japanese speaker begins to take Thai language classes, an emergence of the shared third language (L3), Thai, is observed.

This is not the traditional conceptualisation of 'language development' as the change is not on a trajectory towards a standard-like language use. However, from an interactional competence and CDST perspective, the speakers are mutually adapting to each other's language preferences and proficiency, which facilitates a smoother conversation and reflects the closer social relationship. As R.F. Young (2019) correctly indicates, the majority of longitudinal CA studies focus purely on the target speaker (frequently the so-called 'learner'), and little attention has been paid to how the interlocutor or the surrounding community may be changing and adapting to the speaker(s). Lemke (2000) states, 'There is still a strong individualist bias in our modernist traditions of research' (288).

Therefore, the current study conceptualises 'development' as visible changes as a result of adaptation to the local interactional environment. Development is therefore viewed as a non-linear process that entails the four aspects of language development mentioned above that include the expansion of linguistic items, the expansion of the context of the use of a linguistic item, the increase in participation of a social context, and the co-adaptation between the speakers.

2.3.4 LONGITUDINAL CHANGE OF L2 WORD SEARCH SEQUENCES

In terms of our target linguistic feature of word searches and longitudinal development, a number of studies have investigated how word searches may change in interaction over time (Eskildsen 2011; Hellermann 2009a; Pekarek Doehler and Berger 2019; Pekarek Doehler and Skogmyr Marian 2022; Siegel 2015; Skogmyr Marian and Pekarek Doehler 2022). The findings of these studies match the above mentioned framework of development. They describe how speakers have (1) diversified their method of initiating word searches (Eskildsen 2011), (2) expanded the contexts in which a word search marker is used (Eskildsen 2011), (3) expanded the use of a word search marker, from inviting repair to keeping a turn (Pekarek Doehler and Berger 2019; Siegel 2015; Skogmyr Marian and Pekarek Doehler 2022), and (4) shown gradual mutual adaptation to each other (Siegel 2015).

For example, Eskildsen (2011) displays the expansion of multi-word expressions using the auxiliary word 'do' as well as the expansion of the function of the use of the multi-word expression 'what do you say' of an L2 user of English in a classroom setting over a one-year period. 'What do you say' was initially used for an invitation for lexical help or display thinking, then later used for asking or challenging something previously done or said by the interlocutor, then used for eliciting other people's thoughts or opinions.

Similarly, Pekarek Doehler and her colleagues (Pekarek Doehler and Berger 2019; Pekarek Doehler and Skogmyr Marian 2022; Skogmyr Marian and Pekarek Doehler 2022) describe how an L2 user of French through her 15-month stay in France shows a change in use of '*comment on dit*' (how do you say) from the literal use (request for word) to a discourse-marker-like use (displaying solitary search). This corroborates Hellermann's (2009a) study in the classroom where he found an increase in the frequency of self-initiated self-repair sequences. Siegel (2015), however, brings an adaptive view of word searches and demonstrates how the interlocutor shifts their participation framework during the word searches and shows increased recognition of the speaker's possible ability to self-complete the search.

Although a cross-sectional study, D.R. Kim (2020) found novice speakers using self-repair for word searches, while intermediate speakers used it for grammatical searches. Moreover, while the advanced speakers would use self-repairs for specifying the item (e.g., book to novel), novices would tend to broaden the terms of reference of the item when attempting to resolve the word search (e.g., community to people). D.R. Kim (2020) therefore concludes that this 'proactive self-repair' or pre-emptive repair done by advanced speakers is significant evidence of recipient design and demonstrates the speakers' sensitivity to the context and collaborative efforts to reach mutual understanding.

As shown above, we are slowly gaining some insights into longitudinal change of L2 word search sequences. Yet, there is much we still do not know. None of the studies has explored how the development of word searches can be seen from a CDST perspective as involving complex adaptive systems. They take a linear perspective of development, and have not explored how individuals may show similarities and differences from the group. Moreover, Siegel (2015) is the only longitudinal study conducted in an ELF context, and thus word search features emerging in ELF contexts are still largely unexplored. These gaps in research we aim to fill through the analyses in Chapters 4 and 5.

2.4 COMPLEX DYNAMIC SYSTEMS THEORY AND L2 INTERACTION

2.4.1 COMPLEX DYNAMIC SYSTEMS THEORY IN APPLIED LINGUISTICS

Here, we revisit the discussion of Complex Dynamic Systems Theory (CDST) which we briefly started in Chapter 1, and introduce the principles which we will be employing in the analysis. CDST is a scientific framework that studies non-linear phenomena and attempts to understand them from a holistic perspective. It is characterised by the occurrence of periodic and apparently random events in a deterministic system, resulting in unpredictable behaviour and changing patterns that partly repeat but never quite repeat (Sardar and Abrams 2004). CDST emerged from experimental mathematics, and one of its pioneers was Edward Lorenz, who used a computer model for weather predictions in the 1960s. Lorenz discovered that small changes in initial conditions, such as rounding errors in numbers, can lead to drastically different results, which became known as the 'butterfly effect' (Gribbin 2004; J. Smith and Jenks 2006).

The 'theory' in CDST does not refer to theory in the sense of hypothesis testing or set of rules, but rather as a perspective to understand the complex and dynamic nature of life-related systems, including the social world. In the social world, the relation between cause and effect is complex. Effects or outcomes derive from multiple causes and vary depending on the context. In spite of this, much positivistic scientific and social science research in the past has assumed that groups are homogeneous, development is linear and causes are dividable into separate variables. By contrast, CDST holistically embraces the multiple, dynamic, non-linear nature of life-related systems. Larsen-Freeman (2013) refers to CDST as a 'meta-theory' which is 'a set of coherent principles of reality (i.e., ontological ideas) and principles of knowing (i.e., epistemological ideas)' (Hiver and Al-Hoorie 2020: 20). As Larsen-Freeman (2010) explains, 'As two language users interact, they adapt to each other. This co-adaptation process results in a transformation of the language resources of each participant, and ultimately, on a longer time-scale and at another level, across a speech community' (58).

Other terms besides CDST are used to refer to similar phenomena, including Complexity Theory, Emergent Systems Theory, Chaos Theory and Dynamic Systems Theory.[1] Complex Dynamic Systems Theory (CDST) (de Bot 2017) is becoming more accepted in the field of SLA, thus is used for this book.

---

[1] The term 'Evolving Systems' has also been introduced. A new law of physics has recently been proposed (Wong et al. 2023) to explain how complex systems evolve, namely the 'Law of Increasing Functional Information'. This states that the functional information of a system will increase (i.e.,

CDST describes how life-supporting real-world systems function. Gell-Mann (1994b) explains:

> [A] complex adaptive system acquires information about its environment and its own interaction with that environment, identifying regularities in that information, condensing those regularities into a kind of 'schema' or model, and acting in the real world on the basis of that schema. In each case, there are various competing schemata, and the results of that action in the real world feed back to influence the competition among those schemata. (17)

The bottom-line goal of this complexity science – the study of CDST and complex adaptive systems – is to 'understand, predict and control such emergent phenomena – in particular, potentially catastrophic crowd-like effects such as market crashes, traffic jams, epidemics, illnesses such as cancer, human conflicts, and environmental change' (N.F. Johnson 2007: 5). In terms of social interaction, we are interested how spoken human interaction functions as a complex adaptive system: the emergent patterns of interaction, how mutual understanding is achieved, and the ways in which utterances affect the interlocutor and the interaction.

2.4.2 PRINCIPLES OF COMPLEX ADAPTIVE SYSTEMS

When analysing CDST, 'principles' are commonly used to describe the features which a complex adaptive system should have, which can be verified by observing the behaviours which the phenomena should then show (N.F. Johnson 2007). Researchers have different explanations of what components comprise complex adaptive systems; therefore, there is no agreement on a single list of principles for a complex adaptive system. The principles of a complex adaptive system vary depending on the field and the researcher, and are selected based on the phenomena that are being studied.

Holland (1992, 1995) was one of the first to discuss the core principles of a complex adaptive system. From a mathematical point of view, Holland (1992, 1995) introduces the following principles:

1. Aggregation: (property) Complexity emerges from the interaction of smaller components, which themselves may be the products of systems.
2. Tagging: (mechanism) Agents are differentiated and possess a manner in which to discriminate agents with particular properties.
3. Non-linearity: (property) Agents interact in dynamical and non-linear ways.
4. Flows: (property) Agents organise into networks of interaction in which one interaction may trigger (flow) following interactions.

---

the system will evolve) if many different configurations of the system are subjected to selection for one or more functions. This force towards greater complexity counteracts the movement towards entropy deriving from the second law of thermodynamics.

5. Diversity: (property) Agents evolve to fill diverse niches, which are defined by the specifics of agent interactions. The concept of a niche outlives the inhabiting agents, and the evolution of niches has a larger impact on the system than the evolution of agents (levels of abstraction and control).
6. Internal models: (mechanism) Agents are changed through their interactions, and the changes bias future actions (agents adapt). The internal representations possess information as how to exploit the regularity of their interactions, without necessarily explicitly defining that regularity.
7. Building blocks: (mechanism) Components are reused for multiple purposes.

In contrast, from the field of physics, Gell-Mann (1994a) lists the following principles:

1. Coarse graining: Trade-off between the coarseness for manageability of information and fineness for adequate detail in information.
2. Identification: Sorting out of regularities from randomness in information from the environment.
3. Compression: Perceived regularities are compressed into a schema.
4. Variation: Variation and improvement of schema (adaptation or evolution).
5. Application: Use of schema to the systems environment, also considered decompression of schema.
6. Selection: The consequences of selective pressures in the real world providing feedback and affecting competition for schemata.

With the expansion of interest in CDST and complex adaptive systems, the discussion of what are the principles of a complex adaptive system in language and language development has recently begun in the field of applied linguistics. Focusing on applied linguistics, Larsen-Freeman and Cameron (2008a) list the simplified following five properties:

1. heterogeneity of elements or agents
2. dynamics
3. non-linearity
4. openness
5. adaptation.

The Five Graces Group (2009), which Larsen-Freeman is a member of, state that the following features are key when observing language evolution as a complex adaptive system:

1. The system consists of multiple agents (the speakers in the speech community) interacting with one another.
2. The system is adaptive; that is, speakers' behaviour is based on their past interactions, and current and past interactions together feed forward into future behaviour.

3. A speaker's behaviour is the consequence of competing factors ranging from perceptual mechanics to social motivations.
4. The structures of language emerge from inter-related patterns of experience, social interaction and cognitive processes.

More recently, Hiver and Al-Hoorie (2020) have suggested the following principles when conceptualising CDST and conducting research in the field of SLA:

1. Time and sensitive dependence on initial conditions.
2. Adaptation to the environment and other systems.
3. Feedback and self-organised criticality.
4. Openness to context.
5. Soft-assembly.

Despite the considerable overlap, there are differences between these lists of principles. However, in some cases the differences may be more of terminology than of substance. Which principles and terms to employ could be determined depending on the research questions and the phenomena that are being observed (Hiver and Al-Hoorie 2020). The principles of complex adaptive systems one employs may depend on how CDST is looked upon and utilised in one's research field or specialisation. For our study, we employ Seedhouse's (2010) principles of complex adaptive systems as presented below:

1. Self-organisation and adaptation of many interacting agents.
2. Non-linearity.
3. Surface complexity arising out of deep simplicity.
4. Sensitivity to initial conditions.
5. Complex systems adapt feedback from the environment and from themselves.
6. Complex adaptive systems arise from the interaction of their parts and function as a whole which is more than the sum of its parts.
7. Complex adaptive systems display both homogeneity and heterogeneity.
8. Complex adaptive systems display self-similarity on various scales and levels.
9. There are universal properties of non-linear systems: different systems behave in the same ways.

Seedhouse's (2010) set of principles will be adapted since it attempts to subsume most of the principles proposed by other researchers mentioned above (e.g., Gell-Mann 1994a; Hiver and Al-Hoorie 2020; Holland 1992, 1995; Larsen-Freeman and Cameron 2008a; The Five Graces Group 2009). It attempts to be relevant to applied linguistics and has been employed in L2 interactional studies. Due to the longitudinal nature of the study, we also add the tenth principle of 'different timescales' (Lemke 2000) and 'nested timescales' (L.B. Smith and Thelen 2003) as this is vital to the analysis. In what follows, we briefly explain what these ten principles entail.

2.4.2.1 Self-organisation and adaptation of many interacting agents

Complex adaptive systems consist of many components, connections between which undergo continuous change through interacting, reacting and adapting to each other (Larsen-Freeman and Cameron 2008a).

For example, the human brain constantly organises and reorganises its billions of neural connections so as to make sense of experience. This also applies at the macro level of society: people trying to satisfy their material needs unconsciously organise themselves into an economy through numerous individual acts of buying and selling. This happens without anyone being in charge or consciously planning it (Waldrop 1994). In other words, in a complex adaptive system, there is no one central controller or organiser of systems, only independent agents. As a result, changes are based on locally available resources. This occurs because systems interact with their environment, react to feedback from their environment and feed back on themselves. They are consequently able to self-organise and form new organisations at more complex levels. Therefore, when seeing language as a complex adaptive system, it can be said that the individual humans are the agents and 'Language is emergent from ongoing human social interactions' (The Five Graces Group 2009: 17).

2.4.2.2 Non-linearity

Complex adaptive systems are non-linear, that is, they do not progress in a straight line. As such, it is not always possible to predict what happens next. Holland (1995) states, 'A function is linear if the value of the function, for any set of values assigned to its arguments, is simply a weighted sum of those values' (15). Put differently, in linear systems the relations of cause and effect are clear, and small causes result in small effects, and large effects are results of the adding up of the small causes (Lee et al. 2009). Therefore, in linear equations, results can be predicted, generalised and applied to other situations. In contrast, in non-linear systems like a complex adaptive system, small causes do not always add up to create a proportionate effect, nor are the changes always smooth and incremental. Rather, changes can be disproportionate and 'occur with spurts, plateaus, and even regressions' (Thelen and Smith 1994: 84). As a result, non-linear systems are almost always more complicated than linear systems (Holland 1995).

2.4.2.3 Surface complexity arising out of deep simplicity

Related to the feature of non-linearity, in a complex adaptive system, surface complexity arises out of deep simplicity. Holland (1998) notes that in a complex adaptive system, 'the behavior of the whole is much more complex than the behavior of the parts' (2). The principle refers to the phenomenon of simple changes bringing about large and complex effects (Gribbin 2004). A system may manifest significantly different characteristics from those resulting from adding up its components, which is known as emergent behaviour. The organisation of the whole system is created from the non-linear interactions of numerous much smaller elements. Instead, it is necessary to adopt a holistic perspective and look at the whole system (Hawkins and Gell-Mann 1992). This is due to the system's nature of reaction where 'systems interact with their environment, react to feedback from their environment and feed back on themselves' (Seedhouse 2010: 6).

2.4.2.4 Sensitivity to initial conditions

Complex adaptive systems are sensitive to initial conditions; thus, initial differences may lead to extremely different results. L.B. Smith and Thelen (2003) state that small differences in one or more components of the system 'can lead to reorganisation and to large differences in behaviour' (347). This is what Lorenz (1993) discovered with his weather model simulation, where a decimal point difference in the initial setting led to completely different results on the second run. This principle is connected to the non-linear aspect of complex adaptive systems, where simple initial conditions can lead to unexpected complex structural patterns. Initial conditions with language development could be, for example, the speakers' language proficiency or the context in which the conversation took place.

2.4.2.5 Complex systems adapt feedback from the environment and from themselves

S. Johnson (2001) states that feedback is a principle of complex adaptive systems and 'all decentralized systems rely extensively on feedback for both growth and self-regulation' (133). This principle is similar to the point made in the first principle regarding language use, where agents make adjustments based on the feedback from the environment or the interlocutor, but also from themselves and how they use the language. Thus, complex adaptive systems are 'open systems' (J.H. Brown 1994), that is, they are sensitive to the environment and are not fixed or stable. Lee et al. (2009) demonstrate that the feedback system can be seen in language as well, in that the more people use a certain word or form, the more it will be accepted and used by others.

2.4.2.6 Complex adaptive systems arise from the interaction of their parts and function as a whole which is more than the sum of its parts

According to the above mentioned principles of non-linearity, feedback and adaptation, complex adaptive systems arise from the interaction of their parts and function as a whole which is more than the sum of its parts. Holland (1998) refers to this as 'emergence – much coming from little' (1). This is due to the nature of non-linear systems where direct inspection of individual parts of the system cannot reveal or explain the system's behaviour as a whole. Therefore, 'subsequent activities can be determined only by extended examination and experiment' (Holland 1998: 225). In other words, complex adaptive systems 'cannot, in general, be successfully analysed by isolating properties or variables that are studied separately and then combining those partial approaches' (Seedhouse 2010: 8). In complex adaptive systems, the whole is more than the sum of its parts.

2.4.2.7 Complex adaptive systems display both homogeneity and heterogeneity

Systems can seem very similar at one level but different at another, which is the principle of complex adaptive systems displaying both homogeneity and heterogeneity. This phenomenon is connected to the nature of complex adaptive systems displaying fractal features which are homogeneous, but it is also connected to adaptations and emergence that result in heterogeneity. Miller and Page (2007) state, 'in adaptive social systems we find that the agents' rules often respond to the phenomena that they generate, creating multiple layers of feedback that result in a diverse set of emergent behaviours, both for the agents and the system at large' (107). For instance, snowflakes may be identical at the beginning with the same amount of moisture and temperature, but with the wind and other environmental feedback, the snowflakes that come down from the sky will never be identical (Gleick 1987, 1993).

The scale at which we view a system also affects the degree of homogeneity and heterogeneity we see. To the naked eye, all snowflakes on the ground look identical. However, under the microscope no two ever look identical, because each snowflake takes a slightly different trajectory to the ground on descent, receiving slightly different feedback from the environment.

2.4.2.8 Complex adaptive systems display self-similarity on various scales and levels

Complex adaptive systems are associated with fractal structures, where patterns are repeated, and the patterns are self-similar at different scales. The word 'fractal' (coined by Mandelbrot) is used to denote shapes which are irregular all over (fractional) and which have the same degree of irregularity on all scales. A fractal object looks the same when examined from far away or nearby; it is self-similar, which implies that any subsystem of a fractal system is equivalent to the whole system (Sardar and Abrams 2004). Romanesco broccoli and coastlines are often raised as examples of fractals, where the same shape is repeated to form a shape of a larger scale. The edges of a clover leaf will be bristling with smaller clover shapes that will bristle with still smaller clover shapes, and so on indefinitely (Coveney and Highfield 1995). In complex adaptive systems there are 'attractors', which are points or paths that are taken and/or eventually stabilise regardless of the starting point or initial condition (Thelen and Smith 2006). This feature of complex adaptive systems allows fractals to be formed (Larsen-Freeman 1997).

Holland (1995) explains that an agent at one level serves as a building block for agents at a higher level, which then serve as a building block for agents at the next level. Furthermore, the agents of a higher level can be more complex than those of a lower level. Therefore, although there is a pattern that repeats itself at different level, there is a hierarchical structure. West (2017: 15) explains the importance of scale (how things change with size) for understanding life-associated systems. Using the lens of scale, cities, plants, human bodies and tumours show surprising similarity in the ways they are organised and function. N.F. Johnson (2007) notes that fractals are not always observable, 'just that they can be' (50).

2.4.2.9 There are universal properties of non-linear systems: Different systems behave in the same ways

We have explained that complex adaptive systems adapt and emerge into various different systems, and that these systems can show self-similarities. In addition to this, different systems can also display universal features, as with the snowflake example in the seventh principle (see Section 2.4.2.7). N.F. Johnson (2007) notes, 'patterns which emerge from such Complex Systems can be so similar – or in techno-speak, the emergent phenomena have some universal properties' (70). He then uses people as an example and explains:

> even though there are many differences between all our different personality types, these differences may cancel out to some extent when we are in a large enough group – and hence the group as a whole behaves in such a way that these individual differences don't matter so much. (N.F. Johnson 2007: 68)

As a result, overall behaviours of different groups or systems can be quite similar. For instance, traffic jams appear quite similar among different countries, such as Japan, the UK and the USA (N.F. Johnson 2007).

Why should it be that such diverse systems should function in the same fundamental ways? Gribbin (2004: 163) explains that this is because all of these systems are built on networks, interconnections between the simple parts that make up a complex system. Since all life on Earth has a common ancestry, it is inevitable that all current life-related systems and networks will share similarities in the way they function. West (2017) explains the common conceptual framework underlying the disparate phenomena of life and shows how their dynamics, growth and organisation are subject to similar generic laws.

2.4.2.10 Different and nested timescales

The final complex adaptive system principle pertains to time. Complex adaptive systems assume that developmental changes occur across different timescales, ranging from milliseconds to years or millennia, depending on the focal context and phenomenon. For example, some words can be memorised instantly while others may take weeks or months to memorise. These timescales are not isolated, but instead are on a continuum and are nested within other timescales, resulting in a interaction between them (L.B. Smith and Thelen 2003). For instance, a change in the neural activity is nested within a larger system of physical growth and language development, which is also embedded in a large system of an educational system and world systems, which themselves change at different rates and can affect each other (Lemke 2000; L.B. Smith and Thelen 2003; Thelen and Smith 2006).

2.4.3 CDST, 'LEARNING' AND 'DEVELOPMENT'

Larsen-Freeman (1997) was one of the first to write about viewing SLA from a CDST perspective. She writes that language learning is 'the constant adaptation of their linguistic resources in the service of meaning-making in response to the affordances that emerge in the communicative situation, which is, in turn, affected by learners' adaptivity' (Larsen-Freeman 2010: 67). An individual's linguistic system is thus continuously changed by the ongoing interaction and adaptation. From this viewpoint, as mentioned previously, we define 'learning' as not only occurring in the individual mind and the learner taking in linguistic knowledge, but also as the process of adapting to and making changes to the communicative context, including the interlocutor. Moreover, we define 'development' as the visible changes as a result of 'learning' that can be understood as the changes to the individual linguistic system and the communicative situation that manifest themselves in the ongoing interaction. One of the pioneers of the areas of complexity science, Gell-Mann, also argues that the process of learning grammar exhibits features of a complex adaptive system. He writes:

> The process of learning grammar also demonstrates the other features of a complex adaptive system in operation. A schema is subject to variation, and the different variants are tried out in the real world. In order to try them out, it is necessary to fill in details, such as the ones that were thrown away in creating the schema ... Finally, what happens in the real world influences which variants of the schema survive. (Gell-Mann 1994b: 54)

As such, we also understand that 'development' has no end point, as the learner adapts to the constantly changing and various contexts.

Many publications since then have found supporting evidence of L2 development displaying complex adaptive system features (e.g., Chan et al. 2015; de Bot et al. 2007; de Bot 2008; N.C. Ellis 2008; N.C. Ellis and Larsen-Freeman 2009a; Jessner 2008; Larsen-Freeman and Cameron 2008a, 2008b; Lesonen et al. 2017; Yu and Lowie 2020).

The CDST view of SLA is not isolated or new, as other perspectives in the field of SLA have also acknowledged the cognitive and social aspects of language learning and their inseparability. For example, the 'ecological perspective' emphasises the organic, emergent and adaptive features of agents in language learning and development (Kramsch 2003, 2008; van Lier 1996, 2000, 2004). It views the learner as being immersed in an environment full of potential meanings, which become available gradually as the learner acts and interacts within and with this environment (van Lier 2000). The ecological perspective captures the organic, emergent and adaptive feature of the agents in language learning and development.

The sociocognitive perspective argues that all forms of language use have both a social and cognitive dimension that are interdependent, with performance (a social phenomenon) and competence (a cognitive phenomenon) of language use continually related through co-constructed interaction (Batstone 2010a, 2010b; R. Ellis 2010). People bring their own prior experiences and knowledge to conversations, using these language experiences to communicate and reach mutual understanding. This adaptation and adjustment of language to the activity and new patterns of discourse is thus 'learning', and also never ending (Batstone 2010a).

Finally, the usage-based perspective views language as a collection of semiotic resources that are acquired through language use (Eskildsen 2012; Eskildsen and Cadierno 2015; Tomasello 2000), and thus sees language development as non-linear and grounded in language use (e.g., Roehr-Brackin 2014; Tomasello 2009; Verspoor et al. 2012). This perspective is gaining increasing acceptance, particularly among conversation analysts studying language change in interaction, and has shown how individuals' language evolves during conversation and across time (Cadierno and Eskildsen 2015; Eskildsen 2012; Theodórsdóttir and Eskildsen 2022; Van Compernolle 2019).

However, the ecological perspective comes from the institutional setting of a language classroom, while the sociocognitive perspective was created while moving away from the social and cognitive dichotomy in the field. The usage-based perspective originated from linguistics and analyses emergent patterns of vocabulary and grammar with an emphasis on the agent. In contrast, CDST derives from real-world observations, with no connections to preconceptualised theories. This mirrors the methodological data-driven position of CA, thus suggesting a natural alignment of the two approaches, as will be discussed further in Chapter 3.

Larsen-Freeman (2010) discusses language learning as a process of co-adaptation as two language users interact, resulting in transformation of linguistic resources at both individual and community levels. Language learning involves creating new patterns from old, using language resources differently with different people, and constantly adapting linguistic resources to make meaning in response to the communicative situation. Thus, learners' perceptual, conceptual and linguistic systems are continually being updated through their participation in the ongoing flow of experience, reflecting their adaptivity (Larsen-Freeman 2010: 67).

The existence of some kind of interaction engine prior to the evolution of language is alluded to in the literature on **language** as a complex adaptive system. The Five Graces Group (2009) in their position paper state, 'language evolved in the context of an already highly interactive social existence. This intensive interaction suggests that the evolution of language cannot be understood outside of a social context' (3). In this study, in order to specify and exemplify the characteristics of human spoken interaction as a complex adaptive system, we have needed to separate and differentiate it as much as possible from the complex adaptive system of language, which has already received considerable attention (N.C. Ellis and Larsen-Freeman 2009b).

2.4.4 COMPLEX DYNAMIC SYSTEMS THEORY AND L2 LONGITUDINAL STUDIES

Since Larsen-Freeman (2012) stated that CDST in SLA is in its 'infancy' (83), an increasing number of studies have adopted the perspective of CDST to analyse various aspects of SLA (see Hiver et al. 2022 for a scoping review of CDST-informed SLA studies). Scholars have discussed how language (Cooper 1999; N.C. Ellis and Larsen-Freeman 2009b; Larsen-Freeman and Cameron 2008a), the language learning process as a whole (de Bot 2008; van Geert 2008, 2009) and classroom interaction (Seedhouse 2010) function as complex systems.

CDST has been used to study the developmental patterns of various aspects of L2 learners, including the four skills (reading, writing, listening and speaking) with a focus on measuring accuracy, complexity and fluency in their use of vocabulary and grammar (e.g., Chang and Zhang 2021; Gui et al. 2021; Peng et al. 2022; Wu et al. 2023). In addition, CDST has also been employed to describe the motivation levels of L2 learners (e.g., Castro 2018; Papi and Hiver 2020). These studies have shown that L2 development does indeed demonstrate CDST features, such as sensitivity to initial conditions, non-linear change, and variability and similarity within and between groups. The approach these studies apply to their data is to describe various complex systems and patterns of change using established qualitative or quantitative analytical methodologies, and to compare them with CDST principles to discuss if the data corresponds to the components of a complex system.

An increasing number of studies are examining spoken texts in the context of L2 speaking (Chan et al. 2015; Larsen-Freeman 2006; Lesonen et al. 2017; Yu and Lowie 2020). These quantitative-oriented studies, similarly to research on L2 reading and writing, have identified developmental patterns that reflect a CDST framework, including variability within and between learners, non-linear development, and the emergence of non-target-like features (Chan et al. 2015; Lesonen et al. 2017; Yu and Lowie 2020). For example, Lesonen et al. (2017) observed a high variability in the use of verb constructions at the beginning of their data collection, but noted a decrease in variability over time, with participants settling on a simple verb construction that may not be structurally complex but was found to be most effective for the speakers. However, the existing CDST-informed SLA studies use predominantly quantitative approaches to data. Limited attention is given to the interactional aspects of language use, particularly from a CA approach in the context of multiple speakers and their evolving interactional patterns over time.

While not explicitly adopting a CDST framework, similar findings of changes in variability over time have been reported in studies using CA. For example, studies investigating the use of L2 negation (Eskildsen 2012; Hauser 2013c; Van Compernolle 2019) have found high variability in the early stages of data collection, followed by a gradual narrowing of variability and stabilisation of non-target-like features, reflecting the developmental patterns of L2 negation within a CDST framework. D. Atkinson et al. (2007), although using only one video-recorded session, were able to demonstrate through the methodology of CA and CDST that some micro linguistic features used in interaction, such as gaze, laughter, worksheet, gestures and jokes, are used to 'adapt', or in CA terms 'align', to each other in creating scaffolding and leading to learning of a grammatical feature.

Other CA studies informed by a complex adaptive system framework suggest that 'metaphor performance' is a social and cognitive process where the metaphors are 'attractors' and are used and adapted to within talk and through different times (e.g., Cameron and Deignan 2006; Gibbs and Cameron 2008). For instance, Cameron and Deignan (2006) found a teacher commenting on a student's drawing of trees as 'lollipop', then moments later as 'lollipop trees'. They then later discovered a student using the word 'lollipop trees', thus exemplifying that the emergent new word had been adapted and become a part of the group's repertoire. Larsen-Freeman and Cameron (2008a) state, 'Students learning English through participation in subject classes have different language-using experiences from students learning English as a foreign language, and will develop different language-using patterns' (220). This is because 'Learners' attention to language adapts in response to classroom demands' (Larsen-Freeman and Cameron 2008a: 220). Inevitably, learners will adapt in response to the interaction in the ELF environment of the international university dormitory.

The current field of SLA has tended to oversimplify the complexity of development by omitting the features fundamental to a complex, non-linear dynamical system of development (Larsen-Freeman and Cameron 2008b). The same can be said about developmental research on interactional competence. However, from a CDST perspective, development needs to be analysed holistically, including the individual, the system and the individual within the system. Larsen-Freeman and Cameron (2008a) illustrate this by giving the following example:

> if we see the speech community as a complex system, then it will also have within it sociocultural groups that themselves function as complex systems; individuals within these subgroups can be seen as complex systems, as can their individual brain systems. There are complex systems at all levels, from the social level to the neurological levels. (201)

Therefore, to understand the language learning process, Larsen-Freeman and Cameron (2008a) suggest collecting data about individuals, the group, the individual as a member of a group, and the individual working alone. Based on this, the analysis of the longitudinal data in this research will therefore take two steps. In the first step, transcriptional data will be analysed using the CA principles, observing how certain pragmatic features are used to do what, and their sequential organisation and position in the interaction (Chapters 4 and 5). The second step will be applying the CDST perspective to the interaction and comparing those instances in terms of timelines and the principles of complex adaptive systems (Chapter 6).

No previous CDST-informed longitudinal SLA studies have investigated how the unfolding of the interaction leads to change in the interaction over time. Therefore, investigating the development of L2 interactional competence from a longitudinal developmental perspective using the approach of CA and the framework of CDST will provide new insights into L2 interaction and development.

2.5 SUMMARY AND RESEARCH GAP

The aim of the current book is to examine how human spoken interaction functions as a complex adaptive system in the context of L2 interaction with a focus on word search sequences. Chapter 2 has set the stage for the subsequent chapters by presenting the features of the focal linguistic phenomenon of word search sequences and recent progress in the area of L2 interactional developmental research, while questioning the status quo of current research. The chapter has outlined the principles of CDST and complex adaptive systems, and criticised the oversimplification of development in the fields of SLA and developmental research on interactional competence, emphasising the need for a holistic CDST perspective. We have also stated that CDST provides the conceptual framework for our concept of development. Within this framework, CA depicts how the complex adaptive system of human spoken interaction unfolds in any sequence and hence portrays the progress of development in terms of interactional competence.

Since the conception of this project, an increasing numbers of studies have adopted longitudinal CA for investigating the development of L2 interactional competence, and an increasing number of studies have started to observe how L2 development is occurring in non-institutional settings (in the wild), where the initial goal of the conversation is not language learning. Various empirical studies of L2 interactional competence have started to document the non-linear and context-specific adaptive nature of L2 development. In terms of L2 development, the literature review has also identified the following gaps that this project aims to fill in Chapters 4 and 5. These are:

1. Longitudinal CA-for-SLA studies need to explicitly conduct or discuss the perspective of CDST.
2. Longitudinal CDST for L2 development studies need to take into account changes in the interactional aspects of language (e.g., word search sequences).
3. Studies need to incorporate the interlocutor and their influence on the 'development' of the L2 speaker.
4. Studies need to investigate non-institutional mundane ELF interaction between peers.

Therefore, it is invaluable to investigate the longitudinal development of L2 interactional competence in mundane ELF interaction from a CDST perspective and using a CA methodology. By utilising a CA-CDST approach, a combination of CDST meta-theory and CA microanalysis, this study argues that the development of L2 interactional competence is indeed dynamic and that spoken interaction can be analysed on different nested levels. In this chapter we have learnt about the key characteristics of complex adaptive systems. From the CDST perspective, there have been many studies of how language functions as a complex adaptive system (e.g., N.C. Ellis and Larsen-Freeman 2009b). There is a major research gap, however, in that there have so far been no studies of how the interaction engine functions as a complex adaptive system. It is this gap which the current study aims to fill, from Chapter 3. Here we give an overview of the basic mechanisms and principles of the interaction engine, showing how this functions as a complex adaptive system, as well as how a CA-CDST approach can be conducted.

3
MIRRORING METHODOLOGY

3.1 INTRODUCTION

This chapter explains **how** exactly we are going to examine the spoken interaction in this corpus, as well as how the interaction engine is organised as a complex adaptive system. This chapter explains how we analyse instances of talk using the methodology of Conversation Analysis (CA). The basic mechanisms and concepts of CA are firstly introduced in this chapter in relation to the baseline of ordinary conversation.[1] We see how the component mechanisms of the interaction engine combine to create an 'architecture of intersubjectivity' which enables people to perform an enormous range of social actions, creating a social world as they see fit; the same architecture enables us to analyse their actions. This is as a preface to showing how these mechanisms **adapt** themselves to mirror institutional or social goals, looking at both L2 classroom interaction and the L2 talk in our corpus. We argue that CA is able to portray how spoken interaction functions as a complex adaptive system because CA is itself a complex system which adapts itself to and mirrors the interaction which it analyses. We show in this chapter (1) how spoken interaction is organised as a complex adaptive system, (2) how CA functions as a complex adaptive system, (3) how CA can be applied to L2 talk in this informal setting, and (4) how CA relates to CDST and how they can be combined. The chapter describes the basics of how the interaction engine functions as a complex adaptive system by describing how CA works; this is possible as CA is a mirroring methodology, and we explain below what is meant by this. We use the term 'CA-CDST approach' to refer to our application of CA to analysing human spoken interaction as a complex adaptive system, discussed in Section 3.6.4.

3.2 BASIC PRINCIPLES AND PROCEDURES OF CONVERSATION ANALYSIS

The analytical methodology employed in this study is ethnomethodological CA, which studies the organisation and order of social action in interaction. This organisation and order is produced by the interactants by means of their talk and is oriented to by them. The analyst's task is to develop an 'emic' or participants' perspective, to

---

[1] The discussion is partly based on Seedhouse (2004) and Seedhouse and Nakatsuhara (2018).

uncover and describe what Sacks (1992: vol. 2: 169) termed the underlying *machinery* which enables interactants to achieve this organisation and order:

> Our aim is to get into a position to transform, in an almost literal, physical sense, our view of 'what happened,' from a matter of a particular interaction done by particular people, to a matter of interactions as products of a machinery. We are trying to find the machinery. (Sacks 1984: 26)

At the current time of writing, however, we might prefer to rephrase and update this goal as follows: we are trying to reveal the complex adaptive system of the interaction engine. The argument we develop in this study is that CDST and CA have in effect been working in parallel for decades; CA has been focusing narrowly and uniquely on showing how human spoken interaction functions as a complex adaptive system (but using different terminology) whilst CDST has been operating on an incomparably broader scale, showing how complex adaptive systems function throughout life on Earth. We suggest that CDST and CA have been approaching their respective tasks in similar ways but on different scales and using different terminology, and that CA was designed from the start as a self-similar, adaptive, mirroring methodology in relation to the phenomenon it studies (spoken interaction), following ethnomethodological principles. Although there has previously been little awareness of the similarities between CA and CDST as they have developed independently for decades, the time is now ripe to examine these, which we do in Section 3.6. A common misconception is that CA is obsessed with micro-detail and has nothing to say about interactional organisation on a larger scale. However, Schegloff, Sacks and Jefferson presented their early work as having general application. Their seminal account of the organisation of turn-taking was of general application to ordinary conversation in English (Sacks et al. 1974). Schegloff, Jefferson and Sacks's (1977) account of the organisation of repair again was designed for universal application to English conversation. In this chapter, then, we are simultaneously introducing CA methodology and explaining how human spoken interaction functions as a complex adaptive system, since the methodology aims to mirror the system of human spoken interaction.

A perennial conundrum is this: the interaction engine is something which humans normally learn the basics of in the first year or two of life, forming the interactional basis for subsequent L1 acquisition. However, it is extremely challenging to provide an explicit account of how human spoken interaction functions as a complex adaptive system. Ethnomethodology (Garfinkel 1967) provides a way of understanding this paradox.[2] Garfinkel's argument was that people must make normative use of a number of principles in order to display their actions to each other and allow others to make sense of them. However, these principles are used on a constant basis in everyday life and have become automatised and implicit to the extent that they have a taken-for-granted or 'seen but unnoticed' status which 'entitle[s] persons to conduct their common conversational affairs without interference' (Garfinkel

---

[2] See Heritage (1984b) and Seedhouse (2004) for an introduction to ethnomethodological principles.

1967: 42). Garfinkel was, then, trying to make explicit and visible those principles which we orient to in everyday life and of which we have implicit knowledge. The basic problem which Garfinkel faced was that of uncovering and identifying these normative practices; as they are 'seen but unnoticed', they are not easily perceptible when the norms are being followed. From this perspective, what we are trying to do in this study is to make explicit that which we as humans know implicitly about how the interaction engine functions as a complex adaptive system; the procedures of ethnomethodological CA are designed to help us do this. Since we acquire the interaction engine before language(s), our knowledge of it is more deeply recessed and implicit than even that of our L1; it is therefore even more taken for granted or 'seen but unnoticed'.

One principal aim of CA is to characterise the organisation of spoken interaction by abstracting from exemplars or specimens of interaction and to uncover the emic or endogenous system underlying this organisation. CA analysts seek to provide a holistic portrayal of talk which reveals the reflexive relationships between form, function, sequence, social identity and social/institutional context. That is, the organisation of the talk is seen to relate directly and reflexively to the social goals and actions of the participants, whether institutional or otherwise. Analysis is bottom-up and data-driven; we should not approach the data with any prior theoretical assumptions or assume that any background or contextual details are relevant.[3] Another way of presenting the principles of CA is in relation to the questions which it asks. The essential question which we must ask at all stages of CA analysis of data is, 'Why that, in that way, right now?' (Seedhouse 2004: 16). This encapsulates the perspective of interaction as action (why that) which is expressed by means of linguistic forms (in that way) in a developing sequence (right now). Talk is conceived of as social action, which is delivered in particular linguistic formatting, as part of an unfolding sequence. An interactant has the possibility, in any sequential environment, of selecting between different social and communicative acts, which can in turn be realised on a linguistic level in different ways. So one needs to consider why a participant produced exactly that utterance at that point and what consequences it had for the interaction. This is a major methodological resource in the analysis of excerpts in this study and enables the participants' orientations to be traced through lengthy sequences. CA places an 'emphasis on the interactional and inferential consequences of the choice between alternative utterances' (Levinson 1983: 287). As with other forms of qualitative research, the principles are not to be considered as a formula or to be applied in a mechanistic fashion. It is essential to adopt a conversation analytic mentality which involves a mindset or attitude, rather than following a static and prescriptive set of instructions (Hutchby and Wooffitt 2008: 89).

Sacks's (1992) key idea was that there is order at all points in interaction. This was an extremely radical idea in the 1960s as the dominant linguistic view was that

---

[3] Essentially, there are no features of context or identity which are **always** relevant to a CA analysis. We need to determine which features of identity or context the participants are orienting to and making relevant in the details of their talk; if it is relevant to them, then it is relevant to us as analysts.

conversation was too disordered to be studied. This idea leads to the concept of 'rational design' (Levinson 1992: 71) in interaction, that is, that talk in interaction is systematically organised, deeply ordered and methodical. Another principal aim of CA is to trace the development of intersubjectivity (mutual understanding) in an action sequence. This does not mean that CA provides direct access to participants' cognitive or psychological states. Rather, it means that analysts trace how participants analyse and interpret each other's actions and develop a shared understanding of the progress of the interaction (see Section 3.4 on socially distributed cognition). So CA practitioners aim to discover how interactants understand and respond to one another in their talk (Hutchby and Wooffitt 2008: 12). As we show below, this is done primarily by reference to the interactional mechanisms of turn-taking, sequence and repair.

A further principle of CA is that no order of detail can be dismissed, a priori, as disorderly, accidental or irrelevant (Heritage 1984b: 241). This principle follows from the previous one and underlies the development of the highly detailed CA transcription system (see Appendix 2), its minute analysis of the detail of naturally occurring data and its highly empirical orientation (Schegloff 2007; ten Have 1999, 2007). For illustrations of the benefits of CA transcription, see Hutchby and Wooffitt (2008). For present purposes we need only note that: CA practitioners regard the recordings of naturally occurring interaction as the primary data;[4] transcripts are designed to make the primary data available for intensive analytic consideration by the analyst and other readers; transcripts are inevitably incomplete, selective renderings of the primary data which invariably involve a trade-off between readability and comprehensiveness.

The first stage of CA analysis has been described as 'unmotivated looking' or being open to discovering patterns or phenomena. Having identified a candidate phenomenon (such as a marker like 'oh' or teachers avoiding correction of grammatical errors), the next phase is normally an inductive search through a database to establish a collection of instances of the phenomenon. The next step is to establish regularities and patterns in relation to occurrences of the phenomenon and to show that these regularities are methodically produced and oriented to by the participants as normative mechanisms of action (Heritage 1988: 131). The specific features of individual cases are investigated in depth and are used to build a general account of a phenomenon or interactional organisation (Heritage 1984b). We can only understand the organisation of the interaction and its emic logic by detailed analysis of individual instances of the interaction. In the current study, when a potential characteristic of interaction was identified, a search was made amongst other recordings to determine how systematic and widespread it was; all characteristics presented here are a result of that process. The aim is, then, to produce an account of the data which is both particularised and generalised, which involves a constant, reflexive interaction between

---

[4] CA generally uses the term 'naturally occurring data' to refer to interaction which has not been invented, in contrast to films and plays in which dialogue has been invented and written down by an author. Also, it has in the past been quite common for linguists to invent dialogues to illustrate particular linguistic phenomena; these would not be considered naturally occurring data for CA purposes.

the specific instance and the interactional system being studied (Seedhouse 2004). Lazaraton (2002: xiii) suggests that CA can best be termed a recursive analytic cycle based on repeated, prolonged engagement with the interactional data.

There is inevitably a tension between the process of CA data analysis (which proceeds as stated above) and the presentation of findings, which proceeds in a rather different fashion. Due to limitations of space, it is necessary to select fairly short excerpts to illustrate characteristics; the examples we display throughout the book have been selected to be representative of such features within the corpus. There is also a tension between homogeneity and heterogeneity in terms of data presentation. Excerpts are chosen to illustrate a specific point or support a generalisation, but at the same time excerpts always have their own unique and idiosyncratic features.

3.3 BASIC INTERACTIONAL MECHANISMS

We will now look at three fundamental and inter-related interactional mechanisms which were uncovered by Sacks and associates by grappling with their data and which can now be employed in analysis by CA practitioners, namely sequence organisation, turn-taking and repair. Turn-taking and sequence are mechanisms for displaying and checking mutual understanding, and the organisation of repair is a mechanism for repairing breakdowns in mutual understanding. The aim of this section is to describe how these mechanisms function in ordinary conversation as a baseline,[5] so that in Section 3.6 and Chapters 4 and 5 we can grasp how they have been adapted to the goal of interacting in an ELF setting. It is important from a CDST perspective to understand that sequence organisation, turn-taking and repair are **adaptive** mechanisms which can follow the phenomena as these evolve (or co-evolve with them), as opposed to rigid rules. By showing how these mechanisms function, we are also presenting how human spoken interaction functions as a complex adaptive system, since CA mirrors the functioning of the system which it studies.

3.3.1 ADJACENCY PAIRS (SEQUENCE ORGANISATION)

The concept of the adjacency pair (e.g., question and answer) is one which (if considered purely as a structural phenomenon) may appear to be so obvious and superficial that it is hardly worth mentioning. However, the action sequence or sequence organisation is the key to understanding how CA analysis works. Therefore, we spend some time considering the adjacency pair as the most common and prevalent manifestation of the concept of linked actions in an action sequence. These are, as

---

[5] Sacks et al. (1974) described the fundamental mechanisms of CA in relation to the baseline of ordinary conversation, rather than to talk in institutions such as courtrooms or classrooms. The contested term 'ordinary' conversation does not imply that institutional talk is somehow extraordinary or superior in any way. Conversation is locally managed by the participants. Sacks et al. state that conversation is very flexible in relation to situations and participants; it is therefore very diverse. In institutional discourse such as courtrooms and classrooms, the same mechanisms may be reorganised in relation to the institutional goal and there may be pre-allocation of who can speak when about what.

Heritage (1984b: 256) puts it, the basic building-blocks of intersubjectivity (mutual understanding or interpersonal alignment). Adjacency pairs are paired utterances, such that on production of the first part of the pair (e.g., question) the second part of the pair (answer) becomes conditionally relevant. If, however, the second part is not immediately produced, it may nonetheless remain relevant and accountable and appear later, or its absence may be accounted for.

Excerpt 3.1 (Sidnell 2010: 103)[6]
```
1    A:    maybe Rebecca, maybe you can move it,
2 →  B:    °move what.°
3 →  A:    move that thing that('s in the lock)/(yo- in the door).
4    B:    okay
```

In the above excerpt, one adjacency pair (lines 2 and 3) is embedded in another (lines 1 and 4). What this sequence also demonstrates is that action sequences do not necessarily unroll in a linear fashion (Q1–A1, Q2–A2) and hence that serial order is not necessarily the same thing as sequential order. When this is the case, the different types of interactional mechanism (here, adjacency pair and turn-taking) combine in a mutually reinforcing fashion to provide normative points of reference which enable interactants (and analysts) to orientate themselves. Furthermore, the adjacency pair concept does not claim that second parts are always provided for first parts. Rather, it is a 'normative' frame of reference which provides a framework for understanding actions and providing accountability. So if we ask a question to someone who does not then provide an answer, we may draw conclusions about that person.[7] Following a first turn, the interaction continues sequentially, with the second speaker's action creating expectations for subsequent speakers and so on. Moving on to the third turn, this displays an analysis of the second speaker's turn, so the second speaker is able to determine how their turn has been interpreted. So the essence of CA is the concept of action sequences or sequence organisation, exemplified by the adjacency pair. Interaction clearly does not consist of an endless succession of adjacency pairs. The point being made is nevertheless that interaction **is** always an action sequence in which a turn will be heard as directed to a prior turn, unless some other technique is used to direct attention elsewhere (Sacks et al. 1974: 728). As Schegloff (2007) and Kendrick et al. (2020) demonstrate, the base adjacency pair (first and second pair parts) can be expanded by an additional pair in advance (pre-expansion), by a pair between the base pair-parts (insert expansion as in Excerpt 3.1) or by a post-pair (post-expansion).

The adjacency pair has been used as an example of next-positioning and linked actions within sequence organisation. It is not only an action template with normative force, but also a template for interpretation. Extrapolating from this, any first

---

[6] Arrows → in the left margin pick out lines of interest. Transcription conventions are in Appendix 2.
[7] There are other possibilities to consider, for example that the question was inadequately framed or inappropriate.

action in interaction is an action template which creates a normative expectation for a next action and a template for interpreting it. The second action displays an interpretation of the first action and itself creates an action and interpretational template for subsequent actions, and so on. This can also be termed the 'next-turn proof procedure' (Sacks et al. 1974: 729), which is the basic methodological tool which analysts can use to develop an emic or participants' perspective and analyse the spoken data. The next turn, then, documents an analysis of the previous turn and displays this analysis not only to the other interactants, but also to us as analysts, providing us with a proof criterion and search procedure. **The analytical procedure emerges from and mirrors the structure of the interaction.** This justifies the claim that CA is a mirroring methodology.

The ethnomethodological principle of reflexivity (Heritage 1984b) states that the same set of methods or procedures are responsible for both the production of actions/language and their interpretation. Sequence organisation is the mechanism by which interactants are able to make their utterances comprehensible and by which co-interactants are able to interpret them. However, it is also the mechanism by which we as analysts are able to analyse the course of the interaction, using data which are publicly available. The CA perspective is that we are able to orientate ourselves in interaction and understand each other by normative reference to interactional mechanisms. Adjacency pairs (and sequence organisation) are called the building blocks of intersubjectivity because interactants use them to display to one another (mirror) their understanding of each other's turns, and this permits us as analysts to follow the progress of their intersubjectivity. We see later in the chapter that this 'mirroring' effect is vital to an understanding of how CA functions as a complex adaptive system itself.

Excerpt 3.2 (Levinson 1983: 102)

```
1   A:    where's Bill?
2   J:    there's a yellow VW outside Sue's house
```

The production of a first turn provides an interpretative basis for the first speaker to interpret the next speaker's actions. Here the second part is interpreted as a tentative answer to A's question rather than as an unconnected observation. However, it can be interpreted in this way solely by virtue of its sequential location after the first part of an adjacency pair. Utterances derive much of their pragmatic force from their sequential location and through their relationship to the interactional mechanisms uncovered by CA.

3.3.2 TURN-TAKING

The exchange of turns is obviously characteristic of ordinary conversation; what is not so obvious is how it is accomplished so efficiently. Human communication is typically done in alternation, taking turns at short bursts of communication, averaging about 2 seconds long, with very rapid transitions of the order of 200 milliseconds between turns. These timings are very similar across languages and cultures

(Levinson 2022). Non-verbal communication cannot explain this, since telephone conversations are actually accomplished with more precise timing than face-to-face conversations (Levinson 1983: 296). The system for turn-taking must be extremely robust, since it works whoever or however many people are speaking and whatever the length or topic of the conversation is. The following is a simplified version of Sacks et al.'s (1974) seminal account of the organisation of turn-taking. There is a mechanism governing turn-taking which is termed a local management system; this means that decisions can be made by the participants, rather than having the turns allocated in advance (pre-allocated), as is the case in a courtroom.

There is a set of norms with options which the participants can select. The basis of the system is 'turn-constructional units' or TCUs, units which can be sentences, clauses or words and which perform a complete social action. Listeners project, then, when a speaker is going to finish a turn, and the point at which speaker change may occur is known as the 'transition relevance place' or TRP. At a TRP the norms governing transition of speakers come into play; the speakers may change at that point, but they do not necessarily do so. These norms apply at the first TRP of any turn:

1. If the current speaker selects the next speaker in the current turn, then the current speaker must stop speaking and the next speaker must speak.
2. If the current speaker does not select a next speaker, then any other participant may select themselves as next speaker: the first person to speak at the TRP gains rights to the next turn.
3. If the current speaker has not selected a next speaker, and if no other participant self-selects as per item (2), then the current speaker may (but need not) continue. The procedure then loops or recycles until the end of the conversation, for which there are of course further norms.

According to Sacks et al. (1974), any turn performs three kinds of sequential work, which can be thought of in terms of past, present and future. Any turn shows how it fits into the sequence so far (past), performs its own social action or contribution to the sequence (present) and thus provides a context for the next turn by another interactant (future).

Excerpt 3.3 (Schegloff 1996: 75)

```
1    Marsha:   en Ilene is going to meet im:. becuz the to:p  wz ripped
2              off'v iz car which is tih say someb'ddy helped th'mselfs.
3 →  Tony:     stolen.
4              (0.4)
5    Marsha:   stolen.=right out in front of my house.
6    Tony:     oh: f'r crying out loud,...
```

In Excerpt 3.3 line 3, we can see that Tony's turn consists of a single TCU of a single word. Yet, this single word not only constitutes an entire turn and social action, but it also performs three kinds of sequential work in the past, present and future, as explained below. This is possible because interactants orient to a normative sequential framework, a holistic framework consisting of the interlocking mechanisms of turn-taking, sequence and repair. Since the normative expectation is that a turn will perform these three kinds of sequential work, Tony can design his turn so that a single word is capable of doing so and Marsha can interpret it as doing so; this is the principle of reflexivity in action. The evidence that the participants are actually orienting to the system described is in the next-turn proof procedure. Marsha in line 5 analyses Tony's turn as commenting retrospectively on what happened to the car, as performing a new social action of confirming understanding of Marsha's news by summarising the content (the top was ripped off) in a new linguistic format (the top was stolen) and as providing a context for her to take the sequence further. In the web of interaction, a single word can perform multiple social actions on multiple levels simultaneously. She displays her understanding of the work performed by his turn in her subsequent turn (line 5) by repeating his turn with the same intonation and adding further information on the theft.

3.3.3 REPAIR ORGANISATION

The mechanisms of sequence and turn-taking provide the basic structural framework of talk. However, the third element, repair, comes into play whenever there are problems in the accomplishment of talk. Repair is the mechanism by which interactants address and resolve trouble in speaking, hearing and understanding and involves treatment of trouble occurring in interactive language use (Schegloff et al. 1977). As discussed in Chapter 2, it is a vital mechanism for the maintenance of intersubjectivity. We have chosen the mechanism of repair as our data focus in this study because it is the point where the 'interaction engine' (see Section 3.4.5) starts feeding back on itself and becoming self-referential.[8] Dingemanse et al. (2015) suggest that repair is one of the places where speakers' theories of mind come to the surface. 'Trouble' is anything which the participants find to be impeding speech production or intersubjectivity; a repairable item is one which constitutes such trouble for the participants. Any element of talk may in principle be the focus of repair, even an element which is well formed, propositionally correct and appropriate. Schegloff et al. (1977: 363) point out that there is nothing in talk which cannot in principle be subject to repair. Repair, trouble and repairable items are participants' constructs in ordinary conversation, meaning that they can be used as and when the participants find it appropriate. Their use may be related to institutional constraints, however. In courtroom cross-examination of a witness by an opposing lawyer, for example, a failure by the witness to answer questions with 'yes' or 'no' may constitute trouble within that institutional setting (Drew 1992). Such a failure is therefore repairable (for example, by the lawyer and/or judge insisting on a yes/no answer) and even legally sanctionable. So within a particular institutional sub-variety of talk, the constitution of trouble and what is repairable may be related to the particular institutional focus at that time. The mechanisms **adapt** themselves to the specific social goals of the participants.

---

[8] Garfinkel (1967) describes his ethnomethodological procedure as starting with familiar scenes and asking what can be done to make trouble; this exposes how the system works.

It is important to distinguish self-initiated repair (i.e., I prompt repair of my mistake) from other-initiated repair (somebody else notices my mistake and initiates repair). Self-repair (I correct myself) must also be distinguished from other-repair (somebody corrects my mistake). There are therefore four basic repair trajectories:

1. Self-initiated self-repair

Excerpt 3.4 (Sidnell 2010: 111)
```
1    A:   okay wul listen ((smile voice))
2         .hh (.)>are=you gonna be at my house at
3 →       what time on uh Fri:-on Sunday?
```

2. Self-initiated other-repair

Excerpt 3.5 (Schegloff et al. 1977: 364)
```
1    B:   he had dis uh Mistuh W- whatever k- I can't
2         think of his first name, Watts on,
3         the one that wrote [that piece
4 →  A:                      [Dan Watts.
```

3. Other-initiated self-repair

Excerpt 3.6 (Schegloff et al. 1977: 370)
```
1    A:   hey the first time they stopped me from
2         selling cigarettes was this morning.
3         (1.0)
4 →  B:   from selling cigarettes?
5 →  A:   from buying cigarettes.
```

4. Other-initiated other-repair

Excerpt 3.7 (Sidnell 2010: 134)
```
1    P:   ... the Black Muslims are certainly more provocative
2         than the Black Muslims ever were.
3 →  J:   the Black Panthers.
4    P:   the Black Panthers. what'd I
5    J:   you said the Black Muslims twice.
```

There is a clear preference structure in the organisation of repair which corresponds with the above listing. This is that self-initiated self-repair is most preferred and other-initiated other-repair least preferred (Sacks and Schegloff 1979). This order also corresponds with frequency of usage in normal conversation, with other-initiated other-repair being rare. There are two kinds of evidence for the preference for self-repair. The first is the inherent structural bias, with the first two opportunities located in the speaker's own turn – during the same turn-constructional unit and at the next transition relevance place. The second is that there are various ways in which turns are designed to facilitate self-repair (Hutchby and Wooffitt 2008: 62).

In this section, we have characterised the interactional mechanisms which work together in complementary fashion to create an architecture of intersubjectivity (Heritage 1984b: 254). They function as action templates or points of reference which interactants may use to orientate themselves in the pursuit of mutual understanding. A vital point is that these interactional mechanisms are **not** to be understood as rigid rules, units or coding schemes in the sense in which these would be understood in a descriptivist linguistic paradigm. Rather, they are a set of normative resources which interactants make use of to display the meaning of their social actions to their partners and to interpret their partners' actions. The mechanisms are part of the context-free (general) machinery which we make use of to orientate ourselves in indexical interaction, that is, we employ them in a context-sensitive (particular) way (Sacks et al. 1974). Similarly, we are only able to interpret the context-sensitive (particular) social actions of others because there is a context-free (general) machinery by reference to which we can make sense of them. For example, the context-free mechanism or norm of turn-taking can be stated as 'one person speaks at a time'. 'One person speaks at a time' is not a rule in the sense in which rules of correct syntax, for example, are stated. People can designedly (Schegloff 2000a: 48) speak with overlap in specific contexts to intensify the affiliative or disaffiliative nature of particular social actions, such as agreeing and disagreeing; for example, when someone disagrees so strongly with a speaker that they deliberately interrupt them. People design their social actions in context-sensitive ways by reference to the 'one person' norm, and the value of their social actions is understood by listeners by reference to that norm. As Levinson (2006: 50) puts it, 'interaction is (1) composed of action sequences, and (2) governed not by rules but only by expectations'. From a CDST perspective, these 'norms' are adaptive mechanisms which can co-evolve with and mirror the phenomena they study (see Section 3.6).

3.4 SOCIALLY DISTRIBUTED COGNITION, INFORMATION EXCHANGE AND TOPIC DEVELOPMENT

In this section, a brief introduction is provided to the CA position on socially distributed cognition (Drew 1995; Schegloff 1991) in relation to ordinary conversation, together with the organisations of information exchange (Heritage 2012b) and topic development. We demonstrate how they are employed in ordinary conversation, by reference to a single excerpt. This will then enable us to clarify how the organisations have become adapted to social goals in Chapters 4 and 5. This section demonstrates how the three mechanisms relate to the progress of intersubjectivity.

3.4.1 SOCIALLY DISTRIBUTED COGNITION

CA is not able to establish the cognitive state of individuals in isolation, nor to gain a direct window into what interactants 'really mean'. What CA is able to portray and explicate, however, is the progress of intersubjectivity or 'socially distributed cognition' or 'socially shared cognition'. CA aims to 'identify ways in which participants themselves orient to, display, and make sense of one another's cognitive states (among other things)' (Drew 1995: 79). Intersubjectivity is mutual understanding or interpersonal alignment, and one of the key objectives of CA is to explicate how we are able to achieve a shared understanding of each other's actions. In conversation, interactants perform social displays of their cognitive states to each other. A social display of a cognitive state may differ from an actual state, as in the case of lying. The mechanisms of sequence, turn-taking and repair are employed by interactants in order to display to each other their social actions and cognitive state and also to display their understandings or analyses of the previous speaker's social actions and cognitive state. We return to the already familiar Excerpt 3.3 in a fuller version in Excerpt 3.8 to illustrate how socially distributed cognition works in ordinary conversation.

Excerpt 3.8 (Schegloff 1996: 75)

```
1    Marsha:   hello:?
2    Tony:     hi: Marsha?
3    Marsha:   ye:ah.
4    Tony:     how are you.
5    Marsha:   fi::ne.
6              (0.2)
7    Marsha:   did Joey get home yet?
8    Tony:     well I wz wondering when 'e left.
9              (0.2)
10   Marsha:   'hhh uh(4) did oh: .h yer not in on what ha:ppen'.(hh)(4)
11   Tony:     no(h)o=
12   Marsha:   =he's flying.
13             (0.2)
14   Marsha:   en Ilene is going to meet im:.. becuz the to:p  wz ripped
15             off'v iz car which is tih say someb'ddy helped
               th'mselfs.
16 → Tony:     stolen.
17             (0.4)
18   Marsha:   stolen.=right out in front of my house.
19   Tony:     oh: f'r crying out loud, =en eez not g'nna eez not
20             g'nna bring it ba:ck?
21   Marsha:   'hh no so it's parked in the g'rage cz it wz so damn
22             co:ld. an' ez a matter fact snowing on the Ridge Route.
```

In Excerpt 3.8 line 16, Tony's turn consists of a single word. As we saw earlier, this provides both an analysis of Marsha's previous turn and a social display of Tony's cognitive state, specifically that he has understood what has happened to the car, namely that the roof of the convertible has been stolen. Marsha in line 18 analyses Tony's turn as commenting retrospectively on what happened to the car, as performing a new social action of confirming understanding of Marsha's news by summarising the content in a new linguistic format, and as providing a context for her to take the sequence further. She displays her understanding of the work performed by his turn in her subsequent turn (line 18) by repeating his turn with the same intonation and adding further information on the theft.

Interactants, then, are always producing in their utterances a social display of their own cognitive state at the same time as they are displaying their understanding of a previous speaker's utterance. The next turn documents an analysis of the previous turn and displays this analysis not only to the other interactants, but also to us as analysts, providing us with a proof criterion and search procedure. Interactants are constantly conducting a social display to each other (and to us as analysts) of their cognitive states and their understanding of each other's utterances by means of and by reference to the interactional mechanisms. This aspect of interaction becomes especially relevant during word search sequences when the first speaker shows their cognitive state of difficulty finding a word and the second speaker displays their understanding of the first speaker through providing candidate solutions. Therefore, word searches display a clear embodiment of how socially distributed cognition works as a collaborative, jointly constructed process. In ordinary conversation, the mechanisms of turn and sequence display and check mutual understanding, and the mechanism of repair repairs breakdowns in mutual understanding. This is the basis for the analysis of socially shared cognition in CA and it follows that this cannot be separated from the study of interaction. This is what Schegloff (1991: 152) terms the inextricable intertwinedness of cognition and interaction. CA analysis demonstrates not only 'what' understandings the interactants display to each other, but also 'how' they do so by normative reference to the interactional mechanisms. The interactional mechanisms adapt themselves to mirror the social actions and cognitive displays of the participants. In other words, we as analysts gain access to their displays of understanding to each other in the same way that the participants gain this access, by reference to the interactional mechanisms; this mirroring procedure is what is meant by developing an emic perspective.

3.4.2 INFORMATION EXCHANGE

Closely related to the mechanism of socially distributed cognition is that of information exchange in talk. A recent development in CA is interest in the 'epistemic engine' (Heritage 2012b) of talk. As mentioned in Chapter 2, Heritage emphasises the significance of epistemic or information imbalances in motivating and driving talk until balance is achieved. Heritage introduces a hydraulic metaphor as follows. A participant may have a K+ (more knowledgeable) or K- (less knowledgeable) epistemic status, and the information imbalance will motivate talk to equalise this imbalance. Although not explicitly stated in Heritage's paper, it follows from this claim that topic development (see next section) provides a key mechanism for information exchange. If we re-examine Excerpt 3.8 with this in mind, we see an information imbalance at the start (with Marsha more knowledgeable and Tony less so) which drives the talk forward until equilibrium is reached in terms of information state. The situation is that Marsha and Tony are the separated parents of teenager Joey, who is to return to his father's house 500 miles away, having spent the holidays with his mother. He was supposed to drive back in the car, but the top has been stolen from it and the cold weather means it is impossible to drive back, so Joey has flown instead. At the time of the call, Tony does not know this news. In terms of information exchange, the first few lines establish who the callers are. In lines 7 and 11, we see that there is information imbalance in that Marsha does not know the reason for Tony's call and Tony does not know about the theft. In line 10, we see from Marsha's 'oh' that she has realised that Tony is not aware of the change in Joey's plans. Then Marsha in lines 12 and 14–15 informs Tony of the change of plan and reason for it, whilst Tony in line 19 works out the implications in terms of the car. Note in this sequence just how much information has been efficiently transmitted by phone in a few short turns in spite of the double imbalance of information at the start, with neither parent knowing where Joey is.

3.4.3 TOPIC DEVELOPMENT

Topic (what is being talked about) is a central concept in the analysis of talk and is co-constructed by participants during the course of the talk. However, it is not part of the context-free architecture of talk and, unlike the mechanisms of adjacency pairs and turn-taking, topic is not oriented to normatively. The research into topic within the CA tradition (Sacks 1992) has tended to focus on how topic initialisations, shifts and endings are managed as an interactional achievement. Topic is the vehicle for information exchange in talk, and in ordinary conversation participants have equal rights to propose a topic to other participants, who may or may not decide to engage with it and develop it.

Revisiting Excerpt 3.8 in terms of topic development, there is an overarching topic (Joey's whereabouts), which is introduced in line 7. Sub-topics are then developed in relation to the overarching topic, namely Joey's possible arrival (line 7), his departure time (line 8), Tony's less knowledgeable state (line 10), Joey's change in mode of transport (line 12), the reason for the change (line 14), the implications for the car (line 19) and the whereabouts of the car (line 21).

We previously introduced the organisations of socially distributed cognition and information exchange in relation to ordinary conversation. We should note here how topic development is key to the exchange of information and the progress of intersubjectivity, with the mechanism of repair available to deal with problems. J.M. Atkinson and Heritage (1984: 165) have suggested that topic is among the most complex conversational phenomena to be researched and amongst the most challenging to analyse. The mechanism of topic has to be extremely elastic and yet robust to be able to carry the load of unpredictable imbalances in information as well as intersubjectivity and social actions, as we have seen in Excerpt 3.8. Topic is a vehicle for the delivery of information exchange in this excerpt. In word search sequences, the conversation moves to a word search 'side sequence' (Jefferson 1972) where the topic shifts momentarily to talk about a word. As will be seen through the data analyses, the speakers need to mutually notice and agree to moving in and out of word search side sequences. Moreover, speakers need to have a shared understanding of the topic of the conversation in order for relevant candidate words to be provided and confirmed.

3.4.4 MAINTAINING INTERSUBJECTIVITY IN INTERACTION

Descriptions of specific languages (in terms of grammars, dictionaries, etc.) do not explain how speakers might be able to maintain intersubjectivity or mutual understanding. Rather, this is one of the main functions of the universal interaction engine. In the section above, we have illustrated how the mechanisms of socially distributed cognition, information exchange and topic contribute to the maintenance of intersubjectivity. However, the CA-CDST perspective is that all of the component mechanisms of the interaction engine work together in interaction to maintain intersubjectivity. Adjacency pairs, for example, are known as the building blocks of intersubjectivity (Heritage 1984a, 2007) and the mechanism of repair tackles trouble with intersubjectivity. We saw in Section 2.4.2 that complex adaptive systems arise from the interaction of their parts and function as an emergent whole which is more than the sum of its parts; this is the case with the maintenance of intersubjectivity in interaction. As we show in our data analyses in Chapters 4 and 5, speakers adapt a wide range of mechanisms and resources in inventive ways to maintain intersubjectivity and perform their social actions.

3.4.5 THE INTERACTION ENGINE: LINGUISTIC AND CULTURAL VARIATION

As we have seen in Section 3.2, CA aims to provide a 'holistic' portrayal of language use which reveals the reflexive relationships between form, function, sequence, social action, identity and context. Or, as Heritage and Clayman (2010) put it, CA analyses are analyses simultaneously of action, context management and intersubjectivity because all of these are the objects of the actors' actions. Broadening the perspective, how do we account for cultural and linguistic variation? Is the fundamental complex adaptive system of spoken interaction stable across languages and cultures or does it vary? Levinson (2006: 40) and Schegloff (2006: 83) explain in detail the rationale for concluding that human interactional abilities are at least partly independent of language and culture. Schegloff (2007: xiii) sees interaction as 'a web of practices that is so deeply rooted that it can transcend linguistic and cultural diversity'. Levinson (2006: 44) proposes the concept of an 'interaction engine' with detailed universal properties, but not as a fixed machine with fixed output. Rather, it works with local principles to generate heterogeneous output. In our study, we conceptualise the interaction engine as synonymous with the complex adaptive system of human spoken interaction. The design features (Levinson 2022) of the interaction engine are: orchestration of multimodal signals; highly controlled timing; manipulation of specific contingencies between initiating signal and response; the ability to attribute detailed intentions to communicative acts. The basic mechanisms of the interaction engine are those detailed in this chapter.

A number of studies have demonstrated the universality of the mechanisms of turn-taking, sequence and repair, allowing Levinson (2022: 2) to conclude that the interaction engine is nearly uniform across the species. Kendrick et al. (2020) argue for the universality of sequence organisation, providing evidence from 11 different language families. Stivers et al. (2009) examine turn-taking in 10 diverse languages and conclude that it forms a single shared infrastructure with some cultural variability. Dingemanse et al. (2015) study the repair systems of 12 diverse languages and show other-initiated repair to be a universal system. These studies suggest that the complex adaptive system of human spoken interaction is primary and universal, although (as with all systems) there is evolution and heterogeneity.

As West (2017: 281) notes, 'The great commonality is the universality of social network structures across the globe', and we argue that the interaction engine is embedded in these networks and co-evolved with them. In the terms of our study, the interaction engine as described above is a complex adaptive system which serves as a bedrock (or homogeneous core) providing a foundational resource that facilitates the heterogeneous development of languages and cultures. Levinson (2022: 2) suggests that human interactional abilities offer a 'machine tool' for producing languages. As humans spread out around the world, new languages and cultures evolved following the principles of variation and selection. New languages evolved to sit within the existing system of human spoken interaction. It is this balance between homogeneity (the interaction engine) and heterogeneity (languages) which then enabled communication between the diverse populations when globalisation put them into contact with each other again at the end of the twentieth century. An example of this can be seen in the setting and corpus for this study. In the present, the interaction engine bedrock still enables speakers of differing languages from different cultures to communicate with each other when they meet (Levinson 2006). The combined use of the human spoken interaction (universal) and language (variable) systems provides talk with enormous generative power.

The existence of some kind of interaction engine prior to the evolution of language is alluded to in the literature on **language** as a complex adaptive system: 'language evolved in the context of an already highly interactive social existence. This intensive interaction suggests that the evolution of language cannot be understood outside of a social context' (The Five Graces Group 2009: 3). In order to specify and exemplify the characteristics of **the interaction engine** as a distinct complex adaptive system, we have needed in this study to separate and differentiate it as much as possible from the complex adaptive system of language, which has already received considerable attention (N.C. Ellis and Larsen-Freeman 2009a). In this study, we do not examine how the two related complex systems of the interaction engine and language(s) work together; this remains an area for future research.

3.5 ADAPTING CA METHODOLOGY TO SOCIAL AND INSTITUTIONAL GOALS

So far in this chapter we have examined how the component mechanisms of the interaction engine work together as a complex system, as revealed by CA. CA has been applied to analyse a range of interactional contexts: social and institutional interaction, as well as L2 and longitudinal interaction, as described in Chapter 2 and in the section to follow. We now examine how exactly CA **adapts** itself to mirror spoken interaction as it varies and adapts itself in relation to social and institutional goals. In other words, we now focus on how CA (and hence the interaction engine) works as an **adaptive** system.

3.5.1 INSTITUTIONAL CA

The first phase of CA research (Sacks et al. 1974; Schegloff et al. 1977) produced descriptions of how talk is organised in the baseline of ordinary conversation. In later phases (Drew and Heritage 1992b; Heritage and Clayman 2010) researchers looked at institutional interaction in settings such as courtrooms and hospitals. Such studies have focused on how the organisation of the interaction is related to the institutional aim and on the ways in which this organisation differs from the benchmark of ordinary conversation. Heritage (1997) proposes six basic places to probe the institutionality of interaction, namely:

1. Turn-taking organisation.
2. Overall structural organisation of the interaction.
3. Sequence organisation.
4. Turn design.
5. Lexical choice.
6. Epistemology and information exchange.

Perhaps the most important analytical consideration is that institutional talk displays goal orientation and rational organisation. Participants in institutional interaction orient to some core goal, task or identity normally associated with the institution (Drew and Heritage 1992a: 22). CA institutional discourse methodology attempts to relate not only the overall organisation of the interaction but also individual interactional devices to the core institutional goal. CA attempts, then, to understand the organisation of the interaction as being *rationally* derived from the core institutional goal.

CA methodology is always concerned with making explicit the interactional orientations and concerns of participants. Clearly participants' concerns will inevitably vary in each institutional or semi-institutional setting, and so CA methodology will evolve in a slightly different way in each institutional setting in order to portray the participants' different concerns and orientations. For example, Drew (1992: 472) explicates a device for producing inconsistency in, and damaging implications for, a witness's evidence during cross-examination in a courtroom trial. Clearly these participants' interactional concerns are unique to this institutional setting. Although Drew is using a CA methodology, he is in effect simultaneously developing a **sub-variety** of CA methodology appropriate to the analysis of cross-examination in courtroom settings: he is selecting for analysis a device which is unique to that institutional setting and explicating the interactional work unique to that setting which the device accomplishes (Seedhouse 1996: 108).

In exactly the same way, this study develops a sub-variety of CA methodology appropriate to the analysis of interaction in an ELF setting because the interactional mechanisms adapt themselves to changing social goals and the methodology must follow suit. This study will select for analysis those concerns and competences which are unique to the specific setting and attempt to explicate how the interaction is accomplished in the ELF setting and what the 'machinery' or system is which produces the interaction. In other words, CA can be seen as an **adaptive methodological system** which mirrors the sociocultural contexts which the participants talk into being. To exemplify this, the next sections will focus on how our main analytical tool, the next-turn proof procedure, adapts itself to mirror both L2 classroom interaction and informal language learning talk; this is the basis for our claim that CA is indeed an adaptive or mirroring methodology.

3.5.2 ADAPTING THE NEXT-TURN PROOF PROCEDURE: IN RELATION TO L2 CLASSROOMS

Seedhouse (2004) provides a detailed explanation of how the mechanisms of turn-taking, sequence and repair have adapted to talk in L2 classrooms, showing that there is a reflexive relationship between the pedagogical focus and the organisation of the interaction. As we saw in Section 3.3.1, the basic analytical procedure developed and used in relation to ordinary conversation was the 'next-turn proof procedure'. In relation to institutional talk, however, the institutional goal shapes the participants' talk and so the analytical procedure may (in general terms) be reframed as the 'next-turn proof procedure in relation to the institutional goal'. Seedhouse (2004) stated the adapted methodology for analysing L2 classroom interaction in these terms:

> The analyst follows exactly the same procedure as the participants and traces the evolving relationship between pedagogy and interaction, using as evidence the analyses of this relationship which the participants display to each other in their own turns. So the methodology which is used for the analysis of L2 classroom interaction is the next-turn proof procedure in relation to the pedagogical focus. (195)

Overwhelmingly in L2 classrooms, the pedagogical focus is introduced by the teacher as part of their professional aims in relation to a curriculum. We look briefly in this next excerpt at how this methodology works.

Excerpt 3.9 (Seedhouse 1996: 314)

```
1    T:    I've got a sofa a sofa say after me I've got a sofa
2    LL:   I've got a sofa
3    T:    very good and now I need Kjartan and Elge(.)
4          can you come up to me please (1.0) and
5          can you give each one a sheet?
6    L:    sheet?
7    T:    sheet of paper (LL hand out sheets with pictures on)
```

Excerpt 3.9 (Seedhouse 1996: 314) (continued)

```
8   T:    now again (2.0) listen to me (3.0) I've got a lamp
9   LL:   [I've] got a lamp
10  T:    [what]
11  T:    don't repeat now, don't say after me now. I: I say it and
12        you and you just listen. I've got a lamp. what have you got?
13        (2.5) raise your hands. what have you got Eirik?
14  L1:   e:r=
15  T:    =can you say=
16  L1:   =I've got a book.
17  T:    right, fine. I've got a telephone. what have you got? (4.0)
          Trygve.
18  L2:   I've got a hammer.
```

In lines 1 and 2 in the above excerpt, the relationship between the pedagogical focus and interaction is that the learners must repeat whatever the teacher says, and the evidence that the learners have understood this is their exact choral repetition in line 2. Subsequently the teacher intends a change in the relationship between the pedagogical focus and interaction, which is prepared by movement around the classroom and the handing out of sheets. The teacher tries in line 7 to make explicit the nature of the new relationship between pedagogy and interaction (i.e., say you've got the object on your sheet). However, some of the learners repeat verbatim in line 8 what the teacher says in line 7, that is, they are continuing the speech exchange system from the previous episode. The teacher makes explicit the new relationship between the pedagogical focus and interaction in lines 10 and 11, and in lines 14 and 16 it is clear that the learners have understood the new relationship. The next-turn proof procedure is related to the pedagogical focus introduced by the teacher. So in line 8 we see evidence of the learners' mistaken analysis of the relationship between the pedagogical focus and interaction, whereas in lines 14 and 16 the proof is that they have understood the new relationship required. The next-turn proof procedure has therefore adapted itself to mirror the participants' orientation to the relationship between pedagogical focus and interaction. As the structure of the interaction evolves, so the methodology must itself evolve in tandem.

3.5.3 ADAPTING THE NEXT-TURN PROOF PROCEDURE: IN RELATION TO L2 INTERACTION

We now come to the analytical methodology to be employed in relation to our data in Chapters 4 and 5. The example comes from our corpus of interactions in an English as a lingua franca (ELF) setting, involving two female Asian students with different L1s at an international university dormitory in Japan. The paired participants do not have a common language apart from English to converse in at the start of the recordings, and they are free to discuss whatever they want. Certainly this is not L2 classroom interaction as no teacher is involved and the participants are in dormitory bedrooms rather than classrooms. On the other hand, we will see that the participants sometimes display a clear orientation to the goal of learning English L2 in the detail of their talk. Is this ordinary conversation? The interactional setting examined in this study could be termed 'pre-institutional' or 'quasi-institutional': it lacks many of the features of institutional talk (Drew and Heritage 1992b) such as a professional to lead it, yet it nonetheless has a number of features in common with language learning talk in institutions, for example goal orientation in relation to L2 learning.

As mentioned in Chapter 2, this variety of talk has a dual character, namely (1) a focus on progressivity or social talk and (2) a focus on language learning. This involves talk in which the participants display an orientation to language learning processes in the details of their talk. This may occur anywhere, at any time and involve any kinds of participants, and it may be very temporary, lasting just for a turn. This orientation to (or foregrounding of) language learning processes may take very many different forms, examples of which are presented in the rest of this book. To exemplify rapid switches between social and language learning talk, we can consider the excerpt below from our data, in which Ami and Hang are discussing the topic of economic disparity of people within both Japan and Vietnam.[9]

Excerpt 3.10 Ami–Hang July Gap

```
1    Ami:    ↑in betna:m ah: are there (0.5) AH BIG?
2            (1.0)
3            mm °big separate° no big (0.7) the:::
4            (0.4) I mean the: (0.4) poor?
5    Hang:   [mm
6    Ami:    [the (0.3) the:: .sss ah the some of student
7            is poor but (.) some of student is very rich?
8    Hang:   ↑mmm[mm::
9    Ami:        [so:: (0.4) are there lot >ah< big
10           (0.6)
11   Ami:    °how do you say° the
12           (1.0)
13   Hang:   big ah: gap?
14   Ami:    ↑YA BIG
15   Hang:   big gap
16   Ami:    gap in be ah in betnam?
17   Hang:   ↑mm[mm:::
18   Ami:       [right?
```

Ami in line 1 is focused on social talk and attempting to formulate a question, but from line 3 to line 11 an additional focus on language learning is talked into being because Ami does not know how to say 'gap' or 'disparity'. Hang engages with the language learning focus by supplying the target vocabulary in lines 13 and 15, and in line 16 Ami is able to talk the language learning focus out of being by returning

---

[9] A more detailed analysis is in Section 5.3.2.

to the social talk. Ami completes asking the question which she started in line 1. So language learning talk can 'pop in' and 'pop out' at any time in any type of talk as speakers alter their focus. In the excerpt above, the short episode of language learning talk is a word search. The topic had already been decided by the speaker but a specific L2 word was missing which would allow successful development of the topic; once that has been located, the topic talk can resume. A few minutes later in the same stretch of interaction, Ami uses the word 'gap' in a new context without any display of trouble. Thus, the sequence above is proved to be successful as a learning moment.

In all instances in our data, when the participants develop a language learning focus, they co-develop a speech exchange system which relates to that focus in some way. The participants display in their own turns their analyses of the evolving relationship between language learning focus and interaction, in other words, how the language learning focus relates to the turns produced. Therefore, the methodology which is used for the analysis of language learning talk when it occurs in this setting is the next-turn proof procedure in relation to the language learning focus as determined by the participants. The participants themselves decide on a turn-by-turn basis whether they will focus on a language learning point in their talk or not, and if so, which point. The speech exchange system they develop is reflexively related to the language learning focus, as will be demonstrated in Chapters 4 and 5.

Why should a research methodology have to adapt itself in the way we have argued above? This is because the phenomena of spoken interaction vary and evolve as the participants' concerns evolve, and the methodology needs to co-vary and co-evolve in order to mirror the phenomena and to represent them adequately from an emic perspective. The methodology must mirror the participants' concerns. The social world which these participants talk into being has a dual nature in that they wish to conduct social talk on topics of their choice. However, as L2 users with no common L1, they often encounter trouble with expressing themselves in L2, necessitating a rapid switch to language learning talk in order to repair the trouble. This duality in turn means that the participants switch between using the next-turn proof procedure (for social talk) and the next-turn proof procedure in relation to the language learning focus (for language learning talk) and can switch back again from turn to turn. The speakers also adapt to each other and the interactional context to improve the process of achieving intersubjectivity. Therefore, CA further adapts itself to the study of the longitudinal adaptive nature of interaction. The analyses in Chapters 4 and 5 provide many examples of how this works in practice.

We argue that a dynamic, constantly shifting complex adaptive system such as spoken interaction could not possibly be portrayed adequately using a static, rigid, invariant research methodology. More broadly, we suggest that research methodologies for studying complex adaptive systems should themselves be adaptive systems, precisely because the phenomena which the methodologies are studying are, by their nature, constantly evolving and adapting to a changing world.

3.6 THE RELATIONSHIP BETWEEN CA AND CDST

3.6.1 INTRODUCTION

In Section 3.3 we considered how the basic mechanisms and concepts of CA work together in relation to ordinary conversation. We have seen how the components combine to create an architecture of intersubjectivity which enables people to perform an enormous range of social actions and create a social world as they see fit. In Chapters 4 and 5 we will see how all of these mechanisms and concepts have become transformed in orientation to the specific goal of informal L2 learning in this setting. The fundamental methodological approach we will be adopting in relation to the data is ethnomethodological CA, and we are also using the CDST lens to understand how the interaction functions as a holistic adaptive system; we term this a CA-CDST approach. The combination of methodologies means that the interactional system can be studied simultaneously in the particular or micro-detail (through CA) and from the general, macro or systemic perspective, with both lenses and levels reflexively informing each other. In this section, we consider the relationship between CA and CDST.

Since the 1960s, CA has in effect been describing how human spoken interaction functions as a complex adaptive system. However, it has been using its own idiosyncratic terminology and procedures for this, based on the sociological discipline of ethnomethodology. The multidisciplinary science of CDST also developed at first in the USA during the 1960s and 1970s and is sometimes said to date from Lorenz's (1963) paper on weather systems. What we propose in our study is this. Although CA and CDST use different procedures and terminologies and have separate histories, they can both portray human spoken interaction as a complex adaptive system which is reflexively linked to many other complex systems.

The argument we develop in this study is that CDST and CA have in effect been working in parallel for decades. We suggest that CDST and CA have been approaching their respective tasks in similar ways but on different scales and using different terminology. CDST has been working at a vastly larger scale, looking at all life-related systems on Earth. CA has been focusing narrowly and uniquely on showing how human spoken interaction functions as a complex adaptive system (without using such terminology). CA was designed from the start as a self-similar, mirroring methodology in relation to the phenomenon it studies, because it was following ethnomethodological principles, whilst CDST has been operating on an incomparably broader scale, showing how complex adaptive systems function throughout life and nature on Earth. However, given that it is generally agreed that the human brain is the most complex object yet discovered, and given that CA studies how human brains communicate via spoken interaction, it may just possibly be that CA has in effect been engaged for decades in one of the most complex CDST studies ever undertaken. Although there has previously been little discussion of the similarities between CA and CDST as they have developed independently for decades, the time is now ripe to examine these.

We now start to approach the relationship between CDST and CA in this section by focusing on the key CDST concept of 'self-similarity' or 'fractality'. According to West (2017: 92), systematic repetitive behaviour is called scale invariance or self-similarity (see Section 2.4.2 on fractals and self-similarities). West (2017: 147) suggests that almost all of the networks that sustain life are approximately self-similar fractals. A fractal object looks the same when examined from far away or nearby (Sardar and Abrams 2004) – it is self-similar, which implies that any subsystem of a fractal system is equivalent to the whole system. The patterns or shapes of complex adaptive systems look similar from different scales, perspectives and levels. This is illustrated in Figure 3.1. This property of endlessly manifesting a motif within a motif is known as self-similarity.

We will be using self-similarity as a guiding principle in this study to help us identify which interactional features to investigate and to locate links between levels of interaction. As West (2017) notes, 'To varying degrees, fractality, scale invariance, and self-similarity are ubiquitous across nature from galaxies and clouds to your cells, your brain, the Internet, companies and cities' (92). We have therefore looked in our research for insights as to how it might manifest itself in human spoken interaction.

We argue that CA itself is a self-similar complex adaptive system which is able to reveal self-similarity in spoken interaction. If this is correct, then CA should be able to reveal self-similarity at multiple levels, (1) in relation to the phenomenon studied, namely talk, (2) in relation to itself as a methodology, and (3) in relation to CDST as a meta-theory. The next sections will consider the evidence in relation to these three areas.

Figure 3.1   Fractal shape form of a Romanesco broccoli

3.6.2 CAN CA REVEAL SELF-SIMILARITY IN INTERACTION?

One way to verify whether CA does indeed work as a self-similar complex adaptive system as claimed is to check whether it is able to uncover fractality or self-similarity in interactional structures. To do this we refer to Seedhouse's (2004) study of L2 classroom interaction. If L2 classroom interaction does indeed function as a complex adaptive system, then we should expect to notice some evidence of self-similarity in the structure of the interaction at different levels. In other words, the macro description of the architecture of L2 classroom interaction should be miniaturised in some way in the micro-interactional detail. The best-known, best-studied interactional phenomenon in L2 classroom interaction is the three-part sequence generally known as IRF (Teacher Initiation, Learner Response and Teacher Follow-Up or Feedback) (Sinclair and Coulthard 1975). This pattern has been identified in numerous research studies as ubiquitous in classrooms throughout the world. As Larsen-Freeman and Cameron (2008a) say in their discussion of complexity theory in relation to discourse:

> The IRF pattern ... can be seen as an attractor on the classroom discourse landscape that shows variability around a very stable form and that has arisen through adaptation in response to particular classroom contingencies. The discourse system will tend to return to the IRF attractor because it is a pattern that works; it is a preferred behaviour of the system. (235)

The importance of the IRF pattern demands explanation if we are to claim that L2 classroom interaction has a rational architecture. First of all, we need to present the three properties of L2 classroom interaction from Seedhouse (2004, 2010) and then compare a typical example of the IRF pattern:

1. Language is both the vehicle and object of instruction.
2. There is a reflexive relationship between pedagogy and interaction, and interactants constantly display their analyses of the evolving relationship between pedagogy and interaction.
3. The linguistic forms and patterns of interaction which the learners produce are subject to evaluation by the teacher in some way.

Next, we examine an example of the IRF pattern.

Excerpt 3.11 (Carr 2006: DVD 14)
```
1    T:    number three:: (0.3) er Dilmo where is the cat?
2    L1:   the cat is inside the box
3    T:    excellent ok inside the box
```

In the context of the overall description of the interactional architecture of the L2 classroom, the IRF pattern can be seen as a **'replication in miniature of the three interactional properties' listed above** (Seedhouse 1996: 354). In line 1, the teacher introduces a pedagogical focus, expecting the learner to reflexively produce a precise pattern of interaction in response (property 2). In line 2, the learner produces an interactional pattern, which is matched against the pedagogical focus and positively evaluated (property 3) by the teacher in line 3. Language is both the vehicle and goal of the interaction (property 1) in that the point of the teacher's prompt (using language) is for the learner to produce a string of linguistic forms for evaluation. The lesson itself has a focus (prepositions, as illustrated in the Initiation), learning outcomes (as evidenced in the Response) and evaluation (as in the Feedback), and its interactional realisation is informed by the properties we identify.

The term used in CDST for a 'replication in miniature' is a 'fractal'. Fractals have significance in CDST as they are a key defining characteristic of a complex, non-linear system (N.F. Johnson 2007) (see Section 2.4.2). Therefore, the well-established universality of the IRF cycle around the world suggests that it is a fractal of the whole interactional architecture of the L2 classroom and provides evidence that language learning talk is indeed a complex adaptive system.

So the functional or rational explanation which we can offer for the importance of the IRF pattern is that it is the most compact vehicle imaginable for the accomplishment of what Drew and Heritage (1992a: 40–1) call the 'institutionalised activity'. Because it is so closely identifiable with the interactional properties and with the institutional business, it is the most economical method of accomplishing a complete cycle of the institutional business. For a complete cycle of the institutional business to be carried out, the minimum requirement is that (1) the teacher introduces a pedagogical focus, (2) the learner produces patterns of interaction in response, and (3) the teacher evaluates the learner response (although this is not always verbalised) by matching (1) to (2). In the case of the previous excerpt, this complete cycle of institutional business is accomplished in only 19 words.

This explains why the IRF pattern has a satisfying, complete feel to it, or is an 'attractor' in the terms of CDST. This provides an illustration of what CA means by the rational design of institutional interaction. Not only can it be shown that the overall interactional architecture of L2 classroom interaction derives from the core goal, but 'surface' features of the micro-interaction, such as the IRF pattern, can be allocated a functional place within that architecture and related directly to the macro levels. In other words, it can be shown **how** the surface feature is accomplishing the institutional business. From a CDST perspective, L2 classroom interaction displays self-similarity at different levels, with the IRF pattern a fractal, mirroring on a miniature scale the interactional properties of L2 classroom interaction.

3.6.3 CA AS A SELF-SIMILAR COMPLEX ADAPTIVE SYSTEM

A methodological aim of this book is to examine the relationship between CA and CDST as well as the extent to which CA and CDST are compatible for the study of language learning interaction. Following the discussion above, we can now reconceptualise this relationship by portraying CA itself as both (1) a complex adaptive system which adapts itself to and mirrors the context talked into being by the participants in order to portray the participants' own (emic) perspectives and (2) a self-similar or fractal system. From this perspective, there is little point in discussing the compatibility of CA and CDST. CDST is a meta-theory; CA is an instantiation or narrow-focus operationalisation of the CDST meta-theory, solely in relation to the analysis of human spoken interaction. Alternatively, CA is a self-similar fractal of CDST, with the two operating on different 'scales' (West 2017). Both are trying to research and understand the functioning of complex adaptive systems, but CA has an extremely narrow focus, specialising in one specific system only, namely human spoken interaction.

In which ways does the methodology of CA display **self-similarity**? CA is based on ethnomethodology (Heritage 1984b), which studies the shared methods people use in their everyday lives to construct their own social reality and attempts to represent these methods and processes from the participants' rather than from the analyst's perspective. Ethnomethodology does not promote specific research methods, because the choice of research method should be related to the nature of the phenomenon being studied and to the participants' emic perspective (Garfinkel 1967). However, ethnomethodology means that the analyst should use the same methods as the participants and as such it is an adaptive approach par excellence. In the study of conversation, the next-turn proof procedure is the basic analytical tool because it is the one being used by the participants themselves.

We argue that methodologies which analyse human behaviour in its own terms and from the participants' emic perspective (ethnomethodologies) must themselves function as complex adaptive systems. This is 'rational design' in that the analytical methodologies must adapt themselves to ever-changing human behaviours (which are themselves complex adaptive systems) if they are to portray the perspectives of the participants themselves in context. The ethnomethodological principle of reflexivity states that the same set of methods or procedures are responsible for both the production of actions/language and its interpretation. It therefore follows that as the actions change in real-world contexts, so the analytical methodology must adapt to these. The same principle applies to the mechanisms of CA: sequence organisation is both the mechanism by which interactants are able to make their utterances comprehensible and the mechanism by which co-interactants (and we as analysts) are able to interpret them. Therefore, there is mirroring or self-similarity at all points within CA methodology. The fact that the methodology employed by CA analysts must precisely mirror the analytical methodology the participants use (in order to make sense of each other's talk) demonstrates that CA is a mirroring or self-similar methodology.

It may sound strange to regard research methodologies themselves as complex systems. However, the arguments are these: (1) methodologies determine how the phenomena are observed and analysed, and (2) research methodologies are products of the human brain, the complex adaptive system par excellence. We know from the CDST research that some products of the human brain are themselves clearly complex adaptive systems. For example, West (2017) demonstrates the fractal organisation of cities. It is therefore rational for us to look for mirroring or self-similarity between research methodologies and the phenomena which they are studying. Indeed, this approach is hinted at by Hiver and Al-Hoorie (2020: 30), who suggest that complex systems are the units of analysis for CDST research and that 'cases' are the methodological equivalent of complex systems. One might therefore legitimately evaluate the degree of self-similarity between a case study and the complex system involved. A further argument is that seeing methodologies as complex adaptive systems integrates the issue of the observer and observership into our epistemology. Stephen Hawking's final theory was that 'the theory of the universe and observership are bound together. We create the universe as much as it creates us' (Hertog 2023: 133).

Research methodologies are all products of the human brain, which itself has been extensively studied as a complex system. West (2017) shows how the fractal organisation of the human brain is mirrored in the organisation of the products of the human brain, such as companies and cities, culminating in the 'outrageous speculation that cities are effectively a scaled representation of the structure of the human brain' (309). Schegloff (1991: 154) suggests that 'the structures of interaction penetrate into the very warp' of cognition, so that, for example, an 'understanding-display' device (i.e., the next-turn proof procedure) is built into the mechanism of turn-taking and sequence. In this case, similarly 'outrageous speculation' might be that the functioning of spoken interaction and intersubjectivity as uncovered by CA may mirror in some way the functioning of the human brain.

To sum up, CA can be described as a self-similar, adaptive methodology that is a complex adaptive system. It is a **self-similar** methodology in four senses. Firstly, it identifies self-similarity or fractals in individual phenomena in relation to the overall interactional architecture, as shown in Section 3.6.2. Secondly, the methodology is inherently based on self-similarity and is fractal in nature because of the way it proceeds – the analytical methodology used by the analyst must mirror precisely the analytical methodology used by the interlocutors in the interaction being studied.[10] Thirdly, CA displays fractals within its own overall structure in that the next-turn proof procedure (the basic analytical tool and internal verification procedure) is a fractal of CA as a whole methodology. Fourthly, CA is in a fractal relationship with CDST as an overarching meta-theory; CA works on a much smaller and much more restricted scale, revealing how human spoken interaction functions as a complex adaptive system. As shown in Section 3.5, CA is also an **adaptive** methodology in that the analytical methodology, next-turn proof procedure and basic mechanisms adapt themselves to mirror the specifics and goals of a particular setting and activity. CA is also a **complex system** in the CDST sense. As we have shown in Section 3.4, a CA analysis involves an emergent form of analysis; the way in which participants employ many component mechanisms to perform their social actions is studied in order to create a holistic analysis. Complex systems arise from the interaction of their parts and function as a whole which is more than the sum of its parts. CA can be seen as a reconstruction of the genesis of the unique complex system of social interaction created by the

---

[10] This derives from the ethnomethodological principle of reflexivity, which states that the same set of methods are responsible for the production of actions and their interpretation.

participants in situ. By reconstructing how the participants have assembled the parts, we create a simulation of the whole interactional episode and transient social world which they talked into being.[11] Because CA itself is a self-similar, complex adaptive system, we propose that it is the most appropriate methodology for analysing human spoken interaction from a CDST perspective. We argue in this study that the approaches and discoveries of CA and CDST are compatible. What does a combined CA-CDST analysis of spoken interaction look like? In Section 6.3 we provide a worked-through example.

3.6.4 CONCLUSIONS: USING CA TO RESEARCH HUMAN SPOKEN INTERACTION AS A COMPLEX ADAPTIVE SYSTEM

In this chapter, we have explained how the universal interaction engine works by describing how CA works. The interaction engine provides the basic exchange mechanisms for humans to understand each other's social actions, whichever language(s) they are speaking. It has often been wrongly assumed that language provides all of the necessary meaning and information for interactants to understand each other. We have argued that the interaction engine provides the basic mechanisms for the co-construction of meaning and intersubjectivity, as well as the transfer of information. However, we do not currently have any means of knowing the relative contributions of the interaction engine and language to the exchange of meaning and information, nor do we understand how the two complex systems work together.

The picture we have at the end of this chapter is that (1) CA is a research methodology which aims to reveal the functioning of human spoken interaction, (2) CDST is an overarching meta-theory which aims to reveal the functioning of all of the non-linear complex adaptive systems in the world including human interaction, and (3) CA is a self-similar fractal of CDST, with the two operating on different scales and materials.

In this chapter we have portrayed human spoken interaction as a universal complex adaptive system and have introduced its fundamental mechanisms, which together constitute the 'interaction engine'. These are able to adapt themselves to and mirror any variety of human activity and goal, whether social, institutional or cultural, which is delivered via any means, verbal and non-verbal, and in any specific overlaid language or blend of languages. The universal mechanisms of turn-taking, sequence and repair provide the structure against which the context-sensitive implementations of social actions in talk can be interpreted and intersubjectivity maintained. The research methodology of CA is able to portray how spoken interaction functions as a complex adaptive system because it is designed to mirror the characteristics of the talk and to adapt itself to the varieties of talk which are

---

[11] We are grateful to Keith Richards (personal communication) for this observation: as CA is an emergent form of analysis investigating the emergent phenomenon of spoken interaction, a CA analysis or explanation can never be complete or final. Similarly, CDST recognises that complete explanations or analyses are impractical (as the butterfly effect illustrates), if not impossible, and the focus is on the workings of the machinery and its component mechanisms – as in CA.

created; CA is itself a complex adaptive system. We propose that a complex adaptive research methodology is necessary to portray the functioning of a complex adaptive system adequately.

We have also argued that it is possible to analyse spoken interaction on both the micro (particular) level and the macro (general) level by employing a combination of CDST meta-theory and CA microanalysis. However, this approach works much better if the CDST concept of self-similarity/fractality is employed as a guiding principle at all levels and if CDST and CA are themselves viewed as complex adaptive systems. From this perspective, CA is a fractal of CDST and the concept of self-similarity illuminates many of CA's principles and procedures, as shown above. Although CA and CDST use different procedures and terminologies and have separate histories, they can both portray human spoken interaction as a complex adaptive system which is reflexively linked to many other complex systems. The difference is that CA has (due to its ethnomethodological origins) to mirror from the participants' perspective how they themselves are organising the interaction. By contrast, the CDST study of other complex systems has no requirement to model the participants' socially distributed cognition in the medium of talk. This explains why a number of CA procedures differ from CDST procedures. Nonetheless, this chapter has described the basics of how human spoken interaction functions as a complex adaptive system by describing how CA works; this was possible as CA is a mirroring methodology.

We therefore suggest that (1) using a CDST lens illuminates how CA functions as a mirroring methodology, and (2) using a CA lens illuminates how the interaction engine relates to the other complex systems. In the very specific context studied here (L2 use in an ELF setting), the specific methodological procedure we will use is the next-turn proof procedure in relation to the language learning focus, as exemplified in Section 3.5.3. This will be applied to data in Chapters 4 and 5. Chapters 4 and 5 will bring a 'narrow' view of word search sequence using CA microanalysis, and Chapter 6 will bring a 'wider' view of how word searches function as a complex adaptive system using the principles of CDST. This methodological approach of analysing the narrow and micro CA view of interaction and making connections with the wider and macro view of human interaction in the community through CDST principles is what we call the CA-CDST approach.

We have looked at the basic CA mechanisms of turn-taking, sequence and repair and shown how these provide participants with a universal, flexible framework to conduct the business of human spoken communication in any language. Having context-free (general) mechanisms provides a structure against which speakers design context-sensitive (particular) meanings and social actions and listeners can interpret meaning and social actions. Having context-sensitive applications of the mechanisms means that they are able to adapt to any new social, cultural or technical innovations required of human spoken interaction in changing times, for instance moving to online communication for work during covid lockdown. This has been a brief account of some aspects of CA; a comprehensive account can be found in Sidnell and Stivers (2013). Levinson (2006, 2022, 2023) elaborates on the design features of the interaction engine.

We finish the chapter with a quotation from Goethe's *Wilhelm Meisters Wanderjahre* which is used by Schegloff (2007: v) as a motto to his *Primer in Conversation Analysis*. This encapsulates rather beautifully how both CA and CDST converge in their approaches to the systems they study:

> There is a delicate form of the empirical which identifies itself so intimately with its object that it thereby becomes theory. The general and the particular converge; the particular is the general appearing under various conditions.

4
PATTERNS OF WORD SEARCH SEQUENCES AT THE GROUP LEVEL

4.1 INTRODUCTION

In Chapter 3, we introduced the broad, general perspective on how human spoken interaction is organised as a complex adaptive system. We also saw that repair is the primary mechanism for maintaining intersubjectivity. In Chapters 4 and 5, we present the narrow, particular view of human interaction through word search sequences, which are a specialised application of the mechanism of repair for the location and production of target lexical items. We display how the speakers in the corpus as a group have adapted the mechanism of the word search in ways that enable social actions in this particular ELF context.

In this chapter, we examine the sequential organisation of the L2 speakers' word search sequences in an informal ELF context. Previous studies on word search sequences in English initiated by L2 speakers have frequently focused on the repair work (or lack of it) by the L1 speaker in interaction (Hosoda 2006; Kurhila 2006). However, the field has started to shift its focus towards what L2 speakers **do** in achieving mutual understanding when one lacks the linguistic resources in completing their utterances (e.g., Carroll 2005; Hauser 2013a; Pekarek Doehler and Berger 2019; Pekarek Doehler and Skogmyr Marian 2022). Using the following framework of a typical sequential organisation of a word search sequence introduced in Chapter 2 (e.g., Koshik and Seo 2012), we analyse the ways in which participants initiate word searches and candidate solutions are provided, and how these candidate solutions are responded to:

Speaker A: Initiates a word search
Speaker A or B: Provides candidate solution
Speaker A or B: Confirms/corrects

Through the analysis of word search sequences, we demonstrate that in ELF interaction, there is a wider variety of sequential patterns than has been suggested in previous studies (e.g., Hosoda 2006; Koshik and Seo 2012; Kurhila 2006; Theodórsdóttir 2018), thus suggesting an emergent phenomenon. In L1 interaction, repair is often done solely by the self or the other (Schegloff et al. 1977). But from the data, it is more usually the case that in L2/ELF interaction, repair is conducted sequentially, and the actual resolving of the word search is done mutually. Thus, mutual understanding of a word is achieved sequentially in and through negotiation.

Furthermore, although the Japanese participants in the data would frequently display their orientations to the interaction as a 'learning opportunity' (Brouwer 2003), we will demonstrate through the analysis that even in ELF interactions there is a preference towards self-repair, similar to L1 interaction (Schegloff et al. 1977). What is more, the analysis displays a negotiation of epistemic stance (Heritage and Raymond 2005; Heritage 2012a, 2013) towards the lexical item or the English language knowledge through the interaction, thus suggesting that participants in ELF interactions are not always on an equal footing (Goffman 1981a), nor are the conversations always cooperative and supportive (Jenks 2012; Konakahara 2017; Seidlhofer 2001). This section of the book contributes to this accumulating area of studies by focusing on word search sequences in informal L2 interaction in ELF settings.

The chapter begins by introducing frequently used word search initiation methods, followed by the variations in frequently used candidate solutions utilised. This chapter will then focus on responses by the interlocutor when the candidate solutions are presented with a rising intonation (i.e., try-marked). The chapter outlines how the speakers as a whole cohort adapt the mechanism of the word search sequences to their specific context and social goals. In other words, we display the basic functioning of word search sequences as a system, prior to focusing on the individual changes and emergent use of the mechanism over time in Chapter 5.

4.2 WORD SEARCH INITIATIONS

Out of the 37 hours of video recording among the 4 core participants, 282 instances were found where the Japanese participant initiated the word search: Ami 86, Maya 92, Tomoko 38, and Yoko 66. These word searches were initiated through typical patterns such as silence, eye gaze away from the interlocutor, cut-offs, repetition and restart of sentences, and elongated vowel sounds, as documented in previous research (e.g., Carroll 2005; M.H. Goodwin 1983b; Schegloff et al. 1977; Schegloff 1984).

The word search sequence collection of this study exhibited additional ways in which word searches were initiated, including the use of 'explicit word search markers' (Brouwer 2003) through variation of 'how do you say', '*nanka*' and what-ending turns. The following section will describe these features in detail and analyse how multimodality and intonation affect the use of these word search initiations.

4.2.1 EXPLICIT WORD SEARCH MARKER: 'HOW DO YOU SAY'

Multi-word phrases such as 'how do you say', 'how to say' or 'how can I say' are common 'explicit word-search markers' (Brouwer 2003) used by L2 speakers to indicate an ongoing word search. These multi-word explicit word search markers have been analysed using CA in various L2 interactions including L2 English (Koshik and Seo 2012; Siegel 2015), L2 French (Pekarek Doehler and Berger 2019; Skogmyr Marian and Pekarek Doehler 2022), L2 Danish (Brouwer 2003), L2 Finnish (Kurhila 2006) and L2 Norwegian (Svennevig 2018).

These explicit word search markers have been described as having a dual function: to account for the word search and to simultaneously point to the hearer's expertise (Brouwer 2003: 540) and create language learning opportunities (Brouwer 2003; Svennevig 2018). However, these explicit word search markers, even for L2 speakers, do not necessarily indicate an invitation for other-repair. Rather, they suggest an ongoing self-search (Pekarek Doehler and Berger 2019; Siegel 2015; Skogmyr Marian and Pekarek Doehler 2022). Moreover, their use can change over time from displaying other-reliance towards displaying more self-reliance on resolving the word searches (Pekarek Doehler and Berger 2019; Siegel 2015; Skogmyr Marian and Pekarek Doehler 2022).

In this section, we analyse word search sequences that use these multi-word explicit word search markers, namely 'how do you say' and 'how to say', and examine how they are accompanied by (1) rising and falling intonation and (2) multimodality, especially the use of gaze. Moreover, the analysis brings insight into how these explicit word search markers are used in L2 interactions in an ELF context. We will look at how this use of explicit word search markers changes over time in Chapter 5.

4.2.1.1 'How to say' for inviting repair

Below, we take a look at cases where speakers use these explicit word search markers to display an initiation of or an ongoing word search. Excerpt 4.1 demonstrates a sequence in which Ami uses 'how do you say' with a rising intonation to invite other-repair.

Excerpt 4.1 Ami–Hang June Damage

```
1     Ami:    so:: (.) if I (.) dyed da hair da (.)
a             gz to H---------------------------
2             | h- hair er    |da hair is very: .ss (0.3)°i°
a             | gz down at hair|gz to H----------------------
3             (0.8)
a             -----
4     Hang:   ↑AH:=
a             -----
5  →  Ami:    =how do you say dat? i-(.)[itamu::
6     Hang:                              [you mea:n
a             ------------------------------------
7     Hang:   ↑AH(.) [you mean
8     Ami:           [°ita:
a             ------------------------------------
9     Hang:   you mean (.) its (.) it will be:
a             ------------------------------------
10            hmm: (0.3) damaged?
a             ------------------------------------
11    Ami:    ↑Dame:ji (.) [↑ya
12    Hang:                [ah::
a             ------------------------------------
```

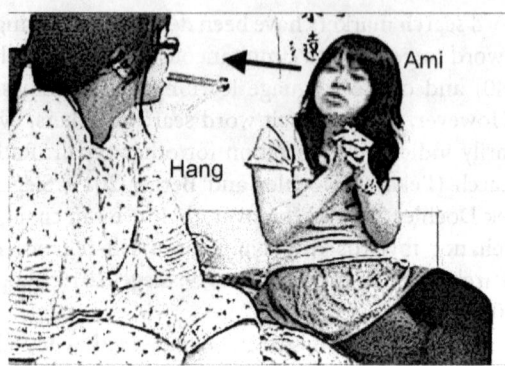

Figure 4.1   Line 5 'how do you say that'

Excerpt 4.1 is between Ami (the Japanese participant) and Hang (from Vietnam) talking about Ami's new permed hairstyle. Ami initiates a word search through her display of hesitancy and pauses (lines 2–3). Hang then shows noticing or understanding through a sharp rising 'ah' (line 4). However, it is unclear what the noticing is referring to. Ami then explicitly displays her trouble of finding the appropriate word by saying 'how do you say that' with a rising intonation (line 5). In addition, while saying 'how do you say that', Ami maintains eye contact with Hang, as shown in Figure 4.1.

This explicit display of a word search is then followed by a Japanese word '*itamu*', meaning 'damage' (line 5). Overlapping with the use of code-switching, Hang begins to display her understanding 'you mean', which is then repeated two more times (lines 6, 7, 9) before she finally provides a candidate word 'damaged' with a rising intonation. Ami then confirms this candidate solution through repetition and 'ya' (line 11).

In line 4, Hang may have understood Ami's intentions ('ah') and moved on with the conversation. However, by Ami explicitly requesting help through a 'how do you say' with a rising intonation and mutual gaze, she is able to move the conversation to a word search side sequence of the word 'damaged'. This was the typical pattern with word search sequences in the corpus using these multi-word phrases accompanied with a rising intonation.

Moreover, these word search sequences were often preceded or followed by a gesture, code-switching or description by the speaker to indicate the nature of the word they were searching for. These strategies will be discussed further in Section 4.3. In addition, these explicit word search markers were used even when mutual understanding was reached in order to create learning opportunities. Examples and discussion of this will be made through this chapter as well.

4.2.1.2 'How to say' for solitary search

'How to say' was found to be also used to indicate solitary search. Excerpt 4.2 is from the same recording as Excerpt 4.1. Here, Ami's solitary search for a word can be observed through the use of 'how to say' without rising intonation and with disengagement of eye contact.

Excerpt 4.2 Ami-Hang June Sour

```
1    Ami:    =↑AND (.) SO:: (.) .sss  |(.)↑hmm
a            gz forward ------------|gz left----
2            (0.9)
a            -------
3  → Ami:    .ss  |>°how do you say°<  |↑ah::
a            ----|gz to H-----------  |gz up ---
4    Hang:   haha
a            -------
5    Ami:    hmm:: (.) .ss |sa (.) sappa?
a            --------------|gz to H ------
```

Figure 4.2   Line 3 'how do you say'   *Figure 4.3   Line 3 'ah::'*

Figure 4.4   Line 5 'sappa?'

Similar to Excerpt 4.1, Ami displays hesitation and pauses and initiates a word search. She then uses 'how do you say' in a soft voice (line 3). While saying 'how do you say' in line 3, Ami looks briefly at Hang (Figure 4.2) then towards the ceiling (Figure 4.3). At this point, compared with Excerpt 4.1, there is no mutual gaze nor a candidate word or sound provided that would allow a candidate completion of the statement by Hang. Rather, Ami continues her solitary search while looking at the ceiling and then presents a candidate production of the word with rising intonation as she moves her gaze to Hang (Figure 4.4). This mutual gaze along with the candidate solution signals Hang to join the search, and leads to several more turns of guessing work and hint-giving by Ami until they reach mutual agreement on the target word (the longer segment that includes this sequence can be found in Excerpt 4.8, Section 4.3.1.2).

Observing these examples, we see the use of 'how do you say' is related to initiating a word search, but the sequential roles it has are contrastive depending on whether it is used with or without a rising intonation and gaze. The lack of rising intonation and mutual gaze suggests that the speaker is conducting a solitary search for a word, while rising intonation and mutual gaze are often connected with a request to the interlocutor to join the word search. For example, the gaze used by Ami is quite different between Figure 4.1 (engaging eye contact) and Figures 4.2–4.3 (slight engagement then disengaging eye contact), despite it being the same recording and despite a similar multi-word phrase being used.

On the one hand, by disengaging her gaze from Hang, Ami displays thinking and the possibility of knowing the target word, as well as her possible K+ position in relation to the word. At the same time, Ami is restricting Hang from joining the word search by looking away and displaying disalignment from the ongoing conversation. On the other hand, through mutual gaze, Ami invites Hang to join the word search and requests support or confirmation, thus suggesting Ami's K- position towards the candidate word. Through the use of her verbal and non-verbal (i.e., eye contact) moves in the sequence, Ami is able to manage the degree of co-construction of the word search. This is similar to how Buckwalter (2001) distinguishes between 'how do you say' as a request and a 'delaying tactic' (387) or 'floor-holding device' (386). This is also consistent with Pekarek Doehler and Berger (2019) on the use of 'how to say' in L2 French. However, unlike the findings from Pekarek Doehler and her colleagues (Pekarek Doehler and Berger 2019; Pekarek Doehler and Skogmyr Marian 2022; Skogmyr Marian and Pekarek Doehler 2022), the utterance of 'how to say' and the disengagement of the eyes are not necessarily synchronised. In our data, there are cases where the disengagement and 'how to say' co-occur, but it is not always the case, and mutual gaze may be delayed even when inviting the hearer to join the word search. Thus, one can utter 'how to say' to warn the interlocutor of an upcoming word search, but the degree and the timing with which the partner can join are determined by the gaze work of the speaker.

What we also see from the data is that in informal L2 interaction in an ELF setting, such as the context of this corpus, the use of 'how to say' for initiating other-repair for potential language learning opportunity is not as common as one may assume. This is possibly due to the context not being an institutional 'language learning' setting. Moreover, considering that the use of other-repaired 'how to say' sequences is relatively more frequent during the earlier months of joining the community and the project, one can interpret that the participants are changing their participation framework from a 'language learning' orientation to something different. This point will be discussed further as we analyse data longitudinally in Chapter 5.

4.2.2 EXPLICIT WORD SEARCH MARKER IN JAPANESE

In the data set, there were also frequent cases of initiating word searching or showing an ongoing word search through the use in Japanese of '*nani*' (what), '*nanka*' (like), as well as '*nandakke*', '*nanteiuno*', '*nanda*' and the like, which could be considered as the Japanese equivalent of the explicit English word search markers 'what is it' or 'how do you say'. Thirty-two cases were identified where the Japanese speaker used these phrases, but only two of the four core participants used these expressions: Yoko and Maya.

Below is an example of the use of '*nandakke*' by Yoko, when talking with her partner Shitora (from Uzbekistan). The two are talking about summer vacation plans and Yoko's volunteer club activity in Thailand.

Excerpt 4.3 Yoko–Shitora June Teach

```
1      Yoko:      ↑this year |>I go to Thailand<
y                 gz to S---|gz up-------------
2                 |a::nd (1.0) mm::
y                 |hand cover eyes---
3                 (2.3)
y                 gz forward
4  →   Yoko:      nandakke.
                  *what is it*
y                 gz left-----
5                 (3.3)
y                 -----
6      Yoko:      Tit
y                 ------
7                 (1.8)
y                 gz forward--
8      Yoko:      not teach but ku=
y                 ------------------
9      Shitora:   =|like teacher assistant,
y                  |gz to S----------------
10     Yoko:      (0.3) >↑yes yes yes<
y                 ---------------------
11     Shitora:   |mm::
y                 |gz forward
```

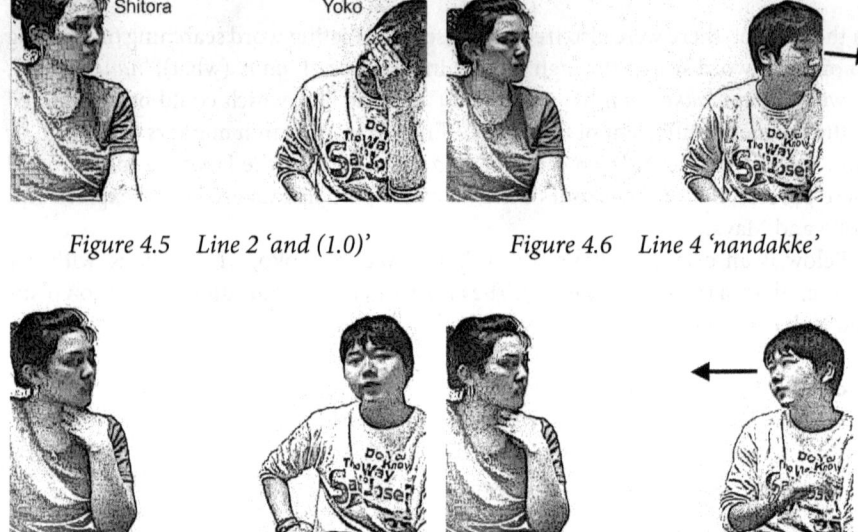

Figure 4.5   Line 2 'and (1.0)'   Figure 4.6   Line 4 'nandakke'

Figure 4.7   Line 8 'not teach but'   Figure 4.8   Line 9 'like teacher assistant'

In line 1 Yoko states that she will be going to Thailand. She then pauses for an extended amount of time while covering her eyes (lines 2–3, Figure 4.5) before saying 'nandakke' (what is it) (line 4), indicating that she is searching for a word. While saying 'nandakke', Yoko looks away from Shitora (Figure 4.6). By doing this, Yoko makes it clear that she is not referring to Shitora, but to herself. Moreover, this clear disengagement allows Yoko to continue to think for an extended amount of time (3.3 seconds), which is a relatively long silence to have in a mundane conversation. Yoko then provides negative clues (Kurhila 2006) about the word she is searching for, that it is 'not teach' (line 8), while continuing the disengagement of the eyes (Figure 4.7). Shitora then provides a candidate understanding of a 'teacher assistant' preceded by 'like' (line 9) while Yoko is turning her head towards Shitora and re-engaging her eyes with her (Figure 4.8). Due to the close co-timing of Yoko's body movement and Shitora's utterance, it is unclear if Yoko re-engages eye contact to seek help or because Shitora starts providing help. Either way, by turning her head back to Shitora and re-engaging eye contact, Yoko physically displays her availability to other-repair or candidate understanding. This candidate understanding is then confirmed by Yoko (line 10).

Therefore, 'nandakke' with no rising intonation can be seen as equivalent to the English 'how do you say' with no rising intonation indicating a solitary search of a word. It allows the current speaker to hold the floor while searching for the appropriate word. This is consistent with Hayashi's (2003) finding in Japanese L1–L1 interactional word searches, where the use of 'nanka' and 'nani' and disengagement of eye contact indicates a solitary word search.

Hence, from the word search initiation methods and the responses that were found in the ELF interactions, it can be said that the interlocutors display orientation to the preference for self-repair compared with other-repair, and avoid shifting towards a word search side sequence. Hosoda (2006) and Kurhila (2004) found that when L2 speakers explicitly display trouble in talk through the use of these word search initiation markers, it shifts the participation framework to solving the word search and the L1 speaker provides repair. However, the excerpts here have demonstrated that this is not always the case. These self-addressed word searches can be considered as self-talk or 'private speech' (Vygotsky 1987), displaying an attempt to self-repair. In addition, by explicitly presenting the solitary word search through verbal (the speaker's L1) and non-verbal behaviour, the interlocutor (hearer) orients to this by providing space in the interaction until the solitary searches are completed or until a request for other-repair or help is received through the speaker's use of gaze or candidate solution. As a result, the participants in talk can avoid assuming the identities of English language expert or novice. Rather, they focus on the progression of the content of the talk.

4.2.3 WHAT-ENDINGS

In connection to the simultaneous use of gaze with phrases or words with rising intonation in initiating a word search, there were also cases where the participant would end her turn with 'what' to initiate a word search. The use of these 'what-endings' to signal an initiation or an ongoing word search has not been documented in previous CA studies to our knowledge. Excerpt 4.4a is an example of a search for a referential (i.e., name of an academic course) which uses this 'what-ending' in a recording between Maya, Taman and Yanti, in October.

Excerpt 4.4a Maya-Yanti-Taman October What-ending

```
1    Maya:   uh::: I (.) I had (0.3) da:: (.)
m            gz to Y & T------------------
2            |↑last semester=
m            |point left ----
3    Yanti:  =°mh huh°=
m            ----------
4    Maya:   =I had (0.5)uh::: asia pacifics::
m            ------------------------------------
5            |(0.8)
m            |stop hand
6    Maya:   |uhu?
m            |gz up, move brows
7            (1.1)
m            ------
8    Maya:   |mhh nne ne nation?(.)of? (.)
m            |gz slightly left------------
9→           |what?
m            |lean left, stick hd out ----
```

Excerpt 4.4a Maya-Yanti-Taman October What-ending (continued)

```
10         |(0.5)|
m          -------
y          |gz right|
11  Taman: >aha<
m          -----
12         (0.6)
m          -----
13  Maya:  UH:::: (0.3) |ah I forgot
m                       |hand to forehead, tilt hd right
14  Yanti: [hehhehehehhe
15  Taman: [(         )
m          ---------------
```

Figure 4.9   Lines 9–10 'what (0.5)'

In line 4, Maya starts naming the class she took last semester, where she starts to display trouble locating the name through elongated sounds, hesitation markers, pauses, 'uhu?' and disengagement of gaze (lines 4–7). In lines 8–9, Maya restarts by stating 'nation' and 'of', but with a rising intonation showing a lack of confidence (line 8), which is then followed with a 'what?', again with a rising intonation (line 9). At the same time, she embodies literal searching for the word by turning her head to the left and staring at something in her room, possibly her course schedule or textbook. This action by Maya prompts Yanti to look the same way (Figure 4.9). Taman responds with a giggle (line 11), but does not provide any support for the word search. This laughter by Taman is open to interpretation, but one way to view it is that Taman is 'laughing at' (Glenn 1995) Maya's turn as the butt of a joke (Stokoe 2008). Stokoe (2008) argues that in sitcoms, laughter is placed after interactional breaches are made, such as unmitigated dispreferred responses. In this case, Maya replaced the next word following 'nation of' with 'what', and breached the expectation of the listener, which provoked laughter from Taman.

What is noteworthy here is that Maya's disengagement of eye contact and shift in the posture towards the left suggests that the 'what' (line 9) is not addressed to the interlocutors but it is a self-addressed first pair part of a question–answer adjacency pair. Moreover, there are no candidate sounds or words provided that would allow candidate solutions from the interlocutors. The second pair part of this adjacency pair is 'I forgot' (line 13), referring to the knowledge that she is having difficulty in retrieving rather than not knowing (e.g., I don't know), and suggesting the possibility of retrieval if given time. As a result, Maya is able to extend her self-repair sequence and keep the floor while specifying the position of the word in the utterance.

It is not until a few turns later in the dialogue (Excerpt 4.4b), when Maya restarts her presentation of the course name with a more specific key term (i.e., 'religion' in line 20) with mutual gaze, that Yanti is able to join the word search and present her understanding of the course name (lines 23, 26), and the word search is completed.

Excerpt 4.4b Maya–Yanti–Taman October What-ending

```
13     Maya:     UH:::: (0.3) ah I forgot
m                ----------------------
14     Yanti:    [hehhehehehhe
15     Taman:    [(              )
m                ---------------
16     Maya:     $subject name$ |hh=
m                -------------- |hd up, gz Y T
17     Taman:    =yeah
m                ------
18     Maya:     (0.3) |uh:::: (.)mh?
m                ----- |gz up-------
19                     (1.3) | (0.6)
m                ----- |snap fingers
20     Maya:     ↑religion and  | (0.5)[nations?
21     Yanti:                         [(         )
m                -------------- |gz Y T--------
22               (0.3)
m                -----
23 →   Yanti     rel- people en religion?
m                -----------------------
24     Taman:    ↑AH=
m                -------
25     Maya:     =people en religion
m                -------------------
26 →   Yanti:    °in da°    [°asia pacific?°
27     Maya:                |[>yeaha:h<
m                ---------- |nod----------
28     Taman:    [AHhhhh
29     Yanti:    [ah:::::
m                -------
```

Drew (1997) indicates cases where a 'partial repeat + what' is used as a repair initiator by the hearer to locate the word which they had difficulty hearing or understanding. Thus, the 'what' substitutes for the lexical item that is under search. However, what Drew (1997) indicates is done by the hearer, and not by the speaker. Rather, the 'what-ending word search initiation' is more similar to the use of '*are*' (that) in Japanese (Hayashi 2003) which the speaker uses as a placeholder for the word in search. However, the use of the what-ending word search initiation was also used by a non-Japanese participant, suggesting that it is not a linguistic transfer of Japanese '*are*' (that) or '*nani*' (what), but possibly a more commonly used word search initiation method in L2 interactions.

By initiating a word search through the use of what-endings, the speaker is able to keep the turn and maintain their K+ epistemic position in relation to the concept or content, while continuing to search for the L2 lexical item. In other words, it is the social display of the cognitive state of the speaker and allows the hearer to recognise the exact position in the utterance where the missing word should be placed, thus creating a socially distributed cognitive state.

Word search initiations in the informal ELF context were generally similar to previous findings in L1–L1 interactions as described in Section 2.2, including the use of gaze. Some of the exceptions, as demonstrated in this section, were the use of code-switching and 'what?' final turns. Elongation of vowel sounds were found to be used by non-Japanese participants as well (cf. Carroll 2005). In addition, the word searches initiated by the L2 speaker tended to involve self-repair if there was indication of a solitary search, whereas support from the interlocutor tended to come if co-participation in the search was invited through gaze and rising intonation. We will look at how this use of explicit word search markers changed over time in Chapter 5.

In the following section, we move on to analyse how candidate solutions to word searches are presented.

4.3 CANDIDATE SOLUTION OF WORD SEARCHES

Of the 282 word search sequences initiated by the Japanese participants, the vast majority of 239 (84.8%) cases were followed by a candidate solution by the Japanese participants: Ami 81, Maya 83, Tomoko 25 and Yoko 50 cases. This excludes all single turn self-initiated self-repair sequences. Therefore, even after initiating a word search and not being able to repair it immediately, there is still a preference towards self-repair of the word search, which suggests the speakers' orientation towards reaching a mutual understanding.

This section will focus on this particular pattern of attempted resolution of the word search by the Japanese participants, the type of strategies used, and the responses by the interlocutor, and will discuss how mutual understanding is achieved. The major resolution methods used by the Japanese participants were the following:

1. Candidate word.
2. Code-switching.

3. Semantic contiguity (word descriptions, explanations, and associations).
4. Gestures.
5. Using the dictionary.

In most cases, the Japanese participants utilised a combination of these methods. In the following section, however, we will introduce the relatively clear cases in which these resolving methods were utilised.

4.3.1 CANDIDATE WORDS AND SOUNDS

The most common method the Japanese participants employed was providing candidate words or sounds, with 134 out of 282 cases. These cases include the provision of a sound associated with the word in search and non-standard English language use.

4.3.1.1 Candidate words

One of the most common resolution moves by the speaker was presenting a candidate word after the initiation of a word search. These were often accompanied by rising intonation, although not always. In the first example, Excerpt 4.5, Yoko is comparing Korean and Japanese food.

Excerpt 4.5 Yoko-Cheng May Snacks
```
1     Yoko:    but mm::
2              (2.8)
3  →  Yoko:    nanyaro
               *what is it*
4              (2.9)
5  →  Yoko:    snacks? or:: sweets are
6              very:: similar I think
7     Cheng:   °mm: mmh°
```

In lines 2–3, Yoko pauses and uses '*nanyaro*' (what is it) to display that her search for a word is ongoing. Yoko then presents a candidate word 'snacks' with rising intonation. This is then followed by another candidate word, 'sweets' (line 5). Cheng shows understanding through backchannelling after Yoko completes her turn (line 7). Therefore, by using the previously mentioned 'word search markers' and presenting candidate words that were intelligible and congruent, Yoko was able to self-complete (self-repair) the search at hand. This candidate word use is the same as 'try-marking' (Sacks and Schegloff 1979) where rising intonation is used after a word to display that the speaker anticipates that the hearer may have trouble recognising it.

Often in the collection, unlike in Excerpt 4.5, the candidate words were followed by a confirmation request, repair or a request for further information from the interlocutor. An example of this is shown in Excerpt 4.6, a segment from Ami and Soo's conversation in June. The two are talking about the starting age for the Korean military conscription system.

Excerpt 4.6 Ami–Soo June Minimum

```
1    Ami:   =↑how old (0.4) d- did (.) do people
a           hand moving front and back----------
2           have to go da|(0.4)  |BA (.) ba:i?
a           ------------|gz down|horizontal move of hands
3 →         ah: |(0.5) da    | meene (.)|meene (.)
a           ----|hands stop--| clap     |gz to S/ clap
4 →         |meenemam?=
a           |tilts head--
5    Soo:   =minimum?=
a           ----------
6    Ami:   =minimum?=
a           ----------
7    Soo:   =↓ah: (0.4)|minimum is: ss (.) minimum is
a           -----------|head up  ---------------------
8           ss (0.3) <eighteen>, and maxshimum is
a           -------------------------------------
9           (0.4) there is n- (.) actually there is
a           ---------------------------------------
10          no maximum
a           ------------------
11   Ami:   (0.4)|oh really?=
a                |lean forward---
```

 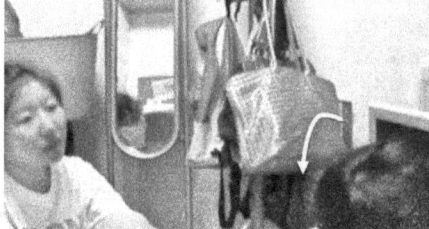

Figure 4.10   Line 3 Ami claps   *Figure 4.11   Line 4 Ami tilts head*

In line 3, Ami pauses and repeats the sound 'meene', displaying trouble with the item. She then completes her turn with a candidate word 'meenemam' with a rising intonation (line 4). While presenting her candidate word, Ami claps (Figure 4.10) and tilts her head (Figure 4.11) while keeping eye contact with Soo. Ami's use of prosody and body language suggests her ambivalent stance towards the candidate word; completing her turn with the clap suggests that there was a change of state and Ami was able to recall the word she is searching for, while the rising intonation and head tilt also suggests that Ami is unsure of the accuracy of the candidate word or anticipating that Soo may have trouble understanding the word she had just presented. And this uncertainty is confirmed in the next turn.

With no hesitation, Soo requests confirmation through a presentation of her understanding (and her version of the pronunciation), saying 'minimum' with a rising intonation (line 5). This is then repeated by Ami in a similar way (line 6). Upon hearing this, Soo takes this as a confirmation of the repair ('ah') and starts to answer Ami's question (line 7). Therefore, it could be said that they have reached a mutual understanding and resolution of the word search. Moreover, we can see that after the Japanese participant's non-standard English word use (pronunciation), a candidate understanding from the interlocutor is presented before the conversation can move on (i.e., 'minimum').

However, unlike Koshik and Seo's (2012) study, where they only found confirmation or correction, in the ELF corpus of this study there were cases where there was no explicit response by the interlocutor, even in cases of unconventional or non-standard English language use. Instead, continuous gaze or backchannelling was used to suggest that the Japanese speaker should continue with the talk. The example below between Maya and Yanti in November illustrates this point. Excerpt 4.7 begins when Maya is sharing her surprise when learning that Americans wear bathing suits in hot springs.

Excerpt 4.7 Maya–Yanti November Swimsuits
```
1    Maya:    they (0.5) take (0.8) nh,
2             (0.4) wo (.) <water> (0.3)
3  →          °water° (0.2) clothes?
4    Yanti:   ↑MH::::: °yeah°
```

In lines 1–2, Maya displays trouble through cut-offs and repetition of 'water'. She then completes her turn with 'clothes' with a rising intonation (line 3). This is possibly a direct translation of the Japanese word for swimsuit ('*mizugi*') which is a combination of two characters of water and clothing (水着). This 'water clothes' with the use of a soft voice, pause and prosody could be seen as not only a try-marking of a candidate word but also what Firth (2009) calls 'flagging for markedness' whereby an L2 speaker marks the way they are phrasing something that is possibly incorrect, and that they are aware of it. Yanti then shows strong agreement through a high-pitched and loud elongated 'mh' followed by 'yeah' with no delay (line 4). Yanti is thus displaying understanding of Maya's utterance. Therefore, in accordance with Firth's (1996) noticing of 'normalising' behaviours in ELF talks, not all unconventional language uses are policed and repaired in the interaction.

4.3.1.2 Candidate sounds

The above excerpts demonstrated candidate 'words' used as candidate solutions for the self-initiated word search. However, at times the candidate word would come out as a 'sound' or an approximated sound of the target word. The first example is between Ami and Hang in June. The topic of the talk is about the difference in Korean and Japanese *kimchi* (fermented pickled cabbage).

Excerpt 4.8 Ami–Hang June Sour

```
1     Ami:    =BUT (.) Koreas kimuchi is:
a                     gz to H --------------------
2     Hang:        ↑hehe
a                  --------
3     Ami:         <↓spi[cy::>
4     Hang:            [very spicy:?=
a                  --------------------
5     Ami:         =↑AND |(.) SO::(.).sss (.)↑hmm
a                  ------|gz front---------------
6                  (0.9)
a                  -----
7     Ami:         .ss  |>°how do you say°< |↑ah::
a                  ----|gz to H -----------|gz up---
8     Hang:        hah:
a                  ----
9 →   Ami:         hmm::(.).ss sa(.)|sappa:?
a                  -----------------|gz to H
10                 (0.6)
a                  -----
11    Hang:        °sappa°
a                  -------
12    Ami:         sappa?=
a                  -------
13    Hang:        =<↑sup(.)↓per>(.)↑sup↓per
a                  -------------------------
14    Ami:         |↑sup↓per? it's
a                  |head tilt ---------------
15                 |(1.3)
a                  |holds mouth
16    Hang:        wo?
a                  ---
17                 (0.6)
a                  -----
18    Ami:         ah:  |supper?
a                  -----|gz front---
19                 (1.2)
a                  -----
20 →  Ami:         |°sssup° (0.6) like a lehmohn?(.)lemon=
a                  |gz to H --------------------------------
21    Hang:        =suppai?=
                   *sour*
a                  ---------
22    Ami:         =↑SUPPAI
                    *sour*
a                  ---------
```

Excerpt 4.8 Ami–Hang June Sour (continued)

```
23    Hang:      (0.4) ↑ah:: so:r
a                -----------------
24    Ami:       (0.4) so[:r?
25    Hang:           [so:r
a                -----------------
26    Ami:       |(0.4) [so:r: ohohoho  |$do you$(.)$do you:$
27    Hang:             [↑hmm
a                |gz front ----------|gz to H-------------
28    Ami:       (.)$do you kno:w (.) ss <suppai?>$
                                        *sour*
a                -------------------------------------
29    Ami:       [|hahahaha
30    Hang:      [un ya hehehe
a                 |close eyes--
31    Ami:       | $okay suppai$ ehehehe=
a                | gz to H ---------------
32    Hang:      =hehehehehe
a                -----------
```

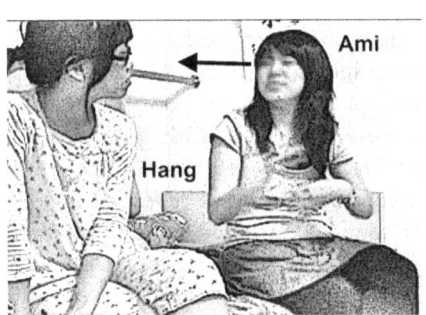

Figure 4.12   Line 7 'how do you say'

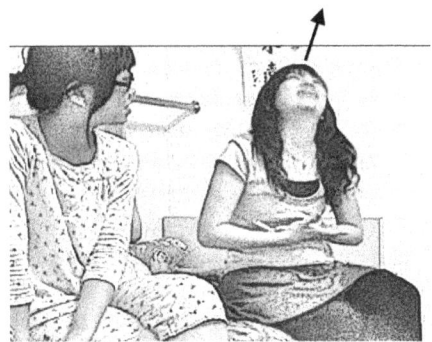

Figure 4.13   Line 7 'ah:::'

Figure 4.14   Line 9 'sappa?'

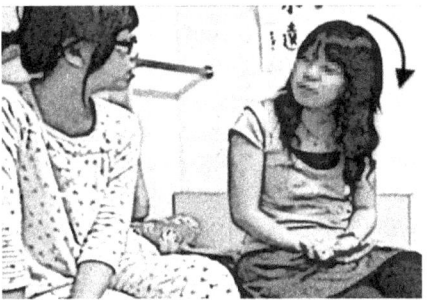

Figure 4.15   Line 14 'supper?'

Figure 4.16   Line 15 Ami holds mouth

From line 5, Ami begins to hedge, uses pauses and displays trouble locating the next item. In line 7, she says, 'how do you say' with mutual gaze (Figure 4.12). Ami immediately disengages eye contact and shows progression towards the target word through approximate sounds (lines 7–9, Figure 4.13). Ami then presents a candidate sound 'sappa' with a rising intonation and eye contact to elicit confirmation (line 9, Figure 4.14). Hang, after a short delay, repeats 'sappa' with a soft voice (line 11), which Ami repeats again (line 12). This can be understood as Hang displaying thinking or non-understanding, with Ami interpreting Hang's repetition as a hearing issue.

Hang then presents a candidate understanding of 'supper' (line 13). Ami repeats this with a similar intonation, but with a rising intonation and tilting of the head (line 14, Figure 4.15), suggesting that Ami does not agree with or is unsure about the accuracy of the repair. Ami then moves on to use gestures of holding her lips and spreading it to the sides, possibly making a 'sour' face (line 15, Figure 4.16). However, Hang again shows non-understanding with 'wo?' (line 16). After repeating 'supper' again and a long silence, Ami repeats the 's' sound, showing that the word she is searching for most likely has an 's' sound, and provides a clue, 'like a lemon' (line 20). Hang then presents a Japanese candidate understanding of '*suppai*' (sour) (line 21). Ami strongly agrees and accepts this candidate word by repeating this with a high pitch and loud voice (line 22). When Ami confirms Hang's candidate understanding and that mutual understanding has been reached, Hang then presents the English equivalent, 'sour' (line 23). Although Hang's pronunciation is not standard, Ami accepts it through multiple repetitions of the word with a similar pronunciation to Hang (lines 24, 26).

As demonstrated through this excerpt, when a candidate word for a word search is presented tentatively as a 'sound', a longer side sequence for negotiation tends to take place. Moreover, in most cases, the side sequence continued until the interlocutors reached a mutual understanding. What is noteworthy here, is that once Ami acknowledges that Hang knows the Japanese word for sour, she suggests using the Japanese word '*suppai*' (sour) as the common expression (line 31). Ami shows a bias towards the Japanese word, suggesting that in an ELF environment, the preferred language is not predetermined, and the language of the host country seems to have a strong influence on the speaking environment (Siegel 2021; Vetchinnikova 2021).

To sum up, the use of candidate word or sound was the most common word search candidate solution method, and these words and sounds were most commonly marked with rising prosody, inviting comment by the interlocutor. Unconventional or non-standard candidate words were not always repaired by the interlocutor, demonstrating the preference of the interaction towards progressivity and self-repair. In other words, although the rising prosody and candidate words demonstrate lack of confidence in the speaker's word choice, this was not commonly oriented to by the interlocutor, thus maintaining an equal epistemic position in terms of the English language knowledge among the participants in the talk. However, when candidate sounds which hindered mutual understanding were used, the word search side sequences tended to become longer and continued until mutual understanding was reached, as seen in Excerpt 4.8.

4.3.2 CODE-SWITCHING

Code-switching was the second most common candidate solution employed by the Japanese participants. Based on the analysis of the collection, we categorised the type of code-switching practices into two: the use of (1) loan words and (2) Japanese. Below, we will exemplify cases where loan words were used, followed by cases where Japanese was used as a candidate solution for the self-initiated word searches, and the shift of frequency of use over time.

4.3.2.1 Using *katakana* words (loan words)

Kurhila (2006) discusses the notion of 'Fennicised words' which are used by the L2 speakers in attempt to resolve word searches. These 'Fennicised words' refer to non-Finnish words whose phonology and/or morphology were adjusted to have Finnish phonology or morphology. In our corpus, there were similar cases where a speaker would use English loan words which have become part of the Japanese language, which are called *gairaigo* (foreign words) or *katakana* words (loan words) when attempting to resolve self-initiated word searches. These words are often English words pronounced with additional or changed vowel sounds (e.g., pickles as *pikurusu*) or other languages adapted to the Japanese language (e.g., *Arbeit*, labour in German, as *arubaito*, part-time job in Japanese). The language of origin is not differentiated, thus Japanese L2 speakers of English may, and would often, assume that all *katakana* words are from English, and apply them to English interactions.

The first example is between Ami and Hang in May when the two are sharing their thoughts about the cafeteria food and where the pineapples are located in the cafeteria.

Excerpt 4.9 Ami-Hang May Cashier
```
1    Ami:    ah: near da l- reji? (0.3)°reji°.
a            right hand up to show location----
2            (0.9)
a            -------
3    Hang:   neji?=
a            -------
4    Ami:    =re↓ji
a            ------
5    Hang:   (0.2) ↑ymh: |reji
a            ------------|typing
6    Hang:   CAshier
a            -------
7    Ami:    cashe:r? (0.3) | and near the le-
a            ---------------| right hand up to show location
8            ah: cashe:r,
a            ------------
9    Hang:   Mhh
             -------
```

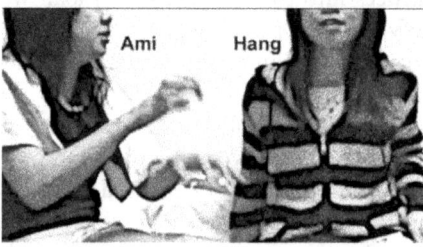

Figure 4.17   Line 6 Typing

In line 1, Ami cuts off the 'l' sound and then utters the Japanese *katakana* word '*reji*' (cashier, originating from 'register') with a rising intonation. After a slight pause, Ami then repeats '*reji*' with a soft voice and falling intonation, suggesting her lack of confidence in her word choice. After a relatively long pause, Hang presents her candidate understanding of 'neji' with a rising intonation (line 3), which is then declined and repaired by Ami (line 4). Hang then shows a change of state through a high-pitched 'ymh' and repeating of '*reji*' (line 5), as Ami starts her typing gesture to describe the object (Figure 4.17). Although it is not clear if Ami's gesture supported Hang's understanding, Hang is able to provide her version of the word, 'cashier' (line 7). Ami repeats 'cashier' with a rising intonation, possibly to request confirmation (line 8). When there is no negative response from Hang, Ami stops the typing gesture and raises her right hand to restart describing the location; at the same time, she recycles the original statement in line 1, 'near the', but replaces '*reji*' with 'cashier' (line 9). As a result of using *katakana* as a candidate solution, the two speakers were able to reach a mutual understanding.

Moreover, through the repair work, different membership categorisations were emerging. In Excerpt 4.9, we can see the Japanese participant, Ami, using the *katakana* word ('*reji*') and being repaired by the interlocutor, Hang. Furthermore, the repair work by Hang is done naturally through multiple steps. Hang first shows understanding of Ami's utterance by using a change of state token 'ymh' and then repeating the presented word '*reji*' to acknowledge Ami's word choice. She then presents her version of the word 'cashier' as an exposed other-correction. Ami orients to this as a possible learning opportunity and restates her initial sentence with the newly presented word, and thus displays 'doing learning'. In this segment, the differences in the speakers' relative linguistic levels become apparent. That is, through Hang's explicit repair work, she presents herself in the K+ position in relation to the English word 'cashier', or takes the role of a relative English language expert. By contrast, Ami's orientation to this segment as a learning opportunity displays her K- position as a relative novice. This is contrastive to Excerpt 4.1, where Hang did not repair Ami until explicitly prompted.

However, the use of *katakana* words as a candidate solution did not necessarily lead to accurate mutual understandings or create learning opportunities. An example of this can be found in Excerpt 4.10. This excerpt is from Maya and Kei in July. The two are talking about the Japanese culture course Maya is taking, and the 'cute culture' which was introduced in class.

Excerpt 4.10 Maya–Kei July 30 Lace aura

```
1      Maya:   ↑colour of (0.4) pink? |(1.0)
m              gz to K --------------|gz forward
2  →           o:r (1.2) |re:s? (0.4) le- leesu,
m                        |gz to K---------------
3      Kei:    lace?
m              --------
4      Maya:   lace?
m              --------
5              |(1.0)
m              |gz down
6      Maya:   a::nd-
m              --------
7              |(2.0)
m              |gz down/ twirl hands next to body
8  →   Maya:   HH (1.2) |ahula? (1.0) oh:la?
m                       |gz to K / hands next to body
9              (1.8)
m              --------
10     Maya:   [|>$kira kira kira$< hh
                 *sparkle sparkle sparkle*
m              |gz to K/twirl hands next to body
11     Kei:    [°ahura,°
```

Excerpt 4.10 Maya-Kei July 30 Lace aura (continued)

```
12    Maya:    hahah (0.8) |n::=
m                          ------------|gz forward/ hands down
13    Kei:     =twinkle twinkle.
m              --------------------
14    Maya:    twinkle?
m              gz to K ---
15    Kei:     yeah. (0.6) bling bling.
m              ----------------------
16    Maya:    blin, | ↑ah: blin. |(1.2) a:ndu un.
m              ------| big nod----|gz down -------
```

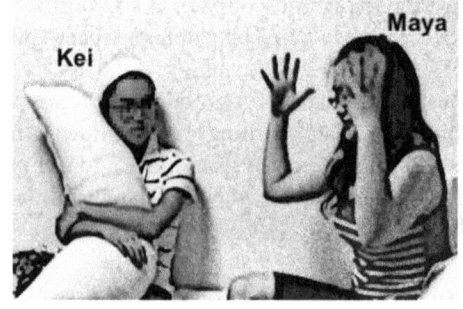

Figure 4.18   Line 7 (2.0)

Figure 4.19   Line 8 'ahula'

Figure 4.20   Line 10 'kira kira kira'

In order to explain the idea of 'cute culture', Maya introduces associated images such as 'pink' (line 1) and after long pauses introduces the idea of 'lace', however with a *katakana* pronunciation of 'leesu' with added vowel sounds (line 2). Kei then introduces a Standard English (North American) pronunciation 'lace' with a rising intonation (line 3). Maya then repeats this with a similar pronunciation (line 4). Kei's utterance in line 3 could be seen as a repair or a request for repair, which is then responded to by Maya with a repetition.

When Kei does not provide a confirmation (line 5), Maya attempts to continue with her explanation (line 6). However, Maya pauses again and while disengaging eye contact, moves her hands along the side of her body while twisting her wrist and displays a solitary word search (lines 5–8, Figure 4.18). She then presents her candidate *katakana* word 'ahula' with a rising intonation and a short version of the gesture (line 8, Figure 4.19). When there is no immediate response from Kei (line 8), she changes the first vowel sound of the word and presents another candidate *katakana* 'ohla' (line 8) and waits for a response. However, Kei does not respond (line 9).

Maya then uses Japanese onomatopoeia '*kira kira kira*' (sparkle sparkle sparkle) to describe the word she is attempting to express with a similar gesture she used in line 7 (line 10, Figure 4.20). However, this is followed by her laughter (line 12), thus marking the word (Firth 2009) and displaying that she understands it is not a conventional word to use, nor is it the preferred language for the interaction. Kei then finally shows his candidate understanding of Maya's utterance as 'twinkle twinkle' (line 13). When Maya displays non-understanding or uncertainty through a repetition with a rising intonation (line 14), Kei introduces a different expression, 'bling bling' (line 15).

'*Kira kira*' and 'bling bling' hold different connotations and describe different attributes of a person. For instance, a girl who is '*kira kira*' could mean someone wearing cute pink clothes and curled long hair, while 'bling bling' could refer to a person wearing sexy clothes and gaudy jewellery. Nevertheless, Maya shows a change of state through 'ah' with a big nod, and repeats the word 'bling'. She then returns to the description of the course (line 16). Kei does not explain what 'twinkle' or 'bling' means, suggesting that he understood Maya's 'ah' and repetition as a confirmation and a sign of understanding. Similarly, Maya does not further pursue the meaning of 'twinkle twinkle' or 'bling bling'.

This example suggests (although it cannot be proven solely using the method of CA) that even though the interactants indicate that they have reached a 'mutual understanding' as a sequence, it may not be an accurate understanding. This also suggests that L2–L2 interactions have the potential to lead to inaccurate L2 learning. This point will be discussed further in the following example and in Section 4.3.5.

Furthermore, as Maya does not request the meaning of 'twinkle twinkle' and 'bling bling', this shows that not all word search sequences are oriented to as learning opportunities. In contrast, progressivity of the talk seems to have been prioritised.

4.3.2.2 Using Japanese words

Excerpts 4.9 and 4.10 demonstrated cases where *katakana* words (loan words) were used. Below, we will introduce cases where the Japanese participants use Japanese in order to potentially solve the word searches. What is interesting to note here is that there were many more cases where the Japanese participants would use Japanese with no hesitation during word search sequences, especially at the early stages of joining the dormitory (i.e., April). The first example is from April between Maya and Kei. Maya is sharing her first-day-of-class experience.

Excerpt 4.11 Maya–Kei April Between

```
1    Kei:    diju have a break?
2 →  Maya:   (0.5) yeah ah::::: (0.7) °ai°
3    Kei:    (0.3) mh?
4 →  Maya:   °aida°
             *between*
5    Kei:    between?
6    Maya:   between?
7    Kei:    yeah
8    Maya:   (1.0) five (.) minutes(.) break
9    Kei:    ↑AH FIVE minutes break
```

In line 2, Maya uses an elongated 'ah' and cuts off the 'ai' or 'I' after a pause, displaying trouble finding the next word that follows. When Kei presents an open class repair initiation 'mh' (line 3), Maya switches to Japanese '*aida*' (between). The lack of prosody after the Japanese word suggests that Maya expects Kei to know the word '*aida*'. Thus Maya presents her lack of knowledge of the English word 'between' and positions Kei as the 'knower' (K+) for both the English and the Japanese word. Kei does an exposed correction with the direct translation of the word 'between' with rising intonation (line 5), and Maya repeats this exactly with the same rising intonation (line 6). Kei then confirms this in the next turn (line 7). This word search sequence can also be seen as an Initiation Response Feedback (IRF) sequence (Sinclair and Coulthard 1975) common in classroom practice (see Section 3.6.2).

```
5    Kei:    between?    --Initiation
6    Maya:   between?    --Response
7    Kei:    yeah        --Feedback
```

Here, Kei talks into being a teacher-like identity even in a non-classroom ELF interaction, and possibly displays superiority in his English language knowledge over Maya. Similar patterns have been reported in L1–L2 interactions (Hosoda 2006; Theodórsdóttir 2018) where the L1 speaker will other-repair or correct the L2 speaker, which is followed by an uptake in a form of repetition, which is then assessed by the L1 speaker before they return to the main topic of interaction. This IRF sequence was a common practice observed between Maya and Kei. However, this was not commonly found between Maya and other partners, or among other participants. This may be due to Kei being a Residential Assistant (RA) and/or having confidence in his English proficiency due to his experience of living in English speaking countries (see Siegel 2016).

The use of Japanese may not have been the immediate method of achieving mutual understanding in the sequences found in this study's collection. Yet, from the excerpts, it can be observed that code-switching was chosen as the first method over others in attempting to resolve the word search in many cases. Therefore, code-switching could be understood as one of the most accessible affordances for the Japanese participants as a candidate solution in word search sequences.

However, the preference towards code-switching also seems to change in ELF interactions once the participants either develop their English language skills or discover that code-switching does not always work. This can be seen in the frequency of the use of code-switching as a candidate solution which is shown in Figures 4.21 and 4.22. Figure 4.21 displays the overall frequency of the use of code-switching as a candidate solution over time.

As can be seen from the graphs, there is frequent use of code-switching by the Japanese participant in the early stages of the study in April. As time goes by, the Japanese participants are less reliant on code-switching, and there is an overall linear regression (bold line). However, as seen from the dotted line, the changes in frequency are not exactly linear. The frequent use of code-switching in resolving word searches at the early stages may suggest (1) the Japanese participants' reliance on their L1, (2) their assumptions that the interlocutor shares the same Japanese knowledge, or (3) the knowledge that their partners are taking Japanese language classes (regardless of proficiency level). This underlying assumption of a shared L2 can be said to be a feature specific to an ELF context situated in the relatively monolingual country of Japan. Moreover, from the graph, we can observe the relative decrease in the use of code-switching over time, possibly due to the participants (1) realising that code-switching has minimal impact on resolving word searches, and (2) emergence and utilisation of other candidate solution methods. However, code-switching is consistently used. This change in the frequency of use of code-switching could therefore be considered as a calibrated strategy where the Japanese participants adjusted their use as they learnt more about their interlocutor's Japanese ability and as their partners increased their Japanese proficiency.

To summarise, the use of a Japanese or *katakana* word in attempting to solve the word search is similar to bilingual interactions where the speaker would switch to

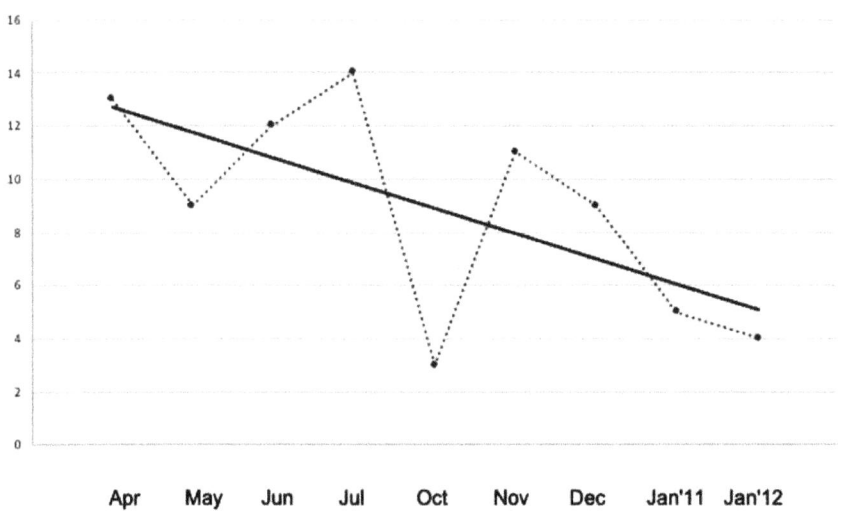

Figure 4.21 Frequency of code-switching use in resolving a word search by Japanese participants

another commonly shared language in resolving the trouble in talk or word search (e.g., Greer 2013b). However, unlike bilingual interactions where speakers anticipate or expect that the other will know the word, in ELF interaction that is not always the case; speakers consistently need to monitor the interlocutor's knowledge of the other language. Furthermore, the use of code-switching tends to expose the participants' linguistic ability in the original language they were talking in or the language that was switched into. Therefore, depending on the interlocutor's linguistic knowledge, some word searches were solved rather quickly, while other sequences took multiple turns to reach a mutual understanding after the use of code-switching as a candidate solution. What is more, the preference towards using code-switching as a main method of producing a candidate solution for a word search seems to shift as the participants become more immersed in the ELF setting.

4.3.3 SEMANTIC CONTIGUITY (DESCRIPTIONS, EXPLANATIONS AND ASSOCIATIONS)

The third most common candidate solution method used by the Japanese participants was using their linguistic knowledge, such as providing definitions, synonyms or associated words. This is similar to what Kurhila (2006) calls 'semantic contiguity' used by the speaker in resolving the word search. Speakers employ semantic contiguity when 'trying to describe an unknown referent so that the speaker tries to make the referent identifiable through synonymic, metonymic, anatomic or superordinate relations to other words she knows and remembers' (Kurhila 2006: 117).

Excerpt 4.12 is a typical example of the use of semantic contiguity from the corpus of this study between Ami and Soo in June. They are talking about Ami's trip to Korea and a survey conducted regarding plastic surgery in Korea.

Excerpt 4.12 Ami–Soo June Plastic surgery

```
1    Ami:   (0.5) so (.) ↑ah (0.5) da another grou:p?
2           ah: very I'm interested in (.) da: research?
3  → 	      beco:use (.) dey resea:ch about the: (0.5)
4  → 	      hmm::: $change the face:$? hh=
5    Soo:   =change?
6    Ami:   .hh
7  → Soo:   [ah: plastic surgery?
8    Ami:   [↑ah::
9           (0.5)
10   Ami:   >↑ya real so [ya yes<
11   Soo:                [↑AH::
```

Ami initiates a word search through hedging and elongated vowel sounds (line 3), then presents a candidate solution 'change of face' (line 4). This use of semantic contiguity is accompanied with a smiley voice and laughter and is 'flagging for markedness' (Firth 2009) of the word choice. Therefore, it suggests Ami's recognition that it is a non-standard language use and that Soo may have difficulty understanding it.

Soo then requests repair through the repetition of 'change' with a rising intonation (line 5). However, before Ami can repair, Soo presents a candidate understanding of 'plastic surgery' (line 7), which is confirmed by Ami (line 10). It is highly possible that Soo is able to understand Ami's use of semantic contiguity due to the fact that she is from Korea, and Ami is talking about Korean culture. These word searches using the strategy of semantic contiguity seem to evoke high dependence on the interlocutor's cooperation and knowledge.

A similar example is displayed in Excerpt 4.13. This sequence is from Maya and Kei in February at the final recording session, when Maya is talking about her landlord.

Excerpt 4.13 Maya–Kei February 2012 Mental

```
1     Kei:    >uh< so the owner doesn't like Korean.
2             (0.4) Chinese (.) a:nd Japanese.
3     Maya:   umh::. but owner is Japanese.
4     Kei:    ° okay. °
5     Maya:   ° umh hh. °
6             (0.6)
m             | turning finger near head
7     Kei:    ° umh. °
8     Maya:   spiritual (0.7) sick?
9             (0.4)
10    Maya:   eh?=
              *what*
11    Kei:    =mentally sick.
12    Maya:   mentally sick. [un.
                             *yeah*
13    Kei:                   [mh huh
```

In line 8, Maya describes the owner as 'spiritual sick' with a relatively long pause of 0.7 seconds in between and rising intonation. This is then followed by '*eh*' (line 10) with a rising intonation, indicating that she is unsure of the word choice (Hayashi 2009). Kei repairs Maya by saying 'mentally sick' with a falling intonation (line 11), displaying his sureness of his repair. This is then repeated and confirmed by Maya (line 12). Similar to the previous example, although Maya attempts to resolve her word search in English, by using semantic contiguity, she is apt to rely on Kei's cooperation and linguistic knowledge in reaching a mutual understanding. As a result, Maya displays her relatively novice position (K-).

When semantic contiguity was used in other excerpts than the ones shown here, the Japanese participants were found providing hints of the colour, shape or meaning of the word, making the word search into a type of guessing game. What is noteworthy is that in all the cases, the interlocutor was cooperative and willing to join the 'guessing game' of what the word in search may be. They were cooperative in ways such as showing attentive listening through gaze and nodding, providing candidate words, negotiating what the word is, or at times showing understanding (without reaching a consensus on what the word is), and signalling the speaker to progress with the content of the talk.

106 HUMAN SPOKEN INTERACTION AS A COMPLEX ADAPTIVE SYSTEM

To summarise, the use of semantic contiguity by the speaker in word search sequences ranges from a strong reliance on the partner's cooperation and knowledge to less reliance and more use of the speaker's own linguistic knowledge.

4.3.4 GAZE AND HAND GESTURES

As seen from the previous excerpts, hand gestures are frequently used in combination with eye gaze during word search sequences. The type of hand gestures, such as beats or iconic, were not categorised or analysed in detail. Instead, this section analyses the interactive features of hand gestures and the role they play during attempts to solve self-initiated word searches.

The first example displays the co-construction of mutual understanding through imitating the other's gesture. Excerpt 4.14 is from Ami and Hang's interaction recorded in May. Ami is explaining about the steak she ate when travelling to New Zealand.

Excerpt 4.14 Ami–Hang May Thick

```
1 →   Ami:      but |erh (.) because ern (.) steak?
a                   |raise hand & show thickness with fingers
h               gz toward A --------------------------------
2 →             (.) en (0.5) | very: (0.5) [sick?
3     Hang:                                [ah:
a               -------------| widest spread of fingers ---
h               -------------------------------------------
4     Ami:      sick?=
a               -------
h               -------
5 →   Hang:     =tick (.) [|tick
6 →   Ami:                [ sick
a               -----------------
h               ----------|raise hand & show thickness with fingers
7     Hang:     <a tsui>?=
                 *thick*
a               ----------
h               ----------
8     Ami:      =ya (.) |atsui (.)      |
                         *thick*
a               --------|push hand forward|
h               -------------------------------
9     Hang:     atsui  |un[un
                *thick  yeah yeah*
10    Ami:             [|>un un un<
                        *yeah yeah yeah*
a               ------------|lowers hand & nods
h               --------|nods-----------
```

Excerpt 4.14 Ami-Hang May Thick (continued)
```
11    Hang:    |ah: its hard to (.)        | ak
h              |stops nod, lowers hand ----| eating hamburger
a              |stops nod--------------------------------
```

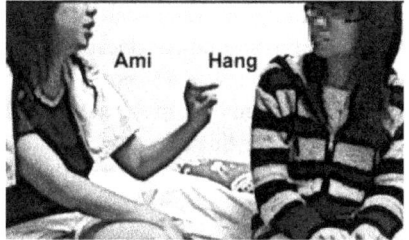

Figure 4.22 Line 1 'steak'

Figure 4.23 Line 2 'very sick'

Figure 4.24 Lines 5-9 'thick'

Figure 4.25 Line 11 hamburger

In line 1, Ami begins her gesturing with her fingers, as shown in Figure 4.23, while rephrasing her initial utterance 'but' to 'because'. She continues to hold the gesture while introducing the topic 'steak'. However, while changing the width of her fingers, Ami uses pauses and elongated vowel sounds to display possible trouble locating a word (line 2). She then says 'thick' (although it sounds like 'sick') with a rising intonation while the width of her fingers becomes the widest (Figure 4.23). Overlapping, Hang responds with an acknowledgement, 'ah' (line 3), suggesting that Hang had anticipated the turn ending prior to Ami's turn completion. Therefore, it could be interpreted that not only the example of the steak, but also the gesturing by Ami supported Hang's understanding. This is similar to Hayashi's (2003) finding in L1 Japanese interactions that the gesturing by the speaker during the initiation of a word search supported mutual understanding and prompted other-repair.

Although Hang displayed understanding, Ami repeats 'thick' (pronounced as 'sick') again with a rising intonation (line 4), and requests repair from Hang, and creates a learning opportunity. Hang then presents her version of the pronunciation, 'tick', twice with a falling intonation (line 5). The second time is accompanied by a similar gesture to Ami's (Figure 4.24). As a result, Hang repairs Ami's pronunciation, and shows that she understands Ami through her gesture.

When Ami's repetition is still slightly different from her pronunciation (line 6), Hang uses Japanese, 'atsui' (thick), with a slow pace and rising intonation while maintaining the same gesture (line 7). This mirrored use of gesture physically demonstrates the state of mutual understanding. It is unclear if Hang uses Japanese here to secure mutual understanding, or if she is trying out her Japanese knowledge. Nevertheless, Ami confirms this through 'ya', repetition, and the similar gesture (line 8), visually demonstrating that they are referring to the same concept. Hang repeats 'atsui' again, as if she is practising her Japanese, followed by 'un un' (yeah yeah) and showing understanding or satisfaction (line 9). Ami then presents another positive feedback in Japanese while nodding (line 10). After this exchange, the two finally return to the main topic of food and Hang displays her clear understanding of the thick meat (line 11, Figure 4.25).

Ami's word search sequence and English learning opportunity in lines 1–6 then transforms into a Japanese practice activity for Hang between lines 7 and 10. This demonstrates the different orientations of the participants towards the interaction and the fluid participation framework used by interlocutors in L2 interaction in informal ELF contexts. There is no negotiation by Hang of the switch to learning Japanese; the switch is simply made and accepted by Ami in line 8.

To summarise, hand gestures during word search sequences play an important role. Gestures function as a placeholder or replacement of the next item in the utterance, as well as supporting other-repair and self-repair in achieving mutual understanding.

4.3.5 ELECTRONIC DICTIONARY USE

The final candidate solution method used that will be introduced is cases in which word searches were attempted to be resolved through the use of a dictionary or the Internet. Only a few studies thus far have analysed the use of the dictionary in L2 interactions using CA (e.g., Barrow 2009, 2010; Greer 2019b; Hauser 2014). These studies have identified that self-initiation of a word search occurs prior to the dictionary 'look-up', such as cut-offs, sound stretches and change of gaze (Barrow 2009). It was also found that dictionaries were used not only during self-initiated self-repairs, but also during self-initiated other-repairs and other-initiated other-repairs (Greer 2019; Hauser 2014). What is interesting is that a participant in Hauser's (2014) research referred to the use of the dictionary as 'cheating', and the one using the dictionary returned it to his bag. Hauser shares his interpretation that during language classroom tasks, the use of the dictionary may or may not be viewed as legitimate. In contrast, the dictionary use in Greer (2019) occurs after a candidate translation to a Japanese word is provided and the dictionary is used for confirming the accuracy of the translation. Thus, the dictionary use and confirmation process seems to support the Japanese L2 learner in internalising the Japanese word.

However, both Barrow's (2009, 2010) and Hauser's (2014) studies were conducted in language classroom settings where the goal of learning, using words accurately or being assessed on their language ability was a shared understanding among the

Figure 4.26   Example of electronic dictionary use

participants; Greer's (2019) study takes place at a hair salon between a customer and a staff member. The current data was collected in a non-classroom setting between peers, thus bringing a different dynamic and meaning to the use of the dictionary during the talk-in-interaction.

From the current collection of word search sequences, only four recordings were identified where the participants used the dictionary to resolve their word search. Two out of the four Japanese participants used this method, and three out of the four recordings were by Maya, as shown in Figure 4.26.

Despite our assumption that using the dictionary would be more prevalent at the start of the study, when the Japanese participants are still at the early stages of joining the ELF environment and need extra linguistic support, the majority of dictionary use was found later in the data collection in December. One possible reason for this is that dictionary use during a conversation is interruptive to the flow of the conversation, as shown below. During the earlier months of the recording, the participants may have been focusing on continuing the interaction and building a social relationship, rather than explicitly pausing the conversation for language accuracy. Excerpt 4.15 is an example from December when Maya and Yanti are talking about classes they disliked in high school.

Excerpt 4.15 Maya–Yanti December Physics

```
1      Maya:    °so° bi ology is (.) | mh (0.3)
m               gz forward---------| nod-----
2               [interesting]
3      Yanti:   |[better?    ] huhuhuh=
m               |gz to Y--------------
4      Maya:    =bedder (0.3)    |bedder than mathematics
m               --------------   |gz down-------------------
5 →             o::r |   (0.6)   |nani? °↑ah: nandakke°
                                  *what*      *what was it*
m               ---- | gz forwad|gz down, look up dictionary---
6 →             (2.5)
m               -----
```

Excerpt 4.15 Maya–Yanti December Physics (continued)

```
7      Yanti:    physics, physics is
m                --------------------
8      Maya:     ↑physics .sssss |(0.9) HU::
m                ----------------|head up shakes head
```

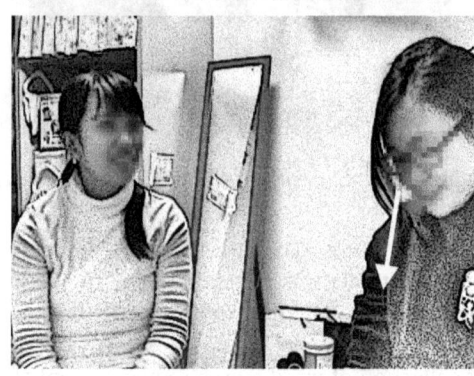

Figure 4.27   Line 5 'nani ah nandakke'

In line 5, Maya attempts to compare biology with another subject, when she elongates the vowel sounds, uses '*nani*' (what) and '*nandakke*' (what was it) to display she is searching for a word (see Section 2.2.3). She does not seek help from Yanti or use other strategies such as description, but uses the electronic dictionary right away in her search for the word (line 5, Figure 4.27). When Yanti utters 'physics' in line 7, Maya is still looking down at her dictionary. In other words, Maya is not attending to the ongoing talk, and slightly impedes the flow of the conversation. When Maya completes her search in the dictionary, she finally confirms Yanti's candidate word through repetition of 'physics', looks up from her dictionary, and expresses her dislike of the subject through a long sigh (line 8).

Despite Yanti's candidate word (line 7), Maya does not display immediate orientation towards it and instead shows reliance on the dictionary. The lack of orientation to Yanti's candidate solution could be due to Maya's lack of linguistic knowledge or non-hearing because she is focusing on the dictionary. However, by not orienting to and displaying reliance on Yanti's other-repair, Maya avoids positioning Yanti as the one with more English knowledge. Instead, she delegates the linguistic authority or the K+ position to the dictionary. Maya could have also employed other possible means of solving the word search. Nevertheless, by using the dictionary, which is readily available in the dormitory room, Maya was able to solve the word search quickly and accurately.

In one interesting case, a dictionary was used when the interlocutor challenged a candidate solution by the Japanese participant, who then attempted to defend her language use through the use of a dictionary. The excerpt below is from July between Maya and Kei when they are talking about what Maya learnt in her environment class regarding a type of fish, namely a carp.

Excerpt 4.16 Maya–Kei July 30 Carp

```
1 →  Maya:   the (.) |>↑ca:p ca:p< |(.)°n?°   |ca:pu?
     m              |snap fingers --|gz left --|gz to K
2            (0.7)
     m       - - - - -
3    Maya:   |fish (0.5)
     m       |fish swim gesture---
4    Kei:    <co:d.>
     m       - - - - - - - -
5    Maya:   |ka- kard?
     m       |stop hands--
6    Kei:    cod.
     m       - - - - - - - -
7            (0.6)
     m       - - - - -
8    Maya:   |ah::.
     m       |gz down
9            (1.2)
     m       - - - - -
10   Kei:    see oh |[dee? ((C-O-D))
11   Maya:          |[cod
     m       -------|gz to K
12           |(1.6)
     m       |gz down-----------------
13   Maya:   ma:ybe::.
     m       - - - - - - - - - - - - -
14   Kei:    |i- >itsa< ↑white fish right?
     m       |gz to K ---------------------
15   Maya:   |↑white and (.) |red.
     m       |gz front -----|gz K, spread fingers
16           (0.6)
     m       - - - - -
17   Kei:    >no no.< |I mean the meat is (.) white.
     m       --------|lower hands-------------------
18   Maya:   white?
     m       - - - - -
19           (1.0)
     m       - - - - -
20   Kei:    meat.
     m       - - - - -
21   Maya:   meat. |[mi- >meat<?
22   Kei:          [the- the-
     m       -----|stick head forward
23           the <fish's ↑meat is white>.
     m       ---------------------------
```

Excerpt 4.16 Maya–Kei July 30 Carp (continued)

```
24              |(0.7)        |(0.5)
 m              |gz forward   | shake head
25   Kei:       <cod>.=
 m              --------
26   Maya:      =>I |I< haven't eat (0.6) the (0.4)
 m              ----|gz to K ---------------------
27              |co- co:p?
 m              | stick head forward
28              (1.2)
 m              -------
29   Maya:      |↑Japanese    |sound (.) is.
 m              |gz forward--|touch ears --
30              (1.0)
 m              |gz K >> gz forward
31   Maya:      |EH? (0.6) co-    |>AH< (.)    |↑CAh: (.) pu.
 m              |turn head left--|wave hand -|lower hand, gz K
32              (1.0)
 m              -----
33   Maya:      ° ca:p. ° (.)  | fish. (0.8) in Japan
 m              --------------| raise hands --------------
34              |re- red (.) ca:p. (0.6) or black $ca:p.$
 m              |make vertical shape with hands-----------
35              |(1.4)
 m              |lower hands
36   Kei:       red and black?
 m              --------------
37              (0.4)
 m              --------------
38   Maya:      |$plea:se hhh my(h) di(h)ctionary::$ .hhh
 m              |reaches out arms-----------------------
39              |(2.4)
 k              |passes dict.to M
 m              ------------------
40   Maya:      |ca:p.(.) >do you: know Hiroshima|ca:p<? (.)
 m              |takes dict., opens case--------|gz to K-------
41              ° in ° (.) Japanese (.) baseball (.) cheam,
 m              ------------------------
42              |(1.2)
 k              |shakes head
 m              -------------
43   Maya:      |°eh:°
 m              |gz down, search in dict.
44              (9.2)
 m              --------
```

Excerpt 4.16 Maya–Kei July 30 Carp (continued)

```
45    Dict:    °carp°
m              --------
46             |(1.8)
m              |shows dict. to K, gz to K
47    Kei:     °carp° (    )[(      )
48    Maya:              [↑ca:p
m              ------------------------
49             |(0.8)
k              |takes dict., looks till line 61
m              |gives dict. to K
50    Maya:    |fish
m              |fish gesture
51             (1.2)
m              ----------
52    Maya:    |Hiroshima (.) ca:p.
m              |gz hand, continue fish gesture to line 56
53    Kei:     |$hh$
m              |gz K
54             (1.8)
m              --------
55 →  Kei:     °n::↑::°.
m              ----------------
56             (2.2)
m              ------------------------
57 →  Maya:    |the ↑ca:p change the:
m              |pointing with index fingers
58             (0.4)
m              ---------------------------
59    Kei:     |↑AH:::↓:: (0.4) it-
m              |make into fist --------
60    Maya:    |[m-
61    Kei:     [they yeah. >they they<
m              |open hands ------------
62    Maya:    male=
m              ---------------------------
63    Kei:     =>yeah yeah yeah yeah yeah<
m              ---------------------------------
64             [>yeah yeah yeah yeah yeah<]
65    Maya:    |[   t o   f e m a l e?   ]
m              |point left with index fingers--
66    Kei:     |>yeah yeah<
m              |lower hands ---
```

Excerpt 4.16 Maya–Kei July 30 Carp (continued)

```
67    Maya:      |°un.°|
                 *yeah*
m                |nod  |
68    Kei:       its- (.) its  because of those |chemical.        |
m                                               |reach for dict.  |
69    Maya:      |°un.°|
                 *yeah*
m                |lower hands|
```
*Dict: Dictionary

Figure 4.28 Line 3 'fish'

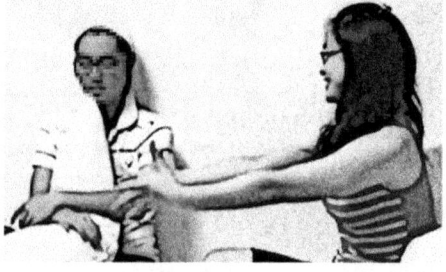

Figure 4.29 Line 38 'please my dictionary'

Figure 4.30 Line 46 Showing dictionary

Figure 4.31 Line 51 Kei looks at dictionary. Maya fish gesture

In line 1, Maya introduces the topic 'carp' with cut-offs, pauses and hesitation, and a rising intonation displaying a possible search and uncertainty about her word choice. Maya provides a semantic contiguity 'fish' and a gesture of a fish while keeping mutual gaze in order to attempt to gain mutual understanding (line 3, Figure 4.28). Kei, as is his frequent practice, then repairs Maya with 'cod' (line 4). When Maya does not repeat it in the same manner (line 5), Kei presents his version of the pronunciation again (line 6). Maya does not respond to this second repair immediately (lines 7–9), and Kei further attempts to seek mutual understanding by presenting the spelling 'C-O-D' with a rising intonation to prompt response (line 10). However, Maya still does not provide a clear confirmation to Kei's prompt (lines 11–13). Kei then attempts to resolve the non-understanding through describing the meat colour (lines 14, 17, 20), but again fails due to Maya describing the colour of the scale of the fish (line 15). Maya then explains that she has never eaten the fish (lines 26–27). Maya then introduces her 'Japanese sound' of the word 'carp' (lines 31–33) and then describes the colour (line 34).

When these negotiation turns do not work towards resolving the word search, Maya then requests her dictionary (line 38, Figure 4.29). While she is looking up the word, she demonstrates her accuracy of the word choice through asking Kei if he knows the Japanese baseball team called 'Hiroshima carp' (lines 40–1). When there is no response, Maya plays the audio of the dictionary (line 45) and shows it to Kei to support her claim (line 46, Figure 4.30). This pronunciation is then repeated by Kei (line 47) and Maya (line 48). Not until Kei looks at the dictionary closely (lines 49–61, Figure 4.31) does he display acceptance or understanding through a soft but a rising utterance of 'n' (line 55). Maya, noticing that Kei has accepted her self-repair and has reached a mutual understanding, continues with her story telling.

Maya and Kei used candidate pronunciations, spelling, gestures and semantic contiguity in the attempt to reach an accurate intersubjectivity in relation to the target word. In this case, the dictionary was the last method that Maya could resort to in supporting her word choice and to convince Kei of her accuracy. At first glance, the two interlocutors seem cooperative in reaching a mutual understanding. However, when analysing the interaction closely, we can see a different dynamic in the negotiation context. That is, Maya is convincing Kei of the accuracy of her word choice.

Even with Maya's questioning of the candidate word 'cod' and evidence of the baseball team name to support her claim of 'carp', Kei does not accept this. On the contrary, he attempts to confirm his accuracy through confirming the fish's meat colour, and does not present any sign of change of epistemic state until he sees the dictionary. This non-acceptance of Maya's word choice could be due to Maya's display of lack of confidence through the try-marking, hedging, the non-English like *katakana* pronunciation, or other social factors such as their past conversations together where Maya was clearly 'doing learning'. Nevertheless, until Maya demonstrates and supports the accuracy of her candidate solution to her word search, using the evidence from the dictionary, Kei does not show alignment.

Researchers have argued that ELF interactions are 'cooperative' and 'supportive' (e.g., Firth 1996; Kaur 2011; Seidlhofer 2001). Seidlhofer (2001) states that 'ELF interactions often are consensus-oriented, cooperative and mutually supportive' (143) where participants in the talk use various affordances to facilitate the progress of communication. Others have found in academic learning situations that L2 users would support each other through repair sequences to reach mutual understandings (Kaur 2011), or in business interactions, that the interlocutor would ignore any linguistic mistakes in order to make 'the other's "abnormal" talk appear "normal"' (Firth 1996: 245). However, in the case of Maya and Kei, there is a negotiation of the K+ position in terms of the English word. At the end, the dictionary became the tool for Maya to use to legitimise her word choice. Therefore, it can be said that the dictionary holds an authoritative role in the interaction in terms of word accuracy. Phillipson (2008) claims, 'Labelling English as a lingua franca, if this is understood as a culturally neutral medium that puts everyone on an equal footing, is simply false' (5). This segment demonstrates that even in ELF interactions, there is a delicate negotiation of epistemic stance in relation to the English language or the word at search, and not all speakers are positioned equally at all times.

Although this issue is rarely discussed or problematised, similar cases where an L2 learner's 'correct' word use is questioned by a peer can be identified in other ELF data. For example, Källkvist et al. (2022) present a negotiation sequence during a classroom discussion, where the male students collaboratively and strongly reject the female student's presentation of the word 'ring' used to phone someone, as a result making her change her understanding of the word. If the female student had had access to a dictionary, perhaps she would have been able to defend her word choice and create a learning opportunity for the male students. Instead, the results turn out to be a missed learning opportunity for the male students and a negative language learning experience for the female student. Although peer interactions can create large numbers of opportunities for language learning as demonstrated through previous studies and data shown above, more discussion and research are needed in regard to cases where incorrect learning can occur, or where particular students are silenced despite their accurate language choices.

This section displayed the methods adopted by the Japanese participants as a candidate solution to their self-initiated word searches. The analysis introduced five common methods used by the participants: candidate words, code-switching, semantic contiguity, gestures and using the dictionary. These strategies were often used in combination. Furthermore, detailed analysis of the participants' orientations to each other displayed a delicate negotiation of epistemic stance regarding the participants' relative knowledge and authority in relation to the English language or the particular word. Therefore, the methods used in attempting to solve the word search varied according to the orientation of the interlocutor.

The final section of this chapter will focus on responses by the interlocutor, in particular the responses to prosody-marked candidate solutions used by the Japanese participants.

4.4 RESPONSES TO CANDIDATE SOLUTIONS

When looking back at the excerpts provided above, we notice that the initial verbal resolving moves made by the Japanese speaker are often accompanied by a rising intonation. Of the 239 word search sequences which used a candidate solution, 136 (56.9%) were accompanied by a rising intonation. This tendency suggests that using a rising intonation is a common feature employed in attempting to self-resolve a word search. We will call this 'prosody-marked candidate solutions'.

This tendency to use prosody-marked candidate solutions is consistent with Koshik and Seo's (2012) results in their study of word searches. However, the authors only found limited responses from the interlocutor to the prosody-marked candidate solution: either 'confirm' or 'correct'; we argue, from analysing the ELF interaction corpus, that this binary response is not the case.

Below, we will document the responses by the interlocutor after prosody-marked candidate solutions of word searches delivered by the Japanese participant. The interlocutors not only (1) confirmed and (2) corrected, but also (3) presented candidate understandings and (4) requested further information. These responses to the candidate solutions, and what they entail as social actions, will be explained in detail below.

4.4.1 CONFIRMATION

Confirmation was a common practice as a response to candidate solutions, similar to what Koshik and Seo (2012) have noted. The first example, Excerpt 4.17, is from Ami and Hang in May, when the two are talking about what happened that day in class.

Excerpt 4.17 Ami–Hang May Concentrate
```
1    Ami:    yahhh I can't concen(.)
2            concentrate? concen[trate
3    Hang:                      [↑unuh
4            [↑concen↓trate
5    Ami:    [ya::
6            (0.4)
7    Ami:    °I'm very [hungry:°]
8    Hang:             [↑ah::   ]so all day
```

In line 1, Ami cuts off 'concen' then redoes 'concentrate' with a rising intonation, thus initiating a word search and presenting a candidate word. Ami repeats 'concentrate' while Hang confirms this through backchannelling and a repetition (lines 3–4). Once Ami receives the confirmation, she returns to the main topic of the conversation. Similar cases were found with other participants. Excerpt 4.18 is a recording from Maya and Yanti in November, discussing the course choices they made.

Excerpt 4.18 Maya–Yanti November Regret
```
1    Maya:   so:: ↓mh::
m            gz down, nod-----
2            (1.0)
m            --------
3    Maya:   °kokai° (.) kokai [mmhh
             *regret*    *regret*
4    Yanti:                    [kokanihehehe
m            ---------------------------------
5            |(1.0)
m            |hand on mouth
6    Maya:   |I regret (.) |regret?
             |hand down ---|gz to Y
7    Yanti:  ↓mm↑huh mhh
m            ------------
8    Maya:   |mh  |regret to take da
             |nod |gz down --------
9            ↓mh  |$↑English ↑base$
m            -----|shake hd--------
```

In lines 1–2, Maya displays she is searching for a word through elongated sounds and a long pause. She then code-switches and says, '*kokai*' (regret) followed by '*tte nani*' (what is it) with no mutual gaze, suggesting a solitary search. Yanti does not join the word search, but repeats a similar sound that Maya has just said with laughter (line 4). It is unclear at this moment if Yanti understands '*kokai*'. Maya then presents a candidate word 'I regret' twice, the second time with a rising intonation and mutual gaze. Yanti responds minimally with 'mh huh' and 'mhh', accompanied with nodding, suggesting that she had understood Maya (line 7). Once Maya has received this confirmation of her word choice and acknowledges there is mutual understanding, she returns to the main topic. She does so by repeating the trouble source 'regret' (line 9), as if practising the word.

Taking another look at Excerpts 4.17 and 4.18, we can see that the Japanese participants would put the main topic of conversation on hold until they had received confirmation of the accuracy of their word choice. As a result, it could be said that they were orienting to the interaction as a learning opportunity (Brouwer 2003).

Below is a clear case of this orientation to the word search sequence as a learning opportunity. Excerpt 4.19 is from Maya and Kei in July. Maya is sharing what she learnt in class that day about the government supporting athletes.

Excerpt 4.19 Maya–Kei July 30 Represent

```
1    Maya:    represent- (0.4) n, present?=
2    Kei:     =>yeah yeah yeah.<=
3    Maya:    =>°↑present repre↓sent,°<
4    Kei:     represent.
5    Maya     like (1.8) in Korea:(0.4) Kim Yona,
```

In line 1, Maya cuts off the end of 'represent', then pauses and says 'n' with a slight rising intonation, displaying uncertainty of the word choice and initiation of a word search. She then presents an alternative candidate word, 'present', with a rising intonation, possibly requesting a confirmation. Kei confirms this with no hesitation (line 2).

Although Kei is displaying understanding, Maya pursues accuracy of the word choice by presenting the two choices of 'present' and 'represent' with a slight rising intonation, and requests for a confirmation (line 3). Kei then confirms, 'represent' (line 4). Only when Maya receives the answer she requested does she continue with her story telling (line 5).

As Koshik and Seo (2012) note, it is not always clear if the prosody-marked candidate solutions are proffering confirmation or a particular word. Similar situations were found in the current data. However, what is different in our data is that when the Japanese participants were pursuing accuracy, they would attempt to elicit the word through using additional turns. This is similar to Hosoda's (2006) study between L1 and L2 Japanese speakers where the L2 speaker continued to pursue linguistic accuracy even when the L1 speaker did not correct their word choice, leading to the conclusion that the L2 speakers were 'doing being a language learner'. L2–L2 interactions, such as the data shown above, also demonstrated such phenomena where Japanese participants would display orientations to the sequence as a learning opportunity and position their partners as the one with relatively more English language knowledge.

However, it is interesting to note that while the Japanese participants occasionally positioned their interlocutors as relative English experts, those interlocutors did not always accept the expert role and join the word search. As noted above, L1 interlocutors have been reported to orient to the teaching opportunity or view their role as a 'helper' to find the precise word, which would be a distinguishing trait of L1–L2 interaction. In contrast, the partners of the Japanese participants in the current corpus either did not always recognise that they were being positioned as the expert, or they opted out of collaborating in locating the exact word. This suggests that the partners did not always view the pursuit of the precise word as important. Rather, they saw meaning, mutual understanding and progressivity as more important.

This observation demonstrates that there can be uncertainty or imbalance relating to expert–novice positioning in ELF interactions at times: participants can opt to align with or resist this expert–novice positioning, or they may be unaware that they are being assigned certain roles. This finding is distinct from those of previous studies in which L1 English users typically acknowledge and take on the role of linguistic expert (Hosoda 2006; Kurhila 2006).

4.4.2 CORRECTION

Another common response to candidate solutions was corrections. Correction responses to the prosody-marked candidate solutions were also done often with minimal turns. In the current collection, there were corrections of word choice, form and pronunciation. The example shown below is Maya and Kei's from April, where Maya's candidate word is corrected. Maya is talking about the transportation system in her hometown.

Excerpt 4.20 Maya–Kei April 1 Subway

```
1    Kei:    so what's the transportation in Fukuoka.
2            (.) bus?
3    Maya:   (0.8) bus a:nd (0.2) train,(.) a:nd
4            (1.2)
5 →  Maya:   <underground> (.) °train°,=
6    Kei:    =↑subway=
7    Maya:   =↑subway,=
8    Kei:    =↑uuhhh
```

After a long pause in line 4 where Maya conducts a solitary word search, Maya presents a candidate word 'underground train' with a slight rising intonation (line 5). Kei, with no hesitation, in the next turn says, 'subway'. 'Underground train' and 'subway' are synonymous, and Kei's turn is not necessarily correcting the accuracy of the word from an etic perspective. However, Maya then repeats the correction turn with a similar pronunciation, and treats Kei's turn as a correction. Kei then accepts this repetition and the two speakers move on with the topic.

Prosody-marking may be a signal to invite other-repair. However, Kei's correction is exposed (Jefferson 1987) and overt. The sequence therefore becomes similar to an IRF sequence (Sinclair and Coulthard 1975) or pedagogic interactions (McHoul 1990). As a result, Kei can be seen as displaying his teacher-like identity towards Maya.

Similar cases were found between Ami and Hang, and an example from May is shown in Excerpt 4.21. Ami is explaining about a magazine she made as a class project and the article she wrote about Hang. In this case, Hang corrects Ami's word form.

Excerpt 4.21 Ami–Hang May Representation
```
1     Hang    [ahhh
2     Ami:    [yu- (.) you are betnamese=
3     Hang:   =↑un
4  →  Ami:    represent(0.4)°tation°?=
5     Hang:   =un=
6     Ami:    =ya?=
7  →  Hang:   =representeitive
8  →  Ami:    represen↑tei↓tive=
9     Hang:   =↑un
10    Ami:    ↑un un un un
11            (0.5)
12    Hang:   ha::::
```

In line 4, Ami pauses mid-word and starts a word search. She then attempts to resolve it through a soft voice and a prosody-marked 'representation'. Hang then shows understanding through 'un' (line 5). Although ambiguous, this could be understood as 'yeah' in Japanese. However, Ami does not return to the main topic, but quickly pursues confirmation through 'ya' with a rising intonation (line 6). Hang, with no hesitation, repairs Ami's previous turn as 'representative' (line 7) with emphasis on the corrected part of the word. Ami then repeats this with a similar pronunciation, similar to what Maya did in the previous example (Excerpt 4.20), displaying her orientation to the sequence as a learning opportunity, and with her partner aligning to it without hesitation.

Although Kei and Hang are both correcting the Japanese participants' prior utterances, there is a difference in their participation framework. That is, Kei is demonstrating an overt display of his K+ position and a pedagogic orientation by providing an outright correction while Hang does not correct Ami until solicited for the second time.

This subsection has introduced ways in which corrections were done as responses to candidate solutions. In most cases in the data set, the Japanese participant would present a candidate solution for the word search with a rising intonation, then the partner would present an alternative word, form or pronunciation with no rising intonation. The compact nature of the sequences and the lack of prosody at the end of the repair turn of these correction sequences suggest that the interlocutor has reached a mutual understanding prior to the correction turn.

However, differences were found among the sequences depending on how and when the correction turn was done. When the corrections were explicit, the Japanese participants would repeat the repair and display their orientation to this as a possible learning opportunity. Moreover, corrections were explicitly prompted by the Japanese speakers in some cases, while in other cases, corrections were outright without any prompting. This suggested differences in the partners' orientations to the interactional goal and self-positioning of their English language expertise.

Schegloff et al. (1977) note that other-correction is typically marked with uncertainty and mitigated through phrases such as 'I think'. However, the examples observed here did not display any mitigation in the correction turn by the partners. From these observations, it could be concluded that even in L2–L2 interactions there can be unequal epistemic positioning in relation to participants' linguistic knowledge and identities.

4.4.3 CANDIDATE UNDERSTANDING

A response to candidate solutions that was not systematically documented by Koshik and Seo (2012) or other word search studies was a case where a candidate understanding was presented by the interlocutor with a rising intonation. Excerpt 4.22, from Ami and Hang in October, exemplifies this. The two are talking about their summer vacation experiences.

Excerpt 4.22 Ami–Hang October Experience

```
1    Ami:    so (.)ah:: what what things ah:::
a            gz down -----------------------
2            how to say that .hhh (0.3)
a            ---------------------------
3            what |thing?
a            -----|gz to H
4            mmm (0.5)ah::: do you like the ↓best
a            ------------------------------------
5            (.) I mean da (.)|whats mm:::
a            -----------------|gz up -----
6            (.) whats |happen? or=
a            ----------|gz to H----
7    Hang:   =mmm
a            -------
8            |(0.5)
a            |gz to H/hands together
9    Ami:    .su:::=
a            --------
```

Excerpt 4.22 Ami–Hang October Experience (continued)
```
10 → Hang:   =experience?=
11   Ami:    =du (.) ↑yeah experience ↑ah:::=
12   Hang:   =ex↑perience
13   Ami:    >yeah yeah yeah<
```

As discussed previously in Section 4.3.3, Ami attempts to resolve the self-initiated word search through describing the concept as 'thing' (line 3) or 'happen' (line 7) with a rising intonation. Hang only replies through a 'mmm' (line 7). However, when Ami halts her candidate solution work (line 9), Hang then presents a candidate understanding of 'experience' with a rising intonation (line 10). Ami then confirms this in the following turn through positive feedback 'yeah' and repetition (line 11). Hang then repeats 'experience', demonstrating that mutual understanding has been reached (line 12).

In this sequence, Hang presents her understanding with uncertainty and waits for Ami's positive reinforcement. Once Ami displays confirmation through multiple turns, the two speakers confirm that a mutual understanding has been reached, and the speakers are able to return to the main conversation topic. Hence, comparing this excerpt with the previous examples of confirmation or correction responses, it could be said that at the point where the candidate understanding is presented by the hearer, intersubjectivity has not been reached, so confirmation or negotiation work is needed before the talk can be progressed.

4.4.4 REQUESTING REPAIR THROUGH PARTIAL OR FULL REPETITION

Displays of non-understanding or requesting repair after a candidate solution were also found in the current corpus. Similar to the candidate understanding responses, these displays of non-understanding and request for repair were done by way of partial or full repetition which ensured that the speaker did not lose face. An example of this is shown in Excerpt 4.23, which was recorded between Ami and Hang in April. Ami is explaining a traditional Japanese sport, sumo, and that many of the recent sumo players come from Mongolia.

Excerpt 4.23 Ami–Hang April Mongolia
```
1    Ami:   $°sumo° people$ ah::: (.) come to::
2           (.) °come to:° (.) °°from°°
3           (1.1)
4  → Ami:   mo- ↑momgol? mongol=
5    Hang:  =↑mon (0.4) mongol?=
6    Ami:   =↑yeah
```

Excerpt 4.23 Ami–Hang April Mongolia (continued)
```
7  → Hang: mongolia?=
8    Ami:  =mongolian
9    Hang: [↑hahhh
10   Ami:  [ahhhh got a lot of (.)mongolian?
11   Hang: ahhhh
12   Ami:  in Japan,
```

After restarts, a long pause and a cut-off to suggest a trouble source to follow (lines 1–4), Ami presents a candidate solution in a *katakana* word 'mongol' with a rising intonation, followed by a restatement (line 4). Hang then responds to this through a partial repetition, then a full repetition with a rising intonation (line 5), requesting a next turn repair. However, Ami takes Hang's response as a display of a hearing trouble or a surprise and confirms Hang's hearing with 'yeah' (line 6). When Hang presents a more explicit repair initiation of 'mongolia' with a rising intonation (line 7), Ami repairs with an adjustment of 'mongolian' (line 8). After the repair by Ami, Hang finally displays understanding and surprise through a high-pitched 'hahhh' (line 9). Moreover, Ami repairs again through a restatement of her initial idea (line 10), possibly orienting to the repair as an English learning and practising opportunity.

Therefore, in some cases, the function of the initial repetition of the candidate solution by the interlocutor was ambiguous. The reason for the prosody could be a confirmation check of hearing, displaying surprise or requesting for repair. Not until the following turns when further negotiations occur does the reason for the prosody become clear. However, because of this lack of explicitness, the repair initiation is not face-threatening to the speaker in challenging their English language knowledge.

This section has described the response turns to prosody-marked candidate solutions. The analysis demonstrated that the responses were not limited to confirmation and correction (Koshik and Seo 2012), but also include candidate understandings and requests for repair. As seen from the excerpts, the sequences were relatively compact, suggesting that candidate solutions play an important role in facilitating the process of reaching a mutual understanding. However, it was also confirmed that prosody-marked candidate solutions are ambiguous regarding whether they are eliciting a confirmation or a specific word. There were no clear patterns found as to how the responses differed in relation to the prior turn. Responses seemed to be related to the partner's orientation, and whether the sequences could be seen as a teaching–learning opportunity or not. Regardless of the type of response, it affected the rest of the unfolding of the word search sequence.

The analysis of word search sequences with prosody-marked candidate solutions displayed the Japanese participants' relatively strong orientation to the sequence as a language learning opportunity and 'doing being a language learner'. At the same time, the Japanese participants were often found to position their partners as having relatively more English language knowledge. However, the partners demonstrated their option to accept or refuse this positioning of the English language expert and language teacher. Thus, in doing so, speakers are displaying a novel dynamic of ELF talk, specifically one where the roles of novice and expert are interchangeable, based on the participants' views and acceptance of those roles.

4.5 SUMMARY AND DISCUSSION

The current chapter set out to explore the common features found in ELF word search sequences utilised by speakers of different L1s in interactions outside the classroom setting. The chapter presented the narrow view of the patterns of word search sequences at a group level within the corpus. The analysis particularly focused on word search sequences initiated by the Japanese participants followed by attempts to self-repair. It described the common features found among the four participants in terms of word search initiation patterns, the candidate solutions, as well as the partners' responses to prosody-marked candidate solutions done by the Japanese participants. From the detailed analysis of the interactions, two observations can be made from the analyses of word search sequences in relation to ELF interaction: (1) preference organisation and (2) learning opportunities.

As previous researchers have claimed, there is a preference for self-repair of self-initiated word searches (Schegloff et al. 1977), and this preference was found to be true even in ELF interactions. Frequently, the Japanese participants would attempt to resolve the word search through various means, such as candidate words or sounds, code-switching, descriptions or synonyms, gestures and the use of the dictionary. At times several different strategies were found used in the same sequence until the word search was resolved. This was a consistent trend across all four participants.

Moreover, when verbal candidate solutions were used, they were often accompanied by prosody, requesting or leaving space for the interlocutor to respond. These prosody-marked candidate solutions by the Japanese participants were responded to by the partner through confirmation, correction, candidate understanding and request for repair. This was different from previous findings in L1–L2 word search sequences, where findings were limited to confirmation or corrections.

In addition, some Japanese participants showed a stronger orientation towards the interaction as a learning opportunity than others. Even after the partner had indicated that they had reached a mutual understanding, the Japanese participant was often found requesting the target word. The Japanese participants were also frequently found repeating the repaired or the target word after the partner's correction or display of candidate understanding. Therefore, participants were displaying different orientations and interactional goals.

Through a mutual orientation to the word search sequence as a learning opportunity, the participants' epistemic stance in terms of English language knowledge became apparent, often with the Japanese participant as the novice and the partner as the expert. This demonstrates that, even in ELF interactions, participants are not always on equal footing or positioned equally in the interaction. Participants were found carefully monitoring their positions, as well as their word choices through the talk in order to save the face of the interlocutor. There were also cases where the partner would opt out of this other-positioning as the English language expert through ignoring the elicitation for other-repair, thus displaying preference towards progressing the talk. This suggests that, unlike some L1–L2 interactions (e.g., Funayama 2002), K+ and K- positions in terms of the English language in ELF interactions are fluid and negotiable.

As can be seen from the detailed analyses, word search sequences are one of the interactional resources which speakers employ to perform their social actions. In other words, a 'word search sequence' is indeed a complex system that displays systematic patterns at the level of the group, as well as at the individual level; differences emerge when speakers develop their own idiosyncratic social actions, relationships and identities. The interaction simultaneously displays both homogeneity and heterogeneity, which is a characteristic of complex adaptive systems (see Section 2.4.2). The balance of homogeneity and heterogeneity which we discover depends on the lens which we adopt. When we look at the micro level using CA, we find that each word search is unique. When we look at how word searches are enacted by a collection of speakers in the same setting, as in this chapter, we find a balance between homogeneity and heterogeneity. When the focus is on the commonalities of how the word search system as a whole functions (as shown through this chapter), then the emphasis is on homogeneity.

This chapter has established the basic functioning in this setting of the mechanism of word search sequences as complex systems. Chapter 5 will move on to examine the changes in the word search sequences of the four participants individually and will demonstrate how their individual uses of the system of word search sequences develop over time. The lens in the next chapter will therefore emphasise heterogeneity. The changes will be examined through the use of quantification and microanalysis of the interactions using CA. Furthermore, the analyses will examine the word search patterns over time through the interaction with their fixed partners while reflecting on the features of ELF word search sequences found in Chapter 4.

5
LONGITUDINAL CHANGES IN WORD SEARCH SEQUENCES

5.1 INTRODUCTION

Chapter 4 illustrated the patterns of word search sequences among the participants in L2 interactions in an ELF context as a large group (i.e., a complex system). We focused on the initiation of word searches, attempts to recover the self-initiated word searches, and the ways in which prosody-initiated recovery attempts are responded to by their partners. Chapter 5 investigates if the word search sequences initiated by four Japanese participants changed over time. It examines the patterns in the use of word search sequences over time between the four lead participants and their interlocutors.

The chapter is divided into five subsections. First, we will analyse the overall patterns of change found among the four Japanese participants, namely Ami, Maya, Yoko and Tomoko. This includes the participants' overall English language proficiency and the quantified frequency of word search sequences. We will then give a detailed analysis of the word search sequence patterns of the four main participants and their fixed partners as shown below:

1. Ami–Hang.
2. Maya–Kei, Maya–Yanti.
3. Yoko–Shitora, Yoko–Jacy.
4. Tomoko–Anh, Tomoko–Pham.

By analysing the data by time and by participants, the chapter examines the individual differences as well as commonalities as this small cohort of four L2 speakers adapts to their ELF interactional environment and interlocutors. We reveal the relative levels of homogeneity and heterogeneity in relation to the word search sequences employed by these four participants over time.

Chapter 6 will then interpret the findings from a holistic perspective in order to relate the changes in word search sequences to the ELF environment of a university dormitory. It aims to connect the micro changes in interaction and the language development of the participants to the CDST perspective, and to widen our understanding of the development of discursive pragmatics and the nature of interaction in ELF environments. The analysis will be done by applying the complex adaptive system framework to the results from Chapter 5. We re-analyse the data in terms of the development of word search sequences in L2 interaction in the ELF context from a CDST perspective, and will argue the following three points:

1. There are features of word searches in ELF interactions identified in this particular population that have not been reported in previous studies.
2. The identified features were not taught but emerged in the interaction through adaptation to the interlocutor and interactional environment.
3. The development of interactional competence displays features of complex adaptive systems.

5.2 QUANTIFIED CHANGES IN THE PARTICIPANTS OVER TIME

5.2.1 OVERALL ENGLISH LANGUAGE PROFICIENCY

This section analyses changes in the four participants' overall English language proficiency over time as measured by the TOEFL (Test of English as a Foreign Language). The participants took the TOEFL ITP (Institutional Testing Program) administered by the university four times during their first year. The first test was taken in April 2010, during their university orientation week (i.e., the first week at university before classes start). Subsequent tests were administered by the university in July and October 2010 and then in January 2011. TOEFL is referred to here as a benchmark for overall change in L2 proficiency and for comparison with studies in SLA and CDST-informed SLA studies that often use proficiency as an independent variable, despite the understanding that measurement of proficiency can differ based on various internal and external factors.

The TOEFL ITP has the same grading scale as the TOEFL PBT (Paper-Based Test), with the score range of 310–677, and uses standardised scores. In other words, the scores the participants received are not raw scores, but are scores that rank the students in comparison with other test takers. The test sections include listening, vocabulary and structure (grammar). There was no speaking component. The total scores of the TOEFL ITP or PBT are found to be a reliable source that reflects overall English language proficiency (J.D. Brown 1999).

As displayed in Figure 5.1, the average score of the four participants improved from 438.25 in April 2010 to 481 in January 2011. This is a 42.75-point increase as a group. However, when examining individual scores over time, variations in the change can be observed, as displayed in Figure 5.2. Ami and Maya had similar scores at the beginning of the recording session in April with 407 and 413, respectively. As a result, the two were placed into the same English language course level ('Fundamental English', the second out of three levels) at the university. In January, however, a large difference was found between the two: Ami with 500 points while Maya with 447 points, a 53-point difference.

Yoko received 483 and Tomoko 450 in April and they were both placed into the same 'Intermediate English' course level at the university, one level above the 'Fundamental English' course. Yoko's scores fluctuated, with a highest of 527 in July, 44 points higher than the first test. Then in January, she received a score of 510.

In contrast, Tomoko's scores plateaued, and showed almost no change. Tomoko's highest score was 467, only 17 points higher than in April. Tomoko did not take the test in July for personal reasons.

Therefore, it can be said there is an overall linear improvement in the English language proficiency among the four participants as measured by the TOEFL test. However, at the individual level, the changes do not necessary display linearity, and there is a variation in the pattern of change in the scores. Furthermore, as may be expected, the change in the overall proficiency level and their use of word search sequences did not necessarily correlate.

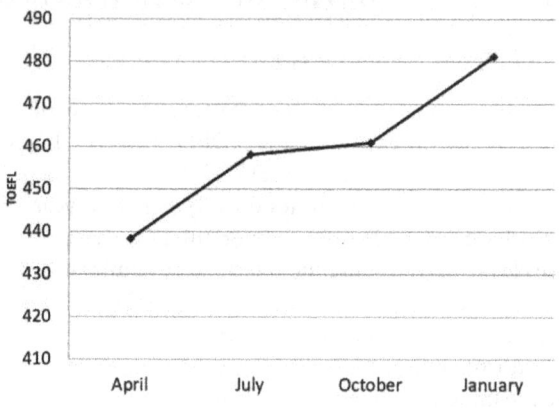

Figure 5.1 Average of TOEFL ITP scores

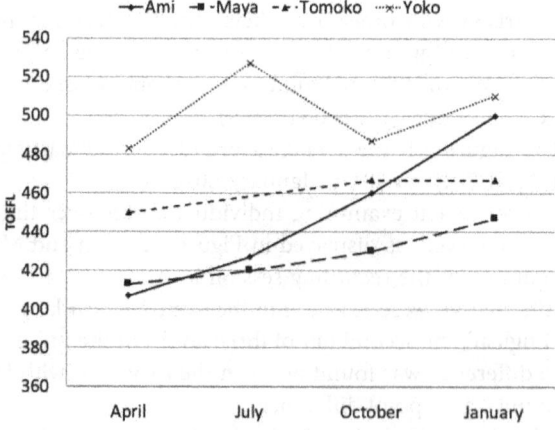

Figure 5.2 Individual TOEFL scores

5.2.2 FREQUENCY OF WORD SEARCH SEQUENCES

In this section, we will determine the overall frequency over time of the word search candidate solutions used by the Japanese participants of this study. This was done by using quantification after the CA analyses.

Figure 5.3 presents the total number of word search sequences and candidate solution turns for the sub-cohort of four participants. As the graph shows, there is not an enormous difference between April 2010 and January 2011 in terms of the frequency of use. Between January 2011 and the last recording in January 2012, there is a sudden large drop in the use of word search sequences (29 times to 14 times). However, overall, it can be argued that the participants did not display significant changes in the frequency of word search sequences during the data collection period, based solely on this data.

Similarly, Figure 5.4 displays the frequency of the three most common candidate solutions for the sub-cohort. As discussed in Section 4.3.2, the use of code-switching decreased from approximately 13 cases in April 2010 to 9 cases in January 2011. In contrast, the use of semantic contiguity strategies gradually increased from 5 cases in April to 12 cases in January 2011. The use of candidate words was constantly high, with 12 cases being the lowest in June and 19 cases being the highest in July (an average of 14.7 cases per month). Therefore, it seems that the participants changed their pattern of candidate solution use over time.

In January 2012, there was a change in the frequencies of the strategies, and the use of candidate words became the most common strategy, while the use of semantic contiguity strategies became the least common. The decrease in the use of semantic contiguity could be due to the overall decrease in the word search sequences. This suggests the continuous tendency towards the use of candidate words among the participants. However, Figures 5.3 and 5.4 only display the frequency of the word search sequences,

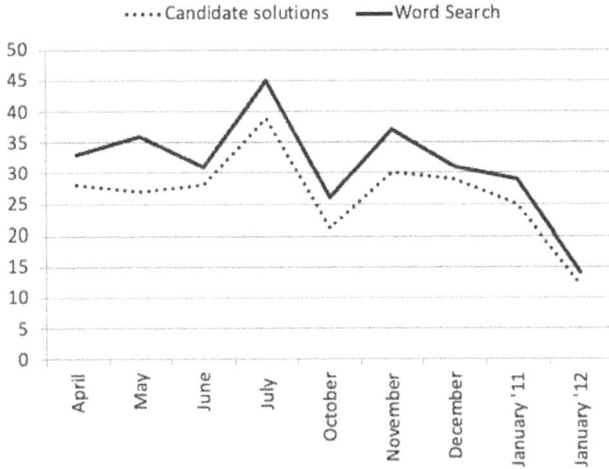

Figure 5.3 Frequency of word search sequences and candidate solutions

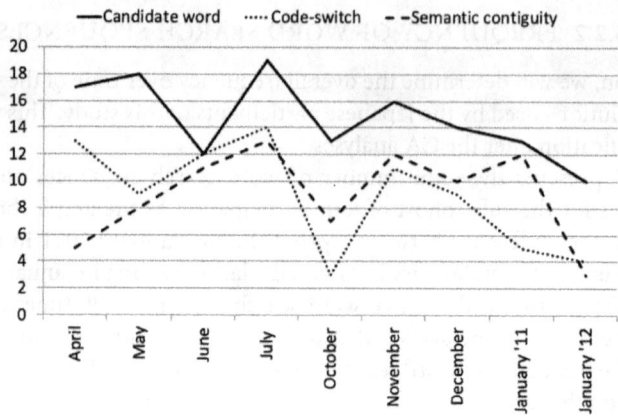

Figure 5.4 Frequency of strategies used as candidate solutions

and the lengths of the recordings vary. In other words, the frequency is based on different parameters and the reliability of the changes cannot be accounted for.

Moreover, when observing the use of the candidate solutions among the individual participants, discrepancies emerge compared with the overall tendencies of the group. Figure 5.5 displays the individual frequency of the self-initiated word search sequences and prosody-marked candidate solutions, which were frequently identified, as discussed in Chapter 4. Figure 5.6 displays the frequency of the candidate solutions used by the individual participants.

According to the data, Maya displayed relatively higher frequency of word search use than other participants. Ami and Yoko displayed some increase in the use of semantic contiguity strategies in resolving word searches, while Maya and Tomoko displayed a tendency to use candidate words and code-switching more frequently. Therefore, it is difficult to reach any decisive conclusions on the changes in the use of word search sequences based only on the frequency of the usage.

Nevertheless, two interpretations can be drawn from the frequency and the figures from the quantification of the word search sequences. Firstly, when the initial overall proficiency level is higher, the participants tend to use fewer word search sequences. As displayed in Figure 5.5, Ami and Maya used relatively more word searches than Yoko and Tomoko throughout the data collection period. Secondly, while Ami and Maya showed increasingly more instances of prosody-marked candidate solutions, Yoko and Tomoko used this method of resolving word searches minimally. In total, Ami used the prosody-marked candidate solutions 62 times, and Maya 54 times, while Yoko used them 13 times, and Tomoko only 7 times.

Therefore, it could be claimed that the lower the overall language proficiency L2 users have, (1) the more they will tend to use word search sequences, and (2) the more they will use prosody-marked candidate solutions during word search sequences. To some extent, this may be interpreted as being consistent with previous SLA researchers' claims that frequency of word search use is associated with level of linguistic ability (e.g., Hilton 2008; Koizumi and In'nami 2013).

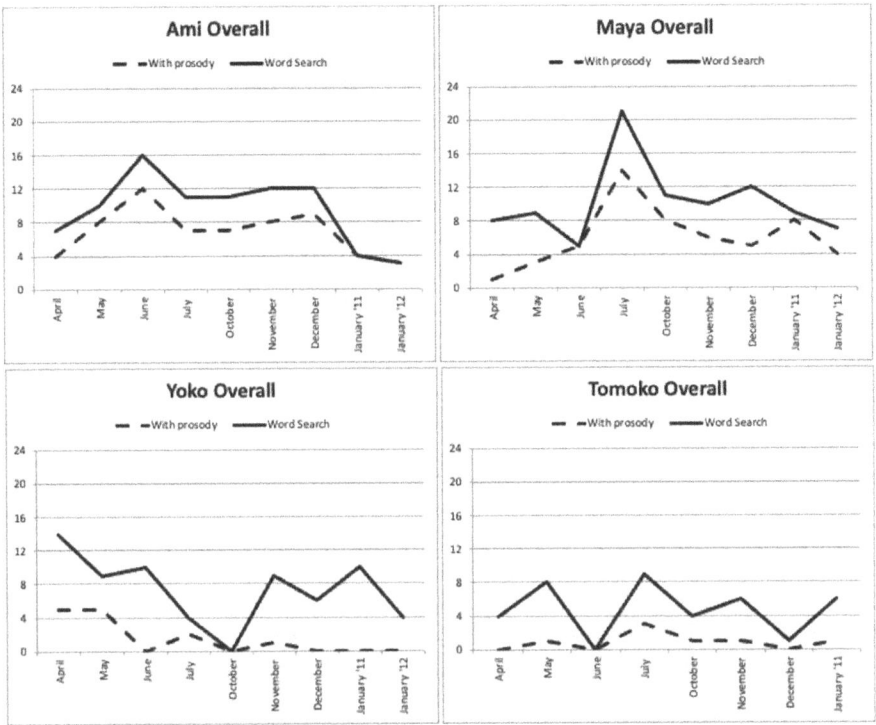

Figure 5.5 Individual frequency of word searches and prosody-marked candidate solutions

However, as mentioned previously, this claim is only based on a simple quantification of single occurrences and does not incorporate other variables such as the different partners, nor the length and the topic of the conversations. Therefore, the changes that are observed through the quantified data are only one way of attempting to understand 'change' in the use of word search sequences. Furthermore, changes in frequency do not hold practical implications towards understanding the use of word search sequences in L2 interactions in an ELF setting.

When we analysed the actual sequences in more detail, however, a different perspective on change over time was observed that provides deeper insights into how word search interactions are organised in L2 conversations in an ELF context and how they change over time. In the following sections, we will analyse the word search sequences of the four participants individually. Namely, we will focus on repair during word searches initiated by the four Japanese participants with their fixed partners, and demonstrate the changes that are displayed from an emic perspective. By focusing on the fixed partners, we highlight the patterns that are created in the localised interactions, as well as the emergent changes that occur over time.

Below, we will analyse the four participants in the order of Ami, Maya, Yoko and Tomoko. Their use of word search sequences, mainly with their fixed partners, will

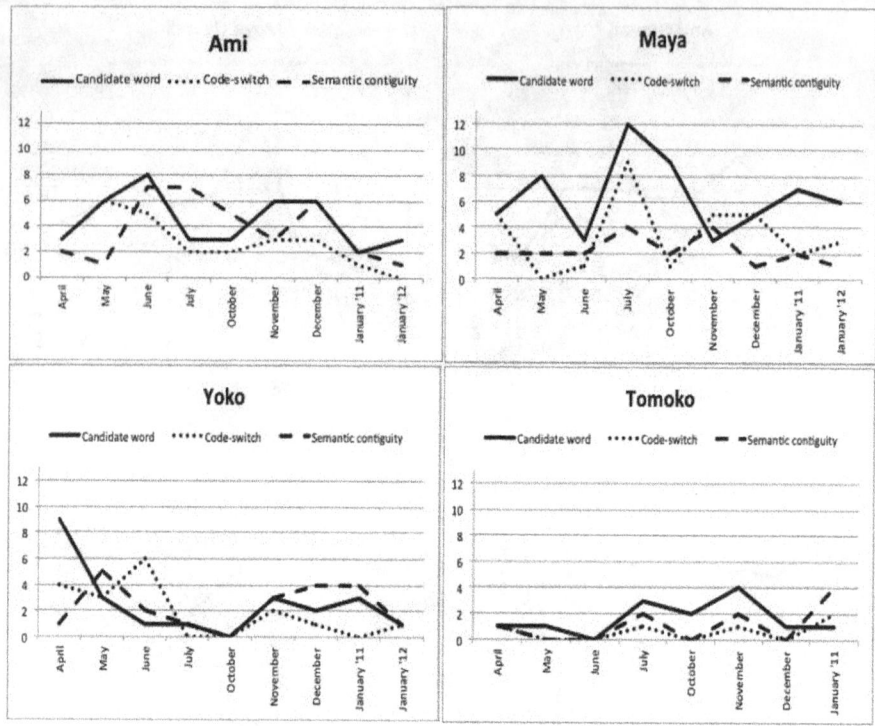

Figure 5.6 Individual frequency of strategies used as candidate solutions

be analysed in terms of frequency, details of the interactional sequence, and then their orientation to the interaction.

5.3 AMI'S CASE

Ami's fixed partner was Hang, and the two recorded together for the whole duration of the study. When analysing Ami's word searches, three main changes in Ami's word search sequences with Hang were identified: (1) the overall frequency of word searches, (2) Hang's responses to Ami's prosody-marked candidate solutions, and (3) Ami's change in the reason for her use of the prosody-marked candidate solutions.

5.3.1 FREQUENCY OF AMI'S WORD SEARCHES

The first change was in terms of quantity. As shown in Figure 5.7, Ami's overall other-involved word search initiation use decreased over time. The most frequent use was ten times in May and June, and the lowest was twice in January 2012. On average, Ami had six word search sequences per month, and approximately 75% of the word search candidate solutions were accompanied with a rising intonation. This suggests that the use of prosody was Ami's favoured strategy in such situations.

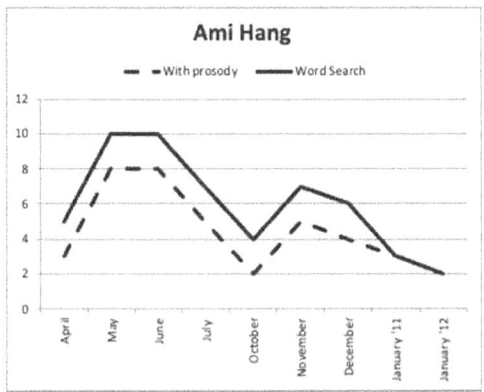

Figure 5.7   Ami's word searches with Hang

5.3.2 CHANGE IN PARTNER'S ORIENTATION FROM LEARNING TO PROGRESSIVITY

Along with the change in the frequency of prosody-marked candidate solutions, Hang's response to Ami's self-initiated word searches showed a change. That is, Hang's orientation changed from initially helping Ami with learning opportunities to progressing the talk.

Excerpt 5.1 is a typical example of a word search during the first three months of recording between Hang and Ami. In this excerpt, Ami is talking about her nail polish purchased during her trip to Korea, and we see Hang's orientation to the sequence as a possible learning opportunity for Ami.

Excerpt 5.1 Ami–Hang June Light pink

```
1       Hang:   so wh- (.) ↑which colour,
2               you buy (0.3) in Korea?
3       Ami:    (0.4) ah- (.) ↑hmm (.) like (.) a pink?
4               but (.) .suu mhh ↑nea:r the hwhi:te.
5       Hang:   ↑ah::=
6       Ami:    =hmm=
7   →   Hang:   =↑light (.) pink.
8   →   Ami:    light pink,
9   →   Hang:   ↑hmm=
10      Ami:    =↓ah
11      Hang:   ↑°ah::°
12      Ami:    [°light pink°
13      Hang:   [°light pink°
14      Ami:    I think its (.) cute
```

Ami uses semantic contiguity ('pink but near the white') in attempting to solve her word search (lines 3–4). Hang then shows understanding through 'ah' (line 5).

Instead of returning to the main topic, Hang corrects Ami and recasts her understanding of the colour as 'light pink' (line 7) with a clear enunciation and stress on each word. Ami aligns to this other-correction through repeating the word twice, the first time confirmed by Hang and the second time softly but in a choral co-production with Hang (lines 8–9, 11–12). This sequential pattern is similar to an IRF sequence (Sinclair and Coulthard 1975) with Hang modelling, Ami repeating and positive feedback by Hang, similar to a classroom practice and Hang taking on the teacher-like role. Thus, the sequence mirrors a pedagogic sequence and displays the participants' orientation to this sequence as a learning–teaching opportunity. Similar cases can be found in previously analysed excerpts such as Excerpt 4.21 (Section 4.4.2) where corrections were explicitly done by Hang with a clear orientation to promoting Ami's L2 learning. This could be due to Hang having a clearly higher English language proficiency over Ami at this moment in the data collection.

However, from the fourth month (July) onwards, there was a change in Hang's reaction to Ami's candidate solutions. Excerpt 5.2 is from July, and Ami and Hang are talking about the different dialects of English.

Excerpt 5.2 Ami–Hang July Learn

```
1      Ami:      because ↑I (0.5) mmh ↑I heard
2                (.)↑I has (.) be::n lu' (0.4)
3   →            la (0.3) learn?
4   →            (0.6)
5      Ami:      I has been learn da:=
6      Hang:     =mm
7      Ami:      American English? s[ince
8      Hang:                        [mmh
9      Ami:      my: °elemen° uhh (.) since
10               uh (.) elementary school [°student°?
11     Hang:                              [mmh
12     Ami:      so it's .hhh maybe difficult fo:r us t[o:
13     Hang:                                           [yeah
14     Ami:      (0.4) speak
15     Hang:     mm
16     Ami:      da New Zealand English hhahahh
```

Figure 5.8   Line 4 (0.6)

In line 2, Ami initiates a word search with silence, cut-offs and elongated vowel sounds. She then provides a candidate solution 'learn' with a rising intonation (line 3). Hang does not respond to this while keeping firm eye contact with Ami (line 4, Figure 5.8). Ami then restates the phrase with the potential trouble source (line 5). Hang responds to Ami with a 'mm' (line 6). By Ami continuing her story after this, we can interpret that Hang's utterance was recognised as 'showing listening' or as a continuer, rather than as a confirmation of the accuracy of the word Ami chose.

Comparing Excerpts 5.1 and 5.2, we can see that Hang in Excerpt 5.2 is not participating in Ami's word search. As a result, the sequence becomes a self-repair sequence, which is known to be 'preferred action' (Pomerantz 1984) in L1 speech (Sacks and Schegloff 1979). Hang is showing her orientation to the interaction as a mundane conversation rather than learning or teaching opportunity, and 'letting it pass' (Firth 1996). Thus, Ami is not positioned as an L2 novice in Excerpt 5.2. Furthermore, the two participants are displaying their preference towards the progressivity of the talk (Heritage 2007; Stivers and Robinson 2006) over accuracy of language choice or learning.

This difference in orientation towards the conversation, and Hang not positioning Ami as an L2 speaker, was only seen from July onwards. Excerpt 5.3 is another example from July where a difference in their interactional goal can be observed. The two are discussing the income gap in Vietnam, where Hang is from.

Excerpt 5.3 Ami–Hang July Gap

```
1    Ami:    |↑in betna:m ah: are there  |  (0.5) AH BIG?
a            |turning head right -------|  arms up, gz up----
h            gz A------------------------------------------
2            |(1.0)
a            |move arms up/down (gap gesture)
h            ------------------
3            mm °big separate°  |no        |big (0.7) the:::
a            ------------------|shake hd  |turn to H, small gap gesture
h            ------------------------------------------
4            (0.4) I mean  |the: (0.4)              |poor?
a            --------------|gz right, open arms|gz H
h            ------------------------------------------
5    Hang:   |[mm|
6    Ami:    |[the (0.3)    |the:: .sss ah the  |some of student
a            |hands together |hands to right----|hands left--------
h            |nod| -------------------------------------
7            is poor but (.) |some of student is    |very rich?
a            ----------------|hands right, gz up --|gz H, rotate hand
h            ----------------|tilt head/ gz left --------------------
```

Excerpt 5.3 Ami–Hang July Gap (continued)

```
8    Hang:   |↑mmm[mm::
9  → Ami:            |[so:: (0.4)  |are there lot |>ah< big
a            ----|open arms ---|gap gesture----------
h            |nod, close eyes--|gz A----------|gz down ----
10 →                 (0.6)
a            -----
h            -----
11 → Ami:    |°how do you say° the
a            ------------------
h            |gz A---------------
12                   (1.0)
a            -----
h            -----
13   Hang:   |big ah: |gap?
a            |touch nose---------
h            |gz up --|gz A, gap gesture
14   Ami:    |↑YA    |BIG
a            |big nod|gap gesture
h            ------------------
15   Hang:   big gap
a            -------
h            -------
16   Ami:    gap |in be ah   |in betnam?
a            ----|hands down |vertical clap
h            ----|nod -------|hands down, fix glasses
17   Hang:   | ↑mm[mm::::
18   Ami:        |[right?
a            ----|hands down
h            |nod, gz up (thinking face)
```

Figure 5.9   Line 2 (1.0) gap gesture   *Figure 5.10   Line 8 'mmm'*

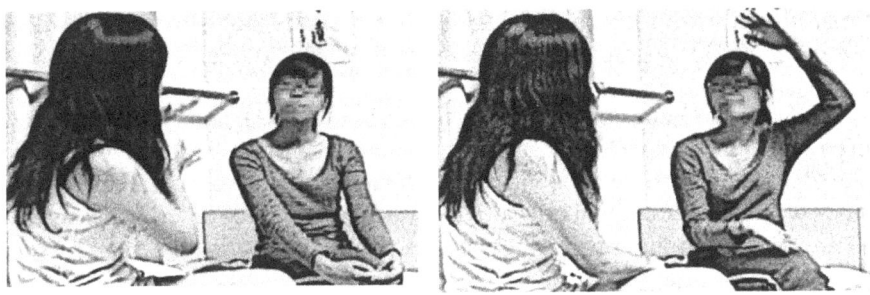

Figure 5.11   Line 12 (1.0) gap gesture   *Figure 5.12   Line 13 'gap?'*

In line 1, Ami specifies Hang's home country, Vietnam, and attempts to start a question 'are there a big', when she pauses and displays a gesture (line 2, Figure 5.9) to embody the word that follows. Ami then presents a candidate word 'big separate' but then rejects it and continues searching for the word through a display of pause and elongated vowel sound (line 3). After a slight pause, Ami takes a different strategy in resolving her word search by using 'I mean' (Sacks 1992) and providing an explanation of the previous utterance (or a semantic contiguity). In line 6, Ami explains that there are some poor students but there are also very rich students. In the next turn, Hang backchannels with a high pitch and disengages eye contact from Ami (line 8, Figure 5.10). This suggests that Hang has understood Ami and is thinking of the answer. However, before Hang can answer the question, Ami overlaps and restarts the original question with 'so' and this time with quantity ('lot') and a stressed 'big' followed by a pause (line 9).

When Hang does not take the turn after 'big' (line 10), Ami then clarifies that she is searching for a target word by saying 'how do you say the' followed by the gesture of a gap (line 12, Figure 5.11). Hang then aligns to Ami's word search by repeating the last word 'big', followed by a short hesitation while doing the same gesture as Ami (Figure 5.12) and a candidate understanding of 'gap' with a rising intonation (line 13). By doing a similar 'gap gesture', Hang specifically displays that she is aligning to Ami and her word search. This candidate understanding is then accepted by Ami with a loud high pitched 'ya' (line 14).

However, Ami displays trouble producing the word and stops after 'big' (line 14). Hang, unlike in line 9, this time aligns to this word search by repeating 'big gap' (line 15). Ami repeats the 'gap' and displays her attempt to learn. Only then does she complete her original question of 'gap in Vietnam' and the conversation shifts back to the main topic (line 16). Hang backchannels, which is then followed by a confirmation request by Ami using a tag question 'right' (lines 17–18).

Comparing lines 8–11 and lines 14–15, it could be said that in the former segment there was a difference between Ami and Hang in the orientation towards the talk. While Ami was orienting towards searching for the word, Hang was orienting towards understanding and responding to the question (lines 8–11). In contrast, in the latter segment (lines 14–15), both participants are orienting towards Ami's word search and learning of the word 'gap'. However, this does not occur until Ami explicitly requests the search by asking, 'how do you say' (line 11).

This feature of Hang not immediately orienting to the word search or not providing a word unless explicitly requested only appeared after the fourth month of the recording (July) between Hang and Ami. This suggests there is a change emerging in terms of Hang's attitude and orientation towards Ami and the interactional goal, as well as the relationship between the two participants.

5.3.3 ADAPTING TO THE PARTNER'S LANGUAGE DEVELOPMENT: CHANGE IN REASON FOR USING PROSODY-MARKED CANDIDATE SOLUTIONS

The final change we introduce is the context in which Ami used rising intonation with the candidate solution. As seen in previously presented excerpts, the typical use of the prosody-marked candidate solution is to elicit Hang's confirmation or correction. However, after the third month, Ami started to use the prosody-marked candidate solution differently. Excerpt 5.4 is from November, the sixth recording between Ami and Hang. The two are talking about the school festival.

Excerpt 5.4 Ami–Hang November *Mogiten*

```
1      Ami:    but ac- (.) actually ah
2              (.)I was joini:n' da:
3              (0.3)
4      Hang:   [°un°
5      Ami:    [| ah (0.2) | like |
a                | roof ----| wall |
6      Ami:    mogite:n?
               'booth/store'
7→             (0.4)
8→     Hang:   [°mo°
9→     Ami:    [mogiten is ↓shop
                *booth/store*
10             (0.5)
11     Hang:   [↑ah::
12     Ami:    [it was sho:p
13     Hang:   food?
14     Ami:    (0.4) ya [food shop (.) food shop
15     Hang:            [(         )
16             mm (0.2)
```

Figure 5.13   Line 5 Roof   *Figure 5.14   Line 5 Walls*

In line 5 (Figures 5.13–5.14) Ami uses an iconic gesture and silence to initiate a word search, followed by a candidate solution of '*mogiten*' (booth/store) with rising intonation (line 6). However, Hang does not respond immediately (line 7). Rather than moving on to a longer sequence of negotiating the meaning of the word (which tended to happen in April and May) while overlapping with Hang, Ami moves on to translate *mogiten* as a 'shop' (line 9), and Hang acknowledges this in line 11. As a result, the conversation does not develop into an extended word search side sequence.

By Ami using a prosody-marked candidate solution that translates the word into English, Ami is not seeking a correction or confirmation of the word choice from Hang. Instead, Ami is checking Hang's understanding of the culturally specific Japanese word, to ensure that Hang knows the word. Hang confirms understanding in line 11. Hang's increase in her Japanese knowledge had been seen through the interactions, such as in Excerpt 4.8 (Section 4.3.1.2) with *suppai* (sour) and Excerpt 4.14 (Section 4.3.4) with *atsui* (thick). Therefore, over time, not only did Ami display changes, but also the interactional environment (specifically Hang as partner) displayed changes.

Ami seems to position Hang as a user of Japanese L2, while at the same time she is not positioning herself as an 'English language learner'. Ami's action is similar to what Sert (2013) calls 'epistemic status check' where speakers make sure that there is a mutual understanding before proceeding with the talk. In this case, Ami displayed a K+ stance towards Hang in relation to Japanese. Again, this phenomenon was only found after the third month.

To summarise this section, Ami's word search sequences displayed changes in terms of (1) a decrease in overall frequency of word searches, (2) the partner's change in orientation towards Ami's word search sequences, and (3) change in use of prosody-marked candidate solutions. In other words, Ami displayed adaptation to her partner Hang as part of the interactional environment. That is, Ami adapted to Hang's increase in Japanese ability and started to use Japanese to describe objects that she knew the word for in English, and initiated explicit word searches when Hang did not respond. Moreover, we can observe that Ami is using English to explain Japanese concepts to Hang, reflecting the superdiverse lingua franca setting where multiple language use is omnipresent and English does not have to be the main language of communication. Thus, Ami displays a result of adaptations to her interlocutor to reach her interactional goal of achieving mutual understanding and language learning. Furthermore, by Hang not foregrounding the interaction as a language learning opportunity and viewing Ami as an 'English language user', rather than an 'English language learner', we see a progressive change of epistemic stances, with the interlocutors becoming closer in their epistemic status.

5.4 MAYA'S CASE

Next, we move on to examine a different participant, namely Maya. Maya had two different fixed partners, Kei and Yanti. Maya started her recordings with Kei in the first semester between April and July 2010. Then, due to scheduling issues, she changed her fixed partner to Yanti during the second semester, October 2010 to January 2011. From the analysis, there were three major changes identified through the interactions with her fixed partners: (1) a change in her effectiveness in using candidate solutions, (2) a change in her partner's orientation towards the interactional goal, and (3) an emergent method for securing intersubjectivity. What did not change was Maya's overall frequency of word search sequences.

5.4.1 SUMMARY OF MAYA

In terms of the frequency of word searches with her fixed partners, Maya's use did not change overall through the collection. The frequency of word search sequences and those accompanied with prosody are displayed in Figure 5.15. The July 8 recording between Maya and Kei is marked as done in June in order to be consistent with the other participants in terms of the number of recordings.

Maya on average had approximately 7.3 word searches per month with Kei, of which four used a prosody-marked strategy on average. With Yanti, Maya had an average of 8.5 word searches per month, and on average 5.5 word search sequences per month were attempted to be resolved with a prosody-marked strategy. In total, Maya had an average of approximately 7.9 word search sequences per month, of which 60% used a prosody-marked strategy. This is similar to Ami, where the prosody-marked candidate solution was commonly used, and displayed an increase in the use during the first few months of the recording.

No clear changes in terms of reaction to prosody-marked candidate solutions were identified between Kei and Maya. In most cases, Kei provided a solution (candidate word) with or without prosody in response. Not until July did Kei ignore or use a 'let it pass' strategy (Firth 1996) without a correction. In contrast, Yanti tended not to engage in the 'teaching' interactional role and displayed focus more on the content and progressivity of the talk.

In the recording with Kei in January 2012, Maya used seven word search sequences, of which four were accompanied with prosody. This recording is excluded from Figure 5.15 since there was a large gap in time between recordings since the last recording with Kei in July 2010.

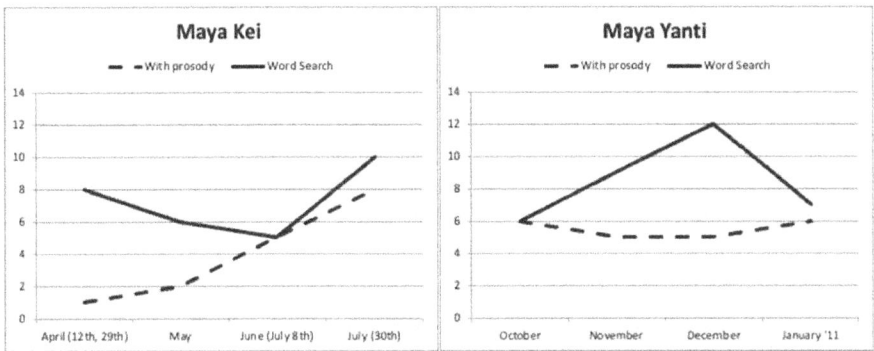

Figure 5.15   Maya word search sequences with Kei and Yanti

5.4.2 CHANGE IN EFFECTIVENESS OF CANDIDATE SOLUTIONS

Although there were no significant changes in Maya's use of candidate solutions during word search sequences over time in terms of frequency, changes in the effectiveness of using strategies and in relying on the interlocutor to achieve mutual understanding were identified. In other words, Maya was found using candidate solutions that relied less on the interlocutor's superior linguistic knowledge in achieving mutual understanding.

In her early recordings, Maya was found to rely heavily on the interlocutor's scaffolding, although she was using various word search resolving methods such as code-switching, gesture and semantic contiguity (explanations). This tendency is shown in Excerpt 5.5, the first recording done between Maya and Kei in April. Kei asked Maya what activities he could do if he visited her hometown.

Excerpt 5.5 Maya–Kei April Fireworks

```
1 → Maya:    a:::hh (1.7) doing (0.8) hanabi.
                                      *fireworks*
  m          gz down ----------------------------
  k          gz M ------------------------------
2   Kei:    |(0.4) hana|bi.
  m          |gz K ----------
  k          -----------|nod-
3   Maya:   |hanabi |(0.4) do you kno:w?
             *fireworks*
  m          |one nod|gz K----------------
  k          nod, gz M---------------------
4   Kei:    (0.4) |°umh:°   |what's hanabi.=
  m          ----------------------------------
  k          ------|shake hd |gz M----------
```

Excerpt 5.5 Maya-Kei April Fireworks (continued)

```
 5 → Maya:    |=hanabi (.) is (0.9) JAPAnese|cultures
              *fireworks*
   m          |gz down --------------------|gz K--------
   k          ---------------------------------------
 6            |(1.2)    |a::h Japanese culture|a:::nd
   m          ------- -|gz down-------------|touch hair
   k          | one nod |gz M----------------------------
 7            (0.6) hhanabi.
                     *fireworks*
   m          -----------------------
   k          -----------------------
 8            (2.3)
   m          -----------------------
   k          -----------------------
 9   Kei:     what do you do:?=
   m          -----------------------
   k          -----------------------
10 → Maya:    |=flower fire |.hh [HUH HH
11   Kei:                    |[huh?
   m          |lower hand --|gz K--------
   k          -----------------|stick hd forward
12   Maya:    $flow(h)er fi(h)|re$hh=
   m          ----------------|raise arms palms up
   k          ---------------------------------------
13   Kei:     =°$flow(h)er|f(h)ire$°[huhh
14   Maya:                          |[huhhuhh
   m          -----------------------|launching gesture
   k          ------------|lean back----------
15 → Kei:     |↑OH (.)    |↑FIrework
   m          ----------  |touch nose---------
   k          | gz up--- |gz M-----------
16   Maya:    ↑firework?=
   m          ------------
   k          ------------
17   Kei:     |=unh
   m          |hand down
   k          |nod
```

Figure 5.16 Line 14 Launching of fireworks

After a few long pauses, Maya uses Japanese '*hanabi*' (fireworks) (line 1). This use of the pause in line 1 is ambiguous, whether Maya was thinking about the content or the word choice. When Kei repeats '*hanabi*', Maya confirms through repeating (lines 2–3). Then she asks if he understands, which could be interpreted that Maya recognises the possible problematic word choice. Therefore, the pauses in line 1 are likely to be due to Maya searching for a word in English.

Kei, after a slight pause, requests an explanation of *hanabi* (line 4), and Maya starts her attempt of explaining *hanabi*. However, the extent of her explanation is that it is 'Japanese culture' (lines 5–6). When Kei prompts a question 'what you do' (line 9), Maya provides a literal translation of the Chinese characters for *hanabi* (花火 flower fire) followed by laughter, marking the word choice (Firth 2009) and displaying her understanding that it is an unconventional word use. Overlapping, Kei responds with an open class repair initiator, 'huh?' (line 11). Maya then repeats 'flower fire', again with laughter (line 12), possibly displaying embarrassment and the laughter functioning as a face-saving device (Adelswärd 1989). 'Flower fire' is repeated by Kei also with laughter (line 13), which is then joined by Maya's laughter. As a result, Maya's candidate solution of 'flower fire' is jointly treated as a laughable item. While laughing, Maya uses gesture to describe the launching of fireworks (Figure 5.16). This seems to prompt Kei's understanding and he shows a change of state ('oh'). Kei then provides the English equivalent, 'firework' (line 15). Maya repeats this, which is confirmed by Kei (lines 16–17).

Here, we see that Maya is incapable of using semantic contiguity to explain the word she is searching for. Rather, she expands the concept as 'Japanese culture', reflecting previous studies on how lower proficiency learners use semantic contiguity (e.g., D.R. Kim 2020). Furthermore, she relies on Kei's scaffolding of suggestive questions and linguistic knowledge in order to resolve the word search.

However, in the later months, Maya displays a more effective use of candidate solutions, which involves less reliance on the interlocutor's linguistic expertise and scaffolding. An example of this can be found in Excerpt 5.6, Maya's recording in October with Yanti and Taman. Maya is explaining a beach event where she sold Indonesian food.

Excerpt 5.6 Maya–Yanti–Taman October Seconds

```
1       Maya:       mmh. becuz ah:: (1.0) >abecuz<
2                   >no no no no< (0.5) da (.)
3  →                I can  (1.0) re (0.4) <re(.)take>?
4                   retake
5       Taman:      uh=
6       Yanti:      =mh rekate [(    )?
7       Taman:                 [retake
8       Maya:       >yeah yeah hh<=
9       Yanti:      =↑ah:::
10      Maya:       uh. I (.) I finish eatin' uh:::=
11      Yanti:      =ah[::::
12      Maya:          [>please< $please o:ne hh mmmo(h)re$
13                  hhahah[hhh
14      Taman:            [↑AH:[::
15      Maya:                  [mhhh=
16      Taman:      =↑AH::: sugoi
                            *great*
```

In lines 3–5, Maya displays that she is searching for a word through the multiple pauses, cut-off and a candidate word 'retake' with rising intonation, which is then repeated. Similar to Excerpt 5.5 with 'flower fire', 'retake' is possibly the literal translation or language transfer of the Japanese word '*okawari*', which means 'a refill' or 'seconds'. Taman responds with 'uh' and repetition, while Yanti responds with a confirmation question. Maya then confirms this (line 8), and Yanti uses a change of state token 'ah', displaying acknowledgement (line 9). Unlike what occurred with the previous Excerpt 5.5, Maya continues to explain what she means by 'retake' without any scaffolding from the interlocutors (lines 10, 12). Yanti then finally displays a change of state or understanding and presents her assessment in Japanese as '*sugoi*' (great) (lines 14, 16). Thus, despite Maya's unconventional language use, the three displayed reaching intersubjectivity with minimal scaffolding effort.

Maya also displayed more independence in her candidate solutions with Kei in relation to a more complex concept. Excerpt 5.7 is between Maya and Kei recorded in early July. Maya is explaining her presentation topic of *doshusei*, the state and county system in Japan.

Excerpt 5.7 Maya-Kei July 8 State system

```
1    Kei:     so what are you guys presenting about.
2 →  Maya:    (0.5) ↑a::hh (0.6) do:shyu:sei?
                                  *state system*
3             (0.4)
4    Maya:    [do you know?
5    Kei:     [°do:shyu:sei°
6             |(0.5)
k             |Kei shakes head
7 →           |(2.0)
m             |Maya picks up dictionary→puts down
8 →  Maya:    >dosyusei like< (0.5) u::m (3.4)
              *state system*
9             a:hh (0.5) the government=
10   Kei:     =°uh huh°
11            (2.0)
12   Maya:    °mh°(0.4) separated the: (0.3)
13            Japanese (.) ja- (.) Japan?
14            (0.8)
15   Maya:    [so
16   Kei:     [°uhm°
17            (0.6)
18   Maya:    °nh?°
19   Kei:     from where
20   Maya:    (0.4) fro::m=
21   Kei:     =separation bu' (.) [Japanese: land
22   Maya:                        [Japan
23   Kei:     From
24            (0.8)
25   Maya:    trom?
26            (0.5)
27   Kei:     from?
28   Maya:    from? (0.5).hhhh u:::m:::
29            (1.3)
30   Maya:    except (1.0) Hokkaido?
31   Kei:     °umhuh°
32            (1.0)
33   Maya:    e::hh (0.8) Honshyu: (0.3) Shikoku.(0.5)
34   Kei:     [°uhm°(.)°mhh°
35   Maya:    [Kyu:syu
36            (1.4)
37   Maya:    oh (1.0) about (0.8) eight? (0.8) eight
38            (.) to: (1.6) °about° (1.2) fifteen? (.)
39            fifteens (1.0) a::hh (2.1) divide.
40   Kei:     (0.4) °uh huh::°
```

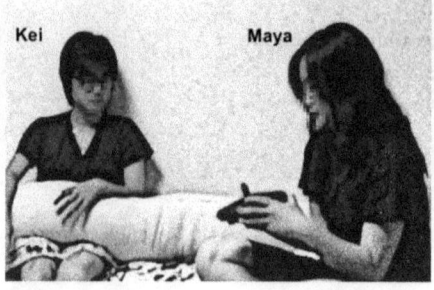 

Figure 5.17 Line 7 Picks up dictionary *Figure 5.18 Line 7 Puts dictionary down*

After Kei's question about the presentation topic, Maya shows thinking through pauses and hesitation, and then states in Japanese '*doshusei*' (state county system) with a rising intonation (line 2). It is unclear at this point if the thinking action relates to recalling the topic or searching for the word. However, after a slight pause, Maya asks Kei if he knows the word, displaying her understanding that the word choice (*doshusei*) may have been problematic for Kei to understand. Kei, as Maya predicted, repeats *doshusei* and then shakes his head to display that he does not know the word (lines 5–6).

At this point, Maya picks up her dictionary and seems as if she is going to look up the word (line 7). However, she puts the dictionary down (Figures 5.17–5.18), and attempts to resolve the non-understanding through her independent explanation (lines 8–39). Although the repair work by Maya is extended over multiple turns with Kei requesting clarification at some points (lines 19, 21), unlike Excerpt 5.5 with fireworks, Maya continues to explain the concept of *doshusei* with minimal scaffolding. In line 40, Kei uses backchannelling to suggest that he has understood, and the conversation moves on to the next topic regarding members of the presentation group.

Kei may not have initiated an outright repair due to the unique concept that Maya was explaining and the fact that he did not have any knowledge of it. Nevertheless, Maya does not abandon the explanation and search-resolving process as she had done previously. Rather, she displays persistence in continuing to attempt to achieve mutual understanding without help from the dictionary or excessive interactive support from the interlocutor. This change cannot be due to her expertise in the topic knowledge, considering the simple concept of 'fireworks' and the more advanced concept of '*doshusei*', regardless of Maya having researched it.

The change described in this section displays the change in Maya's engagement and increased ability in independently resolving her word searches. She demonstrated more autonomy in achieving mutual understanding after her initial failure to locate the word, without extensive scaffolding from the interlocutor. This can therefore be considered as Maya's adaptation and a positive change in her ability to reach a mutual understanding in word search sequences more efficiently.

5.4.3 CHANGE IN PARTNER'S ORIENTATIONS: PREFERENCE TOWARDS PROGRESSIVITY

In addition to the change in Maya's method of resolving word search sequences, a change in Maya's self-positioning as a 'learner' and other-positioning towards Kei as the English language 'expert' was observed. Excerpt 5.8 is from their second recording. Maya is explaining about a video game for studying English that can check pronunciation.

Excerpt 5.8 Maya-Kei May Tells me/pronunciation

```
1  →   Maya:   ah::::  (1.0) da game (0.5) tell tell
2              (0.6)
3  →   Kei:    told me
4  →   Maya:   told me=
5      Kei:    =tells me
6      Maya:   tells   me?
 m                   | gz to K
7              |(0.6)
 k             |quick nod
8      Maya:   ah::m (1.4) pronunshes:(0.3)
9  →           <pronunciate>?
10             |(0.5)
 m             | gz to K
11 →   Kei:    pronuncia:tion
12 →   Maya:   pronunciation (.) is
13 →           (0.3)   noun?
 m                   | gz to K
14             (0.6)
15 →   Maya:   pronunciate (0.6) is verb?
16     Kei:    °mh huh°
17 →   Maya:   pronunciate (0.4) thiss ssentence
18     Kei:    °mh huh°
```

In line 1, Maya displays thinking and trouble searching for a word through hesitation, pauses and repeating of 'tell'. After a slight pause, Kei presents a candidate word 'told me' (lines 2–3). Maya repeats this, when Kei provides a different candidate word 'tells me' (lines 4–5). Maya then repeats this again, but this time with a rising intonation and gazes at Kei, seeking a response (line 6). Kei nods to display acceptance or to confirm the accuracy of the word (line 7). By not questioning Kei's word choice, and repeating it twice, Maya is displaying her lack of linguistic authority. In contrast, Kei is positioned to have more linguistic authority over Maya.

Once the verb ('tells') is agreed on, Maya continues her story telling. However, Maya quickly faces more trouble in selecting a word. She pauses, presents a candidate word 'pronounces' but then provides another alternative 'pronunciate' with a rising intonation and gazes at Kei (lines 8–10), displaying an invitation to take part in the word search (M.H. Goodwin 1983b). Kei repairs with 'pronunciation' (line 11). What is different here from the prior turns is that, in the next turn, Maya asks for confirmation of the part of speech of the word 'pronunciation' and 'pronunciate' (lines 12–15). Once Maya knows that the verb form ('pronunciate') is what she is searching for, she continues her telling. Although 'pronunciate' is not the accurate verb form of 'pronunciation', it is accepted as such in this interaction (Firth 1996; Seidlhofer 2011).

Furthermore, the sequence in lines 2–6, where Maya simply repeats what Kei says with no questioning, and then in lines 12–13 and 15, where she asks Kei for the appropriate form, clearly suggests Maya is lacking confidence in the English language. At the same time, she positions Kei as the English language expert by relying on his other-repair. The sequence demonstrates them both orienting to this particular sequence as a possible language learning and teaching opportunity.

This orientation to the interaction as a learning opportunity was a commonly observed behaviour between Maya and Kei throughout their recordings, especially during the first three months (April, May, June). However, in July, a slight change in Kei's orientation towards Maya's word search sequences was observed. Excerpt 5.9 is from July, the fourth recording between Maya and Kei, approximately 22 minutes into the recording. Maya is explaining about the homework she has from that day's class. Here, we see a change in Kei's orientation towards the sequence as a learning opportunity, while Maya shows no change.

Excerpt 5.9 Maya–Kei July 30 Paragraph

```
1       Maya:    ple- >$please$< (0.4) please (1.0)
2                mention. (0.6)  |°mention?°
m                                | gz to K
3                °please° | (1.2)
m                         | writing gesture
4                write (.) the (1.6) sentence (.)
5  →             |lo:ng sentence.
m                |long gesture
6                (0.5)
7  →    Kei:     |paragraph.
k                |gz right
8                (0.4)
9  →    Maya:    paragraph,
10               (1.0)
11      Maya:    °un.°
                 *yeah*
```

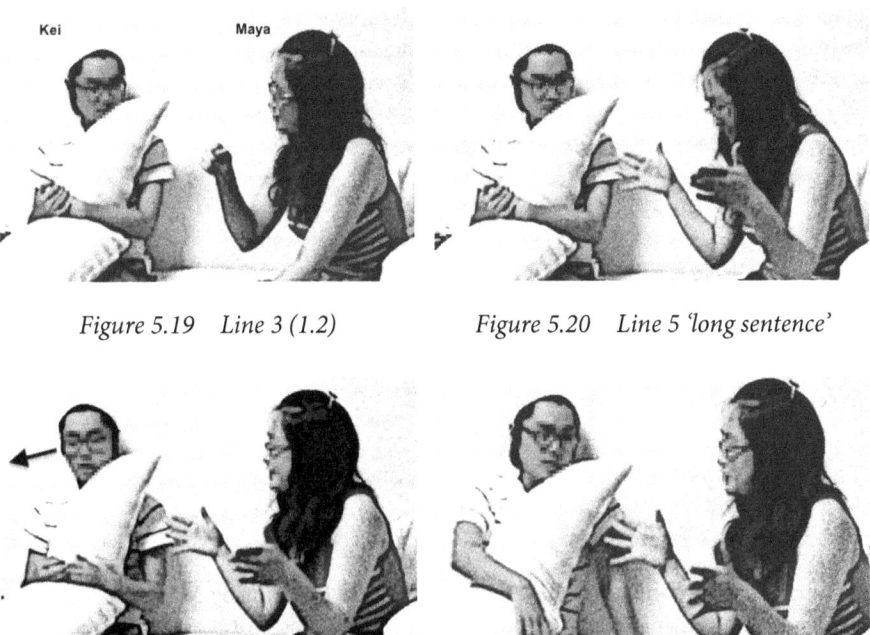

Figure 5.19   Line 3 (1.2)   *Figure 5.20   Line 5 'long sentence'*

Figure 5.21   Line 7 'paragraph'   *Figure 5.22   Line 9 'paragraph'*

After a cut-off and repetition of 'please', Maya has a long pause (line 1). She then says 'mention', but then pauses, and repeats it again with a rising intonation accompanied with a gaze towards Kei (line 2). However, Kei does not respond, and Maya continues the turn by saying 'please' again (line 3). By doing so, it is clear that Maya is searching for a word or thinking of how to phrase her idea in words. In line 3, Maya then uses the gesture of writing in the air (Figure 5.19), then states 'write the sentence'. This is then rephrased as 'long sentence' accompanied with a gesture of describing length with both hands (line 5, Figure 5.20).

Although Kei had been looking at Maya's gestures up till this point, he then looks away from Maya (Figure 5.21) and repairs Maya's prior turn as 'paragraph' (line 7). When Maya repeats 'paragraph', with a slight rising intonation (line 9), although Kei is looking back at Maya (Figure 5.22), he provides no response (line 10) and Maya continues with her story telling.

Comparing Excerpt 5.10 with Excerpt 5.11 (previously introduced as Excerpt 4.20, Section 4.4.2) between Maya and Kei, differences in Kei's engagement with the word search sequences can be identified. In April, as shown in Excerpt 5.11, after Maya provides the candidate word 'underground train', Kei immediately corrects her turn as 'subway', accompanied with gaze and without hesitation. In contrast, in July, after Maya presents her candidate word 'long sentence', Kei does not immediately correct her. Instead, there is a slight pause and Kei looks away just when uttering the repair 'paragraph'. In addition, when Maya repeats the other-correction in April, Kei responds immediately again with an uptake. However, in July, there is no uptake, and Maya continues with her talk after a pause (lack of uptake). Therefore, there is a quite a difference in Kei's engagement with Maya's word search.

Excerpt 5.10 Maya–Kei July 30 Paragraph
```
5    Maya:    lo:ng sentence.
6             (0.5)
7    Kei:     paragraph. ((no gaze))
8             (0.4)
9    Maya:    paragraph?
10            (1.0)
```

Excerpt 5.11 Maya–Kei April Subway
```
5    Maya:    <underground> (.) °train°,=
6    Kei:     =↑subway= ((with gaze))
7    Maya:    =↑subway,=
8    Kei:     =↑uuhhh
```

Thus, it can be concluded that in Excerpt 5.10 in July, during Maya's word search sequence, Kei is displaying a lack of interest in repairing word searches initiated by Maya. As a result, Maya is given the opportunity to self-repair (lines 3–5), and is *not* overtly positioned as the 'language learner' (lines 7–10). Other cases such as this were found in recordings between Maya and Kei during the latter recording sessions.

Approximately 2 minutes after Excerpt 5.10 and 25 minutes into the recording, a clearer case of changed orientations towards talk between Maya and Kei was observed. This sequence was analysed previously in Section 4.4.1 as Excerpt 4.19.

Excerpt 5.12 Maya–Kei July 30 Represent
```
1    Maya:    represent- (0.4) n, present?=
2    Kei:     =>yeah yeah yeah.<=
3    Maya:    =>°↑present repre↓sent,°<
4    Kei:     represent.
5    Maya     like (1.8) in Korea:(0.4) Kim Yona,
```

In line 1, Maya focuses on achieving the 'accurate' word choice by displaying two alternatives, 'represent' and 'present'. In contrast, Kei displays understanding and does not repair Maya until he is explicitly confronted with the two choices of 'present' or 'represent' by Maya the second time (lines 2–3). As a result, compared with the previous segments, there is a clear difference in Kei's orientation towards the talk. That is, while Maya is focusing on learning, Kei is focused on the progressivity of the talk.

This could be due to the fact that this was their fourth (and last) recording together and that Kei has become indifferent to Maya's English language learning. Moreover, as shown from the TOEFL scores, Maya's overall proficiency has slightly improved (Figure 5.2). In Excerpts 5.9 and 5.12, Maya does not self-position herself as a competent user of English and requests repair. Nevertheless, due to the difference in the initial orientation towards the word search sequences, Maya's position as the 'learner' is initially less apparent in the sequences. This is similar to what occurred between Ami and Hang (as discussed in Section 5.3.2), where Hang would not repair Ami unless overtly prompted. The change in Kei's orientation does not prove Maya's development directly, yet it does socially display Maya as a capable speaker.

However, in the same recording and prior to these excerpts, Maya displays confidence as an English language user and defends her word choice as analysed in Section 4.3.5, Excerpt 4.16 ('carp'). Maya was describing the content of the course she had that day regarding environmental chemicals affecting species' reproduction system, and Maya used the dictionary for the first time during a recorded interaction to defend her position and word choice. This suggests that there is a possible emerging change between Maya and Kei in terms of their respective orientations to the conversation and how they display their confidence and certainty of their word choices. Furthermore, Maya displays more confidence and accuracy in her word search sequences, most likely due to the fact that she was the one who attended the lecture. As a result, Kei's engagement in the word search sequences may have been influenced throughout the rest of the July conversation as demonstrated in Excerpts 5.9 and 5.12.

This is similar to the idea of the butterfly effect (Lorenz 1993), that is, that small changes lead to larger-scale changes. The small change in Maya's behaviour towards word search sequences may have led to the change in Kei's orientation towards the interaction and treatment of Maya during word search sequences.

Unfortunately, the two stopped recording together after this and further changes beyond July 2010 could not be analysed, Moreover, when recorded approximately 1.5 years later in January 2012, Maya had completed the required English language classes, moved out of the dormitory, and started studying Korean. As a result, she had not been using English for a while and displayed lack of fluency and confidence in her English use once again. She displayed more requests for repair from Kei, and Kei displayed alignment to this through his responses. This can be seen in the following segment from the recording done in January 2012. The recording was done on campus in an empty office space. Maya is explaining about her apartment owner and his/her unusual behaviour.

Excerpt 5.13 Kei–Maya January 2012 Mentally sick

1	Kei:	>uh< so the owner doesn't like Korean.
2		(0.4) Chinese (.) a:nd Japanese.
3	Maya:	umh::. but owner is Japanese.
4	Kei:	°okay.°
5	Maya:	°umh hh.°
6		|(0.6)
m		|turning finger near head
7	Kei:	°umh.°
8	Maya:	spiritual (0.7) sick?

Excerpt 5.13 Kei–Maya January 2012 Mentally sick (continued)

```
9                 (0.4)
10    Maya:       eh?=
                  *what*
11    Kei:        =mentally sick.
12    Maya:       mentally sick. [un.
                                  *yeah*
13    Kei:                       [mh huh
```

Figure 5.23   Line 6 (0.6)

In line 6, Maya presents a gesture of her finger twirling near the head (Figure 5.23), describing the landlord's unusual or unstable state of mind. Maya then says 'spiritual', but pauses, and presents a candidate word of 'sick' with a rising intonation. By doing so Maya displays her uncertainty regarding her word choice. She then pauses and questions her own word choice with 'eh?' Kei displays his interpretation of this as Maya having trouble searching for the word and inviting him to join. He immediately responds with a correction of 'mentally sick'. Maya then repeats this with a similar intonation to Kei. This sequence is similar to the other-correction sequences shown in Excerpt 5.11 ('subway') from April, with Maya utilising Kei's language ability and expertise to complete the word search and achieve mutual understanding. Moreover, in an interview directly after this recording, Maya shared that she had not been studying English and instead had been studying Korean and Chinese, so her confidence in English had decreased and it took time to express her thoughts in English. These points suggest the non-linearity of development, and the possibility of attrition in English language ability.

5.4.4 ADAPTING TO THE PARTNER'S ORIENTATION: SECURING INTERSUBJECTIVITY

A similar pattern of change in orientation towards the interaction was found between Maya and Yanti. The two conducted their recordings between October 2010 and January 2011. During the first recording in October, especially, orientation to the conversation as a learning opportunity could be observed. Excerpt 5.14 is one example where Maya's orientation to the interaction as a learning opportunity and Yanti as the English language expert is apparent.

Excerpt 5.14 Maya–Yanti October Taught

```
1        Yanti:   nh >I donno< hehehe
2        Maya:    (0.5) be- bery (.) olda: dan you::
3                 (.) >$maybe$< [hehehhe
4        Yanti:                 [hehehhehe=
5   →    Maya:    =heh.hhhh (.) ↓mhh (0.5) she: (.) she
6   →             (0.8) taught (.) °n?°
7                 (0.4)
8   →    Maya:    tea- teached?
9   →             (0.6)
10  →    Yanti:   °taught°
11  →    Maya:    taught? [ehhe
12       Yanti:           [mh
13       Maya:    she taught (.) us (.) nhh Indonesian
14       Yanti:   yeah:
15       Maya:    ↑nhh
```

In line 5, Maya starts a sentence with 'she' but then repeats it, pauses and continues with a candidate word 'taught'. However, she questions her own word choice through a prosody-marked 'n' and pause, displaying thinking. She then self-repairs with 'teached' (line 8). Yanti does not respond right away, but then provides the word 'taught' (line 10). Maya repeats 'taught' with a rising intonation followed with laughter (line 11). Yanti confirms this while overlapping with Maya's laughter, but does not laugh along as she did in line 4. This suggests that this laughter in line 11 is related to Maya, 'treating delicate and potentially embarrassing displays of incompetence as laughable' (Wilkinson 2007: 566). Furthermore, in a similar way to the later months between Maya and Kei, Maya had to prompt support from Yanti in order to receive correction.

The difference in Maya's and Yanti's orientation towards the interaction becomes clearer in the following months. Excerpts 5.15 and 5.16 are from their recording in November. The segment displays the different interactional goals the interlocutors have, with Yanti focusing on progressing the talk, while Maya is focusing on learning.

Excerpt 5.15 Maya–Yanti November Swimsuits

```
1        Maya:    they (0.5) take (0.8) nh,
2                 (0.4) wo (.) <water> (0.3)
3   →             °water° (0.2) clothes?
4   →    Yanti:   ↑MH::::: [°yeah°
5   →    Maya:             [wha wha
6   →             >how do you say<=
7        Yanti:   =ss swim swim
8        Maya:    ah SWIM? (0.5) swim °suit°?
9        Yanti:   swim swimsuits
10       Maya:    swimsuits [mh::
11       Yanti:             [yes
```

In line 3, after hesitation, repetition and pauses, Maya projects a candidate word 'water clothes' with a rising intonation. Yanti shows understanding with a strong backchannelling ('mh') and 'yeah' (line 4). Although Yanti displays that she has understood Maya's prior turn, Maya continues to pursue the exact word she is searching for by using 'what' and 'how do you say' (lines 5–6). Yanti then starts to repair by providing the word 'swim'. Maya then completes this as 'swimsuit' (line 8), which is further repaired by Yanti as 'swimsuits' (line 9). This made the word search a collaborative effort or a co-completion. However, the word search side sequence would not have occurred if Maya had not explicitly initiated it through using 'how do you say'. Up to line 4 in the sequence, Yanti did not show any orientation towards searching for the more 'accurate' word as Maya did. Therefore, Maya is displaying orientation towards learning, while Yanti displays orientation towards progressing the talk, unless there is an explicit request for repair or support in searching for Maya's target word.

In the later months, Maya starts to align to Yanti's orientation towards progressing the talk, rather than starting a word search side sequence. This was found only from their third recording in December onwards. Excerpt 5.16 is from December and the two are talking about Yanti's trip to Kyoto.

Excerpt 5.16   Maya–Yanti December Transportation fee

```
1        Yanti:    Kyoto is so::: expensi::ve [everything like
2        Maya:                                [ah::::
3        Yanti:    da foods en (.) °mm°
4    →   Maya:     (0.5) nara nani (.) traffic (0.5) pay
                   *then what*
5        Yanti:    [yah::::::
6    →   Maya:     [>nani< (.) bus
                   *what*
7        Yanti:    yeah (.) that's too
```

In line 4, Maya starts to give an example of other items that are expensive in Kyoto, that is, the transportation fee. However, Maya pauses, uses '*nara*' (then) and '*nani*' (what) and shows that she is searching for a word. Then she says 'traffic pay' with a pause in between, suggesting lack of confidence with the candidate word. Unlike Kei and similar to the previous excerpt, Yanti displays understanding and acceptance with 'yah' (line 5). Overlapping with this, Maya retries with '*nani*' (what) but only says 'bus' (line 6), which is again confirmed by Yanti (line 7).

This sequence may resemble earlier interactions where Maya relies on Kei's linguistic expertise and scaffolding. However, Maya does not orient to learning by pursuing the conventional English expression. Instead, she self-repairs and uses a more specific form of semantic contiguity ('traffic pay' to 'bus') to secure intersubjectivity. This suggests positive progress in her use of semantic contiguity compared to April (e.g. Excerpt 5.5, 'fireworks', Section 5.4.2) (D. R. Kim, 2020).

To summarise, Maya and her partners demonstrated the following three changes: (1) less reliance on the partner's linguistic resources to resolve self-initiated word searches, (2) the partner's change in orientation towards the word search sequences, and (3) emergence of a new strategy to secure intersubjectivity (pre-emptive repair). Similar to Ami, Maya demonstrated adaptation to the interactional environment of Yanti in securing intersubjectivity through the use of extra turns when there was no explicit repair. Furthermore, through the use of more effective candidate solutions and a change in Kei's orientation to the interaction, Maya also started to display her interactional identity as an 'English language user' rather than an 'English language learner', thus closing the gap in epistemic stance in terms of English language knowledge.

Ami and Maya started their recordings with lower-intermediate level English language proficiency, as shown in Section 5.2. The detailed analyses revealed changes in their interactions and orientations during their word search sequences. One of the changes was the emergence of the L2 speaker's interactional strategies such as the new use of prosody-marked candidate solutions and additional turns to secure intersubjectivity. Another was social changes, in other words, the change in the interlocutor's orientation to the word search sequences and treating the co-participant more as an autonomous English language 'user' rather than an English language 'learner'.

In the following two sections, we analyse the two participants who started with relatively higher English language proficiency, Yoko and Tomoko.

5.5 YOKO'S CASE

Yoko and Shitora were fixed partners for the whole duration of the recording, except for October. Although the two had their own individual bedrooms, there was a sliding door between their rooms. Therefore, although not recorded, it is imaginable that Yoko and Shitora interacted with each other on a daily basis. Yoko also conducted recordings with another partner, Jacy, five times, although she was not the 'fixed' partner. Furthermore, since Yoko was placed into the 'Intermediate English' level of the university English language courses, she only had one semester of English language instruction at the university. In the second semester (starting in October), Yoko enrolled in Thai language classes. There were no substantial changes in Yoko's frequency of use of word search sequences or resolving methods in English. Moreover, there was little change in the orientation of the partner towards the interaction. The changes that were observed regarding Yoko's word search sequences include (1) methods of initiating word searches, (2) knowledge of her partner's culture, and (3) the developing relationship with her partner. These will be described in the subsequent sections.

5.5.1 SUMMARY OF YOKO

Compared with Ami and Maya, Yoko used relatively fewer word search sequences in her recordings. As a result, there was overall low frequency of candidate solutions. With her fixed partner Shitora, Yoko used only a few word search sequences, and very few prosody-marked candidate solutions as well.

As displayed in Figure 5.24, Yoko used an average of 4.75 word search sequences per month with Shitora, and a relatively similar number throughout their eight

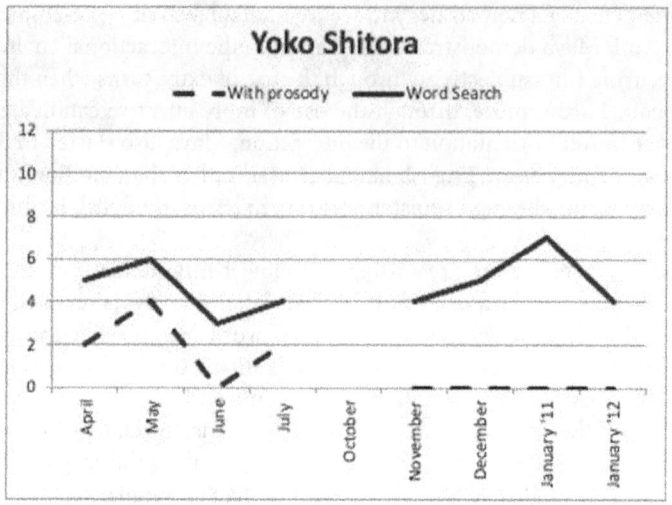

Figure 5.24   Yoko's word search sequences with Shitora

recordings (no recording was done in October). In addition, prosody-marked candidate solutions were not used in the later months of the recordings. Furthermore, possibly due to the overall low frequency of word search sequences, there was little change found in the type of candidate solutions used (Figure 5.25).

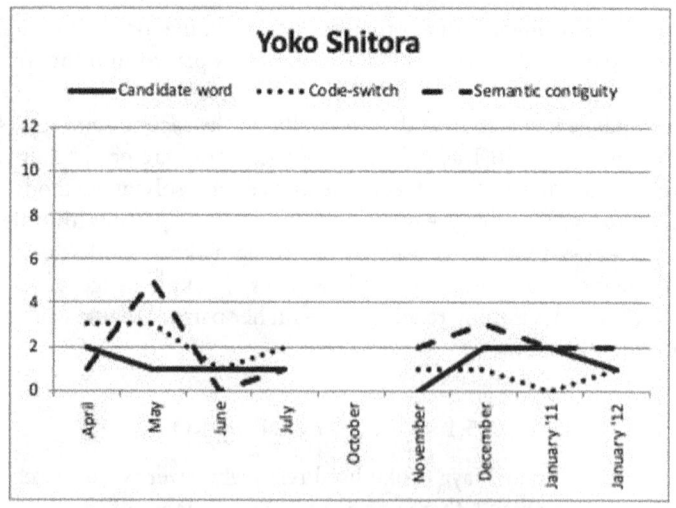

Figure 5.25   Candidate solutions with Shitora

5.5.2 LACK OF CHANGE IN PARTNER'S ORIENTATION

Unlike Ami and Maya, little change was found with how Yoko's fixed partner oriented to Yoko's word searches. Shitora, Yoko's fixed partner from Uzbekistan, frequently used other-initiated repairs in order to display her understanding of the word Yoko was searching for. Excerpt 5.17 is the second recording between Yoko and Shitora in May. Yoko is explaining her family trips during summer vacations. This is an example where Shitora displays her understanding of Yoko's word search, thus engaging in progressing the conversation.

Excerpt 5.17 Yoko–Shitora May Best days

```
1       Shitora:    that's good (1.0) beside you:
2                   don't have so many (0.8)
3                   opportunities to be with your family
4                   (0.3)
5       Yoko:       [mm:
6       Shitora:    [very often (.) [you are he:re
7       Yoko:                       [mm:
8       Shitora:    and your family [is in Kobehh
9       Yoko:                       [mmh:::
10                  yeah
11      Shitora:    yes=
12  →   Yoko:       =very (0.7) mm: (0.7) very:
13  →               (1.3)
14  →   Shitora:    one of the best days
15      Yoko:       ↑yeahh=
16      Shitora:    =aha[ha ha ha .hh ::
17      Yoko:           [yaha ha ha
```

In line 12, Yoko displays difficulty locating the word through repetition of 'very' and multiple extended pauses. After a long 1.3 second pause, Shitora responds to Yoko's difficulty and displays her understanding ('one of the best days') in line 14. This is similar to what Kurhila (2006) calls 'forward looking candidate understanding' where the L1 speaker responds to difficulty displayed by the L2 speaker, and as a result speeds up the conversation. Yoko then confirms this in the following turn. Unlike the interactions between Ami and Hang, and Maya and Kei or Yanti, the 'forward looking candidate understanding' was a common interactional behaviour by Shitora as a response to Yoko's difficulty searching for a word.

A similar situation continues even in December, their sixth recording together, nine months after Yoko entered the university. In Excerpt 5.18, Yoko and Shitora are discussing the education system in their countries. Prior to this segment, Shitora introduced how schools in larger cities in Uzbekistan have better teachers and better education due to the higher salaries.

Excerpt 5.18 Yoko–Shitora December Can receive education

```
1       Yoko:       ↑Ohita    | is not (2.7)       | high level?
y                   gz left---| horizontal hand move| gz S vertical hand
2                   [but
3       Shitora:    [mm hm
y                   ------
4→      Yoko:       | ah::    |(1.4) there're (0.7) >I mean<
y                   | gz up---|circular hand move----------
5→                  | ah:: (0.3) >°nandakke°< (1.5)
                              *what was it*
y                   | stop hand, gz down-----------
6→                  what should I say (0.3) AH::
y                   --------------------------------
7                   | (2.3) ↑everyone
y                   | circular hand move
8       Shitora:    | mhh=
y                   | gz S
9       Yoko:       | =can
y                   | gz up
10                  | (3.7)
y                   | circular >>small fan inward move
11→     Yoko:       | can=
y                   | big fan outward
12→     Shitora:    | =>can receive education,<
y                   | gz S, stop hand ---------
13      Yoko:       | yeah    |can receive education?
y                   | nod---  | small fan inward ---
14                  a:nd (0.5)|↑everyone
y                   ----------| hand up---
15                  | (3.3) is about
y                   | horizontal hand move
16                  | (3.0)
y                   | vertical hand move>> pointing
17      Yoko:       | ss:same
y                   | big vertical hand move
18                  (0.7)
y                   -------
19      Shitora:    ↑mmh mhhm::
y                   ---------
```

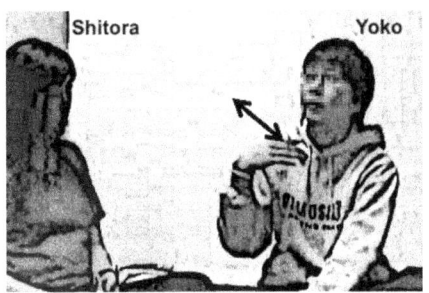
Figure 5.26   Line 10 (3.7)

Figure 5.27   Line 11 'can'

Figure 5.28   Line 15 'is about'

Figure 5.29   Line 16 (3.0)

In lines 4–5, Yoko displays hesitation, pauses and a restart using 'I mean', and word search initiations in Japanese ('*nandakke*') and English ('what should I say'). Yoko tries continuing but shows difficulty completing her statement (lines 7, 10). Shitora indicates that she is listening through backchannelling and a nod, but does not display any candidate understandings at this point. Yoko uses gestures of fanning or accepting by moving her hand towards her (Figure 5.26) then a larger arm movement outward (Figure 5.27). There is no mutual gaze during Yoko's gesture and silence, but Shitora in line 12 displays her candidate understanding of 'can receive education' with a slight rising intonation.

Yoko repeats Shitora's utterance and accepts the candidate understanding, and attempts to add more information 'and everyone'. However, she again demonstrates difficulty locating the target word through the long pauses and multiple gestures (Figures 5.28–5.29). Not until line 17 is Yoko able to articulate the target word, 'same'.

Although lines 14–16 are similar to lines 7–11 in that Yoko displays difficulty in locating a word and uses gesture with no mutual gaze, in lines 14–16, Shitora does not present a candidate understanding. This suggests that Shitora was able to guess 'receive education' not because of attention to Yoko's gestures, but possibly because of the grammar ('not high level but', 'everyone can') and the content of the prior talk ('education'). Therefore, although we have shown that gestures were frequently used during resolving word searches, gestures do not necessarily function as a meaning-providing device by the speaker to the listener in prompting other-repair during word searches. Rather, as Iverson and Goldin-Meadow (1998) have suggested, gestures seem to support L2 production.

Furthermore, these excerpts have demonstrated that forward looking candidate understandings do not only occur with an L1 speaker action towards L2 speakers' word searches, but are also used by L2 speaker peers in ELF interactions. In addition, the interlocutor, Yoko in this case, can then accept or reject the candidate understanding.

5.5.3 EMERGENCE OF THE L3 FOR WORD SEARCH INITIATIONS

As shown in Excerpt 5.18, Yoko is searching for relatively simple words such as 'receive/get' and 'same'. One reason for the lack of change in Yoko's word search sequences and this trouble locating relatively simple and high-frequency words could be due to her starting to study Thai from the second semester, October.

This can be seen from the interactions between Yoko and Jacy, a Thai student. The two conducted their recordings in July, October, November and December 2010 and February of 2011. Yoko was found code-switching between English, Japanese and Thai in these recordings. And in December, Yoko used Thai in initiating an English word search, as displayed in Excerpt 5.19. Yoko and Jacy are talking about a friend who got a good deal buying a new digital camera.

Excerpt 5.19 Yoko–Jacy December Shopper

```
1        Yoko:    Naba:n is good (0.5) shoppin' (0.8)
y                 gz J------------------------------
2 →               good. |(.) °arai na:°,
                        #what's that again#
y                 ------|turn hd, gz forward----
3                 (1.3)
y                 --------
4 →      Jacy:    shopper
y                 --------
5 →      Yoko:    (0.6) good |shopper hh
y                 -----------|turn hd, gz to J, smile
6        Jacy:    mhh hhu hh=
y                 -----------
7        Yoko:    |=>I donno<=
y                 |turn hd, gz forward
8        Jacy:    =he he he[hhh
9        Yoko:             [yah
y                 -------------
10       Jacy:    mm=
y                 -----
11       Yoko:    =maybe:: |(0.3) did (0.6) good (0.7)
y                 ---------|gz up, turn hd to J -----
12                shoppin'
y                 --------
```

In line 2, after a pause and repeating of 'good', Yoko uses '*arai na*' an equivalent of 'what is it' or 'what's that again' in the Thai language. Yoko looks away, displaying an ongoing solitary search, when Jacy presents a candidate understanding of 'shopper' (line 4).

Although Yoko had been identified using Thai with Jacy since their first recording together in October, Yoko would often initiate a word search in Japanese or English. This was the first time that Yoko used Thai to indicate an ongoing word search.

Switching languages from English to Thai only to indicate that there is word search going on suggests two things: firstly, Yoko and Jacy are becoming more comfortable interacting in Thai; secondly, although there is no mutual gaze in line 3, Yoko is requesting Jacy to join the search for the word.

Although code-switching between English and Japanese were frequently found in other participants, Yoko was the only participant who started conversing in and doing word searches in a third language during the video recording. This again is a typical feature of ELF interactions and the ELF environment, where the language choice is not limited to one or two, but many, as long as they are shared language resources. Therefore, the data empirically support Jenkins's (2015) argument for ELF interactions potentially being multilingual.

5.5.4 YOKO'S OVERALL ORIENTATION TO THE CONVERSATIONS

Despite the lack of change in Yoko's use of word search candidate solutions, the partner's orientation towards Yoko's word search sequences, and even Yoko remembering relatively simple English words, Yoko did present some changes through her interactions. These related to learning her partner's culture.

Excerpt 5.20 is from Yoko's first recording with Shitora in April, right after they moved into the dormitory and started living next to each other.

Excerpt 5.20 Yoko–Shitora April Dried fruits

```
1        Shitora:   a:nd different kind of (.) fru:its?
2        Yoko:      mmh:
3   →    Shitora:   a↑hah (0.4) a:nd >fruit< dried fruits
4        Yoko:      mmh: mmh: mmh:
5                   (1.3)
6        Shitora:   and that's all (too thin) (.)
7                   [ha ha ha .hh
8        Yoko:      [↑ha ha hu ha
9                   (1.3)
10       Yoko:      don't you: eat (0.7) ah: (3.0) ↑not
11  →               (0.4) not dri:ed fruits?
12                  (1.0)
13  →    Shitora:   no either are (.) a ↑lot of ahahh
14                  (0.4) fruits.
15       Yoko:      mhh
```

Excerpt 5.20 Yoko-Shitora April Dried fruits (continued)

```
16      Shitora:    in Uzbekistan (0.5).hh a:nd
17                  its not so expensive $like here(h)$
18                  $in$ [$Japan$ hh
19      Yoko:            [↑haha hh
```

In this segment, Shitora is introducing the food culture in Uzbekistan, when she brings up the topic of fruits. She explains that there are different kinds of fruits (line 1), including dried fruits (line 3). Yoko picks up on this and requests clarification whether Uzbeks eat fresh fruits (lines 10–11). Shitora responds as 'no either are a lot of fruits' (line 13). The meaning of this turn is unclear from an outsider (etic) perspective, but Yoko displays understanding through backchannelling and does not initiate further repair (line 15). Shitora then continues to explain the cheapness of the fruits in Uzbekistan compared with Japan.

The next reference to fruits or dried fruits in their talk does not occur until three months later, in their fourth recording together in July. Prior to this segment, Shitora was explaining how humid it is in Japan during the summer compared with Uzbekistan, where it is hotter but dry. This is when Yoko then jokes about the climate in Uzbekistan as presented in Excerpt 5.21.

Excerpt 5.21 Yoko-Shitora July Dried fruits

```
1       Yoko:       >maybe< (0.5) i i:: (.) i in: (0.9)
2                   i: if you: (.) don't use(.) air
3                   conditioner, (.)in Uzbekistan. (.)
4   →               you: will be (.) dry: (0.4) dried
5   →               (0.5) dried fruits?
6                   (1.2)
7       Shitora:    dry fruits?=
8       Yoko:       =mhhuhu no:: .hh hhhh=
9       Shitora:    =[hahaha  HAHHHAHH .hh ha ha]
10      Yoko:        [>just kid-< $just kidding$]
11      Shitora:    Ha.hh:
12      Yoko:       [you'll be]
13      Shitora:    [haha hhah] AHAHAHHA=
14      Yoko:       =.hh $you$:
15      Shitora:    .huhuhuu hh  (.) ma::y↑be .hh=
16      Yoko:       =haha hahh .hh::
17      Shitora:    [$ma(h)ybe(h)$ ha[haaha haha
18      Yoko:                        [hah hhh   hhh
19      Shitora:    but it's impossible.
20      Yoko:       ↑HuHHhh hh:[aha ha ha ha ha ha
21      Shitora:               [↑not to use (.)$air$
22                  $conditioner$ i- if it is fourt-
23                  forty degree:s=
24      Yoko:       =ah:::=
```

Excerpt 5.21 Yoko–Shitora July Dried fruits (continued)

```
25      Shitora:    =or forty five
26      Yoko:       $↑fo:rty$? hahhh
27  →   Shitora:    Ye:s then you will die just there
28      Yoko:       [$die$ >yah yah yah<
29  →   Shitora:    [you'll really (.) you'll ↑really
30  →               become dry [frui:ts right?
31      Yoko:                  [mmhm:: hehhhehaha
32      Shitora:    [>dried fruits<
33      Yoko:       [hehhehh .hhhhehhh hh[hhh
34  →   Shitora:                         [not only ↑dry
35  →               [bu' they're black. hahaha
36      Yoko:       [hhuhuhhh hu .hh hhuhhuhu
```

In lines 1–3, Yoko presents a hypothetical situation 'if you don't use air conditioner' and then jokes 'you will be dried fruits' with a rising intonation. Shitora does not respond right away (line 6) and then initiates a repair by repeating 'dry fruits' (line 7).

Yoko with no gap starts laughing and explains that she is 'just kidding' (lines 8, 10). Once Shitora figures out that it is a joke from Yoko's laughter, she joins the laughter and aligns herself to the joke (e.g., 'maybe' in line 17). Shitora then upgrades the joke that if there is no air conditioner, 'you will die' (line 27), 'you'll really become dry fruits' (lines 29–30), and even 'black' (line 25).

There was no reference to 'dried fruits' in the May and June recordings. However, it is clear that Yoko has referenced 'dried fruits' as explaining Uzbekistan's climate due to her prior knowledge of Uzbekistan food culture, and possibly the previous conversation she had with Shitora. Furthermore, the July interaction demonstrates Yoko's closer relationship with Shitora through the initiation of a cultural joke and alignment from Shitora.

To summarise Yoko's change of word search sequences, her English word search candidate solutions displayed little change. Furthermore, there was little change in the partner's orientation towards Yoko's word search sequences. Therefore, it could be said that there was little development in Yoko's word search sequences. However, Yoko showed change in (1) her expansion in language varieties, by using Thai in initiating word searches, and displaying her newly emerging competence in a third shared language with her partner. This indexed that Yoko had adapted to the interlocutor's language and the interactional environment. Despite the lack of change in her individual English language use, Yoko did display (2) change in her knowledge of her partner's culture, and (3) the development of a closer relationship with her partner where joking about their culture is acceptable. Therefore, although there was no clear 'language development' identified, there certainly was a development in 'knowledge' and the 'interactional environment' as reflected in the interaction.

5.6 TOMOKO'S CASE

In this section, we will analyse the fourth participant, Tomoko. Similarly to Yoko, Tomoko was placed into the 'Intermediate English' level university English language course for one semester. Therefore, in the second semester, she did not enrol in any English language class, and it is unclear if she enrolled in any additional language classes as Yoko did. Tomoko had two fixed partners, Anh and Pham, both from Vietnam. However, Tomoko conducted more recordings with Anh, with whom she shared a room.

Through the analysis, there were no identifiable changes found in the ways candidate solutions were conducted by Tomoko. Tomoko displayed a change that was different from the other three lead participants, that is, showing more reliance on the partner during word search sequences. In addition, although not a longitudinal change, Tomoko responded differently to other-corrections depending on the interlocutor.

5.6.1 SUMMARY OF TOMOKO

Overall, Tomoko used a minimal number of word search sequences throughout the recordings. As displayed in Figure 5.30, Tomoko used very few word searches or candidate solutions with prosody. Furthermore, no clear changes in the use of word search candidate solutions could be identified, nor were there clearly identified changes with the partner's orientations to Tomoko's word searches.

5.6.2 RESPONSES TO PROSODY-MARKED CANDIDATE SOLUTIONS

Despite the few changes in Tomoko's overall word search frequency, there was a change identified in terms of other-orientation to Tomoko's self-initiated word searches. In other words, similarly to Ami's and Maya's partners such as Hang and Kei, Pham's reaction towards Tomoko's word search sequences changed, especially towards Tomoko's prosody-marked candidate solutions.

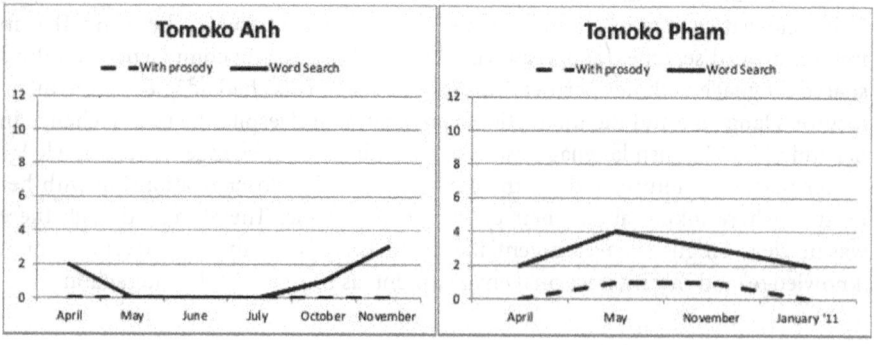

Figure 5.30 Tomoko's frequency of word search sequences

The following excerpt is the first recording made between Tomoko and Pham, right after Tomoko entered the university dormitory. Tomoko is sharing her future dream of living in Austria.

Excerpt 5.22 Tomoko–Pham April Austria
```
1     Tomoko:    someday I wanna li::v in (.) Vienna?
2                (0.4)
3     Tomoko:    >I mean< (.) Austrilia
4     Pham:      ↑mh huh. (0.8) Austria? right.=
5     Tomoko:    =Austrilia (.) not Austa↑railia
6     Pham:      (0.3) yeah Austria.
7                (0.6)
8     Tomoko:    Aus[tria.
9     Pham:         [°yeah°
10    Tomoko:    (0.4) °some° (0.4) ↑music city
11    Pham:      ↑mh huh.
```

In line 1, Tomoko elongates the vowel sound in 'live', with a slight pause afterwards suggesting that she is thinking of the word that follows. She then completes her turn with a prosody-marked 'Vienna'. Pham does not respond right away (line 2). Tomoko then initiates a redo with 'I mean' and completes her turn with 'Austrilia', a pronunciation which could be perceived as a combination of Austria and Australia (line 3). Pham responds to this with backchannelling and then a candidate understanding of 'Austria' with a rising intonation (line 4). Pham does not wait for Tomoko's response to the candidate understanding, and displays her understanding with 'right' (line 4). From this action, it could be interpreted that Pham's candidate understanding ('Austria') was not meant to repair Tomoko's previous turn, but to display her understanding of it.

Nevertheless, Tomoko responds to Pham's utterance as a possible other-initiated repair by repeating 'Austrilia' and comparing it with 'Austarailia' (written here as pronounced by Tomoko) (line 5). By repeating her original pronunciation, and then contrasting it to a different word, Tomoko is displaying her confidence in the word choice she had made, whilst at the same time resisting the possible correction by Pham.

Pham then responds to this by confirming her understanding, at the same time, presenting her version of the word 'Austria' again (line 6). After a slight silence (line 7), Tomoko accepts this as a repair and repeats 'Austria' in a similar way to Pham's version of the pronunciation (line 8). This orienting to and adjusting one's pronunciation mirrors Brouwer's (2004) term 'doing pronunciation', where L1 speakers would repair L2 speakers' pronunciation.

Tomoko continues and attempts to secure mutual understanding through adding information 'music city' (line 10). This is similar to what Maya started to do at the end of her recording sessions, namely adding information in attempting to secure intersubjectivity (see Excerpt 5.16 'transportation fee', Section 5.4.4). Pham then confirms this through backchannelling (line 11). Although very subtle, this sequence can be seen as Tomoko initially resisting Pham's correction, but then accepting it.

A similar case was identified in the following month, as shown in Excerpt 5.23. This was the second recording between Tomoko and Pham. Tomoko is explaining the courses she is currently taking.

Excerpt 5.23 Tomoko–Pham May Introduction

```
1         Tomoko:     an I ha:ve (2.2) AH:ah
2                     |(1.0)
t                     | claps
3  →      Tomoko:     the intransi(.)i'o:f (.)eei pee(.)°yuu°?=
4  →      Pham:       =$ohohoho an introduction$
5                     [$of eei pee yoo: ((APU)) (.)right?$
6  →      Tomoko:     [>$introduction.(.) sorry$<
7                     >$introduction$<
8         Pham:       .hhh [$oh ai see$
9         Tomoko:          [>$ya: introduction of$<
10                    (.) DAT was (.) prii: (.) good
```

Tomoko displays uncertainty and a possible word search through pauses and hedges, followed by a rising intonation (line 3). Pham shows understanding and shares her candidate understanding ('introduction') accompanied with a smiley voice and a tag-question (lines 4–5). By doing so, Pham reforms the other-correction into a less face-threatening display of candidate understanding. Tomoko, however, self-repairs following Pham's previous turn 'introduction', with a fast-paced smiley voice and a 'sorry' (line 6). Tomoko does this while overlapping with Pham and then quickly repeats 'introduction', again with a smiley voice (line 7).

Again, although aligning herself to Pham's indication of a possible mispronunciation of a word, unlike in Maya's case shown in Excerpt 4.10 (Section 4.3.2.1) with 'lace', Tomoko displays a negative reaction to the correction. In Excerpt 5.23, Tomoko self-repairs quickly with a smiley voice, suggesting a display of embarrassment for her mistake (Wilkinson 2007). At the same time, Tomoko says 'sorry' to reformulate the repair as a simple 'mistake' rather than 'non-knowing'. In this way she still maintains her position as a 'knower' of the word.

However, in their third recording together in November, six months after the last recording, Tomoko displayed a different orientation towards Pham and her English pronunciation. This is displayed in Excerpt 5.24. Pham indicated that she would like to visit Okinawa, a Pacific island of Japan, then Tomoko started to share her experience of visiting there.

LONGITUDINAL CHANGES IN WORD SEARCH SEQUENCES   167

Excerpt 5.24 Tomoko–Pham November Swam

```
1      Tomoko:   a::nd (2.1) the-   (.) the           ↑first time
t                gz forward--------|tap finger table|gz to P--------
2                (1.2)   |was (1.2)|with my: family?
t                turn hd |gz down  |tap finger on table -|
3      Pham:     (0.3)   |mh ↑hu:h=
t                        |gz P>>gz down
4      Tomoko:   =when I was ah:(0.4) |fourtee:n? (.)
t                |gz up, tap finger --|draw 14 with finger|
5                |when I was(.) >a junior↑high school< student
t                |gz P, tap finger -----------------------------
6      Pham:     |mh hu:h
t                |gz front
7  →   Tomoko:   (0.7) ↑A:nd (.) I |swom?
t                ------------------|gz P, wave hand
8  →             (1.4)
t                --------
9  →   Tomoko:   °swum°?
t                -----------
p                nod
10     Pham:     |ya:
t                |gz front
11               (1.7)
t                ----------
12     Tomoko:   °hmm° (.) de- ocean was ↑really| beautiful.
t                -------------------------------| gz P
```

Figure 5.31   Line 7 Swom   *Figure 5.32   Line 8 (1.4)*

Figure 5.33   Line 9 Swum   *Figure 5.34   Line 11 (1.7)*

In line 7, Tomoko starts a new sentence 'and I swum' with a rising intonation, accompanied by a gesture that could be interpreted as her doing a small breast stroke (Figures 5.31–5.32). In line 8, when there is no explicit verbal response from Pham but only a slight smile (Figure 5.32), Tomoko speeds up her breast stroke gesture, and repeats 'swum' again, this time with a slightly stronger 'u' sound while keeping eye contact with Pham (line 9). When Pham finally nods (line 9) and gives a verbal response 'ya' (line 10), Tomoko disengages eye contact from Pham and looks away, shows thinking while pausing (line 11, Figure 5.34), and then continues with her story.

Tomoko's action in lines 7–9 is similar to Ami and Hang in Excerpt 5.3 ('gap', Section 5.3.2) and Maya and Kei's case in Excerpt 5.12 ('represent', Section 5.4.3), where Maya and Ami are seeking other- correction or confirmation while their partners orient to progressing the talk. Therefore, when comparing the three sequences (i.e., Excerpts 5.22–5.24) of Tomoko and Pham regarding their orientation towards English pronunciation, it could be understood that Tomoko is displaying less confidence in her word choice and more reliance on Pham's English language expertise.

Tomoko here can be interpreted as regressing in terms of presenting herself as a competent user of the English language. This is different from the previous participants analysed in this chapter, especially with Ami and Maya displaying increasing confidence in their word choices during word search sequences with their fixed partners.

In developmental studies of second languages, there have been few cases that have indicated regression of competence or confidence. Nevertheless, as attrition research has shown, people do forget words and grammar (Cohen 1986; de Bot and Weltens 1995; Weltens and Cohen 1989). As displayed here in this case, confidence and independence of one's word choice in interaction, similarly, can display signs of regression and increase in other-reliance. It is noteworthy that during the first interview with the researcher, Tomoko displayed confidence in her English proficiency and in particular her English pronunciation. She described how she practised repeating lines from movies and looked at herself in the mirror to see her mouth movements while pronouncing English words. However, in and through the ELF interactions over time, Tomoko displayed less confidence in her pronunciation.

5.6.3 LACK OF ORIENTATION AS 'LEARNING OPPORTUNITIES'

Although no direct or clear connections can be made, the lack of change in Tomoko's word search strategies could be associated with her lack of orientation to the conversations overall as learning opportunities.

There were very few word searches between Tomoko and Anh. However, there were cases where Anh would correct Tomoko's word choice or pronunciation. In these cases, Tomoko would display a negative reaction to the other-correction. An example is displayed in Excerpt 5.25. This was the first recording made between Tomoko and Anh in April, and the two are discussing the courses they are taking.

Excerpt 5.25 Tomoko–Anh April Fundamental

```
1     Tomoko:     okay ah:::m (.) >are you in< (0.5)
t                 gz A-----------------------------
2                 fundamental Japane:se?
t                 ----------------------
3                 (.) or intermediate,
t                 --------------------
4                 (0.8)
t                 -----
5     Anh:        first (.) I: (.) s- (.) sta:'ed
t                 -------------------------------
6                 (0.8) °em:° (.) |fou'dation.(0.4) mhh
t                 ---------------|gz forward nod---
7                 |Japanese foundation[class
8     Tomoko:                        [fundam(.)
t                 |gz A-----------------------------
9                 fundation     |sorry=
t                 --------------|gz down
10→   Anh:        |=no fou'dation
t                 |gz A----------------------------
11→   Tomoko:     (0.5)fundation =
t                 -------------------------
12→   Anh:        =>iie< fun jya nai (.) <fou'dation>
                  *no*  *it's not 'fun'*
t                 -----------------------------------
13→   Tomoko:     (0.4) |yah:?|
t                 ------|nod--|
14    Anh:        (0.7)<fundamental> (.) I think it's just
t                 gz A------------------------------------
15                for (0.7) Engliss cla'(.)fundamental
t                 -----------------------------------
16                Engliss (.) fou'dation Engliss (.) then
t                 --------------------------------------
```

Excerpt 5.25 Tomoko–Anh April Fundamental (continued)

```
17                    (.)  chukyu    Engliss  >something like that<
                           *intermediate*
t                     ------------------------------------------------
18                    (0.5) >intermediate Engliss |I mean< ya?
t                     -----------------------------|straighten back
19                    (0.5)
t                     ------
20        Anh:        |it's for e- Japanese (.)>ah<
t                     |turn hd, gz down-------------
21                    it's for Engliss cla'(0.4) Japanese cla'
t                     -------------------------------------------
22                    |'ave a (.) difference
t →                   |gz at nails
23                    |(1.1)
t                     |gz A
```

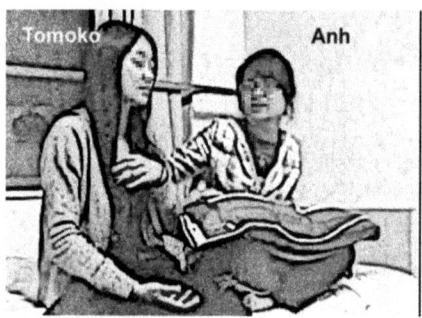 

Figure 5.35 Line 20 Looks away   *Figure 5.36 Line 22 Looks at nails*

Tomoko asks Anh if she is in 'fundamental Japanese' class or not (lines 1–2), and Anh responds that she started in 'foundation' Japanese class (lines 5–7). Tomoko then recognises the difference in the sound of the course name and self-repairs as 'fundation' with a 'sorry' (line 9). However, Anh responds to Tomoko quickly with a clear 'no' and a correction which can be heard as 'foudation' (line 12). Tomoko then presents her version of the pronunciation 'fundation' similar to line 9 again (line 11). Anh, however, rejects this again, this time in Japanese *'iie fun ja nai'* (no, it's not 'fun') and repeats her version of the pronunciation (line 12). Tomoko does not show alignment to Anh's repeated correction, and responds with a prosody-marked 'yah' and nodding (line 13). This displays Tomoko's ambivalent position of questioning the accuracy of Anh's pronunciation or showing listening and letting Anh continue. Anh then continues to explain how the English programme and the Japanese programme have different words for explaining the entry-level class (i.e., fundamental and foundation).

During Anh's explanation, Tomoko displays a loss of interest through disengagement of eye contact (line 20, Figure 5.35), and then looking at her nails (line 22, Figure 5.36). There was no mutual agreement on the pronunciation or word choice of the course name, and Tomoko changed the topic regarding her English teacher once Anh finished her turn.

Therefore, although Tomoko could have oriented to this sequence as a learning opportunity, she decided to opt out and disengage from the interaction. This could have been due to Anh's rather direct correction method or Anh having a less 'native-like' English pronunciation. Nevertheless, Tomoko is displaying lack of interest in and orientation to Anh's other-correction and its explanation. Tomoko's lack of orientation to Anh's corrections and explanations or display of non-interest in Anh's talk were found in other recordings, suggesting that it was a common action taken by Tomoko towards Anh.

Cases were found when Tomoko was not orienting to the possible learning opportunity and not attempting to achieve mutual understanding with interlocutors besides Anh as well. Excerpt 5.26 is an example case of this where Tomoko is introducing the food for the Japanese New Year, but not showing an attempt to achieve a clear agreement on the object she is referring to.

Excerpt 5.26 Tomoko–Lee January Chestnut

```
1 →   Tomoko:   a::nd (1.4) and  kuri?
                                  *chestnut*
t                gz forward------|gz L, round gesture
2                (0.6)
t                ----------
3 →   Tomoko:   ma↑ron?
t                ----------
4                |(2.4)
t                |fold fingers
5     Tomoko:   |maro:n (.)       |[ha::s
6 →   Lee:                        [>yeah I donno.< (.) °that°
t                |big round gesture| gz front>>gz L----------
7                |(0.5)
t                |gz front
8     Lee:      [(                                )
9 →   Tomoko:   [|we (.) >we w'll< (.) >we'll be: able<
t                |gz L-------------------------------
10               to:: rich
t                ----------
11               (1.0)
t                ----------
12    Lee:      [oh.
13 →  Tomoko:   [|>we w'll< be able to be |↑rich
t                |wave finger-------------|touch eye
```

Excerpt 5.26 Tomoko–Lee January Chestnut (continued)

```
14                (1.0)
t        gz L--
15   Lee:         it is kind of (bean)=
t                 ---------------------
16→  Tomoko:      =[marin?
17   Lee:          [beca- because of China: ((continues))
t                 ---------------------------------------
```

Figure 5.37   Line 1 'ku-'   Figure 5.38   Line 1 '-ri'

Figure 5.39   Line 4 'ma-'   Figure 5.40   Line 4 '-ron'

Tomoko in line 1 uses a pause and then a Japanese word '*kuri*' (chestnut) with a rising intonation. The projection of '*kuri*' was accompanied with a hand gesture describing the shape of the nut, although not in the accurate proportion (Figures 5.37–5.38). The use of the prosody and gesturing suggests that Tomoko is aware of the possibility that her partner Lee may not be aware of the Japanese word '*kuri*'.

Tomoko then presents an alternative in French, '*marron*' (chestnut), again with a rising intonation and a similar gesture (Figures 5.39–5.40). However, Lee does not respond to either word, and when Tomoko attempts to continue with her talk, he explicitly states that he does not know the object (lines 4–6). Tomoko, however, does not respond to Lee's statement of non-understanding and continues with her explanation (lines 9, 13). There is no pursuit by Tomoko in achieving or securing accurate mutual understanding through the use of multiple turns and various candidate solutions, unlike what other participants such as Maya did (e.g., Excerpt 5.7, Section 5.4.2).

Lee requests clarification by asking if 'it is a kind of bean' (line 15), and continues to explain a similar culture in China. Tomoko does not respond to Lee's question, but presents a different pronunciation 'marin' (line 16). However, the conversation moves on and the two do not display a mutual understanding of the object Tomoko is referring to (i.e., chestnut).

This sequence could have been an opportunity for Tomoko to learn the English equivalent for '*kuri*' or '*marron*'. Nevertheless, it was not utilised for the purpose, and the two participants displayed their orientation towards progressing the talk, and sharing their different culinary cultures.

Although Tomoko presented herself in the initial interview as a confident speaker with a 'native like' pronunciation, a relatively high overall proficiency level as measured by the TOEFL, and fewer word search sequences overall, she was found regressing in terms of self-confidence and self-reliance during word searches, especially with pronunciation. This may be connected to Tomoko (unlike other participants in this research) displaying a lack of orientation to word search sequences or lexical repair sequences as learning opportunities. She also displayed different orientations towards other-corrections depending on the partner.

To summarise, in Tomoko's case, (1) there were changes identified in the partner's orientation towards the word search sequences, as a result (2) displaying Tomoko as being more reliant on the partner during word search sequences. In addition, although not a longitudinal change, (3) Tomoko exhibited different responses towards other-correction depending on the interlocutor during word search sequences. In other words, there was no 'development' identified in terms of word search sequences in a positive direction. In contrast, there was change found in a negative direction of Tomoko moving her own position from an 'English language user' to an 'English language learner'.

Although no clear correlation could be made between the lack of interest in the interaction as a learning opportunity and her increase in other-reliance during word searches, it can be said that Tomoko did have multiple missed opportunities for language learning through the interactions. In addition, unlike Yoko, we were not able to find any evidence of cultural learning with the fixed partners either. This suggests that Tomoko may have oriented to the video recordings overall as a task to fulfil the researcher's request, rather than a joint interactive moment to exchange ideas or as a learning opportunity of any kind.

Thus, Tomoko's case suggests that 'just talking' does not necessarily lead to 'development', and a conscious orientation to the individual moments in talk as a learning opportunity may be crucial in leading to language or cultural development. This is similar to Hellermann and Pekarek Doehler's (2010) study, where they found different behaviours among the students despite the fact that they were assigned the same task by the teacher. They note, 'learning potentials in task construction hinge on the participants' joint understanding of the task and on how they coordinate their mutual orientations to the task by means of a multitude of verbal and non-verbal resources' (Hellermann and Pekarek Doehler 2010: 42).

In other words, language development through interaction is a mutual and conscious action of utilising 'learning potentials' (Hellermann and Pekarek Doehler 2010), and how participants orient to it may be influenced by their personal agendas and topics of conversation, as well as their relationship with and perceptions of their interlocutor. Therefore, in Tomoko's case, she may have had multiple missed learning opportunities, hence not displaying any development in her word search sequences.

5.7 DISCUSSION: VARIATION AND PATTERNS OF CHANGE

The first part of the chapter analysed the changes in word search sequences of the four participants: firstly in terms of frequency as a group of four, then individually from an emic perspective. From the analysis three major points were identified: individual differences, adaptation to the interlocutor by the participants and changes in the partners.

One of the findings revealed large individual differences within the changes in word search sequences. For instance, while Ami's overall frequency of word searches decreased, Maya's, Yoko's and Tomoko's did not change. Moreover, Maya became less reliant on the partner's linguistic resources, but Tomoko became more reliant.

The analysis also demonstrated the participants' adaptations to the interlocutor. For instance, Ami started to use prosody-marked candidate solutions to test Hang's Japanese ability due to Hang's increase in her Japanese ability. Maya started to add additional turns to secure intersubjectivity during her word searches, possibly related to Yanti's lack of other-correction. Moreover, Yoko displayed her increasing ability in her third language, Thai, which is also Jacy's L1.

These adaptations of the Japanese participants could be associated with their interlocutor's changes during word search sequences. Ami's, Maya's and Tomoko's partners performed fewer other-corrections during the word search sequences over the course of time. As a result, their partners displayed their perspective towards them as an English language 'user' rather than a 'learner'. At the same time, the Japanese participants displayed adaptation to the interlocutor to secure intersubjectivity by using new strategies during word search sequences. Other findings demonstrated cultural learning of the partner, a closer relationship between the interlocutors, and variety in responses depending on the interlocutor. In contrast, Tomoko displayed lack of change in the positive direction compared with other participants in the study, suggesting that her lack of interest in orienting to the interaction as a learning opportunity influenced her degree of change in the type of word search sequences she used, her orientation to word search sequences and her partners, as well as her overall English language proficiency.

Despite accumulating research evidence that context is important and that interlocutors do affect performance in talk, there has been little mention in the literature of how the surrounding language community itself changes around the L2 speakers and how that may affect their performance as a speaker. Developmental studies of interactional competence have not considered sufficiently the impact of the interlocutor and their own changes and development either.

Our findings support the claim that the interactional environment, especially the interlocutor, plays a crucial role in conversation and in development. Furthermore, the effects of the interlocutor became evident through the adaptation of the Japanese participants in their interaction during word search sequences. At the same time, the partners, or the interactional environment itself, displayed changes during the word search sequences. The partners displayed less linguistic superiority in English towards the Japanese participants. As a result in most cases, the participants had fairly equal epistemic stances in terms of English language knowledge. In sum, we were able to observe changes involving the interlocutors, as well as in how both participants treated and positioned each other. We have shown how many changes over time in the four participants' conduct of word searches are adaptations to their interactional environment and partners. From a CDST perspective, the chapter demonstrates that it is possible to study these dyadic interactions themselves as complex systems which adapt over time to changes in the participants, their partners and the environment. We stated in Chapter 1 that our choice of sample, setting and specific focus on word search sequences functions as a test case of how the human interaction engine facilitates communication across cultures and languages involving lingua franca use. Our analyses in Chapters 4 and 5 have demonstrated that the universal mechanism of repair has proven highly adaptable across languages, cultures and settings; we argue that this is possible because of the bedrock of the universal interaction engine. This functions as a homogeneous foundation for human communication which enables everyone to orientate themselves when speaking to people of different cultures, languages and traditions.

The next chapter will compare these findings with CDST principles to determine the extent to which these converge. In Chapter 7, we discuss further how these findings display homogeneity and heterogeneity and consider implications.

6
SEEING HUMAN SPOKEN INTERACTION AS A COMPLEX ADAPTIVE SYSTEM

6.1 INTRODUCTION

We saw in Chapter 4 how a particular cohort of users adapted word search sequences (part of the repair mechanism) to perform their social actions, and to further the progressivity of their talk and their L2 learning. In Chapter 5, we have shown how many changes over time in the four participants' conduct of word search are adaptations to their interactional environment and partners. Our analyses revealed a paradox: the speakers made expert, inventive use of the universal interaction engine to convey sophisticated levels of meaning, even though they are not expert learners of the L2. The analyses in these chapters laid the ground work for the possibility of studying dyadic interactions themselves as complex systems which adapt to changes in the participants, their partners and the environment.

In this chapter, we attempt to show how the interaction engine functions as a complex adaptive system, using two different presentations. We will first demonstrate how the data from this study can be understood from a macro CDST perspective by matching its principles to the results from the CA analyses. We then apply the principles to one short excerpt from the corpus in Section 6.3, explaining how CDST principles are evident at the micro level in its functioning. This also provides a worked-through example of how the CA-CDST approach works. The following ten principles of complex adaptive systems as outlined in Section 2.4.2 will be used as the framework in Section 6.2:

1. Self-organisation and adaptation of many interacting agents.
2. Non-linearity.
3. Surface complexity arising out of deep simplicity.
4. Sensitivity to initial conditions.
5. Complex systems adapt feedback from the environment and from themselves.
6. Complex adaptive systems arise from the interaction of their parts and function as a whole which is more than the sum of its parts.
7. Complex adaptive systems display both homogeneity and heterogeneity.
8. Complex adaptive systems display self-similarity on various scales and levels.
9. There are universal properties of non-linear systems: different systems behave in the same ways.
10. Different systems function on different timescales and timescales interact.

The subsequent sections will relate the findings from the data to these principles and make comparisons.

6.2 MATCHING THE TEN CDST PRINCIPLES TO FINDINGS FROM THE DATA ANALYSES

6.2.1 SELF-ORGANISATION AND ADAPTATION OF MANY INTERACTING AGENTS

This CDST principle relates to self-organisation and adaptation of agents (see Section 2.4.2.1). When seeing the individual participants as agents, adaptation to partner (i.e., the interactional environment) was observed. Ami displayed changes in the reason for her use of prosody-marked candidate words, Maya displayed a new strategy of adding an extra turn to secure intersubjectivity, and Yoko displayed use of Thai in initiating word searches. These adaptations of the Japanese participants can be connected to their partner's linguistic ability or strategies in the interaction. As a result, different adaptations were observed among the participants. In other words, the changes in the Japanese participants during their word search sequences were self-organised and emerged through the interaction rather than from instructions from a teacher. This is consistent with The Five Graces Group's (2009) points regarding the emergent nature of language from human social interactions.

Apart from the participants, it is worth considering what the self-organising interacting adaptive agents are which are employed by the participants in human spoken interaction. We have argued that the interaction engine is employed, the basic mechanisms of which were introduced in Chapter 3, namely turn-taking, sequence, repair, socially distributed cognition, information exchange and topic development. In Section 6.3, we demonstrate, by working through an excerpt, how exactly these interacting agents self-organise, adapt and combine in human spoken interaction. Of course, language plays a major part, but this is studied separately in CDST as a distinct (although intimately connected) complex adaptive system. In this study, our focus is solely on the functioning of the interaction engine, so language is mentioned only peripherally.

In Chapters 3 and 4, we also presented holistic analyses of how the interactants used the interaction engine, language and non-verbal resources to perform their social actions and further the progressivity of their talk and their L2 learning. The analyses have attempted to show this: ultimately, each conversation between the partners is a new self-organisation and adaptation of many interacting agents. We argue that the process of self-organisation, variation, selection and adaptation can best be portrayed in situ by using a combination of CA and CDST perspectives. We further exemplify how this CA-CDST approach can be applied to data in Section 6.3.

6.2.2 NON-LINEARITY

Complex adaptive systems also display non-linearity (see Section 2.4.2.2). As seen from the graphs in Figure 5.1 (Section 5.2.1) of the participants' overall English language proficiency and Figure 5.3 (Section 5.2.2) of their overall initiation of word search sequences, there seems to be a linear change. That is, the participants' overall English language proficiency improved, and their overall frequency of initiation of word search sequences decreased. The simple interpretation of this would be that the participants therefore 'improved' over time.

However, observing the individual participants in detail, wide variations were observed. For instance, when examining the individual TOEFL scores, there is a wide variation, with Ami increasing dramatically while Tomoko hardly changed. This is similar to Larsen-Freeman's (2006) analysis of her participants' writing skills: whilst overall improvements were found, there were also large individual differences in their developmental patterns. Moreover, some changes were not always progressive, but at times regressive. With regard to the interactional sequence and orientations, Tomoko displayed an increase in reliance on her partner Pham's linguistic ability to confirm her word choices. In contrast, other participants demonstrated a decrease or no change in their reliance on their partner in resolving their word searches.

Therefore, the non-linear nature of language development can be identified in the data, and this non-linear nature helps explain the wide range of changes among the participants. Despite all four Japanese participants living in a similar ELF university dormitory environment as first year university students, diverse results in tests and development of interactional competence were observed after one academic year.

6.2.3 SURFACE COMPLEXITY ARISING OUT OF DEEP SIMPLICITY

The third principle, closely related to non-linearity, is complexity arising out of simplicity (see Section 2.4.2.3). The data demonstrated that word search initiations have relatively simple and rudimentary patterns of a universal and simple use of pauses, hesitation markers and gaze. Yet, this can lead to (1) large differences in the sequential patterns, (2) variation in candidate solutions among the participants, and (3) complex changes over time in and through the interactions.

More specifically, in the case of Maya in Excerpt 4.16 (Section 4.3.5), she initiated a word search for the word 'carp' using repetition, pause and rising intonation. However, rather than having the word search sequence complete with Kei's exposed correction as in Excerpt 4.20 ('subway', Section 4.4.2), the sequence moves on to a more complex negotiation of the accuracy of the word choice and pronunciation, leading Maya to use her dictionary to defend her word choice. Similar points can be made about the participants' developmental patterns. Although the word search sequences were initiated in a similar pattern, as time passed participants developed various strategies for resolving the word search. For instance, Ami started to use prosody-marked candidate words to check Hang's comprehension rather than to elicit confirmation (Excerpt 5.4 *'mogiten'*, Section 5.3.3), while Maya started to add extra turns after the partner's backchannelling as a means of securing intersubjectivity

(Excerpt 5.16 'transportation fee', Section 5.4.4). These were individually unique changes that were identified only with these particular participants. These examples thus demonstrate that a variety of word search negotiation sequences and changes can arise from a similar and simple word search initiation pattern.

The basic mechanisms of the universal interaction engine are stated with deep simplicity in 'context-free' or general terms in Chapter 3. We then showed in Chapters 4 and 5 how these mechanisms were employed in a 'context-sensitive' or particular way to perform diverse, heterogenous social actions in a superdiverse intercultural setting. It is precisely because speakers are able to match the surface complexity and diversity of the interaction to the deep simplicity of the interaction engine bedrock that they are able to make sense of each other's social actions and maintain intersubjectivity. People orientate themselves in spoken interaction by matching deeply simple mechanisms to surface complexity and diversity, and CA methodology is able to mirror for us how exactly this functions.

The complex adaptive system of the interaction engine provides the deep simplicity bedrock which enables speakers of differing languages from different cultures to understand each other when they meet (Levinson 2006: 40). Our study provides a microcosm of how this works. We follow speakers of different L1s using ELF to perform their social actions using the universal mechanism of repair (specifically word search sequences) to fix trouble so that they can perform their social actions.

6.2.4 SENSITIVITY TO INITIAL CONDITIONS

Sensitivity to initial conditions means that small changes in one or more components of the system can lead to large differences in the behaviour of the system as a whole (L.B. Smith and Thelen 2003) (see Section 2.4.2.4). The data of this study also indicated that participants are sensitive to initial conditions, particularly to their respective overall proficiency levels.

Although the relation of cause and effect cannot be proven, one possibility is that the difference in the participants' proficiency level at the start of joining the ELF environment may have influenced the changes of the participants. Ami and Maya displayed expansion in their range of candidate solutions, while Yoko and Tomoko displayed minimal change. One of the similarities between Ami and Maya, and Yoko and Tomoko is their overall language proficiency, which also influenced their placement in the university English language programme. This aligns with CDST research in SLA where studies have found participants with higher proficiency showing less variation within group and smaller changes over time, while participants with lower proficiency show wider variation within group and larger improvements over time (e.g., Gui et al. 2021).

Moreover, when considering the partner as a condition, the participants displayed different interactional sequences and orientations depending on whom they were talking to. Although at a similar recording time, Tomoko displayed different orientations towards the interaction when the partner was Anh, rather than Pham, who had relatively more knowledge of the English language and more experience abroad. Tomoko displayed orientations towards learning during word search sequences when talking with Pham, while ignoring Anh's repair and not displaying orientation to learning when talking to her.

In sum, initial conditions in terms of the participants' proficiency level at the beginning of the recording and the interactional environment seem to contribute to a wide range of differences through the interaction and over time.

6.2.5 COMPLEX SYSTEMS ADAPT FEEDBACK FROM THE ENVIRONMENT AND FROM THEMSELVES

Complex adaptive systems are 'open systems' (J.H. Brown 1994; L.B. Smith and Thelen 2003) and are constantly adapting based on feedback (see Section 2.4.2.5). As discussed earlier in Section 6.2.1, participants respond to their partner's reactions (i.e., the interactional environment) sensitively. For example, Ami showed recognition of Hang's increase in her Japanese ability through the use of *'suppai'* (sour) in Excerpt 4.8 (Section 4.3.1.2), and possibly used a Japanese word *'mogiten'* (store/booth) in Excerpt 5.4 (Section 5.3.3) in resolving her word search, despite knowing how to explain it in English. However, when she notices that Hang does not understand, Ami readjusts her candidate solution method and explains in English. In short, Ami is adapting based on the feedback she is receiving from Hang, who is also changing. Ami notices the change in the interactional environment based on the feedback she receives (e.g., Hang knowing Japanese, e.g., *suppai*), adapts her candidate solution method and applies it in the interaction (e.g., using Japanese, *mogiten*), receives feedback again (e.g., Hang does not understand the Japanese word), and adapts to the feedback again (e.g., using English, shop).

Other examples of this principle can be found in one interactional sequence. In Excerpt 4.22 ('experience', Section 4.4.3), Ami responds to the lack of feedback from Hang and presents alternative strategies to achieve mutual understanding. First, Ami starts with 'what things' with no rising intonation, then adjusts to 'what thing' with prosody followed by 'do you like the best, 'and then 'what happened'. When Hang suggests 'experience' as a candidate understanding, Ami adapts and uses it, which is then followed by Ami's change of state token ('ah'), displaying 'learning' or cognitive adaptation.

As an example of adaptation to feedback through the word search sequence, there were multiple cases of vocabulary learning. Below is an example after the segment of 'language learning' on 'fireworks' as analysed in Excerpt 5.5 (Section 5.4.2). Excerpt 6.1 shows a sequence from Maya and Yanti from October, six months after Maya encountered the word 'fireworks' when talking with Kei. In Excerpt 6.1, we see Maya using 'fireworks' in a new context (new sentence, new partner), as well as doing an embedded correction while responding to Yanti's confirmation request.

Excerpt 6.1 Maya–Yanti Oct Fireworks

```
1    Maya:    ↑ah:::n (.) ↓den (0.4)
2             you should >you should< go: (0.2)
3             da: festival of (0.8) fireworks?
4    Yanti:   (0.5) °↑ah° >firework?<
```

Excerpt 6.1 Maya–Yanti Oct Fireworks (continued)
```
5    Maya:     fireworks ah:: (0.5) decemba
6              (0.6) °twenny° (0.6) three and
7              (0.4) twenny four?
```

Therefore, adaptation to feedback was observed in one segment of the talk, as well as over time through several discussions. Furthermore, the multiple adaptations to the interactional environment by the participants demonstrates that the interactions between the dyads are 'open systems' and that the language and interaction are influenced by the speakers' surrounding interactional environment.

6.2.6 COMPLEX ADAPTIVE SYSTEMS ARISE FROM THE INTERACTION OF THEIR PARTS AND FUNCTION AS A WHOLE WHICH IS MORE THAN THE SUM OF ITS PARTS

In CDST, 'much comes from little' (Holland 1998) and the whole can be more than the sum of its parts (see Section 2.4.2.6). This study provides an example of how human spoken interaction, examined through the lens of word search sequences, functions as a complex adaptive system. Through the analyses we have demonstrated how various components of interaction are involved in the interactional activity of repair and in its changes of use over time: the speakers' language background and proficiency, the interactional situation, the ongoing conversation topic, the word that is being searched for, and the strategies employed during word search sequences.

We have seen how the specialist repair mechanism of the word search sequence adapts itself to a dual function in this setting, dealing with both progressivity of talk and L2 learning goals. We have also considered how the mechanism of repair adapts itself over time to the business of informal language learning talk, which involves both social actions and L2 development. The data show that use of the word search mechanism by participants tends to decrease as their proficiency increases, a phenomenon already familiar in the literature. Notably, for certain participants, the changes in the word search sequence reflected the shift in their role within the interaction, transitioning from a perceived 'language learner' to a proficient 'English language user'. In other words, this suggests that the whole is more than the sum of its parts.

The overall picture is that spoken interaction in this setting involves the interplay of many components; some of these are in an inversely proportional relationship, as in the above example, whereas others are in a proportional relationship, as with the overall increase in lexical range over time, as exemplified in Excerpt 6.1.

6.2.7 COMPLEX ADAPTIVE SYSTEMS DISPLAY BOTH HOMOGENEITY AND HETEROGENEITY

A specific contribution of this volume is that the CA-CDST approach provides a means of explicating and conceptualising the complementary scales or levels on which an instance of spoken interaction can be viewed, as well as its simultaneous heterogeneity (or particular nature) and homogeneity (or general nature) (see Section 2.4.2.7). This involves portraying any instance of spoken interaction as having a complex personality, as simultaneously displaying both homogeneity and heterogeneity and functioning on a number of different levels at the same time.

As mentioned previously, there were similarities in the word search initiation methods and the candidate solutions used among the four core participants. The use of candidate words, code-switching to Japanese, semantic contiguity and gestures to resolve self-initiated word search sequences was common to all the participants (see Section 4.3). Nevertheless, the outcomes of the word search varied. Some sequences became learning opportunities (e.g., Excerpt 5.1 'light pink', Section 5.3.2), while others did not (e.g., Excerpt 5.25 'fundamental', Section 5.6.3). Similarly, the reaction by the partners to the candidate solutions differed: some oriented to 'teaching' with exposed correction (e.g., Excerpt 4.20 'subway', Section 4.4.2), while others displayed minimal response to the non-standard English use until prompted for other-repair (e.g., Excerpt 5.15 'swimsuits', Section 5.4.4). Despite the sequences having similar patterns as displayed above (Section 6.2.6), with Speaker A initiating the word search and then attempting to resolve it, and Speaker B providing uptake, no two sequences were identical. In other words, word search sequences display both homogeneity and heterogeneity.

There is always a tension between a description of an excerpt of interaction as a unique occurrence, locally produced by the participants, a description of it as an example of interaction within a particular setting, for example informal dormitory talk, and a description of it as an example of human spoken interaction. All three levels of scale are simultaneously manifested in an excerpt. Our CA-CDST analyses in Chapters 4 and 5 are intended to illustrate how the interaction displays both homogeneity (general features) and heterogeneity (particular features) at the same time: in Section 6.3 we provide an exemplary analysis.

On the micro (CA) level, the particular word search produced is variable. We view the interaction as a singular occurrence and the emphasis is on heterogeneity. On an intermediate level, the particular word search has some features in common and some differences compared with other word searches which have occurred in the dormitory setting of Chapter 4. There is a balance in focus between homogeneity and heterogeneity. On the macro (CDST) level, the interaction produced has general or universal features in common with all other instances of word searches, which is the focus we find in Section 4.1; at that level of scale, the emphasis is on homogeneity. All three levels are present in talk at all times, but the lens adopted will tend to focus our attention on a different level of scale. With the model detailed here, the micro level, the intermediate level and the macro level can all be analysed and portrayed simultaneously, with each level feeding the other reflexively. The model thereby provides the basis for this study's empirical finding that all instances of word search have the same general properties and use the same basic sequence organisation, whilst at the same time portraying the extreme diversity, fluidity and complexity of their particular manifestations.

The interaction engine provides a universal bedrock of deep simplicity and homogeneity onto which a heterogenous range of languages and lects can be overlaid in a range of contexts and cultures. The combination of interaction engine and language provides the balance between homogeneity and heterogeneity which enables intersubjectivity to be maintained whilst cultural diversity is enabled. As we have shown in Chapters 4–5, the same interaction engine can be adapted by speakers of different languages to achieve intersubjectivity in intercultural/ELF interaction in a superdiverse setting.

6.2.8 COMPLEX ADAPTIVE SYSTEMS DISPLAY SELF-SIMILARITY ON VARIOUS SCALES AND LEVELS

Our empirical study has focused specifically on word searches as a prominent phenomenon in both the interactional corpus and the literature. From the CDST perspective, it is vital to consider fractal relationships between the important interactional phenomena and macro-level structures. In Section 3.6.2, for example, we saw how the IRF cycle is a fractal of the overall organisation of L2 classroom interaction. The word search sequences also displayed fractal features (see Section 2.4.2.8).

When resolving word searches, they were always in adjacency pairs, such as question and answer or initiation and repair, which then became part of a word search sequence. Several of these word search sequences, on a larger scale, can then be seen as a longer interactional sequence or a conversation. Let us take Excerpt 6.2 (analysed previously as Excerpts 4.19 and 5.12) as an example as shown below. Lines 1 and 2, and lines 3 and 4 can be understood as adjacency pairs of checks and confirmations, characterised by a rising intonation after a candidate word, which in turn prompts an affirmative response ('yeah') or repetition of the candidate word. These two adjacency pairs together can then be understood as a word search sequence involving an initiation and confirmation.

Excerpt 6.2 Maya–Kei July 30 Represent

```
1  Maya:  represent- (0.4) n, present?=
2  Kei:   =>yeah yeah yeah.<=
3  Maya:  =>°↑present repre↓sent,°<
4  Kei:   represent.
5  Maya   like (1.8) in Korea:(0.4) Kim Yona,
```

Fractal features of word search sequences were observed on a different scale as well. For example, we have shown Yoko developing a 'new way' of initiating a word search using Thai (Excerpt 5.19 'shopper', Section 5.5.3), mirroring the language use environment at different levels: it mirrors Yoko's increasing proficiency in Thai (micro), the interlocutor (Jacy) who is a native Thai speaker (intermediate), as well as the multilingual interactional environment of the superdiverse community of the international dormitory (macro). Moreover, the way Yoko uses '*arai na*' mirrors the way she initiated a word search in Japanese (e.g., '*nandakke*' in Excerpt 4.3 'teach', Section 4.2.2; '*nanyaro*' in Excerpt 4.5 'snacks', Section 4.3.1.1) and English (e.g., 'what should I say' in Excerpt 5.18 'Can receive education', Section 5.5.2). These are therefore displaying fractal features. In Section 6.3, we further highlight an innovative adaptation of the word search sequence by Ami. Word search sequences therefore seem to display cohesive patterns through self-organisation and by displaying self-similarity on different scales and levels.

Scale is vital for understanding complex systems: using the lens of scale, many different phenomena show a remarkable similarity in the ways they are organised and function (West 2017). The concept of scale is vital not only to CDST, but also to understanding how human spoken interaction functions and in particular to understanding the complex personality of any instance of interaction. In this study, we have shown that the twin lenses of CA and CDST are not only compatible for the portrayal of spoken interaction, but they also enable analysis on the micro and macro scales at the same time. The functional explanation as to why this should work is as follows. We have argued that CA is a fractal of CDST and their principles are compatible; as CDST is a meta-theory and CA a highly empirical narrow-focus practice, they are the same approach operating on different scales (see Chapter 3). As we saw in Chapter 1 with Gleick's (1993) example of snowflakes, complex systems display simultaneous homogeneity and heterogeneity; the degree one finds depends on the lens employed.

A specific contribution of this volume is that the combination of CA and CDST provides a means of explicating and conceptualising the complementary scales on which an instance of spoken interaction can be viewed, as well as its simultaneous heterogeneity (or particular nature) and homogeneity (or general nature). Scale is then key to understanding how human spoken interaction functions as a complex adaptive system; any instance of talk can be seen on multiple scales or through multiple lenses. What is the relationship between scale and homogeneity/heterogeneity? The largest or macro scale displays the homogeneity or general characteristics of the talk, whereas the smallest or micro scale displays the heterogeneity or particular features. In Section 6.3, we illustrate how all of these elements and scales can be revealed in a data analysis.

6.2.9 THERE ARE UNIVERSAL PROPERTIES OF NON-LINEAR SYSTEMS: DIFFERENT SYSTEMS BEHAVE IN THE SAME WAYS

The interaction engine is a complex adaptive system related to and interlocked with many other complex adaptive systems which have the potential to engage with other complex adaptive systems at all scales throughout life on Earth. From this perspective, it is clear that non-linear emergent systems behave in similar ways at different scales (see Section 2.4.2.9). We have argued that human spoken interaction behaves in the same fundamental ways as other emergent systems. As humans have evolved together with other life forms in the same planetary ecosystem, it is inevitable that networks and systems involving humans are remarkably similar (West 2017) to those involving other life forms.

However, this CDST principle can be the most difficult one to relate to on a human level. People may believe that human beings have free will, agency and intelligence to make their own choices in terms of spoken interaction and behaviour. So how could people accept that human spoken interaction and behaviour could possibly follow the same principles which govern the development of locust populations, snowflakes and the weather? People may complain that humans are so much more advanced and conscious than anything in nature and that this principle makes humans sound like automatons. The above complaint is contradicted by our study (and Section 6.3). This has shown that the combined power of the interaction engine and language enables agency, creativity, imagination and heterogeneity in talk, whilst retaining the systematic homogeneity required to make talk comprehensible to each other. The similar functioning of the interaction engine and non-human systems does not stifle our individuality or creativity; rather, it provides the homogeneity against which the heterogeneity can be understood. In Chapters 4 and 5, we have demonstrated the range in the English language proficiency of the participants, the difference in frequency of the word search sequences initiated, the diversity of conversational topics, and the various interlocutors the Japanese participants conversed with. Yet, the participants demonstrated use of common word search initiation strategies and candidate solutions to resolve word searches, indicating certain universal properties.

6.2.10 DIFFERENT SYSTEMS FUNCTION ON DIFFERENT TIMESCALES AND TIMESCALES INTERACT

The final principle pertains to the notion of time and different timescales functioning at different levels and timescales interacting. We have seen the participants displaying 'learning' of a new word or concept in a matter of seconds through the word search sequences. The cause and effect are easily identified within the interaction. In contrast, the changes to the use of word search markers and self- and other-positioning during word search sequences seem to evolve over longer stretches of time. Moreover, the causes of the changes are more difficult to identify, and at times the changes seem to emerge suddenly. The changes in their increased lexical knowledge may be connected to the increase in their overall English proficiency score (see Section 5.2.1), which is also changing on a different timescale. Therefore, when analysing the development of features of discourse, one must take into account the complexity of the feature itself and its individualistic and non-linear developmental patterns. In other words, development does not occur in stage-like progression; rather, changes occur over different timescales (de Bot 2014; Lemke 2000; L.B. Smith and Thelen 2003).

6.3 HOW DO ALL THE COMPONENTS COMBINE IN SPOKEN INTERACTION?

So far in this chapter, we have taken a more macro view of interaction and demonstrated how the ten CDST principles (see Chapter 2) can be observed in the corpus of L2 interaction in an ELF context, analysing the narrow and wide perspectives of word search sequences used between the pairs, as a cohort and community, and across time. In this section, we focus on a single short excerpt and provide a worked-through illustration of how all of the mechanisms of human spoken interaction (identified in Chapter 3) combine to enable speakers to perform their social actions and maintain intersubjectivity. In addition, we show how speakers make use of the mechanisms of human spoken interaction. From the macro CA-CDST perspective, we aim to reveal how the diverse elements of a complex adaptive system combine and how the characteristics of complexity manifest themselves in spoken interaction. We are also providing a detailed example of what a micro CA-CDST analysis of human spoken interaction looks like.

6.3.1 INTRODUCTION TO THE ANALYSIS

We now analyse a very brief and familiar excerpt from Chapter 5 (Excerpt 5.1, Section 5.3.2) in which we see an example of a word search during the first three months of recordings. Ami is talking about her nail polish, purchased during a trip to Korea. This excerpt exemplifies how a language learning focus is talked in and out of being during social talk.

Excerpt 6.3 Ami–Hang June Light pink

```
1     Hang:   so wh- (.) ↑which colour,
2             you buy (0.3) in Korea?
3     Ami:    (0.4) ah- (.) ↑hmm (.) like (.) a pink?
4             but (.) .suu mhh ↑nea:r the hwhi:te.
5     Hang:   ↑ah::=
6             Ami: =hmm=
7  →  Hang:   =↑light (.) pink.
8  →  Ami:    light pink,
9  →  Hang:   ↑hmm=
10    Ami:    =↓ah
11    Hang:   ↑°ah::°
12    Ami:    [°light pink°
13    Hang:   [°light pink°
14    Ami:    I think it's (.) cute
```

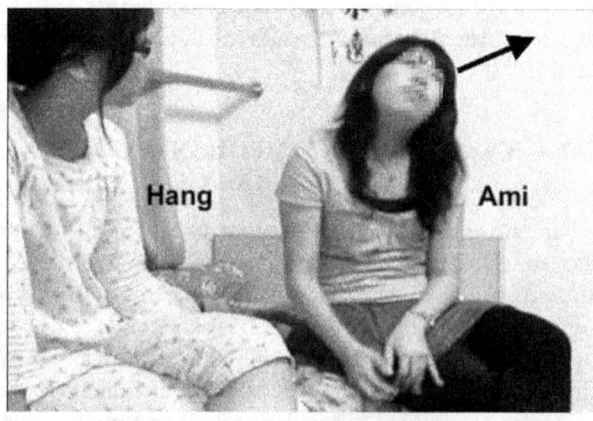

Figure 6.1   Line 3 'hmm'. An embodied display of 'thinking'

In line 3, Ami uses a false start ('ah', 'hmm') and gazes upwards, an embodied display of thinking or searching for the correct word (Figure 6.1). She then provides an approximation token 'like' (Fuller 2003) and then a semantic contiguity (Kurhila 2006) of the colour ('pink but near the white'), attempting to provide a direction for her word search (lines 3–4). Hang then shows understanding through 'ah' (line 5). However, Hang does not stop here, but provides other-repair of this trouble by displaying her understanding of the colour as 'light pink' (line 7) with a clear enunciation and stress on each word. Ami displays uptake of this other-repair through repeating the word twice, the first time confirmed by Hang and the second time softly but in a choral co-repetition with Hang (lines 7–8, 12–13). Although Hang had displayed that she had understood Ami, Hang repeats the target word, which is simultaneously co-repeated by Ami. Choral co-repetition demonstrates agreement (Lerner 2002: 226) and in this case (lines 12–13), it also confirms that the language learning trouble has been successfully concluded, which means that Ami can return to the original social talk focus in line 14. In lines 3–13, the participants briefly develop a language learning focus and a speech exchange system which is appropriate to that focus. Ami and Hang jointly develop a focus on vocabulary and specifically on a colour which Ami phrases as 'like pink', 'but near white'. Hang agrees to this focus by suggesting 'light pink' in line 7 as the target vocabulary item, and the repetitions in lines 8, 12 and 13 display the mutual understanding that the language learning cycle has been successfully negotiated.

6.3.2 HOW THE MECHANISMS ARE ADAPTED

We now examine how the mechanisms of human spoken interaction which we introduced in Chapter 3 co-adapt themselves in this excerpt to enable the participants' social actions. We explained previously that **turn-taking** and **sequence** are mechanisms for displaying and checking mutual understanding, and the organisation of **repair** is a mechanism for repairing breakdowns in mutual understanding. The mechanisms of **socially distributed cognition, information exchange** and **topic development** relate to the progress and flow of intersubjectivity. In the last excerpt, the mechanisms of **turn-taking** and **sequence** combine in Hang's line 1 question to expect an answer in line 3. Ami's answer in line 3 shows hesitation and trouble. Her answer is designed not only to be maximally informative (given her lack of knowledge of the target L2 word) but also to self-initiate **repair** by framing a word search. In terms of **socially distributed cognition**, she displays her lack of knowledge, or K- status from the **information exchange** perspective. The careful design of her turn enables Hang to display K+ status in relation to the target word in line 8. The choral co-production in lines 12 and 13 demonstrates that epistemic exchange has been achieved, trouble repaired and a full answer provided, so a return to **topic** in social talk is warranted in line 14.

The analysis demonstrates not only **what** understandings the interactants display to each other, but also **how** they do so by normative reference to the interactional mechanisms. The interactional mechanisms adapt themselves to mirror the social actions and socially shared cognitive displays of the participants. In other words, we as analysts gain access to their displays of understanding to each other in the same way that the participants gain this access, that is, by reference to the interactional mechanisms; this is a mirroring procedure on all levels.

6.3.3 TWO EMERGENT PHENOMENA: EPISTEMIC NARROWING AND CHORAL CO-PRODUCTION

We now examine two phenomena which are emergent, that is, they are not planned in advance and emerge creatively through the participants' initiative in the flow of interaction. They do not occur often in the word search sequences in our corpus, but they do co-occur in this very short excerpt.

The first phenomenon we examine is '**epistemic narrowing**', a type of semantic contiguity. As stated above, the participants display in their own turns their analyses of the evolving relationship between language learning focus and interaction, that is, how the language learning focus relates to the turns produced. Ami displays in lines 3–4 the wish to establish a language learning focus on a target vocabulary item through two phrases involving colour: 'like pink', 'but near white'. This specific phrasing of two concepts very neatly performs multiple actions simultaneously. It foregrounds the two concepts, to enable Hang to provide the target item of 'light pink'. It also sets up the language learning focus as being on a target vocabulary item and hence starts off the speech exchange system of the word search. It also narrows the epistemic gap for Hang.

One of Sacks's (1992: vol. 2: xxviii) key methodological precepts was to ask 'for which problem is this specific action a solution?'[1] In this case, the epistemic problem which Ami has is that she does not yet know the correct word in L2 English for the exact colour of her nail polish (namely 'light pink'). However, she does know a number of more common colour-related terms in L2 and she can attempt to use the joint resources of the interaction engine together with Hang (who has higher epistemic status in L2 than Ami) to learn the target word. Therefore, Ami's turn in lines 3–4 ('like (.) a pink? But (.) .suu mhh ↑nea:r the hwhi:te.') performs simultaneously a number of actions and solutions on a number of levels at the same time. It provides a maximally informative answer to Hang's question in line 1, given that Ami's L2 level is not high enough to find the precise term. It also self-initiates other-repair; note, though, that this is not explicitly requested, since the linguistic formatting is that of an answer. However, the turn also provides what we term '**epistemic narrowing**', in that it implicitly suggests an epistemic gap and provides clues as to what the target lexical item might be which would provide epistemic fulfilment, namely a shade of pink near the white.

Hang displays understanding that a new language learning focus has been talked into being in line 5 with elongated '↑ah::'. What is required in this new focus is for Hang to take a turn and to specify the required target vocabulary item, which Hang successfully delivers in line 7 with a clear enunciation and stress on each word. This

---

[1] For example, 'How to avoid giving help without refusing it (treat the circumstance as a joke)' (Sacks 1992: vol. 2: xxviii).

is then mirrored by Ami in lines 8 and 12, signifying recognition, acceptance and uptake of the target word search item, confirming that the language learning talk cycle which she initiated in line 3 has been successfully concluded. What exactly is it about Ami's turn in lines 3–4 which enables it to be understood as language learning talk and the initiation of a word search sequence, which is how Hang understands it? It is neither explicit nor linguistically sophisticated. Firstly, it is designed as the answer to the question in line 1. Ami therefore appears to be cooperative in wanting to provide a full answer. The hesitation and hedging together with the embodied display of thinking and with the nomination of two close colours indicate a language learning gap to be filled.

The methodology mirrors the participants' preoccupations. In the above analysis, we have shown that there is a very compatible, reflexive relationship between language learning focus and speech exchange system in this excerpt and a successful outcome in terms of learning as uptake is displayed twice in lines 8 and 12. This does not, however, ensure that the target vocabulary item will be retained in long-term memory. In this informal learning context of a university dormitory, we can see that there was no externally imposed reason for the participants to focus on language learning. They chose a temporary focus on language learning in order to solve a communication problem and reverted to the prior interactional business and topic in line 14 once that was repaired. In the excerpt above, the word search is an integral component of topic development. That is, the topic has already been decided by the speaker but a specific L2 word was missing which would allow successful development of the topic; the word search itself becomes topicalised.

The above sequence provides the clearest evidence possible of two separate complex systems being employed in talk. Ami's level of English L2 is not advanced enough for her to know 'light pink'. However, her native knowledge of the universal interaction engine is expert enough for her to instantly invent a highly appropriate and precise epistemic strategy for obtaining help in finding the exact word she is seeking.

The second phenomenon examined in this section is choral co-production (seen in lines 12–13), a phenomenon which forms part of the universal human interaction engine but is not part of language as a complex adaptive system; it is not mentioned in any language or grammar textbook and is purely a spoken discourse phenomenon. As Lerner (2002: 226) writes, choral co-production (or turn-sharing) can be employed to express agreement. In this case, it also manifests resolution of the trouble/repair sequence and co-production of the answer to the question, hence movement back to social talk, which occurs smoothly on the next line (14). We develop this point further in the next section. The two phenomena are not only emergent, but also function on several different interactional levels. This is possible because of the generative power of the multiple mechanisms of the interaction engine, combined with the complex system of language.

6.3.4 WHERE IN THE INTERACTION CAN WE SEE EVIDENCE OF THE TEN PRINCIPLES?

We now look again at the ten principles characterising complex adaptive systems and consider how they manifest themselves in this short excerpt.

Self-organisation and adaptation of many interacting agents. We have shown in Section 6.3.2 how the many mechanisms of the interaction engine are themselves inter-relating and interacting agents within the system in this excerpt.

In which ways are we showing a complex adaptive system at work here? We see an adaptation by speakers in a shift from a social talk question–answer sequence to a repair side sequence using word search. The mechanisms adapt with the speakers' shift, or alternatively the speakers design their shift by reference to the adaptive mechanisms; this is a reflexive relationship. In Section 3.5.3, we suggest that, when talk shifts from ordinary conversation to a focus on language learning, the next-turn proof procedure also adapts itself to the next-turn proof procedure in relation to the language learning focus as determined by the participants. In this excerpt we see that the movement into the language learning focus in line 3 and out again in line 14 is managed very smoothly. Following the initiation by Ami in line 3 of a word search to locate an L2 word, Hang provides a marker in line 5 of understanding that a language learning focus has started and then provides the candidate solution in line 7, confirmed by Ami in 8. The next-turn proof procedure has adapted itself to the language learning focus without any explicit marking of this adaptation; this suggests that the switching has become routinised with these specific participants. The two participants prove well able to organise the interaction themselves, including seamless changes in activity focus.

Non-linearity occurs in the excerpt in that the topic does not develop 'in a straight line'; the topic cannot be developed nor the question answered without repair work. The topic and social talk do then continue on line 14.

We can see evidence of **surface complexity arising out of deep simplicity** in that the basic mechanisms of the universal interaction engine are stated with deep simplicity in 'context-free' or general terms, as discussed in Chapter 3. We then showed in Section 6.3.2 how these mechanisms were employed in a 'context-sensitive' or particular way to perform diverse, heterogenous social actions. It is precisely because speakers are able to match the surface complexity and diversity of the interaction to the deep simplicity of the interaction engine bedrock that they are able to display and understand each other's social actions and maintain intersubjectivity. In the case of the choral co-production in lines 7–8, for example, the context-free norms are that turn-taking and sequence follow one after the other. However, taking exactly the same turn at exactly the same time (turn-sharing) is a context-sensitive way of expressing empathy, agreement and conclusion of a sequence. We argue that the interactional management of the shifting sequence is very sophisticated and efficient in terms of dealing with trouble, in spite of the fact that they have different L1s and are both speaking an L2 in which they are not fully proficient. We suggest that this is only possible because they both have access to the same universal interaction engine, by reference to which they can design their turns and understand those of others.

To be sure, the interaction does not sound particularly sophisticated or efficient at first glance or hearing. This is because the intricate, sophisticated design of the interaction engine has become so routinised and implicit that we no longer perceive it; it has become 'seen but unnoticed' in ethnomethodological terms. In this study, we have been making explicit that which we all know implicitly in order to understand how the interaction engine functions as a complex adaptive system.

We can see evidence of **sensitivity to initial conditions** in that trouble occurs because the particular nail polish referred to has a less usual colour; had the colour been simply 'red', the question could have been answered straightforwardly.

Complex systems adapt feedback from the environment and from themselves. How does the complex system of the interaction engine relate to the external environment in this excerpt? Hang's question in line 1 refers to the particular colour of the particular nail polish, which has a less common colour. This reference is to the external environment, rather than being internal to the spoken interaction. Ami does not yet know the correct word in L2 English for the exact colour (namely 'light pink'). This trouble could in principle be repaired with feedback from the external environment, for example by Ami locating the actual nail polish, or by use of a dictionary. However, Ami chooses to elicit feedback from within the system of the interaction engine, namely by initiating other-repair from Hang, whose feedback succeeds in repairing the trouble. In general terms, the word search sequence is therefore neatly designed within the overall interaction engine to be able to locate and marshal feedback from all participants and from the environment towards the repair of whatever interactional trouble needs to be dealt with. The interaction engine can adapt feedback from both the external environment and from within the interaction itself to repair trouble.

Complex adaptive systems arise from the interaction of their parts and function as a whole which is more than the sum of its parts. The above excerpt analysis demonstrates how the participants make use of all of the interactional resources and mechanisms at their disposal to perform their social actions to exchange information, repair the trouble and be able to continue to develop the topic. We have looked above at how the speakers make context-sensitive use of the component mechanisms of the interaction engine, namely turn-taking, sequence, repair, socially distributed cognition, information exchange and topic development. However, speakers also employ the separate complex system of language to perform their social actions, and linguistic formatting of turns is also carefully integrated into the whole performance. For example, in lines 3-4 we see how careful linguistic formatting is integrated with the mechanism of repair to narrow the epistemic gap and to maximise its efficiency.

One way we can tell that the whole is more than the sum of its parts in spoken interaction is because any single spoken utterance may be working on a number of different levels at the same time and be carefully designed to do so (Levinson 1983: 287). In the excerpt above, for example, the choral co-production in lines 12-13 demonstrates that epistemic exchange has been achieved, trouble has been repaired and a full answer provided, so a return to developing topic in social talk is warranted. This is because in spoken interaction, the inter-related mechanisms mentioned above are constantly in play. From the perspective of the complex system of language, all there is to see is two people saying 'light pink' at the same time. However, from the perspective of the interaction engine, the linguistic formatting meshes with the mechanisms of turn-taking and sequence as it is able to confirm an answer to Hang's line 1 question. The joint utterance also engages with the mechanism of repair by completing the word search repair started in line 3. The utterance engages at the same time with the mechanisms of socially distributed cognition and information exchange in that it confirms that Ami has moved from K- status in line 3 to K+ status in relation to this lexical item. The mechanism of topic is also engaged, in that this joint utterance confirms that the trouble previously preventing topic development has been repaired, meaning that the topic can be further developed with no delay by Ami in line 14. Because the complex systems of the interaction engine and language are able to combine in this seamless way to create many simultaneous levels of meaning, the generative power of human talk is vast, enormously more than the sum of its parts.

Complex adaptive systems display both homogeneity and heterogeneity and we can see some similarities and some differences between this specific word search sequence and other such sequences in the corpus. On the macro (CDST) level, the interaction produced has general or universal features in common with all other instances of word searches (see Section 4.1). On this level, this is a typical word search displaying homogeneity: speaker A initiates, speaker B provides a candidate solution and speaker A confirms. On the micro (CA) level, however, we view the interaction as a singular occurrence and the emphasis is on heterogeneity. We can note the unique combination of both the 'epistemic narrowing' in lines 3–4 with choral co-production in lines 12–13 in a very short sequence. Depending on the lens and macro/micro scale employed, the excerpt is both firmly typical (homogeneous) and unique (heterogeneous). On an intermediate level, the particular word search has some features in common and some differences compared with other word searches which have occurred in the dormitory setting, as shown in Chapter 4. All three levels are present in talk at all times, but the lens adopted will tend to focus our attention on a different level of scale. With the model detailed here, the micro level, the intermediate level and the macro level can all be analysed and portrayed simultaneously, with each level feeding the other reflexively.

Complex adaptive systems display self-similarity on various scales and levels. As noted previously, we argue that word search sequences display fractal features in relation to the mechanism of repair. What we see in this excerpt is rapid movement between L2 social talk and a focus on language learning, specifically word search. As previously noted (see Section 3.5.3), when viewed from the macro level, talk in this ELF setting has a dual character, namely that the participants are conducting social actions and developing topics of their own selection, while they are also enrolled on English programmes at the university and therefore often take the opportunity to focus on learning English L2. In this sense, the excerpt shows self-similar fractal features in relation to the macro-level dual character of talk in this ELF setting. The way we have approached and analysed the data is based on self-similarity. In Chapter 3, we noted that the CA methodology is fractal in nature because of the way it proceeds: the analytical methodology used by the analyst must mirror precisely the analytical methodology used by the interlocutors in the interaction being studied.

There are universal properties of non-linear systems. Perhaps the key universal characteristic of complex, adaptive, non-linear systems is that of 'emergence' or patterning which emerges from adaptation to the specific and changing needs of the environment (S. Johnson 2001: 20). What happens if you are having a social conversation in a foreign language and you need to reply to a question but do not know the L2 word which would answer the question precisely? There are many possible strategies which could have been employed, but what we see in lines 3-4 is of necessity an emergent solution, since Ami did not know this specific question would be asked by Hang, which changed the interactional environment and created a specific epistemological need. After a brief multimodal display of 'thinking' (Figure 6.1), Ami makes the most of her limited L2 resources by using the epistemic narrowing strategy in an attempt to enlist Hang's help with the word search, and this is very quickly successful. Then there is the question of finding an emergent solution to the issue of how to exit the side sequence of repair/word search to return to the social talk as smoothly as possible. We explained above that their choice of choral co-production is a successful one as it accomplishes closure on three different levels in a very economical way. However, Ami and Hang do not use choral co-production in this way (i.e., isolated choral of a single phrase after intersubjectivity is reached) elsewhere in their talk, so this appears to be an emergent solution arising from the flow of this specific interactional environment: they found themselves jointly doing choral co-production and realised that this moved them elegantly back to social talk.

Different systems function on different timescales and timescales interact. This excerpt is very short at 21 seconds in total, yet we see a change of state of Ami from K- to K+ of the word 'light pink' (i.e., 'development') occurring in such a short time period. In contrast, as discussed through Chapter 5, changes to the use of word search sequences as a system were observed through longer periods of time, suggesting these different systems change at different time scales. Ami does not use 'light pink' or the isolated choral sequence closure in any other recording, thus we cannot analyse how this sequence may have affected their interaction at a later time. However, it is worth considering how much social action on several different levels is condensed into such a short time period of ostensibly unexceptional ELF chit-chat.

In Section 6.3.4, we have reviewed the excerpt in relation to the universal properties which apply to all life-related non-linear systems and shown that these apply equally to the interaction engine; the universal properties are manifest, even in this short excerpt.

6.4 CHAPTER SUMMARY AND CONCLUSIONS

In Section 6.2, we showed how the data from this study can be understood from a macro CA-CDST perspective by matching its principles to the results from the CA analyses. The characteristics of CDST correspond very well to the characteristics uncovered in the analyses. Nonetheless, mere matching does not demonstrate

how exactly spoken interaction functions as a complex adaptive system. Therefore, Section 6.3 provided a detailed, lengthy CA-CDST analysis of a brief excerpt. Use of this approach showed how the macro level can be seen in the micro and vice versa; the different levels mirror each other. The conclusions of this chapter are: (1) the data from Chapters 4 and 5 demonstrate that human spoken interaction displays the characteristics of a complex adaptive system, (2) it is eminently possible to perform joint CA-CDST analyses of spoken interaction which work simultaneously on the micro and macro levels, and (3) the data analysis demonstrates that the L2 speakers make expert, inventive use of the universal interaction engine to convey and resolve meaning, even when they are only inexpert users of the specific overlaid language they are using.

6.4.1 HUMAN INTERACTION AS A COMPLEX ADAPTIVE SYSTEM

The study has illustrated some aspects of how spoken interaction functions as a complex adaptive system: firstly, by outlining the principles and the component mechanisms in Chapters 2 and 3; secondly, by focusing in detail on how word search (as part of the repair mechanism) is adapted by these participants for their purposes in this specific setting in Chapters 4 and 5. In Chapters 4–6, we have seen how the functioning of spoken interaction as a complex adaptive system can be studied both longitudinally (Chapter 5) and cross-sectionally (Section 6.3). We have shown that the universality of the mechanisms of turn-taking, word search sequence, repair, socially distributed cognition, information exchange and topic development enables interaction and L2 learning in ELF across first languages and cultures. Moreover, the analysis from this chapter demonstrated that the changes of word search sequences in the participants of this study do display characteristics of complex adaptive systems. In Section 6.3, we exemplified how exactly the multiple mechanisms combine to enable social action and intersubjectivity.

We have also shown that the joint application of CDST and CA allows simultaneous analysis of macro and micro levels in spoken interaction. Larsen-Freeman and Cameron (2008a) suggest that CA, including longitudinal CA, is compatible with investigating complex adaptive systems, and Seedhouse (2010, 2015) has demonstrated this possibility when analysing L2 classroom interactions. This study takes a step forward in analysing longitudinal CA data as complex adaptive systems, demonstrating that methodologically this is possible.

The analysis revealed that L2 speakers in an ELF setting effectively utilise the universal interaction engine to achieve intersubjectivity, even at intermediate proficiency levels of English in an ELF context. We have focused on word search sequences as a test case of how the human interaction engine facilitates communication across cultures and languages involving lingua franca use. Through the analysis, we have demonstrated the universality of the interaction engine, even in a lingua franca context where different language systems meet and interact. In particular, we have shown systematic patterns of turn-taking, word search sequence, socially distributed cognition, information exchange and topic development working in combination to enable social action and L2 learning in an ELF setting.

Furthermore, the analysis reveals non-linear dynamic features in the development of L2 users' word search sequences in ELF interactions, showcasing adaptability to the immediate interactional environment and interlocutors. We have demonstrated the adaptations the participants make to the different components of the interaction: turn, sequence, topic, interlocutor and the ELF community, which are also simultaneously changing. Moreover, these adaptations were identified in a short excerpt of a few seconds as well as over longer periods of time of weeks and months. In other words, changes in the interactional competence of L2 users are locally situated and adaptive to the feedback from the immediate interactional environment. The analysis also suggests that the identified features of word searches in ELF interactions emerged through adaptation to the interlocutor, who is also changeable. We now move on to our final chapter to draw the conclusions and discuss the implications of this project.

7
CONCLUSIONS AND IMPLICATIONS

7.1 INTRODUCTION

In this final chapter, we summarise the main findings of the study, both on the broad scale in terms of human spoken interaction as a complex adaptive system, as well as in the narrow empirical focus on L2 interaction in this specific informal ELF setting. We then take the discussion further in relation to a number of methodological and theoretical issues which have arisen. The first is the use of self-similarity as a methodological principle, the second is in relation to our use of scales and multiple lenses and the third concerns the design of human talk. We then consider the implications of our study in terms of CDST research. Finally, we look at the limitations of the study and possible directions for future research using a CA-CDST approach.

7.2 SUMMARY OF FINDINGS

In this book we have argued the following: living systems, from the smallest bacteria to the largest cities and ecosystems, are complex adaptive systems (West 2017: 79), and the interaction engine is one such system. CDST is a meta-theory which seeks to understand such systems, but in order to research the functioning of specific systems, appropriate research methodologies are necessary. Given that complex adaptive systems are by their nature adaptive and mutable, we argued that it is necessary to use research methodologies which are able to adapt themselves to and mirror the constantly changing nature of the phenomena which they study, revealing the complex interactions of their multiple components. We have argued that CA is the appropriate methodology par excellence for CDST research of spoken interaction in general and L2 talk in particular. This is because it was developed as a mirroring methodology to track the turn-by-turn mutability of talk and the complex interactions of the components of talk and because CA is a self-similar complex adaptive system itself. In Chapter 3, we described the basics of how human spoken interaction functions as a complex adaptive system by describing how CA works; this was possible precisely because CA is a mirroring methodology.[1] We have argued that the interaction engine applies universally, providing the bedrock for all human spoken interaction (Levinson 2022); languages are portable in spoken interaction and

---

[1] Borges (1984: 29) notes that it only takes two facing mirrors to construct a labyrinth.

language is a separate (though entwined) complex adaptive system. The combined use of the complex adaptive systems of the interaction engine and language provides enormous generative power.

We have demonstrated (Chapter 6) that it is possible to analyse spoken interaction on both the micro (particular) scale and the macro (general) scale by employing a combination of CDST meta-theory and CA microanalysis, which we call CA-CDST. It has also proved possible to portray spoken interaction as simultaneously displaying both homogeneity and heterogeneity. However, this approach works much better if the CDST concept of self-similarity/fractality is employed as a guiding and connecting principle at all scales and if CDST and CA are themselves viewed as complex adaptive systems. From this perspective, CA is a fractal of CDST (both working at different scales) and self-similarity illuminates many of CA's principles and procedures.

We have argued there is a universal complex adaptive system (interaction engine) for human spoken interaction, the mechanisms and workings of which we described in Chapter 3. We examined (in Chapters 4 and 5) data in which one might expect significant cross-linguistic and cross-cultural trouble to occur in interaction. We analysed pairs of speakers with different L1s in a 'superdiverse' setting, each of whom is speaking English as a lingua franca. We showed that in spite of this, they are able to perform their social actions, develop topics and maintain intersubjectivity. We argued that this is possible because they are employing the universal interaction engine to orientate themselves; the system is infinitely adaptable across languages and cultures. The discrepancy between the speakers' expert knowledge of the universal interaction engine and inexpert knowledge of L2 English reinforced our argument that they are employing separate (though related) complex adaptive systems. We explained in Chapter 3 how exactly the interaction engine is able to adapt itself to superdiverse settings and enable intersubjectivity and we then traced usage of word search sequences over time in Chapters 4 and 5. In Chapter 4, we displayed the use and the result of these adaptations of the word search sequences as a cohort, which demonstrated divergent features by comparison with the L1 literature discussed in Chapter 2. In Chapter 5, we observed individual adaptations and how the participants responded to feedback, as manifested through the various uses of language, strategies and epistemic stances towards words, depending on the interlocutor and over time.

The structure of the book has interwoven a CA component with a CDST component as a 'CA-CDST' approach, complementing our argument that CA is a realisation of CDST theory on an empirical level in relation to the analysis of human spoken interaction. We were introduced to CDST as meta-theory in Chapters 1 and 2 and then to the micro-analytic principles and procedures of CA in Chapter 3; this also introduced us to the working of human spoken interaction as a complex adaptive system, as CA aims to reveal the machinery underlying talk. Chapters 4 and 5 used CA to examine the micro-detail of how the repair mechanism (word searches) is adapted by this cohort of users and how their use changes over time. Chapter 6 then re-examined the findings of Chapters 4 and 5 through a CDST lens, demonstrating the compatibility of the two perspectives, then exemplifying the combined CA-CDST approach to data analysis. Indeed, we argue that CA and CDST are the same approach, operating at different scales on different phenomena.

7.3 METHODOLOGICAL ISSUES

7.3.1 SELF-SIMILARITY AS METHODOLOGICAL PRINCIPLE

The reason why we should use self-similarity as a key principle to guide our (qualitative) research into complex systems is the ethnomethodological precept that we should use the same methods as the phenomena we study (Heritage 1984b). Complex systems themselves use self-similarity as an internal means of self-organisation, construction and connection, and our methodology should mirror the functioning of the phenomenon which it studies. In this study, we have therefore identified self-similarity at all possible scales in both the data and the methodologies employed. West (2017) suggests that 'human-engineered systems that have grown organically such as cities ... have unconsciously evolved self-similar fractal structures which have tended to optimise their performance' (154). Given that the two complex systems involved in human talk are also human-engineered and have grown organically, we need to investigate further how self-similarity is built into them.

We have argued that in order to study spoken interaction from a CDST perspective, it is vital to treat not only the phenomena themselves, but also the research methodology employed as complex adaptive systems. We show that CA is well suited to this task as it is a mirroring methodology which adapts itself to the unfolding phenomena. Furthermore, it reveals self-similarity at many scales in the phenomena studied, in the methodology and in their mirroring relationship. We suggest that self-similarity should be at the heart of CDST studies of human spoken interaction in general and L2 talk in particular. The identification of fractals provides a warrant for selecting key interactional features for research amongst the enormous range and diversity of candidate phenomena. Furthermore, fractal features help to reveal links between micro- and macro-level features. For example, in Section 3.6.2 we saw how the micro IRF sequence is a fractal of the overall interactional architecture of the L2 classroom.

However, we should be clear that this is a challenging task. When looking at visual data such as coastlines, it is straightforward to identify fractals. However, it is by no means evident what forms fractals might take in spoken interaction and other areas of human sociality; we should perhaps expect the unexpected.

7.3.2 EMPLOYING MULTIPLE LENSES AND SCALES: HOMOGENEITY AND HETEROGENEITY, MACRO AND MICRO, GENERAL AND PARTICULAR

The concept of scale is vital not only to CDST (West 2017), but also to understanding how human spoken interaction functions and to understanding the complex personality of any instance of interaction. In this study, we have shown that the twin lenses of CA and CDST are not only compatible for the portrayal of spoken interaction, but that they also enable analysis on the micro and macro scales at the same time. The functional explanation as to why this should work is as follows. We have argued that the principles of CA and CDST are compatible; as CDST is a meta-theory and

CA a highly empirical narrow-focus practice, they are the same approach operating on different scales with different phenomena. As we saw in Chapter 1 with Gleick's (1993) example of snowflakes, complex systems display simultaneous homogeneity and heterogeneity; the degree one finds depends on the lens employed. A specific contribution of this volume is that the combination of CA and CDST provides a means of explicating and conceptualising the complementary scales on which any instance of spoken interaction can be viewed, as well as its simultaneous heterogeneity (or particular nature) and homogeneity (or general nature).

This involves portraying any instance of spoken interaction as having a complex personality, as simultaneously displaying both homogeneity and heterogeneity and functioning on a number of different scales at the same time. There is always a tension between a description of an excerpt of interaction as a unique occurrence, locally produced by the participants, a description of it as an example of interaction within a particular setting (e.g., informal dormitory ELF context) and a description of it as an example of human spoken interaction. All three scales are simultaneously manifested in an excerpt, even one as short as Excerpt 6.3 ('light pink', Section 6.3.1). Our CA-CDST analyses are intended to illustrate how the interaction displays both homogeneity (general features) and heterogeneity (particular features) at the same time. The relationship between scale and homogeneity/heterogeneity is as follows: the largest or macro scale displays the homogeneity or general characteristics of the talk, whereas the smallest or micro scale displays the heterogeneity or particular features.

On the micro (CA) scale, the particular word search in Excerpt 6.3 is unique. We view the interaction as a singular occurrence and the emphasis is on heterogeneity. On an intermediate scale, the particular word search has some features in common and some differences compared with other word searches which have occurred in the dormitory setting introduced in Chapters 4 and 5. There is a balance in focus between homogeneity and heterogeneity. On the macro (CDST) scale, the interaction produced has general or universal features in common with all other instances of human spoken interaction, which is the focus we find in Section 6.2; at that scale the emphasis is on homogeneity. All scales are present in talk at all times, but the lens adopted will tend to focus our attention on a different scale.

With the approach detailed here, the micro scale, the intermediate scale and the macro scale of interaction can all be analysed and portrayed simultaneously, with each scale feeding the other reflexively. This is because the CA-CDST approach analyses samples of spoken interaction as manifestations of a complex adaptive system in action, which dissolves the barriers between the micro and macro. Scale is also key to understanding how human spoken interaction functions as a complex adaptive system; any instance of talk can be seen on multiple scales or through multiple lenses. The CA-CDST approach thereby provides the basis for this study's empirical finding that all instances of word search have the same general properties and use the same basic sequence organisation, whilst at the same time portraying the extreme diversity, fluidity and complexity of their particular manifestations.

7.3.3 METHODOLOGICAL REFLECTIONS ON INTERACTION IN THIS SUPERDIVERSE CONTEXT

Throughout this book, we have intentionally used 'ELF' to refer to the interactional context and have used 'L1' and 'L2' to refer to the language of interaction. We attempted to make it clear that multilingualism is omnipresent and it is the speakers that decide on the mode of communication and the goal of the interaction. However, as evidenced by the excerpts in the book, the boundaries between specific languages become blurred in this superdiverse and informal interactional context, challenging traditional categorisations. The speakers' perspectives and their relationship with their own language play a pivotal role in shaping language choice. Whose L1, L2 or even L3 is being used varies depending on the speaker, while confidence in one's own language performance fluctuates based on the feedback received. Additionally, language preference changes according to the speakers' language proficiency levels and their interlocutors; what is more, language proficiency itself is not static. Our analysis also highlighted how speakers seamlessly transition in and out of a 'language learning' focus with subtle but mutually recognised signals that bystanders would miss without close observation; these have become routinised. The interactional findings of Chapters 4 and 5 are therefore possibly unique to these particular participants at these particular moments of interaction at this particular stage of their lives.

While the dynamics of language use may be context-dependent, there are certain commonalities with previous studies reviewed in Chapter 2. In other words, there is a balance between homogeneity and heterogeneity. Students with lower proficiency levels exhibited flexibility and adaptiveness in their language use, displaying more changes over time that would help them progress the conversation. On the other hand, students with higher proficiency levels showed less utilisation of 'new' strategies and fewer changes over time, reflecting consistent patterns observed in other studies within the CDST-applied linguistics field. Furthermore, our research also addresses a key gap identified by Hiver et al. (2022) in CDST-applied linguistics studies: the need to identify interventions or influences on the system. By examining the system of word search sequences and their interlocutor responses, we demonstrated how exactly the feedback shaped the interaction and influenced the speakers' language use (including word search) both in the moment and over time. This offers insights into potential future avenues for further interactional studies within the CA-CDST-applied linguistics framework.

7.3.4 THE DESIGN OF HUMAN TALK: TWO INTERLOCKING COMPLEX SYSTEMS

As noted in Chapter 3, CA attempts to reveal the 'rational design' of interaction; this has some similarities with 'reverse engineering' as applied to the products of human design. Applying these approaches to human talk, we consider a puzzle. Would it not have been much more economical and straightforward for humans to have developed just one single complex system governing human talk rather than two?

The first point to consider is that (according to our current state of knowledge) the two complex systems emerged at very different points in the long evolutionary process. The components of the interaction engine were developed cumulatively over deep time in the Hominidae (great ape family), whose non-human members remained primarily gestural turn-takers. Only humans evolved (through genetic and physical adaptation) to have the modern speech and language capacities to become vocal turn-takers, which process probably took place between 1.6 million and 600,000 years ago (Levinson 2022, 2023). The interaction engine formed the natural ecological niche for the evolution of language as a later overlay.

Could there possibly have been any advantages to humans having developed and used two different complex adaptive systems for talk rather than one? There seem to have been two possible design advantages. Firstly, having the ability to develop new diverse languages in tandem with new cultures in adaptation to new and changing environments as they spread around the globe provided the heterogeneity necessary for evolution. Adaptation to new environments included long-term physical adaptations, while cultural adaptations included food/cooking, clothing, housing, technologies, beliefs/rituals and social structures. Cultural adaptation also included the development of languages; Levinson (2023: 7) notes that vocal language transmission was largely outsourced to culture, with the consequent diversity of languages (around 7,000 at present). However, having retained the universal homogeneous core of the interaction engine meant that groups which had evolved different cultures and languages over time were still able to communicate when they made contact. This has also meant that it has proved perfectly feasible to form our current global, superdiverse mega-cities in which multiple cultural/linguistic groupings co-exist with dominant cultures/languages. The combination of the universal interaction engine and variable languages therefore provided the balance between homogeneity and heterogeneity necessary for human talk to flourish as we spread around the globe over tens of thousands of years and then globalised very rapidly indeed.

The second design advantage to having these two distinct but interlocking complex adaptive systems for communication rather than one is the exponential increase in generative and adaptive power. As Levinson (1983: 287) demonstrates, a single word in the web of interaction can be carefully designed to perform multiple social actions on multiple levels simultaneously by virtue of the additional generative power of the interaction engine. Such a word in such a web can deliver far more meaning than is contained in its dictionary definition, as is illustrated in Section 3.3.2.

7.4 IMPLICATIONS

7.4.1 IMPLICATIONS: SELECTING RESEARCH METHODOLOGIES FOR CDST STUDIES IN THE SOCIAL SCIENCES

Moving to a broader social science perspective, many research methodologies are proposed as possible candidates in the social sciences for studying the functioning of complex adaptive systems (e.g., Hiver and Al-Hoorie 2020). In order to develop criteria to select the most appropriate empirical methodologies, our study suggests that we might ask the following questions:

1. Is it possible to describe how the methodology functions as a complex adaptive system in its own right? In this study we have described how CA functions as a complex adaptive system.
2. When wanting to determine whether a particular research method is suitable for use in a CDST paradigm, one might ask: what is the relationship between the method and the phenomenon being studied? Using CDST principles, if the analytical methodology employed by the participant agents mirrors that used by the researchers, this can be taken as evidence that the empirical studies are indeed being undertaken in a CDST vein. In other words, the verification of the methodology's appropriateness would partly reside in its fractal nature with respect to the phenomenon.
3. To what extent can a specific research methodology adapt itself to the endless adaptations of the complex phenomena studied? How does it accomplish this? Which kinds of methodological mechanisms can be observed adapting themselves to the data? This book has explained how CA manages this, in that the next-turn proof procedure and basic mechanisms adapt themselves to the different social goals manifested in the interaction. The next-turn proof mechanism emerged from the data, from analysis of the structure of the talk as it is used by the participants in talk themselves. This may point to a general way forward for selection of appropriate research methodologies for CDST: can methodologies make explicit what their adaptive mechanisms are which allow them to adapt to the mutable phenomena studied?
4. Which kinds of internal mechanisms seem to be the most common and/or central to the overall functioning of the complex system being studied? Do these mechanisms display fractal relationships with the whole system itself or with other components of the system? Do these mechanisms mirror what is happening in the data in any way? If so, these observations may provide pointers to the use of such mechanisms as the basis for a research methodology, as is the case with CA. Approaches which allow research methodologies to emerge from the data themselves (e.g., the ethnomethodological approach) may prove to be more successful for CDST research than using existing methodologies which were created for other purposes.
5. Can the methodology reveal self-similarity? We saw in Section 3.6.2 that CA reveals self-similarity or fractality at many scales in the phenomena studied. We suggest that the identification of fractality should be at the heart of CDST social science studies and a means of assessing the suitability of research methodologies. The revelation of self-similarity provides a warrant for selecting key interactional features for research amongst the enormous range and diversity of possible candidate phenomena.

CDST offers the social sciences a perspective to re-examine the range of research methodologies that they employ, to consider each methodology as a complex adaptive system in its own right and to reflect on its relationship to the phenomena which it aims to analyse. We propose that a complex adaptive research methodology is necessary to portray the functioning of a complex adaptive system adequately.

7.4.2 IMPLICATIONS FOR INFORMAL LANGUAGE LEARNING AND INTERACTIONAL COMPETENCE

This study has demonstrated that the interaction engine provides a universal resource for L2 speakers to engage in the advanced interactional sequences of a word search. We showed that the interactional practice of word search is indeed an interactional competence which is co-constructed, requiring mutual understanding and mutual adaptation in order to co-create meaning and action together.

In Chapters 4 and 5, we discussed how speakers were able to organise the interaction themselves, perform their social actions and learn aspects of L2 through interaction. Speakers were able to 'do conversation' and 'do learning' at the same time, thus reflecting the dual nature of word search sequences in this setting. Moreover, speakers were using feedback received to adjust their language production to achieve mutual understanding, in real time as well as across extended temporal spans. As a result, the language use that facilitated the progression of the conversation was not necessarily so-called 'native speaker-like' but rather 'context-appropriate'.

Reflecting upon informal language learning and interactional competence in the ELF context, we can now see that 'learning' is the adaptation process and 'development' is the result of the adaptation to the specific context and the needs of the context for language use. The data at hand suggest that 'successful' L2 users exhibit two essential qualities: (1) sensitivity to the language use context and the ability to notice and employ the feedback being provided by the interactional context (e.g., interlocutor), and (2) the ability to appropriately adapt and enhance their language use to the ever-changing context in order to facilitate mutual understanding and progression of the conversation.

The complex adaptive system of the interaction engine is the fundamental, primal resource which can be adapted by users of any language and culture to communicate with users of any other, and to facilitate their cross-linguistic and cross-cultural learning. We are all able to 'speak Human', in combination with any language at any level of expertise. The dominant emphasis in the literature has always been on the approximately 7,000 different languages used in the world, which may sometimes seem to divide us as a human population, especially as the interaction engine has remained 'seen but unnoticed'.[2] Making explicit the foundational, vital contribution of the interaction engine to spoken communication may perhaps help to work against these divisions and bring people closer together. The experience of human spoken interaction is at root universal; it is fundamentally the same, whichever languages, cultures and topics are in play. As we have seen in the data of this study, we can make expert use of the interaction engine to support us in our communication,

---

[2] Despite the best efforts of Levinson (2006) and his colleagues.

even when we are having problems with a specific overlaid language; it enables us to make sense of each other and achieve intersubjectivity, if we wish to do so.

7.5 LIMITATIONS AND DIRECTIONS FOR FUTURE RESEARCH

As this is the first book-length study of how the interaction engine is organised as a complex adaptive system, this is inevitably a limited and tentative first step and much remains to be discovered. Our CA-CDST approach has been employed with one idiosyncratic and specific dataset, for the reasons given in Section 1.6. The set is very limited in terms of the numbers of participants, and in terms of the tight focus on word search sequences, but as a longitudinal study the total amount of video data is huge. There is a substantial CA literature (Sidnell and Stivers 2013) which demonstrates that the methodology can be applied to an enormous variety of interaction types in a massive variety of settings. Since our CA-CDST approach is based on the systematic properties of spoken interaction as a complex adaptive system, we believe that it is applicable to talk in any other setting, but this remains to be tested. In order to develop a better understanding of the advantages, disadvantages and implications of a CA-CDST approach, it needs to be applied to a range of contexts. Besides the mechanism of repair, the contribution of other components of the interaction engine to the functioning of the complex adaptive system needs to be investigated.

It is also clear that much work needs to be done to relate the findings of CA to those of CDST. Both have substantial literatures, but very different terminologies, traditions and procedures, and it is by no means evident how to relate these to each other. However, if we accept the dominant view of CDST as meta-theory (Hiver and Al-Hoorie 2020; Larsen-Freeman 2013) and CA as narrow-focus empirical methodology (and the view of this study that CA is a fractal of CDST), then future studies should be able to discover a way forward. From our perspective as researchers, we have not encountered major conflicts in combining the two; whether using a CA lens and/or a CDST lens, we have always been focused on showing how the spoken interaction has been organised as a system.

West (2017) notes that 'the structure and dynamics of human social networks are very much the same everywhere' (282). We believe that relating the structure and dynamics of spoken interaction (as outlined here) to those of social networks is likely to prove highly productive. For example, West has described how cities and companies function as complex adaptive systems using large-scale quantitative data analyses, which could be complemented by CA-CDST studies of spoken interaction in those settings.

We suggest that the complex adaptive system of human spoken interaction (the interaction engine) needs to be taken seriously in CDST as an object of future research. Our study provides the groundwork for the interaction engine to be studied as a complex adaptive system, and there are grounds for believing that it is one of the most researchable of all complex adaptive systems. It is the most available, observable, recordable and studiable complex system that we can find anywhere in the world, and it is the primary means of delivery for 'what it is to be human', that is, human sociality. CDST phenomena such as feedback are observable directly in spoken interaction in the form of the system of repair. In human spoken interaction, we can observe, record and analyse a complex adaptive system unfolding in real time, feeding back on itself reflexively, mirroring itself and revealing the decision-making processes of the participants. As we have shown, it displays all of the characteristics of a complex adaptive system and adapts itself to the whole range of human activities. It is also relevant to the whole population of the world, who use the system every day for their own vital purposes and invariably have an opinion on talk. Human spoken interaction is a prime site for CDST research.

We also argue that this study makes a unique contribution from the CDST perspective. Human spoken interaction is the only complex adaptive system to have been studied so far in which the aim has been to represent the functioning of the system from the emic perspective of the internal actors or agents within the system, explaining how they use available mechanisms and resources to manage their business. The future is exciting because there is simple access to an unlimited data source together with a proven methodology combining CA and CDST.[3] It is of course difficult for the average person to collect data for themselves on the functioning of earthquakes or insect populations as complex systems, whereas anyone with a mobile phone can now collect high-quality digital data on human spoken interaction as a complex system and use transcription software. As Levinson (2006: 39) states, it is right under our noses: much more accessible than the recesses of our brains or the fossils that track our evolutionary origins, and quite understudied!

We have argued that the interaction engine is a more primal system than language and languages (Levinson 2006) and that 'human language rests on an infrastructure for communicative interaction' (Levinson 2022: 5). The CDST work in language and linguistics so far has tended to focus on how languages function as complex adaptive systems and how they are learnt (N.C. Ellis and Larsen-Freeman 2009b). In this study, we have had to differentiate the system of human spoken interaction as much as possible from that of language in order to clarify their respective characteristics. A major limitation of our study and a major research gap for the future is that we have not investigated **how** the complex systems of the interaction engine and language/languages co-relate and combine. Our focus in the limited space of this book has been solely on establishing the nature and functioning of the interaction engine as complex system.

By the age of about six, the vast majority of children in all cultures have learnt how to combine the interaction engine and (at least one) language well enough to fulfil their basic communicative needs in their family and community. This means that we have acquired **implicit** knowledge of how to do so, but we have learnt this at such an early age that we cannot access the memories. As adults we have become experts in combining the two systems at great speed, but the problem is that as adults we find it extremely challenging to make **explicit** that which we know implicitly.

---

[3] We are grateful to Keith Richards (personal communication) for pointing out that the future is also exciting because of the potential of AI to facilitate the analysis of huge communication data sets. An example of this is the work of Yossi Yovel on bat communication (http://yossiyovel.com), which used a voice recognition program to analyse 15,000 sounds and an algorithm correlating sounds with specific interactions that had been video recorded.

The functioning of the two different complex systems can still be separated and specified, as we have done with the interaction engine in this study. However, the problem appears to be that the two complex systems co-evolved over such a huge stretch of time, developing a 'symbiotic', entwined relationship. The challenge for future research will be to specify how exactly we as users combine the universal system of the interaction engine and the variable system of language(s) to perform our social actions in our talk.

In our study we have concentrated on demonstrating how our CA-CDST approach works by analysing a collection of L2 interactions involving word searches. However, constraints on space meant that we were unable to develop findings in relation to the broad field of language learning. It is worth exploring how L2 learners' already expert knowledge of the interaction engine can best be utilised in L2 learning, as we saw in Section 6.3.3. The CA-CDST approach offers new and original possibilities for researching language learning talk, ELF talk and interactional competence in particular. L2 interaction does not need to be viewed as an unusual, isolated phenomenon, as a 'messy' type of data full of errors, but can be considered and analysed as a complex adaptive system like any other. Research on intercultural communication may also take an interest in the interaction engine, given that Levinson (2023) argues that it 'provides a stable cross-cultural base for the use and acquisition of language' (7).

Research on communication disorders has typically focused on problems with first language acquisition. However, there is emerging research (Levinson 2022: 3) into the possibility that problems may actually have started earlier with acquisition of the interaction engine. Bruner (1974) suggests:

> Any realistic account of language acquisition must take into account the manner in which the child passes from pre-speech communication to the use of language proper ... many of the major organizing features of syntax, semantics, pragmatics, and even phonology have important precursors and prerequisites in the pre-speech communicative acts of infants. (255)

The combination of CA and CDST offers many prospects for future research into spoken interaction. There are universal properties of non-linear systems; the notion of universality means that different complex adaptive systems will behave in the same ways (Sardar and Abrams 2004). As we have shown in this study, the machinery of human spoken interaction functions in the same fundamental ways as other complex adaptive systems. By analysing how human spoken interaction works using a CA-CDST methodology, we are simultaneously conducting an exposition of how a complex adaptive system functions in real time in the real world, following the principle of universality. Integrating CA with CDST presents the prospect of progress in our understanding of spoken interaction as a system and also of the integration of the study of spoken interaction into a much larger scientific project. This would have reciprocal benefits; advances in the study of complex adaptive systems in any field could potentially have implications for our understanding of spoken interaction and vice versa.

However, human spoken interaction does offer one uniquely powerful opportunity to CDST research, in that humans are able to record, analyse and reflect upon their own complex adaptive system of communication. The unique advantage we have in the study of human spoken interaction over the study of any other CDST system is this: we as analysts can have access to the decision-making flow taking place at the heart of the system using the same methods as the participant agents in the system. We refer to the decision-making of speakers using the next-turn proof procedure. Elsewhere it is not possible to gain any access to how participants within a complex adaptive system **themselves** analyse the data flow, evolve and react to it. It is only in the interaction engine that observership, feedback on and repair of data flow are all integral parts of a system to which we as analysts have access using a mirroring methodology. In other words, our approach offers CDST analysts the opportunity to access the perspective from inside a complex adaptive system as it is evolving. As a bonus, the crucial issue of observership is integrated into the heart of the research.

Human spoken interaction is the fundamental system which human brains (the most complex object yet discovered) use to communicate with each other, in combination with overlaid languages. The interaction engine enables us to engage with the other complex adaptive systems in the world. It is also an object of intricate beauty, which has sadly become so implicit and deeply recessed in our psyches and social procedures that we can scarcely perceive it any longer.[4] Its crystalline structure enables endless mirroring between ourselves, our conversational partners and our world.

---

[4] It has become 'seen but unnoticed' in ethnomethodological terms (Garfinkel 1967: 42).

APPENDIX 1
RECORDINGS OF PARTICIPANTS

Table 1   Ami's recordings

Participant	Date	Partner(s)	Country	Length (minutes)
Ami	April 5, 2010	Wei, Umi	China, Japan	30
	April 19, 2010	Hang	Vietnam	39
	May 4, 2010	Ting, Nicole, Yui	China & Thailand, China, Japan	27
	May 1, 2010	Hang	Vietnam	61
	June 8, 2010	Hang	Vietnam	42
	June 27, 2010	Soo	Korea	38
	July 12, 2010	Hang	Vietnam	33
	July 26, 2010	Soo	Korea	34.5
	October 6, 2010	Hang	Vietnam	29
	October 20, 2010	Shuang	China	31
	November 4, 2010	Hang	Vietnam	27
	November 14, 2010	Wei	China	24
	December 1, 2010	Hang	Vietnam	26
	December 12, 2010	Soo	Korea	25.5
	January 7, 2011	Hang	Vietnam	26
	January 28, 2011	Ai	Vietnam	25
	January 12, 2012	Hang	Vietnam	32.5
	Total length of transcribed recording			**550.5**

Table 2 Yoko's recordings

Participant	Date	Partner(s)	Country	Length (minutes)
Yoko	April 1, 2010	Shitora	Uzbekistan	34
	April 19, 2010	Sharon	USA	36.5
	May 3, 2010	Shitora	Uzbekistan	37
	May 17, 2010	Cheng	China	34
	June 14, 2010	Nuru	Botswana	36
	June 30, 2010	Shitora	Uzbekistan	40
	July 14, 2010	Jacy	Thailand	34.5
	July 30, 2010	Shitora	Uzbekistan	40
	October 13, 2010	Jacy, Obb	Thailand	35.5
	October 27, 2010	Jacy, Obb, Pan	Thailand	37* unusable
	November 10, 2010	Shitora	Uzbekistan	36
	November 30, 2010	Jacy	Thailand	37
	December 13, 2010	Jacy	Thailand	38
	December 23, 2010	Shitora	Uzbekistan	69
	January 28, 2011	Shitora	Uzbekistan	42
	February 1, 2011	Jacy	Thailand	33
	January 20, 2012	Shitora	Uzbekistan	30
	Total length of transcribed recording			612.5

Table 3 Maya's recordings

Participant	Date	Partner(s)	Country	Length (minutes)
Maya	April 12, 2010	Kei	Korea (Canada)	27
	April 29, 2010	Kei	Korea (Canada)	42.5
	May 10, 2010	Niel	Korea (USA)	31
	May 24, 2010	Kei	Korea (Canada)	48
	June 23, 2010	Jenny, Tim, Joe, James	USA	37.5* unusable
	July 8, 2010	Kei	Korea (Canada)	25
	July 21, 2010	Cathy	Indonesia	32
	July 30, 2010	Kei	Korea (Canada)	25.5
	October 10, 2010	Yanti	Indonesia	59
	October 26, 2010	Yanti, Taman	Indonesia	33.5
	November 8, 2010	Dao, Angela	Vietnam, USA	34
	November 25, 2010	Yanti	Indonesia	56.5
	December 8, 2010	Bob, Rick, Thomas	China	48* unusable
	December 20, 2010	Yanti	Indonesia	61
	January 16, 2011	Shen	Korea	38
	February 7, 2011	Yanti	Indonesia	48.5
	January 25, 2012	Kei	Korea (Canada)	30
	Total length of transcribed recording			591.5

Table 4 Tomoko's recordings

Participant	Date	Partner(s)	Country	Length (minutes)
Tomoko	April 6, 2010	Pham	Thailand	22
	April 25, 2010	Anh	Vietnam	40
	May 16, 2010	Pham	Thailand	30
	May 24, 2010	Citra	Indonesia	30
	June 23, 2010	Anh	Vietnam	27
	July 7, 2010	Anh	Vietnam	30
	July 22, 2010	Monica	Romania	38.5
	October 1, 2010	Anh	Vietnam	29
	October 16, 2010	Maria	USA	30
	November 1, 2010	Anh	Vietnam	28
	November 12, 2010	Pham	Thailand	28
	November 30, 2010	Alice	China	damaged* unusable
	December 22, 2010	Jin	Korea	34.5
	January 20, 2011	Lee	China	23
	February 10, 2011	Pham	Thailand	36
	February 10, 2011	Keiko, Anh	Japan (USA), Vietnam	30
	Total length of transcribed recording			**456**

APPENDIX 2
TRANSCRIPTION CONVENTIONS

Adaptation of Jefferson's (2004) transcription format for verbal communication and Mondada (2018) and Greer (2019a) for non-verbal communication.

(.)	Short untimed pause
(0.3) (2.6)	Duration of silence in seconds
CAPS	Relatively high volume
↑word	Pitch rise or fall in the next phrase
↓word	
$word$	Smiley voice
A: word [word	Overlapping talk
B: [word	
ha ha huh heh hnh	Laughter, depending on the sounds produced
(h)(hh)	Laughter within a word
.hhh	A dot-prefixed row indicates inbreath
wo:::rd	Elongation of preceding sound
word	Stressed sound
wo-	Cut-off
A: word=	Latching speech
B: =word	
°word°	Utterance that is quieter than the surrounding talk
>word word<	Inwards arrows show faster speech, outward slower
<word word>	
?	Turn final rising intonation
.	Turn final falling intonation
→	Feature of interest to the analyst
(word)	Word or parts of a word transcriber is unsure of
((sobbing))	Other details of the conversational scene

Special Conventions

|	Where embodied action begins in relation to talk
----	Holding gaze or continued action
gz	Gaze
hd	Head
word	Translation of a Japanese word
#word#	Translation of a Thai word

REFERENCES

Adelswärd, V. (1989), 'Laughter and dialogue: The social significance of laughter in institutional discourse', *Nordic Journal of Linguistics*, 12 (2), 107–36.
Appel, J. (2010), 'Participation and instructed language learning', in Seedhouse, P., S. Walsh, and C. Jenks (eds), *Conceptualising 'learning' in applied linguistics* (Houndmills: Palgrave Macmillan), 206–24.
Atkinson, D., E. Churchill, T. Nishino, and H. Okada (2007), 'Alignment and interaction in a sociocognitive approach to second language acquisition', *The Modern Language Journal*, 91 (2), 169–88.
Atkinson, J.M. and J. Heritage (1984), *Structures of social action: Studies in conversation analysis* (Studies in Emotion and Social Interaction; Cambridge: Cambridge University Press).
Auer, P. and E. Zima (2021), 'On word searches, gaze, and co-participation', *Gesprächsforschung. Online-Zeitschrift Zur Verbalen Interaktion*, 22, 390–425.
Balaman, U. (2018), 'Task-induced development of hinting behaviors in online task-oriented L2 interaction', *Language Learning & Technology*, 22 (2), 95–115.
Barrow, J. (2009), 'Electronic dictionary use in novice L2 learner interaction', Unpublished doctoral dissertation, Temple University.
Barrow, J. (2010), 'Electronic dictionary look-up practices of novice English learners', in Greer, T. (ed.), *Observing talk: Conversation analytic studies of second language interaction* (Tokyo: Pragmatics Special Interest Group of JALT), 55–72.
Batstone, R. (2010a), 'Issues and options in sociocognition', in Batstone, R. (ed.), *Sociocognitive perspective on language use and language learning* (Oxford: Oxford University Press), 3–23.
Batstone, R. (ed.) (2010b), *Sociocognitive perspectives on language use and language learning* (Oxford: Oxford University Press).
Bilmes, J. (1986), *Discourse and behavior* (New York: Plenum Press).
Blommaert, J. (2009), 'Language, asylum, and the national order', *Current Anthropology*, 50 (4), 415–41.
Blommaert, J. and B. Rampton (2011), 'Language and superdiversity', *Diversity*, 13 (2), 1–21.
Bolden, G.B. (2003), 'Multiple modalities in collaborative turn sequences', *Gesture*, 3 (2), 187–212.
Borges, J.L. (1984), 'Nightmares', *Seven Nights* (New York: New Directions), 29–32.
Breiteneder, A. (2005), 'The naturalness of English as a European lingua franca: The case of the "third person -s"', *VIenna English Working PaperS (VIEWS)*, 14, 3–26.
Brouwer, C.E. (2003), 'Word searches in NNS-NS interaction: Opportunities for language learning?', *The Modern Language Journal*, 87 (4), 534–45.
Brouwer, C.E. (2004), 'Doing pronunciation: A specific type of repair sequence', in Gardner, R. and J. Wagner (eds), *Second language conversations* (London: Continuum), 93–113.

Brouwer, C.E., G. Rasmussen, and J. Wagner (2004), 'Embedded corrections in second language talk', in Gardner, R. and J. Wagner (eds), *Second language conversations* (London: Continuum), 75–92.

Brouwer, C.E. and J. Wagner (2004), 'Developmental issues in second language conversation', *Journal of Applied Linguistics*, 1 (1), 29–47.

Brown, J.D. (1999), 'The relative importance of persons, items, subtests and languages to TOEFL test variance', *Language Testing*, 16 (2), 217–38.

Brown, J.H. (1994), 'Complex ecological systems', in Cowan, G.A., D. Pines, and D. Meltzer (eds), *Complexity: Metaphors, models, and reality* (Reading, MA: Addison-Wesley), 419–49.

Bruner, J.S. (1974), 'From communication to language – a psychological perspective', *Cognition*, 3 (3), 255–87.

Buckwalter, P. (2001), 'Repair sequences in Spanish L2 dyadic discourse: A descriptive study', *The Modern Language Journal*, 85 (3), 380–97.

Cadierno, T. and S.W. Eskildsen (eds) (2015), *Usage-based perspectives on second language learning* (Berlin; Boston: De Gruyter).

Cameron, L. and A. Deignan (2006), 'The emergence of metaphor in discourse', *Applied Linguistics*, 27 (4), 671–90.

Canale, M. and M. Swain (1980), 'Theoretical bases of communicative approaches to second language teaching and testing', *Applied Linguistics*, 1, 1–47.

Carlin, A.P. and Y. Kim (2021), 'Longitudinal conversation analysis of parent–child interaction: Small data and interdisciplinary work in linguistics and sociology', in *Sage Research Methods Cases Part 1* (SAGE Publications), <https://doi.org/10.4135/9781529757248>.

Carr, D. (2006), *Teacher training DVD series* (Set of 15 DVDs; London: International House).

Carroll, D. (2005), 'Vowel-marking as an interactional resource in Japanese novice ESL conversation', in Richards, K. and P. Seedhouse (eds), *Applying conversation analysis* (Houndmills: Palgrave Macmillan), 214–34.

Castro, E. (2018), 'Complex adaptive systems, language advising, and motivation: A longitudinal case study with a Brazilian student of English', *System*, 74, 138–48.

Cekaite, A. (2007), 'A child's development of interactional competence in a Swedish L2 classroom', *The Modern Language Journal*, 91 (1), 45–62.

Chan, H., M. Verspoor, and L. Vahtrick (2015), 'Dynamic development in speaking versus writing in identical twins', *Language Learning*, 65 (2), 298–325.

Chang, P. and L.J. Zhang (2021), 'A CDST perspective on variability in foreign language learners' listening development', *Frontiers in Psychology*, 12, 601962.

Cogo, A. (2010), 'Strategic use and perceptions of English as a lingua franca', *Poznań Studies in Contemporary Linguistics*, 46 (3), 295–312.

Cogo, A. (2012), 'ELF and super-diversity: A case study of ELF multilingual practices from a business context', *Journal of English as a Lingua Franca*, 1 (2), 287–313.

Cohen, A.D. (1986), 'Forgetting foreign language vocabulary', in Weltens, B., K. de Bot, and T. van Els (eds), *Language attrition in progress* (Dordrecht: Foris), 143–58.

Cooper, D.L. (1999), *Linguistic attractors: The cognitive dynamics of language acquisition and change* (Amsterdam: John Benjamins).

Coveney, P. and R. Highfield (1995), *Frontiers of complexity: The search for order in a chaotic world* (London: Faber and Faber).

de Bot, K. (2008), 'Introduction: Second language development as a dynamic process [Special Issue]', *The Modern Language Journal*, 92 (2), 166–78.

de Bot, K. (2014), 'Rates of change: Timescales in second language development', in Dörnyei, Z., P.D. MacIntyre, and A. Henry (eds), *Motivational dynamics in language learning* (Bristol: Multilingual Matters), 29–37.

de Bot, K. (2017), 'Complexity theory and dynamic systems theory: Same or different?', in Ortega, L. and Z. Han (eds), *Complexity theory and language development: In celebration of Diane Larsen-Freeman* (Amsterdam; Philadelphia: John Benjamins), 51–8.

de Bot, K., W. Lowie, and M. Verspoor (2007), 'A dynamic systems theory approach to second language acquisition', *Bilingualism: Language and Cognition*, 10 (1), 7–21 and 51–5.

de Bot, K. and B. Weltens (1995), 'Foreign language attrition', *Annual Review of Applied Linguistics*, 15 (1), 151–64.

Dingemanse, M., S.G. Roberts, J. Baranova, J. Blythe, P. Drew, S. Floyd, R.S. Gisladottir, K.H. Kendrick, S.C. Levinson, E. Manrique, G. Rossi, and N.J. Enfield (2015), 'Universal principles in the repair of communication problems', *PLOS ONE*, 10 (9), e0136100.

Dressel, D. (2020), 'Multimodal word searches in collaborative storytelling: On the local mobilization and negotiation of coparticipation', *Journal of Pragmatics*, 170, 37–54.

Dressel, D. and A.T. Kalkhoff (2019), 'Co-constructing utterances in face-to-face-interaction: A multimodal analysis of collaborative completions in spoken Spanish', *Social Interaction. Video-Based Studies of Human Sociality*, 2 (2).

Drew, P. (1992), 'Contested evidence in courtroom cross-examination: The case of a trial for rape', in Drew, P. and J. Heritage (eds), *Talk at work: Interaction in institutional settings* (Cambridge: Cambridge University Press), 470–520.

Drew, P. (1995), 'Conversation analysis', in Smith, J.A., R. Harré, and L. Van Langenhove (eds), *Rethinking methods in psychology* (London: Sage Publications), 64–79.

Drew, P. (1997), '"Open" class repair initiators in response to sequential sources of troubles in conversation', *Journal of Pragmatics*, 28 (1), 69–101.

Drew, P. and J. Heritage (1992a), 'Analyzing talk at work: An introduction', in Drew, P. and J. Heritage (eds), *Talk at work: Interaction in institutional settings* (Cambridge: Cambridge University Press), 3–65.

Drew, P. and J. Heritage (eds) (1992b), *Talk at work: Interaction in institutional settings* (Cambridge: Cambridge University Press).

Edwards, D. and J. Potter (1992), *Discursive psychology* (London: Sage Publications).

Ellis, N.C. (2008), 'The dynamics of second language emergence: Cycles of language use, language change, and language acquisition', *The Modern Language Journal*, 92 (2), 232–49.

Ellis, N.C. and D. Larsen-Freeman (2009a), 'Constructing a second language: Analyses and computational simulations of the emergence of linguistic constructions from usage', *Language Learning*, 59 (S1), 90–125.

Ellis, N.C. and D. Larsen-Freeman (eds) (2009b), *Language as a complex adaptive system* (Chichester: Wiley-Blackwell).

Ellis, R. (2010), 'Theoretical pluralism in SLA: Is there a way forward?', in Seedhouse, P., S. Walsh, and C. Jenks (eds), *Conceptualising 'learning' in applied linguistics* (Houndmills: Palgrave Macmillan), 23–51.

Eskildsen, S.W. (2009), 'Constructing another language: Usage-based linguistics in second language acquisition', *Applied Linguistics*, 30 (3), 335–57.

Eskildsen, S.W. (2011), 'The L2 inventory in action: Conversation analysis and usage', in Pallotti, G. and J. Wagner (eds), *L2 learning as social practice: Conversation-analytic perspectives* (Honolulu: National Foreign Language Resource Center, University of Hawai'i at Mānoa), 327–64.

Eskildsen, S.W. (2012), 'L2 negation constructions at work', *Language Learning*, 62 (2), 335–72.

Eskildsen, S.W. (2018), '"We're learning a lot of new words": Encountering new L2 vocabulary outside of class', *The Modern Language Journal*, 102 (S1), 46–63.

Eskildsen, S.W. and T. Cadierno (2015), 'Advancing usage-based approaches to L2 studies', in Cadierno, T. and S.W. Eskildsen (eds), *Usage-based perspectives on second language learning* (Berlin; Boston: De Gruyter).

Færch, C. and Kasper, G. (1983), 'Plans and strategies in foreign language communication', in Færch, C. and G. Kasper (eds), *Strategies in interlanguage communication* (London: Longman), 20–60.

Firth, A. (1996), 'The discursive accomplishment of normality: On "lingua franca" English and conversation analysis', *Journal of Pragmatics*, 26 (2), 237–59.

Firth, A. (2009), 'Doing not being a foreign language learner: English as a lingua franca in the workplace and (some) implications for SLA', *International Review of Applied Linguistics in Language Teaching (IRAL)*, 47 (1), 127–56.

Fuller, J.M. (2003), 'Discourse marker use across speech contexts: A comparison of native and non-native speaker performance', *Multilingua*, 22 (2), 185–208.

Funayama, I. (2002), 'Word-searches in cross-linguistic settings: Teaching–learning collaboration between native and non-native speakers', *Crossroads of Language, Interaction, and Culture*, 4, 33–57.

Garfinkel, H. (1967), *Studies in ethnomethodology* (Englewood Cliffs, NJ: Prentice-Hall).

Gell-Mann, M. (1994a), 'Complex adaptive systems', in Cowan, G.A., D. Pines, and D. Meltzer (eds), *Complexity: Metaphors, models, and reality* (Reading, MA: Addison-Wesley), 17–45.

Gell-Mann, M. (1994b), *The quark and the jaguar: Adventures in the simple and the complex* (New York: W. H. Freeman).

Gibbs, R.W. and L. Cameron (2008), 'The social-cognitive dynamics of metaphor performance', *Cognitive Systems Research*, 9 (1–2), 64–75.

Gleick, J. (1987), *Chaos: Making a new science* (New York: Viking).

Gleick, J. (1993), *Chaos: Making a new science* (2nd edn; New York: Viking).

Glenn, P.J. (1995), 'Laughing at and laughing with: Negotiations of participant alignments through conversational laughter', in ten Have, P. and G. Psathas (eds), *Situated order: Studies in the social organization of talk and embodied activities* (Washington, DC: University Press of America), 43–56.

Goffman, E. (1981a), 'Footing', in Goffman, E. (ed.), *Forms of talk* (Philadelphia: University of Pennsylvania Press), 124–59.

Goffman, E. (1981b), *Forms of talk* (Philadelphia: University of Pennsylvania Press).

Goodwin, C. (1980), 'Restarts, pauses, and the achievement of a state of mutual gaze at turn-beginning', *Sociological Inquiry*, 50 (3–4), 272–302.

Goodwin, C. (1995), 'Co-constructing meaning in conversations with an aphasic man', *Research on Language and Social Interaction*, 28 (3), 233–60.

Goodwin, C. (1996), 'Transparent vision', in Ochs, E., E.A. Schegloff, and S.A. Thompson (eds), *Interaction and grammar* (Cambridge: Cambridge University Press), 370–404.

Goodwin, M.H. (1983a), 'Aggravated correction and disagreement in children's conversations', *Journal of Pragmatics*, 7 (6), 657–77.

Goodwin, M.H. (1983b), 'Searching for a word as an interactive activity', in Deely, J.N. and M.D. Lenhart (eds), *Semiotics* (New York: Plenum), 129–37.

Goodwin, M.H. and C. Goodwin (1986), 'Gesture and coparticipation in the activity of searching for a word', *Semiotica*, 62 (1/2), 51–75.

Greer, T. (2008), 'Accomplishing difference in bilingual interaction: Translation as backwards-oriented medium repair', *Multilingua*, 27 (1–2), 99–127.

Greer, T. (2013a), 'Establishing a pattern of dual-receptive language alternation: Insights from a series of successive haircuts', *Australian Journal of Communication*, 40 (2), 47–61.

Greer, T. (2013b), 'Word search sequences in bilingual interaction: Codeswitching and embodied orientation toward shifting participant constellations', *Journal of Pragmatics*, 57, 100–17.

Greer, T. (2016), 'Learner initiative in action: Post-expansion sequences in a novice ESL survey interview task', *Linguistics and Education*, 35, 78–87.

Greer, T. (2019a), 'Initiating and delivering news of the day: Interactional competence as joint-development', *Journal of Pragmatics*, 146, 150–64.

Greer, T. (2019b), 'Noticing words in the wild', in Hellermann, J., S. Eskildsen, S. Pekarek Doehler, and A. Piirainen-Marsh (eds), *Conversation analytic research on learning-in-action: The complex ecology of second language interaction 'in the wild'* (Cham: Springer), 131–58.

Greer, T. and Z. Nanbu (2022), 'Visualizing emergent turn construction: Seeing writing while speaking', *The Modern Language Journal*, 106 (S1), 69–88.

Gribbin, J. (2004), *Deep simplicity* (London: Penguin Books).

Gudmundsen, J. and J. Svennevig (2020), 'Multimodal displays of understanding in vocabulary-oriented sequences', *Social Interaction. Video-Based Studies of Human Sociality*, 3 (2).

Gui, M., X. Chen, and M. Verspoor (2021), 'The dynamics of reading development in L2 English for academic purposes', *System*, 100, 102546.

Gullberg, M. (2011), 'Multilingual multimodality: Communicative difficulties and their solutions in second-language use', in Streeck, J., C. Goodwin, and C. LeBaron (eds), *Embodied interaction: Language and body in the material world* (New York: Cambridge University Press), 137–51.

Hall, J.K. and S. Pekarek Doehler (2011), 'L2 interactional competence and development', in Hall, J.K., J. Hellermann, and S.P. Doehler (eds), *L2 interactional competence and development* (56; Bristol: Multilingual Matters), 1–15.

Hall, N. (1992), *The New Scientist guide to chaos* (London: Penguin).

Hauser, E. (2010), 'Other-correction of language form following a repair sequence', in Kasper, G., H.T. Nguyen, D.R. Yoshimi, and J.K. Yoshioka (eds), *Pragmatics and language learning* (12; Honolulu: National Foreign Language Resource Center, University of Hawai'i at Mānoa), 277–96.

Hauser, E. (2011), 'On the danger of exogenous theory in CA-for-SLA: A response to Hellermann and Cole (2009)', *Applied Linguistics*, 32 (3), 348–52.

Hauser, E. (2013a), 'Beyond intersubjectivity: Task orientation and first language use in foreign language discussions', *Pragmatics and Society*, 4 (3), 285–316.

Hauser, E. (2013b), 'Expanding resources for marking direct reported speech', in Greer, T., D. Tatsuki, and C. Roever (eds), *Pragmatics and language learning* (13; Honolulu: National Foreign Language Resource Center, University of Hawai'i at Mānoa), 29–53.

Hauser, E. (2013c), 'Stability and change in one adult's second language English negation', *Language Learning*, 63 (3), 463–98.

Hauser, E. (2014), 'Embodied uses of electronic bilingual dictionaries', *JALT Journal*, 36 (1), 5–23.

Hauser, E. (2017), 'Learning and the immediate use (fulness) of a new vocabulary item', *The Modern Language Journal*, 101 (4), 712–28.

Hawkins, J.A. and M. Gell-Mann (eds) (1992), *The evolution of human languages* (Reading, MA: Addison-Wesley).

Hayashi, M. (2003), 'Language and the body as resources for collaborative action: A study of word searches in Japanese conversation', *Research on Language and Social Interaction*, 36 (2), 109–41.

Hayashi, M. (2005), 'Referential problems and turn construction: An exploration of an intersection between grammar and interaction', *Text*, 25 (4), 437–68.
Hayashi, M. (2009), 'Marking a "noticing of departure": Eh-prefaced turns in Japanese conversation', *Journal of Pragmatics*, 41 (10), 2100–29.
He, A.W. (2004), 'CA for SLA: Arguments from the Chinese language classroom', *Modern Language Journal*, 88 (4), 568–82.
He, A.W. and R.F. Young (1998), 'Language proficiency interviews: A discourse approach', in Young, R.F. and A.W. He (eds), *Talking and testing: Discourse approaches to the assessment of oral proficiency* (Philadelphia: John Benjamins), 1–24.
Hellermann, J. (2008), *Social actions for classroom language learning* (Clevedon: Multilingual Matters).
Hellermann, J. (2009a), 'Looking for evidence of language learning in practices for repair: A case study of self-initiated self-repair by an adult learner of English', *Scandinavian Journal of Educational Research*, 53 (2), 113–32.
Hellermann, J. (2009b), 'Practices for dispreferred responses using no by a learner of English', *International Review of Applied Linguistics in Language Teaching (IRAL)*, 47 (1), 95–126.
Hellermann, J. and E. Cole (2008), 'Practices for social interaction in the language-learning classroom: Disengagements from dyadic task interaction', *Applied Linguistics*, 30 (2), 186–215.
Hellermann, J. and S. Pekarek Doehler (2010), 'On the contingent nature of language-learning tasks', *Classroom Discourse*, 1 (1), 25–45.
Heritage, J. (1984a), 'A change-of-state token and aspects of its sequential placement', in Atkinson, J.M. and J. Heritage (eds), *Structures of social action: Studies in conversation analysis* (Cambridge: Cambridge University Press), 299–345.
Heritage, J. (1984b), *Garfinkel and ethnomethodology* (Cambridge: Polity Press).
Heritage, J. (1988), 'Explanations as accounts: A conversation analytic perspective', in Antaki, C. (ed.), *Analysing everyday explanation: A casebook of methods* (London; Newbury Park, CA: Sage Publications), 127–44.
Heritage, J. (1997), 'Conversation analysis and institutional talk: Analyzing data', in Silverman, D. (ed.), *Qualitative research: Theory, method and practice* (London; Thousand Oaks, CA: Sage Publications), 161–82.
Heritage, J. (2007), 'Intersubjectivity and progressivity in person (and place) reference', in Stivers, T. and N.J. Enfield (eds), *Person reference in interaction: Linguistic, cultural and social perspectives* (Cambridge: Cambridge University Press), 255–80.
Heritage, J. (2012a), 'Epistemics in action: Action formation and territories of knowledge', *Research on Language and Social Interaction*, 45 (1), 1–29.
Heritage, J. (2012b), 'The epistemic engine: Sequence organization and territories of knowledge', *Research on Language and Social Interaction*, 45 (1), 30–52.
Heritage, J. (2013), 'Epistemics in conversation', in Sidnell, J. and T. Stivers (eds), *The handbook of conversation analysis* (Boston: Wiley-Blackwell), 370–94.
Heritage, J. and S. Clayman (2010), *Talk in action: Interactions, identities, and institutions* (Chichester: Wiley-Blackwell).
Heritage, J. and G. Raymond (2005), 'The terms of agreement: Indexing epistemic authority and subordination in talk-in-interaction', *Social Psychology Quarterly*, 68 (1), 15–38.
Hertog, T. (2023), *On the origin of time: Stephen Hawking's final theory* (London: Penguin Random House).
Hilton, H. (2008), 'The link between vocabulary knowledge and spoken L2 fluency', *The Language Learning Journal*, 36 (2), 153–66.

Hiver, P. and A.H. Al-Hoorie (2020), *Research methods for complexity theory in applied linguistics* (Bristol: Multilingual Matters).
Hiver, P., A.H. Al-Hoorie, and R. Evans (2022), 'Complex dynamic systems theory in language learning: A scoping review of 25 years of research', *Studies in Second Language Acquisition*, 44 (4), 913-41.
Holland, J.H. (1992), 'Complex adaptive systems', *Daedalus*, 121, 17-30.
Holland, J.H. (1995), *Hidden order: How adaptation builds complexity* (Reading, MA: Perseus).
Holland, J.H. (1998), *Emergence: From chaos to order* (New York: Basic Books).
Hosoda, Y. (2000), 'Other-repair in Japanese conversations between nonnative and native speakers', *Issues in Applied Linguistics*, 11 (1), 39-63.
Hosoda, Y. (2006), 'Repair and relevance of differential language expertise in second language conversations', *Applied Linguistics*, 27 (1), 25-50.
Housen, A. and F. Kuiken (2009), 'Complexity, accuracy, and fluency in second language acquisition', *Applied Linguistics*, 30 (4), 461-73.
Hutchby, I. and R. Wooffitt (2008), *Conversation analysis* (2nd edn; Cambridge: Polity Press).
Hymes, D. (1972), 'On communicative competence', in Pride, J.B. and J. Holmes (eds), *Sociolinguistics: Selected readings* (Harmondsworth: Penguin), 269-93.
Hymes, D. (1974), *Foundations in sociolinguistics: An ethnographic approach* (Philadelphia: University of Pennsylvania Press).
IELTS (n.d.), 'Speaking: Band descriptors', <https://www.ielts.org/-/media/pdfs/speaking-band-descriptors.ashx>, accessed 9 April 2023.
Ishida, M. (2009), 'Development of interactional competence: Changes in the use of *ne* in L2 Japanese during study abroad', in Nguyen, H.T. and G. Kasper (eds), *Talk-in-interaction: Multilingual perspectives* (Honolulu: National Foreign Language Resource Center, University of Hawai'i at Mānoa), 351-85.
Ishida, M. (2011), 'Engaging in another person's telling as a recipient in L2 Japanese: Development of interactional competence during one-year study abroad', in Pallotti, G. and J. Wagner (eds), *L2 learning as social practice: Conversation-analytic perspectives* (Honolulu: National Foreign Language Resource Center, University of Hawai'i at Mānoa), 45-86.
Iverson, J.M. and S. Goldin-Meadow (1998), 'Why people gesture when they speak', *Nature*, 396, 228.
Jefferson, G. (1972), 'Side sequences', in Sudnow, D. (ed.), *Studies in social interaction* (New York: The Free Press), 294-338.
Jefferson, G. (1987), 'On exposed and embedded correction in conversation', in Button, G. and J.R.E. Lee (eds), *Talk and social organization* (Clevedon: Multilingual Matters), 86-100.
Jefferson, G. (2004), 'Glossary of transcript symbols with an introduction', in Lerner, G.H. (ed.), *Conversation analysis: Studies from the first generation* (Philadelphia: John Benjamins), 13-23.
Jenkins, J. (2007), *English as a lingua franca: Attitude and identity* (Oxford: Oxford University Press).
Jenkins, J. (2015), 'Repositioning English and multilingualism in English as a lingua franca', *Englishes in Practice*, 2 (3), 49-85.
Jenkins, J., A. Cogo, and M. Dewey (2011), 'Review of developments in research into English as a lingua franca', *Language Teaching*, 44 (3), 281-315.
Jenks, C. (2010), 'Adaptation in online voice-based chat rooms: Implications for language learning', in Seedhouse, P., S. Walsh, and C. Jenks (eds), *Conceptualising 'learning' in applied linguistics* (Houndmills: Palgrave Macmillan), 147-63.

Jenks, C.J. (2012), 'Doing being reprehensive: Some interactional features of English as a lingua franca in a chat room', *Applied Linguistics*, 33 (4), 386–405.
Jessner, U. (2008), 'A DST model of multilingualism and the role of metalinguistic awareness', *The Modern Language Journal*, 92 (2), 270–83.
Johnson, N.F. (2007), *Two's company, three is complexity* (Oxford: Oneworld Publications).
Johnson, S. (2001), *Emergence: The connected lives of ants, brains, cities and software* (New York: Scribner).
Källkvist, M., E. Sandlund, P. Sundqvist, and H. Gyllstad (2022), 'Interaction in the multilingual classroom', in Kecskes, I. (ed.), *The Cambridge handbook of intercultural pragmatics* (Cambridge Handbooks in Language and Linguistics; Cambridge: Cambridge University Press), 836–68.
Kamio, A. (1994), 'The theory of territory of information: The case of Japanese', *Journal of Pragmatics*, 21 (1), 67–100.
Kamio, A. (1997), *Territory of information* (48; Amsterdam: John Benjamins).
Kärkkäinen, E. (2003), *Epistemic stance in English conversation* (Pragmatics and Beyond New Series; Amsterdam; Philadelphia: John Benjamins).
Kasper, G. (1997), '"A" stands for acquisition: A response to Firth and Wagner', *The Modern Language Journal*, 81 (3), 307–12.
Kasper, G. (2006a), 'Beyond repair', *AILA Review*, 19, 83–99.
Kasper, G. (2006b), 'Speech acts in interaction: Towards discursive pragmatics', in Bardovi-Harlig, K., C.J. Félix-Brasdefer, and A.S. Omar (eds), *Pragmatics and language learning* (11; Honolulu: National Foreign Language Resource Center, University of Hawai'i at Mānoa), 281–314.
Kasper, G. (2009), 'Locating cognition in second language interaction and learning: Inside the skull or in public view?', *International Review of Applied Linguistics in Language Teaching (IRAL)*, 47 (1), 11–36.
Kasper, G. and E. Kellerman (1997), *Communication strategies* (London: Longman).
Kaur, J. (2009), 'Pre-empting problems of understanding in English as a lingua franca', in Mauranen, A. and E. Ranta (eds), *English as a lingua franca: Studies and findings* (Newcastle upon Tyne: Cambridge Scholars Publishing), 107–23.
Kaur, J. (2011), '"Doing being a language expert": The case of the ELF speaker', in Archibald, A., A. Cogo, and J. Jenkins (eds), *Latest trends in ELF research* (Newcastle upon Tyne: Cambridge Scholars Publishing), 53–75.
Kendrick, K.H., P. Brown, M. Dingemanse, S. Floyd, S. Gipper, K. Hayano, E. Hoey, G. Hoymann, E. Manrique, G. Rossi, and S.C. Levinson (2020), 'Sequence organization: A universal infrastructure for social action', *Journal of Pragmatics*, 168, 119–38.
Kılıç, E.T. and U. Balaman (2023), 'Facilitating students' learning of a target construction through teacher interactional resources in EFL kindergarten classrooms', *TESOL Quarterly*, 57 (2), 656–69.
Kim, D.R. (2020), 'Emergence of proactive self-initiated self-repair as an indicator of L2 IC development', *Applied Linguistics*, 41 (6), 901–21.
Kim, S. (2019), '"We limit ten under twenty centu charge okay?": Routinization of an idiosyncratic multi-word expression', in Hellermann, J., S. Eskildsen, S. Pekarek Doehler, and A. Piirainen-Marsh (eds), *Conversation analytic research on learning-in-action: The complex ecology of second language interaction 'in the wild'* (Cham: Springer), 25–49.
Kim, Y. (2009), 'Achieving reference in talk-in-interaction: L1 and L2 English speakers' conversation', Unpublished doctoral dissertation, University of Hawai'i at Mānoa.
Kitzinger, C. (2013), 'Repair', in Sidnell, J. and T. Stivers (eds), *The handbook of conversation analysis* (Boston: Wiley-Blackwell), 229–56.

Koizumi, R. and Y. In'nami (2013), 'Vocabulary knowledge and speaking proficiency among second language learners from novice to intermediate levels', *Journal of Language Teaching and Research*, 4 (5), 900–13.

Konakahara, M. (2017), 'Interactional management of face-threatening acts in casual ELF conversation: An analysis of third-party complaint sequences', *Journal of English as a Lingua Franca*, 6 (2), 313–43.

König, C. (2013), 'Topic management in French L2: A longitudinal conversation analytic study', *EUROSLA Yearbook*, 13, 226–50.

Koshik, I. and M.-S. Seo (2012), 'Word (and other) search sequences initiated by language learners', *Text & Talk*, 32 (2), 167–89.

Kotilainen, L. and S. Kurhila (2020), 'Orientation to language learning over time: A case analysis on the repertoire addition of a lexical item', *The Modern Language Journal*, 104 (3), 647–61.

Kramsch, C. (1986), 'From language proficiency to interactional competence', *The Modern Language Journal*, 70, 366–72.

Kramsch, C. (2003), *Language acquisition and language socialization: Ecological perspectives* (London: Continuum).

Kramsch, C. (2008), 'Ecological perspectives on foreign language education', *Language Teaching*, 41 (3), 389–408.

Kristiansen, E.D., A.K. Marstrand, and J. El Derbas (2017), 'Repeating a searched-for word with an agreement token in "challenged interaction"', *Research on Language and Social Interaction*, 50 (4), 388–403.

Kurhila, S. (2005), 'Different orientations to grammatical correctness', in Richards, K. and P. Seedhouse (eds), *Applying conversation analysis* (Houndmills: Palgrave Macmillan), 143–58.

Kurhila, S. (2006), *Second language interaction* (Amsterdam; Philadelphia: John Benjamins).

Labov, W. and D. Fanshel (1977), *Therapeutic discourse: Psychotherapy as conversation* (New York: Academic Press).

Landsberger, H.A. (1958), *Hawthorne revisited: Management and the worker, its critics, and developments in human relations in industry* (Ithaca, NY: Cornell University).

Larsen-Freeman, D. (1997), 'Chaos/complexity science and second language acquisition', *Applied Linguistics*, 18 (2), 141–65.

Larsen-Freeman, D. (2006), 'The emergence of complexity, fluency, and accuracy in the oral and written production of five Chinese learners of English', *Applied Linguistics*, 27 (4), 590–619.

Larsen-Freeman, D. (2010), 'Having and doing: Learning from a complexity theory perspective', in Seedhouse, P., S. Walsh, and C. Jenks (eds), *Conceptualising 'learning' in applied linguistics* (Houndmills: Palgrave Macmillan), 52–68.

Larsen-Freeman, D. (2012), 'Complexity theory', in Gass, S.M. and A. Mackey (eds), *The Routledge handbook of second language acquisition* (London; New York: Routledge), 73–87.

Larsen-Freeman, D. (2013), 'Complexity theory: A new way to think', *Revista Brasileira de Linguística Aplicada*, 13 (2), 369–73.

Larsen-Freeman, D. and L. Cameron (2008a), *Complex systems and applied linguistics* (Oxford: Oxford University Press).

Larsen-Freeman, D. and L. Cameron (2008b), 'Research methodology on language development from a complex systems perspective', *The Modern Language Journal*, 92 (2), 200–13.

Lave, J. and E. Wenger (1991), *Situated learning: Legitimate peripheral participation* (Cambridge: Cambridge University Press).

Lazaraton, A. (2002), *A qualitative approach to the validation of oral language tests* (Cambridge: Cambridge University Press).
Lee, N., L. Mikesell, A.D.L. Joaquin, A.W. Mates, and J.H. Schumann (2009), *The interactional instinct: The evolution and acquisition of language* (Oxford: Oxford University Press).
Lemke, J.L. (2000), 'Across the scales of time: Artifacts, activities, and meanings in ecosocial systems', *Mind, Culture, and Activity*, 7 (4), 273–90.
Lerner, G.H. (2002), 'Turn-sharing: The choral co-production of talk-in-interaction', in Ford, C.E., B.A. Fox, and S.A. Thompson (eds), *The language of turn and sequence* (Oxford: Oxford University Press), 225–57.
Lesonen, S., M. Suni, R. Steinkrauss, and M. Verspoor (2017), 'From conceptualization to constructions in Finnish as an L2: A case study', *Pragmatics & Cognition*, 24 (2), 212–62.
Levinson, S.C. (1983), *Pragmatics* (Cambridge Textbooks in Linguistics; Cambridge; New York: Cambridge University Press).
Levinson, S.C. (1992), 'Activity types and language', in Drew, P. and J. Heritage (eds), *Talk at work: Interaction in institutional settings* (Cambridge: Cambridge University Press), 66–100.
Levinson, S.C. (2006), 'On the human "interaction engine"', in Enfield, N.J. and S.C. Levinson (eds), *Roots of human sociality* (Oxford: Berg), 39–69.
Levinson, S.C. (2022), 'The interaction engine: Cuteness selection and the evolution of the interactional base for language', *Philosophical Transactions of the Royal Society B: Biological Sciences*, 377 (1859), 20210108.
Levinson, S.C. (2023), 'Gesture, spatial cognition and the evolution of language', *Philosophical Transactions of the Royal Society B: Biological Sciences*, 378 (1875), 20210481.
Lewin, R. (1993), *Complexity: Life at the edge of chaos* (London: Phoenix).
Lorenz, E.N. (1963), 'Deterministic nonperiodic flow', *Journal of Atmospheric Sciences*, 20 (2), 130–41.
Lorenz, E.N. (1993), *The essence of chaos* (The Jessie and John Danz Lectures; Seattle: University of Washington Press).
MacBeth, D. (2004), 'The relevance of repair for classroom correction', *Language in Society*, 33 (5), 703–36.
McHoul, A. (1990), 'The organization of repair in classroom talk', *Language in Society*, 19 (3), 349–77.
Mainzer, K. (1997), *Thinking in complexity* (3rd edn; Berlin: Springer-Verlag).
Markee, N. (2008), 'Toward a learning behavior tracking methodology for CA-for-SLA', *Applied Linguistics*, 29 (3), 404–27.
Markee, N. (2010), 'Doing, and justifying doing, avoidance', *Journal of Pragmatics*, 43 (2), 602–15.
Mauranen, A. (2006), 'Signaling and preventing misunderstanding in English as lingua franca communication', *International Journal of the Sociology of Language*, 177, 123–50.
Miller, J.H. and S.E. Page (2007), *Complex adaptive systems: An introduction to computational models of social life* (Princeton: Princeton University Press).
Mondada, L. (2004), 'Ways of "doing being plurilingual" in international work meetings', Gardner, R. and J. Wagner (eds), *Second language conversations* (London: Continuum), 18–39.
Mondada, L. (2018), 'Multiple temporalities of language and body in interaction: Challenges for transcribing multimodality', *Research on Language and Social Interaction*, 51 (1), 85–106.
Mori, J. and A. Hasegawa (2009), 'Doing being a foreign language learner in a classroom: Embodiment of cognitive states as social events', *International Review of Applied Linguistics in Language Teaching (IRAL)*, 47 (1), 65–94.

Mortensen, J. (2013), 'Notes on English used as a lingua franca as an object of study', *Journal of English as a Lingua Franca*, 2 (1), 25–46.

Murray, N. (2012), 'English as a lingua franca and the development of pragmatic competence', *ELT Journal*, 66 (3), 318–26.

Nguyen, H.T. (2008), 'Sequence organization as local and longitudinal achievement', *Text & Talk*, 28 (4), 501–28.

Nguyen, H.T. (2011), 'A longitudinal microanalysis of a second language learner's participation', in Pallotti, G. and J. Wagner (eds), *L2 learning as social practice: Conversation-analytic perspectives* (Honolulu: National Foreign Langauge Resource Center, University of Hawai'i at Mānoa), 17–44.

Nguyen, H.T. (2012), 'Social interaction and competence development: Learning the structural organization of a communicative practice', *Learning Culture and Social Interaction*, 1 (2), 127–42.

Nguyen, H.T. (2019), 'Turn design as longitudinal achievement: Learning on the shop floor', in Hellermann, J., S. Eskildsen, S. Pekarek Doehler, and A. Piirainen-Marsh (eds), *Conversation analytic research on learning-in-action: The complex ecology of second language interaction 'in the wild'* (Cham: Springer), 77–101.

Oelschlaeger, M.L. and J.S. Damico (2000), 'Partnership in conversation: A study of word search strategies', *Journal of Communication Disorders*, 33 (3), 205–25.

Ohta, A.S. (2001), *Second language acquisition processes in the classroom: Learning Japanese* (Mahwah, NJ: Lawrence Erlbaum Associates).

Ortega, L. and Z. Han (eds), *Complexity theory and language development: In celebration of Diane Larsen-Freeman* (Amsterdam; Philadelphia: John Benjamins).

Papi, M. and P. Hiver (2020), 'Language learning motivation as a complex dynamic system: A global perspective of truth, control, and value', *Modern Language Journal*, 104 (1), 209–32.

Park, J.E. (2007), 'Co-construction of nonnative speaker identity in cross-cultural interaction', *Applied Linguistics*, 28 (3), 339–60.

Pekarek Doehler, S. (2018), 'Elaborations on L2 interactional competence: The development of L2 grammar-for-interaction', *Classroom Discourse*, 9 (1), 3–24.

Pekarek Doehler, S. and E. Berger (2018), 'L2 interactional competence as increased ability for context-sensitive conduct: A longitudinal study of story-openings', *Applied Linguistics*, 39 (4), 555–78.

Pekarek Doehler, S. and E. Berger (2019), 'On the reflexive relation between developing L2 interactional competence and evolving social relationships: A longitudinal study of word-searches in the "wild"', in Hellermann, J., S. Eskildsen, S. Pekarek Doehler, and A. Piirainen-Marsh (eds), *Conversation analytic research on learning-in-action: The complex ecology of second language interaction 'in the wild'* (Cham: Springer), 51–75.

Pekarek Doehler, S. and K. Skogmyr Marian (2022), 'Functional diversification and progressive routinization of a multiword expression in and for social interaction: A longitudinal L2 study', *Modern Language Journal*, 106, 23–45.

Peng, H., W. Lowie, and S. Jager (2022), 'Unravelling the idiosyncrasy and commonality in L2 developmental processes: A time-series clustering methodology', *Applied Linguistics*, 43 (5), 891–911.

Phillipson, R. (2008), 'The new linguistic imperial order: English as an EU lingua franca or lingua frankensteinia?', *Journal of Irish and Scottish Studies*, 1 (2), 189–203.

Pietikäinen, K.S. (2020), 'On second language/nonnative speakerism in conversation analysis: A study of emic orientations to language in multilingual/lingua franca couple interactions', *Journal of Pragmatics*, 169, 136–50.

Pomerantz, A. (1984), 'Agreeing and disagreeing with assessments: Some features of preferred/dispreferred turn shapes', in Atkinson, J.M. and J. Heritage (eds), *Structures of social action: Studies in conversation analysis* (Studies in Emotion and Social Interaction; Cambridge: Cambridge University Press), 57–101.

Raymond, G. and J. Heritage (2006), 'The epistemics of social relations: Owning grandchildren', *Language in Society*, 35 (5), 677–705.

Richards, J.C. and W.A. Renandya (2002), *Methodology in language teaching: An anthology of current practice* (Cambridge: Cambridge University Press).

Roehr-Brackin, K. (2014), 'Explicit knowledge and processes from a usage-based perspective: The developmental trajectory of an instructed L2 learner', *Language Learning*, 64 (4), 771–808.

Rydell, M. (2019), 'Negotiating co-participation: Embodied word searching sequences in paired L2 speaking tests', *Journal of Pragmatics*, 149, 60–77.

Sacks, H. (1984), 'Notes on methodology', in Atkinson, J.M. and J. Heritage (eds), *Structures of social action: Studies in conversation analysis* (Cambridge: Cambridge University Press), 21–7.

Sacks, H. (1989), 'Lecture six: The M. I. R. membership categorization device', in Jefferson, G. (ed.), *Harvey Sacks lectures 1964–1965* (Dordrecht: Kluwer Academic Publishers), 89–99.

Sacks, H. (1992), *Lectures on conversation* (Vols I & II), ed. Jefferson, G. (Cambridge, MA: Blackwell).

Sacks, H. and E.A. Schegloff (1979), 'Two preferences in the organization of reference to persons in conversation and their interaction', in Psathas, G. (ed.), *Everyday language: Studies in ethnomethodology* (New York: Irvington Publishers), 15–21.

Sacks, H., E.A. Schegloff, and G. Jefferson (1974), 'A simplest systematics for the organization of turn-taking for conversation', *Language*, 50 (4), 696–735.

Sardar, Z. and I. Abrams (2004), *Introducing chaos* (Cambridge: Icon Books).

Schegloff, E.A. (1979), 'The relevance of repair to syntax-for-conversation', *Syntax and Semantics*, 12, 261–86.

Schegloff, E.A. (1984), 'On some gestures' relation to talk', in Atkinson, J.M. and J. Heritage (eds), *Structures of social action: Studies in conversation analysis* (Cambridge: Cambridge University Press), 266–96.

Schegloff, E.A. (1991), 'Conversational analysis and socially shared cognition', in Resnick, L.B., J.M. Levine, and S.D. Teasley (eds), *Perspectives on socially shared cognition* (Washington, DC: American Psychological Association), 150–71.

Schegloff, E.A. (1996), 'Turn organization: One intersection of grammar and interaction', in Ochs, E., E.A. Schegloff, and S.A. Thompson (eds), *Interaction and grammar* (Cambridge: Cambridge Univeristy Press), 52–133.

Schegloff, E.A. (2000a), 'Overlapping talk and the organization of turn-taking for conversation', *Language in Society*, 29 (1), 1–63.

Schegloff, E.A. (2000b), 'When "others" initiate repair', *Applied Linguistics*, 21 (2), 205–43.

Schegloff, E.A. (2006), 'Interaction: The infrastructure for social institutions, the natural ecological niche for language, and the arena in which culture is enacted', in Enfield, N.J. and S.C. Levinson (eds), *Roots of human sociality* (Oxford: Berg), 70–96.

Schegloff, E.A. (2007), *A primer in conversation analysis: Sequential organization* (Cambridge: Cambridge University Press).

Schegloff, E.A., G. Jefferson, and H. Sacks (1977), 'The preference for self-correction in the organization of repair in conversation', *Language*, 53 (2), 361–82.

Seedhouse, P. (1996), 'Learning talk: A study of the interactional organisation of the L2 classroom from a CA institutional discourse perspective', Unpublished Doctor of Philosophy (D Phil) thesis, University of York.

Seedhouse, P. (2004), *The interactional architecture of the language classroom: A conversation analysis perspective* (Malden, MA: Blackwell).

Seedhouse, P. (2010), 'Locusts, snowflakes, and recasts: Complexity theory and spoken interaction', *Classroom Discourse*, 1 (1), 4–24.

Seedhouse, P. (2015), 'L2 classroom interaction as a complex adaptive system', in Markee, N. (ed.), *The handbook of classroom discourse and interaction* (Oxford: Wiley-Blackwell), 373–89.

Seedhouse, P. and F. Nakatsuhara (2018), *The discourse of the IELTS speaking test: Interactional design and practice* (Cambridge: Cambridge University Press).

Seidlhofer, B. (2001), 'Closing a conceptual gap: The case for a description of English as a lingua franca', *International Journal of Applied Linguistics*, 11 (2), 133–58.

Seidlhofer, B. (2011), *Understanding English as a lingua franca* (Oxford: Oxford University Press).

Seo, M.-S. and I. Koshik (2010), 'A conversation analytic study of gestures that engender repair in ESL conversational tutoring', *Journal of Pragmatics*, 42 (8), 2219–39.

Sert, O. (2013), 'Epistemic status check as an interactional phenomenon in instructed learning settings', *Journal of Pragmatics*, 45 (1), 13–28.

Sert, O. and M. Amri (2021), 'Learning potentials afforded by a film in task-based language classroom interactions', *The Modern Language Journal*, 105 (S1), 126–41.

Sfard, A. (1998), 'On two metaphors for learning and the dangers of choosing just one', *Educational Researcher*, 27 (2), 4–13.

Shea, D.P. (1994), 'Perspective and production: Structuring conversational participation across cultural borders', *Pragmatics*, 4, 357–89.

Sidnell, J. (2010), *Conversation analysis: An introduction* (Oxford: Wiley-Blackwell).

Sidnell, J. and T. Stivers (2013), *The handbook of conversation analysis* (Boston: Wiley-Blackwell).

Siegel, A. (2015), 'Social epistemics for analyzing longitudinal language learner development', *International Journal of Applied Linguistics*, 25 (1), 83–104.

Siegel, A. (2016), '"Oh no, it's just culture": Multicultural identities in action in ELF interactions', *Journal of Asian Pacific Communication*, 26 (2), 193–215.

Siegel, A. (2018), 'Superficial intersubjectivity in ELF university dormitory interactions', *Journal of English as a Lingua Franca*, 7 (2), 377–402.

Siegel, A. (2021), 'Development of shared multilingual resources in ELF dyadic interaction: A longitudinal case study', in Mauranen, A. and S. Vetchinnikova (eds), *Language change: The impact of English as a lingua franca* (Cambridge: Cambridge University Press), 311–35.

Sinclair, J. and M. Coulthard (1975), *Towards an analysis of discourse* (Oxford: Oxford University Press).

Skogmyr Marian, K. and S. Pekarek Doehler (2022), 'Multimodal word-search trajectories in L2 interaction: The use of gesture and how it changes over time', *Social Interaction. Video-Based Studies of Human Sociality*, 5 (1).

Smith, J. and C. Jenks (2006), *Qualitative complexity* (London: Routledge).

Smith, L.B. and E. Thelen (2003), 'Development as a dynamic system', *Trends in Cognitive Sciences*, 7 (8), 343–8.

Stivers, T., N.J. Enfield, P. Brown, C. Englert, M. Hayashi, T. Heinemann, G. Hoymann, F. Rossano, J.P. De Ruiter, and K.-E. Yoon (2009), 'Universals and cultural variation in turn-taking in conversation', *Proceedings of the National Academy of Sciences*, 106 (26), 10587–92.

Stivers, T. and J.D. Robinson (2006), 'A preference for progressivity in interaction', *Language in Society*, 35 (3), 367–92.

Stokoe, E. (2008), 'Dispreferred actions and other interactional breaches as devices for occasioning audience laughter in television "sitcoms"', *Social Semiotics*, 18 (3), 289–307.

Svennevig, J. (2018), '"What's it called in Norwegian?": Acquiring L2 vocabulary items in the workplace', *Journal of Pragmatics*, 126, 68–77.

Taguchi, N. (2014), 'Development of interactional competence in Japanese as a second language: Use of incomplete sentences as interactional resources', *The Modern Language Journal*, 98 (2), 518–35.

Taleghani-Nikazm, C. (2014), 'From searching for words into bodily enactment', Paper presented at 4th International Conference on Conversation (ICCA), University of California, Los Angeles.

Tarone, E. (1983), 'Some thoughts on the notion of communication strategy', in Færch, C. and G. Kasper (eds), *Strategies in interlanguage communication* (London: Longman), 61–74.

ten Have, P. (1999), *Doing conversation analysis: A practical guide* (London: Sage Publications).

ten Have, P. (2007), *Doing conversation analysis: A practical guide* (2nd edn; London: Sage Publications).

The Five Graces Group (2009), 'Language is a complex adaptive system: Position paper', *Language Learning*, 59, 1–26.

Thelen, E. and L.B. Smith (1994), *A dynamic systems approach to the development of cognition and action* (Cambridge, MA: MIT Press).

Thelen, E. and L.B. Smith (2006), 'Dynamic systems theories', in Lerner, R.M. (ed.), *Handbook of child psychology: Volume 1: Theoretical models of human development* (6th edn; Hoboken, NJ: John Wiley & Sons), 258–312.

Theodórsdóttir, G. (2018), 'L2 teaching in the wild: A closer look at correction and explanation practices in everyday L2 interaction', *The Modern Language Journal*, 102 (S1), 30–45.

Theodórsdóttir, G. and S.W. Eskildsen (2022), 'Accumulating semiotic resources for social actions: A case study of L2 Icelandic in the wild', *The Modern Language Journal*, 106 (S1), 46–68.

Tomasello, M. (2000), 'First steps toward a usage-based theory of language acquisition', *Cognitive Linguistics*, 11 (1/2), 61–82.

Tomasello, M. (2009), *Constructing a language: A usage-based theory of language acquisition* (Boston: Harvard University Press).

van Compernolle, R.A. (2019), 'Constructing a second language sociolinguistic repertoire: A sociocultural usage-based perspective', *Applied Linguistics*, 40 (6), 871–93.

van Geert, P. (2008), 'The dynamic systems approach in the study of L1 and L2 acquisition: An introduction', *The Modern Language Journal*, 92 (2), 179–99.

van Geert, P. (2009), 'A comprehensive dynamic systems theory of language development', in de Bot, K. and R.W. Schrauf (eds), *Language development over the lifespan* (New York: Psychology Press), 60–104.

van Lier, L. (1996), *Interaction in the language curriculum: Awareness, autonomy and authenticity* (London: Longman).

van Lier, L. (2000), 'From input to affordance: Social-interactive learning from an ecological perspective', in Lantolf, J.P. (ed.), *Sociocultural theory and second language learning* (Oxford: Oxford University Press), 245–59.

van Lier, L. (2004), *The ecology and semiotics of language learning: A sociocultural perspective* (Boston: Kluwer Academic Publishers).

Verspoor, M., M.S. Schmid, and X. Xu (2012), 'A dynamic usage based perspective on L2 writing', *Journal of Second Language Writing*, 21 (3), 239–63.

Vertovec, S. (2007), 'Super-diversity and its implications', *Ethnic and Racial Studies*, 30 (6), 1024–54.

Vetchinnikova, S. (2021), 'Zooming in on ELF: Introduction', in Mauranen, A. and S. Vetchinnikova (eds), *Language change: The impact of English as a lingua franca* (Cambridge: Cambridge University Press), 175–8.

Vygotsky, L.S. (1978), *Mind and society* (Cambridge, MA: Harvard University Press).
Vygotsky, L.S. (1987), 'Thinking and speech', in Rieber, R.W. and A.S. Carton (eds), *The collected works of L. S. Vygotsky: Volume 1: Problems of general psychology* (New York: Plenum Press), 39–285.
Wagner, J. and R. Gardner (2004), 'Introduction', in Gardner, R. and J. Wagner (eds), *Second language conversations* (London: Continuum), 1–17.
Waldrop, M.M. (1994), *Complexity: The emerging science at the edge of order and chaos* (London: Penguin).
Watanabe, A. (2017), 'Developing L2 interactional competence: Increasing participation through self-selection in post-expansion sequences', *Classroom Discourse*, 8 (3), 271–93.
Weltens, B. and A.D. Cohen (1989), 'Language attrition research: An introduction', *Studies in Second Language Acquisition*, 11 (2), 127–33.
Wenger, E. (1998), *Communities of practice: Learning, meaning, and identity* (New York: Cambridge University Press).
West, G. (2017), *Scale: The universal laws of life and death in organisms, cities and companies* (London: Weidenfeld & Nicolson).
Wilkinson, R. (2007), 'Managing linguistic incompetence as a delicate issue in aphasic talk-in-interaction: On the use of laughter in prolonged repair sequences', *Journal of Pragmatics*, 39 (3), 542–69.
Wilkinson, R., M. Gower, S. Beeke, and J. Maxim (2007), 'Adapting to conversation as a language-impaired speaker: Changes in aphasic turn construction over time', *Communication & Medicine*, 4 (1), 79–97.
Wong, J. (2000a), 'Delayed next turn repair initiation in native/non-native speaker English conversation', *Applied Linguistics*, 21 (2), 244–67.
Wong, J. (2000b), 'The token "yeah" in nonnative speaker English conversation', *Research on Language and Social Interaction*, 33 (1), 39–67.
Wong, M.L., C.E. Cleland, D. Arend, S. Bartlett, H. James Cleaves, H. Demarest, A. Prabhu, J.I. Lunineg, and R.M. Hazen (2023), 'On the roles of function and selection in evolving systems', *PNAS*, 120 (43), e2310223120.
Wootton, A.J. (1997), *Interaction and the development of mind* (Cambridge: Cambridge University Press).
Wu, M.Y., R. Steinkrauss, and W. Lowie (2023), 'The reliability of single task assessment in longitudinal L2 writing research', *Journal of Second Language Writing*, 59, 100950.
Young, C.H., K.L. Savola, and E. Phelps (1991), *Inventory of longitudinal studies in the social sciences* (Newbury Park, CA: Sage Publications).
Young, R.F. (2008), *Language and interaction: An advanced resource book* (London; New York: Routledge).
Young, R.F. (2019), 'Interactional competence and L2 pragmatics', in Taguchi, N. (ed.), *The Routledge handbook of second language acquisition and pragmatics* (New York: Routledge), 93–110.
Young, R.F. and E.R. Miller (2004), 'Learning as changing participation: Discourse roles in ESL writing conferences', *The Modern Language Journal*, 88 (4), 519–35.
Yu, H. and W. Lowie (2020), 'Dynamic paths of complexity and accuracy in second language speech: A longitudinal case study of Chinese learners', *Applied Linguistics*, 41 (6), 855–77.
Zimmerman, D.H. (1998), 'Identity, context and interaction', in Antaki, C. and S. Widdicombe (eds), *Identities in talk* (Thousand Oaks, CA: Sage Publications), 87–106.

INDEX

action sequence, 52–4, 59
action template, 54–5, 59
adapt, 13–15, 17, 31, 34, 36, 38–9, 41–2, 44–6, 49, 53, 57, 59, 61, 63–7, 69, 73–7, 79–80, 97, 126, 138–9, 152, 163, 175–7, 180–1, 187, 190–1, 194, 196–8, 202–3, 205, 226
adaptation, 5, 10, 16, 24, 33–6, 38–45, 72, 127, 139, 146, 155, 174–7, 180–1, 183, 190, 193, 195, 197, 201–3, 211, 218
adaptive, 11–13, 19, 35, 37–51, 53, 55, 59, 63–6, 69–77, 79, 125–7, 176–81, 183–4, 189–207, 213–15, 218, 221, 224–5
adjacency pair, 53–5, 62–3, 89, 183
affiliative, 59
agents, 5, 37–42, 44, 176–7, 190, 202, 205, 207
agreement, 16, 18, 24, 27, 37, 38, 84, 93, 171, 187, 189–90, 215, 217, 220
alignment, 45, 54, 60, 84, 115, 151, 163, 170, 212, 215
analysis, 1–3, 6, 8–9, 11–12, 15, 28–9, 32, 34, 36, 39, 47–9, 51–5, 60–2, 65–9, 74–81, 97, 116, 123–6, 140, 164, 174, 178, 182, 184, 186–7, 189, 191, 194–5, 197–8, 200, 202, 205, 212–15, 217–20, 222–5
aphasia, 2, 19, 24, 29, 45
argument, 2, 10, 12, 40, 45, 50, 70, 74–5, 161, 197, 217
assessment, 27, 45, 144, 217, 223, 226
association, 91, 104, 223
attractor, 42, 46, 72–3, 213
attrition, 152, 168, 213–14, 226

backchannelling, 25, 91, 93, 117, 146, 154, 159, 162, 165–6, 178
bilingual, 6, 23, 103–4, 152, 214–16

camera, 8, 152, 160
candidate solution, 15, 20–25, 28, 61, 79–80, 82, 84, 87, 89–90, 93, 97–9, 102–4, 108, 110, 115–24, 129–35, 138–41, 143–4, 155–6, 161, 163–5, 173–4, 178–80, 182, 185, 190, 192
candidate sound, 89, 93, 96–7
cause, 5–6, 25, 36, 40, 179, 185
change, 4, 6, 8, 10, 21–2, 27–30, 32, 34–5, 37, 40, 42–4, 46–7, 56, 62, 67, 74, 81, 89, 92, 98–9, 101, 103–5, 108, 113, 115–16, 126–9, 131–4, 138–41, 143–4, 146–8, 151–2, 154–7, 160–1, 163–4, 169, 173–4, 178–80, 193, 213–14, 216, 224–5
Chaos Theory, 36, 89
choral co-production, 187–93, 221
classroom, 5, 29–31, 33, 35, 45–6, 49, 66–7, 72–3, 102, 108–9, 116, 124, 134, 183, 187, 194, 198, 213, 217, 219, 221–4, 226
co-adaptation, 33–4, 45
co-construction, 18, 76, 84, 106, 222
code-switching, 23, 82, 90, 97, 102–4, 116, 124, 129, 130, 141, 160–1, 182
cognition, 9, 14–15, 23, 27, 32, 35, 52, 59–63, 75, 77, 104, 177, 180, 187, 189, 191–2, 194, 205, 212–14, 219, 221, 223, 225
cognitive state, 24, 59–61, 90, 221
collaborative, 9, 15, 18, 26, 35, 61, 116, 154, 212, 214, 216
communicate, 1–4, 44, 64, 70, 201, 203, 207
communication, 1, 8–10, 17, 19, 24, 26, 29, 31, 34, 55–6, 64, 76–7, 115, 140, 175, 189, 194, 201–2, 203, 205–7, 211, 213–15, 219, 221–2, 224–6
communicative competence, 17, 218
complex adaptive system, 1–6, 9–13, 35, 37–51, 53, 55, 63–4, 69–79, 125–7, 176–81, 183–4, 189–92, 194, 196–9, 201–7, 213–15, 218, 221, 224, 225

227

Complex Dynamic Systems Theory (CDST), 3–6, 10–16, 19, 28, 34–9, 43–50, 53, 63, 70–1, 73–8, 126–7, 175–7, 179, 181–5, 192–4, 196–202, 204–7
complex personality, 182, 184, 198–9
complex system, 1, 4–5, 10–11, 36, 39, 41, 43, 45–7, 49, 64, 70, 74–7, 125–6, 175–6, 180, 184, 189, 191–2, 198–202, 204–6, 220
complexity science, 3, 11, 37, 44, 220
Complexity Theory, 5, 36, 72, 214, 218, 220, 222, 224
component, 5, 9–10, 12, 17, 37–8, 40–1, 46, 49, 63–4, 70, 75–6, 127, 179, 181, 185, 189, 191, 194–7, 201–2, 204
confirm, 16, 20–3, 25, 27, 34, 57, 61, 63, 79, 82, 84, 86, 91–3, 96, 101–2, 105, 108, 110, 114–18, 120, 122–4, 134–5, 137–9, 143–4, 147–8, 153–4, 157, 165–6, 168, 178, 180, 183, 187, 189–90, 192
context, 2–6, 9–11, 13, 17–18, 22–3, 28–9, 31, 33–6, 39, 41, 43–8, 51, 56–7, 59, 61–6, 69, 75, 76–7, 79–81, 84, 90, 103, 108, 115, 126–7, 131, 138, 174, 179–80, 182, 185, 189–91, 194, 199–200, 203–4, 213, 215, 222, 226
context-free, 59, 62, 77, 179, 190
context-sensitive, 59, 76–7, 179, 190–1, 222
conversation, 1–2, 4, 6–9, 15–16, 20–1, 23–5, 27–8, 30–31, 33–4, 41, 44–5, 48–53, 55–63, 65–6, 68, 70, 74, 78, 80, 82, 84, 86, 91, 93, 109–10, 115, 117–18, 122, 131, 135, 137, 139, 146, 151–2, 157, 161, 163, 169, 173–5, 177, 181, 183, 185, 190, 193, 200, 203, 207, 211–20, 222–6
Conversation Analysis (CA), 1–3, 6, 10–15, 18–19, 21, 26, 28–9, 31–2, 34, 45–55, 59–66, 69–78, 80, 87, 101, 108, 125, 129, 176, 179, 182, 184, 192–4, 196–200, 202, 204–6
Conversation Analysis – Complex Dynamic Systems Theory (CA-CDST), 6, 70, 77, 176, 186, 193–4, 196–7, 199–200, 204, 206
Conversation Analysis for Second Language Acquisition (CA-for-SLA), 6, 28
cooperative, 18, 80, 105, 115, 189
corpus, 6–7, 9, 49, 53, 64, 67, 79, 82, 84, 93, 97, 104, 116, 119, 122, 124, 176, 183, 185, 188, 192
correct, 16, 18–20, 22, 25, 28, 34, 52, 57–9, 71, 79, 93, 99, 102, 116, 118–24, 134, 138–40, 149, 152–3, 164–6, 168–71, 173–4, 178, 180, 182, 187–8, 191, 213, 215–16, 218, 220–21, 223, 225
correction, 16, 18–19, 22, 25, 52, 93, 99, 102, 119–24, 134, 138–40, 149, 152–3, 164–6, 168–71, 173–4, 178, 180, 182, 213, 215–16, 218, 221, 223, 225
cross-cultural, 2, 12–13, 23, 197, 203, 206, 222
cross-linguistic, 2, 26, 197, 203, 215
culture, 1–2, 4, 7–10, 13, 55, 63–4, 99–100, 105, 142–3, 155, 161–3, 173, 175, 179, 182, 194, 197, 201, 203, 205, 215, 221–4
cut-off, 80, 93, 108, 114, 123, 135, 144, 149, 211

data, 2–3, 6–12, 19, 21, 25, 28–34, 45–7, 51–3, 55, 57, 62–3, 67–70, 77, 79–80, 84–5, 109, 116, 118, 120, 126, 129–31, 134, 161, 176–9, 181, 184, 192–4, 197–8, 202–7, 213, 217
data-driven, 31–2, 45, 51
dataset, 10, 204
description, 63, 65, 72, 82, 91, 101, 104, 110, 124, 182, 199, 224
design, 1, 16, 29, 35, 50–2, 57, 59, 63, 65, 70, 73–4, 76–7, 187, 189–91, 196, 200–1, 222, 224
development, 6, 10–12, 14, 28–36, 38, 41, 43–8, 52, 59, 61–2, 64, 69, 126–7, 138, 151–2, 163, 168, 173–5, 177–8, 181, 184–5, 187, 189, 191, 193–5, 201, 203, 213–14, 216, 218–20, 222–6
dictionary, 91, 108–10, 114–16, 124, 145–6, 151, 178, 191, 201, 212
disaffiliative, 59
discursive, 14, 18, 34, 126, 214–15, 219
disfluency, 16–18
display, 59–61, 65–6, 68–9, 72–5, 79–84, 86–8, 90–3, 96, 99, 101–3, 105–8, 110, 114–16, 118–25, 127–31, 134–5, 137, 139–40, 143–4, 146–7, 150–5, 157, 159–66, 168–71, 173–90, 192–4, 197, 199–200, 202, 205, 216
diversity, 4, 38, 63, 179, 182–3, 185, 190, 198–9, 201–2, 212–13, 225
doing learning, 99, 115, 220
dormitory, 7–8, 46, 67, 101, 110, 126, 151, 161, 165, 178, 182–3, 189, 192, 199, 224
dual, 10, 14, 16, 68–9, 81, 181, 192, 203, 215
dynamic, 3–4, 6, 13, 25–6, 31, 36–8, 43, 45,

47–8, 69, 109, 115, 124, 195, 200, 204, 213–16, 218, 222, 225–6
Dynamic Systems Theory, 3–4, 6, 36, 45, 214, 218, 225

ecological, 1, 5, 44–5, 201, 213, 220, 223, 225
embedded, 11, 16, 43, 54, 64, 180, 213, 218
embodied, 186–7, 189, 211, 215–16, 223
embodiment, 9, 15, 20–2, 61, 221
emerge, 5, 31, 34, 36–7, 39–46, 55, 63, 75–6, 79–80, 103, 125, 127, 130–1, 140, 155, 160, 177, 184–5, 188–9, 193, 195, 201–2, 213–14, 216, 218–20
emergence, 34, 41–2, 46, 103, 155, 160, 193, 213–14, 218–20
Emergent Systems Theory, 36
emic, 2, 28, 49, 51–2, 55, 61, 69, 74, 131, 174, 205, 222
empirical, 6, 10–13, 28, 30, 33–4, 48 52, 78, 161, 182–4, 196–7, 199, 202, 204
English, 2–4, 6–7, 9–12, 21, 25, 30, 33–5, 46, 50, 67–8, 79–80, 85–7, 91, 93, 96–7, 99–100, 102–13, 105, 108, 110, 115–17, 119, 121, 123–4, 126–7, 134, 139–40, 143, 147–8, 150–2, 154–5, 159–61, 163–4, 166, 168, 170–1, 173–5, 178–83, 185, 188–9, 191–2, 194, 197, 212–13, 215–22, 224–6
English as a lingua franca (ELF), 2–4, 10–11, 28, 36, 67, 79–81, 124–5, 126–7, 194–5, 206
environment, 4–6, 9–10, 17–18, 21, 28, 32, 34, 37–42, 44, 46, 51, 96–7, 109–10, 126–7, 139, 151, 155, 161, 163, 175–81, 183, 191, 193, 195, 201
epistemic engine, 61, 217
epistemic narrowing, 188, 192–3
epistemic position, 90, 97, 121
epistemic stance, 26, 28, 80, 116, 124, 140, 155, 175, 197, 219
epistemic state, 115
epistemic status, 26, 61, 139, 188, 224
ethnomethodology, 50, 70, 74, 215, 217, 223
etic, 119, 162
evolution, 10, 38, 45, 65, 201, 205, 216, 221
evolve, 1, 4, 10, 31, 36–7, 45, 53, 59, 64–5, 67, 69, 184–5, 198, 201, 206–7
evolving system, 36, 226
examination, 7, 41, 57, 65, 214
expansion, 31, 33–5, 38, 54, 57, 163, 179, 216, 226

expert, 2, 4, 9–12, 16, 25–8, 81, 87, 99, 119, 121, 123–4, 143, 146–8, 152, 168, 176, 189, 194, 197, 203, 205–6, 218–19
explanation, 25, 37, 66, 72–3, 76, 91, 101, 104, 137, 141, 143, 146, 171, 173, 184, 198, 217, 225
explicit, 11, 21–2, 27–8, 31–2, 38, 46, 48, 50–1, 61, 65, 67, 80–2, 85, 87, 90, 93, 99, 109, 121, 123, 134, 138–9, 150, 154–5, 173, 188–91, 201, 203, 205, 223
exposed, 16, 99, 102, 120, 178, 182, 218
eye contact, 82, 84, 86, 89, 92, 96, 101, 135, 137, 168, 171

feedback, 4, 24, 38–42, 72–3, 102, 108, 122, 134, 176, 180–1, 191, 195, 197, 200, 203–4, 207
fluency, 16–18, 45, 151, 217–18, 220
focus, 57, 62, 65–70, 73–4, 76–7, 79–80, 87, 90, 110, 116, 124–6, 131, 140, 150, 153, 175, 177, 182–5, 187–90, 192, 194, 196, 199–200, 204–6
form, 2, 5, 16, 19, 23–4, 40–2, 51, 63, 71–2, 75–6, 78, 102, 119–20, 148, 201, 205, 216
fractal, 12–13, 16, 41–2, 70–1, 73–7, 183–4, 192, 197–8, 202, 204
frequency, 35, 58, 97, 103, 126, 129–33, 139–41, 155–6, 160, 164, 174, 178, 185
function, 1–3, 5–6, 9–13, 31, 33, 35–7, 39–43, 45, 47–51, 53, 55, 59, 63, 70, 72–7, 80–1, 108, 123, 125, 143, 159, 175–7, 179, 181–2, 184–5, 189, 191, 193–4, 196, 198, 199, 201–6, 222, 226

Garfinkel, H., 215
gaze, 22, 27, 29, 46, 80–4, 87–90, 93, 96, 105–6, 108, 114, 118, 147, 149–50, 159, 161, 178, 187, 211–12, 215
general, 5, 10–12, 15, 17, 19, 23–4, 40–41, 50, 52–3, 59, 66, 70, 72, 77–9, 90, 179, 181–2, 184, 190–2, 196–9, 202
gesture, 2, 21–2, 25, 46, 82, 91, 96, 98, 101, 106–8, 111, 113–16, 124, 135–7, 139, 141–3, 148–9, 152, 159–60, 168, 171–2, 182, 212, 215, 218, 221, 223–4
global, 4, 64, 201, 222
grammar, 18–19, 44–5, 63, 127, 159, 168, 189, 215, 217, 222–3

hedging, 104, 115, 189
Heritage, J., 217

hesitation, 17, 20–2, 88, 93, 101, 114, 118–20, 137, 146–7, 149, 154, 159, 178, 187, 189
hesitation marker, 17, 20, 88, 178
heterogeneity, 5, 12, 17, 38–9, 41–2, 53, 64, 125–6, 175–6, 181–5, 192, 197–201
holistic, 2, 5, 17, 36, 40, 47, 51, 57, 63, 70, 75, 126, 177
homogeneity, 5, 12, 39, 41–2, 53, 64, 125–6, 175–6, 181–2, 184–5, 192, 197, 198–201
human spoken interaction, 45, 47, 49–50, 53, 63–4, 68, 70–1, 74–7, 79, 177, 181, 182, 184–5, 187, 194, 196–9, 203–7

iconic (gesture), 21, 106, 139
identity, 2, 26–7, 51, 63, 65, 102, 120, 155, 218, 222, 226
impact, 11, 38, 103, 175, 224–5
implicit, 5, 11, 39–40, 50–1, 176, 178–9, 182, 188, 190–1, 205, 207, 216
inbreath, 211
inductive, 52
informal, 11, 49, 52, 66, 70, 79–80, 84, 90, 108, 181–2, 189, 196, 199–200, 203
information exchange, 52, 59, 61–2, 65, 177, 187, 191–2, 194
information imbalance, 52, 61–2
initiate, 15, 19–21, 23–4, 26, 35, 58, 64, 79–80, 82–3, 87, 90, 93, 97, 104, 106, 108, 116, 122, 124, 126, 130–1, 133, 135, 139, 146, 150, 154, 161–5, 178, 182–3, 185, 187–8, 192, 217, 219–20, 223
institution, 2–3, 13, 25, 29, 45, 48–9, 51, 53, 57, 64–6, 68, 73, 76, 84, 127, 212, 214, 217, 221, 223
institutional interaction, 35, 65, 73
intention, 17, 63, 82, 200
interaction engine, 76–7, 175–7, 179, 182, 184, 188–94, 196–7, 201, 203–7, 221
interactional competence, 6, 10, 14–15, 17–19, 28–30, 32, 34, 47–8, 127, 175, 178, 195, 203, 206, 213, 216, 218, 220, 222, 225–6
interactional environment, 17–18, 21, 32, 34, 126, 139, 155, 163, 175–7, 180–1, 183, 193, 195
interlocutor, 2, 7, 15, 17, 22, 24, 26–8, 30, 34–5, 37, 41, 44, 48, 80, 84, 87, 90–1, 93, 97, 99, 103, 105, 110, 115–16, 121, 123–4, 127, 140–1, 146, 160, 164, 171, 173–5, 183, 195, 197, 200, 203

international, 6–7, 46, 67, 183, 213, 215, 217, 219, 221, 224
intersubjectivity, 2–4, 10–11, 13, 15, 20, 49, 52, 54–5, 57, 59, 62–3, 69, 75–6, 79, 115, 122, 140, 144, 152, 155, 166, 174, 177–8, 183, 185, 187, 190, 193–4, 197, 204, 216–17, 224
interview, 9, 30, 152, 168, 173, 216
intonation, 20–1, 23, 57, 61, 80–2, 84, 86–8, 90–3, 96, 98, 100–2, 105, 107, 114, 116–23, 132, 135, 137–9, 144, 146–7, 149, 152–4, 159, 163, 165–6, 168, 172, 178, 180, 183, 211
IRF pattern, 72–3

Japan, 6–8, 21, 27, 33–4, 43, 67–8, 80, 82, 84, 86, 90–1, 93, 96–9, 101–5, 107–10, 112, 115–16, 118, 120, 122–4, 126, 129, 131, 139, 142–6, 151, 159–62, 166, 169–72, 174–5, 177–8, 180, 182–3, 185, 208, 210–11, 213, 216, 218–19, 222, 225
Japanese, 6–8, 21, 27, 33–4, 80, 82, 84, 86, 90–1, 93, 96–9, 101–5, 107–10, 112, 115–16, 118, 120, 122–4, 126, 129, 131, 139, 142–6, 151, 159–61, 169–72, 174–5, 177–8, 180, 182–3, 185, 211, 213, 216, 218–19, 222, 225
Jefferson, G., 80, 218, 223

K+, 26, 61, 84, 90, 99, 102, 110, 115, 120, 125, 139, 187, 192–3
K-, 3, 14, 26, 30, 58, 61, 84, 92, 99, 105, 108–9, 112, 125, 141–2, 187, 192–3, 204, 212, 217–19, 221, 224, 226
Katakana, 97–101, 103, 115, 123

L2, 2–3, 5–6, 9–12, 14–37, 39, 41, 43–9, 65–70, 72–3, 77, 79–81, 84, 87, 90, 93, 97, 101–3, 108, 115, 118, 121, 124, 126–7, 130–1, 134–5, 139, 155, 157, 160, 165, 174, 176–7, 181, 183, 185, 187–94, 196–8, 200, 203, 206, 212–14, 216–19, 221–6
L2 classroom, 5, 49, 66–7, 72–3, 183, 194, 198, 213, 223
L2 speaker, 11, 14, 17–21, 23, 25–7, 32–3, 48, 79–80, 87, 90, 93, 97, 102, 118, 126, 135, 155, 157, 160, 165, 174, 194, 203
L2 user, 4, 9, 17, 35, 69, 115, 130, 195, 203
L3, 34, 160, 200; *see also* 'third language'
language, 1–7, 9–11, 13, 16–19, 23, 25–32, 34, 36, 38, 40–1, 43–8, 51, 55, 57, 63–4,

66–9, 72–4, 76–7, 80, 84, 87, 91–3, 96–7, 99, 101–4, 108–10, 116, 118, 121, 123–4, 126–8, 130, 134–5, 138–9, 144, 147–8, 150–2, 155, 161, 163, 168, 174–5, 177–83, 185–94, 196–7, 200–1, 203, 205–7, 212–13, 224–6
language expertise, 26, 121, 168, 218
language learning, 5, 10, 13, 16, 18, 28–30, 43–5, 47, 66, 68–9, 73, 77, 81, 84, 116, 123, 130, 140, 148, 150, 173, 180–1, 186–90, 192, 200, 203, 206, 212–14, 216–20, 222, 225
Larsen-Freeman, D., 220
latch, 211
laugh, 88, 143, 153, 163, 21
laughter, 46, 88, 101, 104, 118, 143, 153, 163, 211, 215, 224, 226
learning, 5–6, 10, 13–14, 16, 18–19, 28–34, 43–8, 66, 68–70, 73, 77, 80, 82, 84, 93, 99, 101, 107–8, 115–16, 118, 120, 123–4, 133–5, 138, 140, 148, 150, 152–4, 161, 169, 171, 173–4, 176–7, 179–82, 185–90, 192, 194, 200, 203, 206, 212–26
learning opportunity, 14, 80, 84, 99, 107–8, 116, 118, 120, 123–4, 133, 140, 148, 152–3, 171, 173–4
lens, 12, 42, 70, 77, 125, 153, 181–2, 184, 192, 196–9, 204
Levinson, S. C., 221
lexical, 11, 15, 17, 19–20, 27, 29, 33, 35, 65, 79, 90, 173, 181, 185, 188, 192, 220
life-related system, 1, 11, 36, 43, 70
limitation, 18, 53, 196, 204–5
linear, 4–6, 31, 34–42, 44, 46, 48, 54, 73, 76, 103, 128, 152, 176, 178, 184–5, 190, 193, 195, 206
linguistic, 2–6, 12, 14, 16–18, 23–6, 28, 30–1, 33–4, 36, 38–9, 43, 45–7, 51–2, 57, 59, 61, 63, 72, 79, 90, 99, 104–5, 109–10, 115, 118–19, 121, 130, 141, 143, 147, 154, 174, 177–8, 188, 191, 197, 200–1, 203, 205, 212–26
linguistic resource, 43, 45, 79, 154, 174
loan word, 97, 101
longitudinal, 6–7, 10–11, 13, 27–9, 31–5, 39, 45, 47–8, 65, 69, 84, 126, 129, 131, 133, 135, 137, 139, 141, 143, 145, 147, 149, 151, 153, 155, 157, 159, 161, 163–5, 167, 169, 171, 173, 175, 194, 204, 213, 220, 222, 224, 226
Lorenz, E. N., 221

machinery, 2, 11, 50, 59, 66, 76, 197, 206, 221
macro, 3, 11–12, 29, 40, 70, 72–3, 77, 176, 182–5, 192–4, 197–9, 221
marker, 17, 20–1, 23, 27, 33, 35, 52, 80–2, 85, 87–8, 90–1, 178, 185, 190, 215
meaning, 2, 5, 9–10, 13–14, 17–18, 20, 32, 43–5, 57, 59, 76–7, 82, 101, 105, 109, 119, 139, 159, 162, 176, 192, 194, 201, 203, 215, 221, 226
mechanism, 1, 4, 9–10, 12, 15–16, 37, 48–9, 52–7, 59, 61–4, 66, 70, 74–7, 79–80, 125, 175–7, 179, 181, 185, 187, 189–92, 194, 197, 202, 204–5
membership, 23–5, 28, 99, 223
membership categorisation, 26, 99
meta-theory, 4, 12, 36, 48, 71, 74–7, 184, 196–8, 204
methodology, 46, 48–51, 53, 55, 57, 59, 61, 63–7, 69–71, 73–7, 179, 189, 192, 196, 198, 202, 204–7, 215, 217, 220–3
micro, 3–4, 11–12, 42, 46, 48, 50, 70, 72–3, 77, 125–6, 176, 179, 182–4, 186, 192, 194, 197–9, 222
microanalysis, 11–12, 48, 77, 125, 197, 222
mirror, 2–3, 45, 49–51, 53, 55, 57, 59, 61, 63, 65–7, 69–70, 73–7, 108, 134, 165, 168, 179, 183, 187, 189, 193, 196, 198, 202, 205, 207
mirroring methodology, 2, 49–51, 53, 55, 57, 59, 61, 63, 65–7, 69–70, 73, 75, 77, 196, 198, 207
mitigation, 121
multicultural, 3, 7, 224
multilingual, 3, 28, 34, 161, 183, 200, 213, 216, 218, 222, 224
multimodal, 2, 22, 29, 63, 80–1, 193, 214, 216, 221, 224
multi-word, 21, 35, 80–2, 84, 219
mutual adaptation, 34, 35, 203

native, 24, 26, 173, 183, 189, 203, 215, 218, 226
nested, 39, 43, 48
network, 37, 43, 64, 71, 184, 204
next-turn proof procedure, 55, 57, 66–7, 69, 74–5, 77, 190, 202, 207
non-institutional, 29, 48
non-linear, 4–6, 31–2, 34, 36–42, 44, 46, 48, 76, 152, 176, 178, 184–5, 190, 193, 195, 206
non-linearity, 37–41, 152, 176, 178, 190
non-native, 24, 26, 215, 226

non-verbal, 8, 9, 33, 56, 76, 84, 87, 174, 177, 211
normative, 50–2, 54–6, 59, 61–2, 187
novice, 16, 27, 35, 87, 99, 105, 119, 124, 135, 212–23, 216, 220

offer, 23, 64, 73, 118, 200, 202, 206–27
ordinary conversation, 49–50, 53, 55, 57, 59–62, 65–6, 68, 70, 119
organic, 44, 198
orientation, 10, 24, 26–8, 32, 51–2, 65, 67–8, 70, 80, 84, 87, 90, 99, 108, 110, 116, 118, 120–1, 123–4, 127, 132–5, 137–40, 147–8, 150, 151–5, 157, 161, 163–4, 166, 168–9, 171, 173–4, 178–9, 216, 220, 222
other-initiated self-repair, 15, 58
other-initiated other-repair, 15, 58
other-repair, 15–6, 18, 22–5, 58, 81, 84, 86–7, 102, 107–8, 110, 120, 125, 148, 159, 182, 187–8, 191, 218
overlap, 39, 59, 82, 107, 137, 139, 143, 153–4, 166, 211, 222

participant, 1–2, 7–10, 14–17, 23–5, 27, 32, 34, 36, 46, 49, 51–3, 55–7, 60–2, 65–70, 74–5, 77, 79–80, 82, 84–5, 87, 90–91, 93, 97, 99, 101–5, 108–10, 115–21, 123–31, 134–5, 137–8, 140, 155, 161, 164, 168 173–82, 185, 187–92, 194–5, 197, 199, 200, 202, 204–5, 207–10, 215
particular, 3, 9, 11–12, 23, 26, 31, 37, 44, 46, 50–52, 57, 59, 70, 72, 75, 77–9, 90, 116, 118, 124, 127, 148, 168, 176, 179, 181–2, 184, 190–2, 194, 196–200, 202, 206
partner, 7–8, 29, 59, 84–5, 102–3, 106, 119–21, 123–6, 131–3, 138–40, 147, 152, 154–5, 157, 161, 163–4, 168, 172–80, 182, 207–10, 222
pattern, 5, 11, 14, 19, 21, 25, 30, 36–7, 39, 41–6, 52, 71–3, 79–80, 82, 85, 87, 89–90, 93, 95, 97, 99, 101–2, 105, 107, 109, 111, 113, 115, 117, 119, 121, 123–6, 128–9, 131, 134, 152, 174, 178–9, 182, 184–5, 193–4, 200, 215
pause, 17, 20, 23, 82, 83, 86, 88, 91–3, 96, 98, 100, 102, 105, 107, 114, 118–20, 123, 137, 143–4, 146–7, 149, 152–4, 157, 159, 161, 165–6, 172, 178, 211, 215
pedagogical, 10, 66–7, 73
pitch, 93, 96, 98, 123, 137, 211
posture, 89

pragmatics, 14, 18, 126, 206, 212, 214–17, 219, 221–2, 224, 226
pre-emptive repair, 25, 35, 155
preference, 16, 18, 22–3, 34, 58, 80, 87, 90, 97, 103–4, 124, 135, 147, 200, 223–4
principle, 5, 12–14, 36–41, 43, 46–52, 55, 57, 63–4, 70–1, 74–5, 77, 175–8, 180, 184–5, 190–1, 193–4, 196–8, 202, 206, 214
proficiency, 16–17, 34, 41, 102–3, 126–8, 130, 134, 143, 150, 155, 168, 173–4, 178–81, 183, 185, 194, 200, 206, 217, 220
progressivity, 24, 33, 68, 97, 101, 119, 133, 135, 140, 147, 150, 176–7, 181, 217, 224
pronunciation, 18–19, 21, 93, 96, 100, 107, 114–15, 119–20, 147–8, 165–6, 168–71, 173, 178, 212
proof criterion, 55, 61
proportional, 4–5, 181
prosody, 92–3, 97, 102, 116, 118–21, 123–4, 126, 130–3, 138–40, 153, 155–6, 164–5, 170, 172, 174, 177–8, 180
prosody-marked, 116, 118–20, 123–4, 130–3, 138–40, 153, 155–6, 164–5, 170, 174, 177–8

qualitative, 46, 51, 198, 217, 221, 224
quantitative, 46, 204, 206
question, 3, 4, 21, 31, 39, 47, 51, 53–5, 57, 68, 89, 93, 115–16, 137, 143–4, 146–7, 152–3, 166, 170, 173, 183, 187–93, 202

rational design, 52, 73–4, 185
record, 7, 8, 30, 32, 46, 52, 67, 80, 82, 84, 87, 105, 106, 109, 117, 122, 127, 129, 130, 132–3, 138, 140–1, 144, 147–8, 150–7, 160–6, 169, 171, 173, 179–80, 185–6, 193, 204–5, 207–10
reflexive, 2, 9, 11–12, 51–2, 63, 66, 69–70, 72, 77, 182, 189–90, 192, 199, 205, 222
reflexivity, 55, 57, 74–5
repair, 1, 9–10, 15–16, 18–20, 22–5, 27–9, 32, 35, 50, 53, 57–8, 60–64, 66, 69, 76–7, 79–81, 84, 86–7, 89–91, 93, 96–100, 102, 105, 107–8, 110, 114–15, 120–4, 131, 135, 143, 146, 148–51, 153–5, 157, 159, 162–3, 165–6, 170, 173, 175–7, 179, 181–3, 187–94, 197, 204, 207, 212–19, 221, 223–4, 226
repetition, 25, 34, 67, 80, 82, 93, 96, 100–2, 105, 108, 110, 117, 120, 122–3, 144, 149, 154, 157, 178, 183, 187

research, 1, 6–8, 10, 14, 28–9, 31–2, 34, 36–7, 39, 46–8, 51, 62, 65, 69, 71–72, 74–6, 80, 104, 108, 115–16, 124, 130, 146, 168, 173–4, 179, 196, 198, 200–7, 213, 215–22, 224, 226
researcher, 7–8, 29, 32, 37, 39, 65, 115, 124, 130, 168, 173, 202, 204
research gap, 14, 47–8, 205
research method, 6, 69, 74–6, 196, 198, 201–2, 213, 218, 220
resolution, 90–1, 93, 189
response, 17, 21, 24–5, 43, 45–6, 63, 72–3, 80, 87–8, 90, 93, 98, 101–2, 114–17, 119–24, 132, 133, 140, 147, 149, 151, 157, 164–5, 168, 173–4, 182–3, 200, 214, 216–17, 219
reverse engineering, 200
rule, 5, 36, 42, 53, 59

Sacks, H., 223
scaffolding, 46, 141, 143–4, 146, 154
scale, 3, 5, 11–13, 26, 36, 39, 42–3, 50, 70–1, 73–6, 115, 127, 151, 176, 181–5, 192–3, 196–9, 202, 204, 213, 221, 223
Schegloff, E. A., 223
schema, 37–8, 44
second language acquisition (SLA), 5
seen but unnoticed, 50–1, 192, 203, 207
self-initiated other-repair, 15, 58, 108
self-initiated self-repair, 15, 35, 58, 90, 108, 217, 219
self-organise, 5, 39–40, 177
self-referential, 9, 57
self-repair, 15–16, 19, 22–3, 35, 58, 80, 87, 89–91, 97, 108, 115, 125, 150, 153, 166, 170, 217, 219
self-similar, 5, 12–13, 39, 42, 50, 70–7, 176, 183, 192, 196–8, 202
self-similarity, 5, 12–13, 39, 42, 70–5, 77, 176, 183, 192, 196–8, 202
semantic contiguity, 23–4, 91, 104–5, 114–16, 129–30, 133, 137, 141, 143, 182, 187–8
sensitivity, 5, 25, 33, 35, 39, 41, 46, 176, 179, 191, 203
sequence, 1–3, 5, 9–28, 32, 35, 38, 47–8, 51–7, 59–66, 69, 72, 74–7, 79–82, 84, 87, 89–90, 93, 96–7, 99, 101–6, 108–9, 111, 113, 115–26, 128–35, 137, 139–41, 143, 146, 148–52, 154–7, 159–61, 163–8, 171, 173–83, 185, 187–95, 197–200, 203–4, 212–13, 216–23, 226
sequence organisation, 53–5, 64–5, 74, 182, 199
side sequence, 15, 20, 25, 62, 82, 87, 96–7, 139, 154, 190, 193, 218
silence, 25, 80, 86, 96, 116, 135, 139, 159, 165, 211
simplicity, 39–40, 176, 178–9, 182, 190, 216
situated learning, 30–3, 220
social action, 1–4, 10, 12, 16, 49, 51, 56–7, 59–63, 70, 75–7, 79, 117, 125, 176–7, 179, 181, 185, 187, 190–4, 197, 201, 203, 206, 212, 217, 219, 223, 225
social epistemics, 26, 224
socially distributed cognition, 9, 15, 52, 59–63, 77, 177, 187, 191–2, 194
sociocognitive, 44–5, 212
sociocultural theory, 30, 32, 225
speaking, 2, 10, 12, 14–15, 24, 33–4, 45–6, 56–7, 76, 97, 102, 127, 175, 190, 197, 213, 216, 218, 220, 223–4
speech, 15–17, 19–20, 23, 29, 33, 36, 38, 47, 57, 67, 69, 87, 135, 148, 187–9, 201, 206, 211, 215–16, 219, 226
speech exchange system, 67, 69, 187–9
speech perturbation, 20
spoken interaction, 45, 47–51, 53, 63–5, 69–71, 74–7, 79, 177, 179, 181–7, 191, 194, 196–9, 202–7, 224
strategy, 16, 23, 103, 105, 129, 132, 137, 140, 155, 170, 189, 193, 225
strategies, 9, 16, 17, 24, 25, 82, 90, 110, 116, 124, 129–30, 132, 141, 155, 169, 174, 177–8, 180–1, 185, 193, 197, 200, 215, 219, 222
strategic competence, 17
superdiverse, 2–4, 6, 9, 12–13, 139, 179, 183, 197, 200
symbiotic, 206

talk, 2–3, 7–12, 14–18, 20, 23–7, 29–30, 32–3, 46, 49, 51–3, 57, 61–2, 64–6, 68–9, 71, 73–4, 76–7, 82, 85, 87, 91, 93, 97, 99, 101–2, 104–5, 109–10, 115, 117, 119, 121–2, 124, 133–5, 137–40, 150, 153–4, 159–60, 162, 168, 171, 173–4, 176–7, 179–82, 184–93, 196–202, 204–6, 211–15, 217–19, 221–3, 226
target word, 84, 93, 96, 115, 124, 137, 154, 159, 187–8

teacher, 32–3, 46, 52, 66–7, 72–3, 85–6, 102, 120, 124, 134, 157, 171, 174, 177, 213, 219
teaching, 119, 123, 134–5, 140, 148, 182, 213, 215, 217–21, 223, 225
Thai, 7–8, 34, 85–6, 155, 160–1, 163, 174, 177, 183, 208–11
theory, 3–6, 12, 30–3, 36, 45, 48, 71–2, 74–8, 184, 196–8, 204, 214, 216–20, 222, 224–5
third language, 34, 161, 174
third turn, 20, 25, 54
third position, 24, 34
timescales, 39, 43, 176, 185, 193, 213
TOEFL, 9, 127–8, 150, 173, 178, 213
topic, 2, 6, 8, 10, 12, 16, 20, 22, 24, 26, 28, 30, 56, 59, 61–3, 68–9, 93, 102, 107–8, 114, 117–18, 120, 122, 131, 134, 137, 144, 146, 162, 171, 174, 177, 181, 185, 187, 189–92, 194–5, 197, 203, 220
tracking, 7, 28, 32, 221
trajectory, 32, 34, 42, 223
transcribe, 8–9, 208–11
transcript, 9, 24, 47, 52, 54, 205, 211, 218
transition relevance place (TRP), 56
translate, 25, 139
translation, 9, 25, 93, 102, 108, 143–4, 211, 215
trouble, 2, 9, 11–12, 15, 17, 19, 21, 24, 57, 63, 69, 82, 87–8, 91–3, 96, 102, 104, 107, 118, 123, 135, 137, 147, 152, 160, 179, 187, 189–92, 197, 214
try-marking, 23, 91, 93, 115
turn, 1, 10, 16, 18, 20–1, 25, 27, 29–30, 35, 43, 50–62, 64–9, 74–7, 87–8, 90–3, 102, 107, 112, 116, 119–23, 135, 137, 148–9, 154, 157, 160, 162, 165–7, 170, 177, 183, 187–91, 194–6, 201–2, 207, 211–12, 216, 221–3, 226
turn-constructional unit (TCU), 56
turn design, 29, 65, 222

turn-taking, 1, 10, 18, 30, 50, 52–5, 57, 59–60, 62, 64–5, 75–7, 177, 187, 190–1, 194, 223

understanding, 4, 9, 11, 13, 15–18, 22–3, 25–6, 28, 32, 35, 37, 42, 44, 50, 52–5, 57, 59–61, 63, 75, 79, 82, 86, 89–93, 96–9, 101–2, 104–8, 114–16, 118–24, 126–7, 131, 133, 137, 139, 141, 143–4, 146, 150, 152, 154, 157, 159–62, 165–6, 168, 171, 173, 180, 184, 187–8, 198–9, 203–4, 206, 216, 219, 221, 224
universal, 1, 2, 4–5, 9–12, 39, 42–3, 50, 63–4, 73, 76–7, 175–6, 178–9, 182, 184–5, 189–90, 192–4, 196–7, 199, 201, 203, 206, 214, 219, 224, 226
universality, 4, 64, 73, 194, 206
university, 6–7, 9, 21, 46, 67, 126–7, 155, 157, 164–5, 178–9, 189, 192, 212, 214–21, 223–6
unmotivated looking, 52
usage-based theory, 31, 225

variation, 1, 21, 33, 38, 44, 63–4, 80, 127, 128, 174, 177–9, 185
verbal, 2, 8–9, 33, 56, 73, 76, 84, 87, 116, 124, 168, 174, 185, 211–12
vocabulary, 2, 18, 45, 68, 127, 180, 185, 187–9, 213–14, 216–17, 220, 225
volume, 181, 184–5, 199, 211, 225–6

West, G., 221
word search, 3, 9–29, 31, 33, 35, 37, 39, 41, 43, 45, 47–8, 61–2, 69, 77, 79–88, 90–1, 93, 97, 99, 101–10, 113, 115–26, 129–33, 135, 137–41, 143, 145–52, 154–7, 159–61, 163–9, 171, 173–83, 185–95, 197, 199–200, 203–4, 206, 212, 214, 216, 222–5
word search marker, 21, 27, 35, 80–2, 85, 90–1, 185

EU representative:
Easy Access System Europe
Mustamäe tee 50, 10621 Tallinn, Estonia
Gpsr.requests@easproject.com

www.ingramcontent.com/pod-product-compliance
Lightning Source LLC
Chambersburg PA
CBHW071708160426
43195CB00012B/1619